Practical C Programming

Solutions for modern C developers to create efficient and well-structured programs

B. M. Harwani

BIRMINGHAM - MUMBAI

Practical C Programming

Copyright © 2020 Packt Publishing

Commissioning Editor: Richa Tripathi
Acquisition Editor: Alok Dhuri
Content Development Editor: Ruvika Rao
Senior Editor: Afshaan Khan
Technical Editor: Pradeep Sahu
Copy Editor: Safis Editing
Project Coordinator: Francy Puthiry
Proofreader: Safis Editing
Indexer: Tejal Daruwale Soni
Production Designer: Arvindkumar Gupta

First published: February 2020

Production reference: 1140220

Published by Packt Publishing Ltd.
Livery Place
35 Livery Street
Birmingham
B3 2PB, UK.

ISBN 978-1-83864-110-8

www.packt.com

`Packt.com`

Subscribe to our online digital library for full access to over 7,000 books and videos, as well as industry leading tools to help you plan your personal development and advance your career. For more information, please visit our website.

Why subscribe?

- Spend less time learning and more time coding with practical eBooks and Videos from over 4,000 industry professionals

- Improve your learning with Skill Plans built especially for you

- Get a free eBook or video every month

- Fully searchable for easy access to vital information

- Copy and paste, print, and bookmark content

Did you know that Packt offers eBook versions of every book published, with PDF and ePub files available? You can upgrade to the eBook version at `www.packt.com` and as a print book customer, you are entitled to a discount on the eBook copy. Get in touch with us at `customercare@packtpub.com` for more details.

At `www.packt.com`, you can also read a collection of free technical articles, sign up for a range of free newsletters, and receive exclusive discounts and offers on Packt books and eBooks.

Contributors

About the author

B. M. Harwani is the founder of Microchip Computer Education, based in Ajmer, India, which provides computer literacy in programming and web development to learners of all ages. He further helps the community by sharing the knowledge and expertise he's gained over 20 years of teaching by writing books. His recent publications include *jQuery Recipes*, published by Apress, *Introduction to Python Programming and Developing GUI Applications with PyQT*, published by Cengage Learning, *The Android Tablet Developer's Cookbook*, published by Addison-Wesley Professional, *UNIX and Shell Programming*, published by Oxford University Press, and *Qt5 Python GUI Programming Cookbook*, published by Packt.

About the reviewer

Nibedit Dey is a software engineer turned serial entrepreneur with over 9 years of experience in building complex software-based products using C and C++. He has been involved in developing new medical devices, oscilloscopes, advanced showering systems, automotive dashboards, and infotainment systems. He is passionate about cutting-edge technologies. Before starting his entrepreneurial journey, he worked for L&T and Tektronix in different R&D roles. He has also reviewed several books on C and C++ programming for Packt.

I would like to thank the online programming communities, bloggers, and my peers from earlier organizations, from whom I have learned a lot over the years.

Packt is searching for authors like you

If you're interested in becoming an author for Packt, please visit `authors.packtpub.com` and apply today. We have worked with thousands of developers and tech professionals, just like you, to help them share their insight with the global tech community. You can make a general application, apply for a specific hot topic that we are recruiting an author for, or submit your own idea.

Table of Contents

Preface

This book is on the C programming language and explores all the important elements of C, such as strings, arrays (including one-dimensional and two-dimensional arrays), functions, pointers, file handling, threads, inter-process communication, database handling, advanced data structures, graphs, and graphics. As this book takes the cookbook approach, the reader will find independent solutions to different problems that they usually come across while making applications. By the end of the book, the reader will have sufficient knowledge to use high- as well as low-level features of the C language and will be able to apply this knowledge to making real-time applications.

Who this book is for

This book is meant for intermediate to advanced programmers and developers who want to make complex and real-time applications in C programming. This book will be of great use for trainers, teachers, and software developers who get stuck while making applications with arrays, pointers, functions, structures, files, databases, inter-process communication, advanced data structures, graphs, and graphics, and wish to see a walkthrough example to find the way out of a given problem.

What this book covers

Chapter 1, *Working with Arrays*, covers some complex but essential operations with arrays. You will learn how to insert an element into an array, multiply two matrices, find the common elements in two arrays, and also how to find the difference between two sets or arrays. Also, you will learn how to find the unique elements in an array and will encounter a technique to help you find out whether a given matrix is a sparse matrix or not. Lastly, we'll look at the procedure to merge two sorted arrays into one array.

Chapter 2, *Managing Strings*, teaches you how to manipulate strings to the extent of characters. You will learn how to find out whether a given string is a palindrome or not, how to find a given occurrence of the first repetitive character in a string, and how to count each character in a string. You will also learn how to count vowels and consonants in a string and the procedure for converting the vowels in a sentence into uppercase.

Chapter 3, *Exploring Functions*, explores the major role played by functions in breaking down a big application into small, independent, and manageable modules. In this chapter, you will learn to make a function that finds whether the supplied argument is an Armstrong number or not. You will also learn how a function returns an array and will make a function that finds the **greatest common divisor (gcd)** of two numbers using recursion. You will also learn to make functions that convert a binary number into hexadecimal. Lastly, you will learn to make a function that determines whether the supplied number is a palindrome or not.

Chapter 4, *Preprocessing and Compilation*, covers a range of topics, including performing preprocessing and compilation, performing conditional compilation with directives, applying assertions for validation, catching errors early with compile-time assertions, applying stringize, and how to use token-pasting operators.

Chapter 5, *Deep Dive into Pointers*, shows you how to use pointers to access content from specific memory locations. You will learn how to reverse a string using pointers, how to find the largest value in an array using pointers, and the procedure to sort a singly linked list. Besides this, the chapter explains how to find the transpose of a matrix using pointers and how to access a structure using pointers.

Chapter 6, *File Handling*, looks at how, when storing data for future use, file handling is very important. In this chapter, you will learn to learn to read a text file and convert all the characters after a period into uppercase. Also, you will learn how to display the content of a random file in reverse order and how to count the number of vowels in a text file. The chapter will also show you how to replace a word in a given text file with another word, and how to keep your file secure from unauthorized access. You will also learn how a file is encrypted.

Chapter 7, *Implementing Concurrency*, covers how concurrency is implemented in order to increase the efficiency of CPU operations. In this chapter, you will learn to do a task using a single thread. You will also learn to do multiple tasks with multiple threads and examine the technique of sharing data between two threads using mutex. Besides this, you will become familiar with situations where deadlock can be created and how such deadlock situations can be avoided.

Chapter 8, *Networking and Inter-Process Communication*, focuses on how to establish communication among processes. You will learn how to communicate between processes using pipes, how to establish communication among processes using FIFO, and how communication is established between the client and server using socket programming. You will also learn to do inter-process communication using the UDP socket, how a message is passed from one process to another using the message queue, and how the two processes communicate using shared memory.

`Chapter` 9, *Sorting and Searching*, covers searching using binary search, sorting numbers using bubble sort, and the use of insertion sort, quick sort, heap sort, selection sort, merge sort, shell sort, and radix sort.

`Chapter` 10, *Working with Graphs*, examines implementing stacks, two-way linked lists, circular linked lists, queues, circular queues, and the dequeue function. You'll also look at performing inorder traversal of a binary search tree recursively, followed by performing postorder traversal of a binary tree non-recursively.

`Chapter` 11, *Advanced Data Structures and Algorithms*, looks at representing graphs using an adjacency matrix and adjacency list, how to do breadth-first and depth-first traversal of graphs, and creating minimum spanning trees using Prim's and Kruskal's algorithms.

`Chapter` 12, *Creativity with Graphics*, covers making different graphical shapes, drawing a line between two mouse clicks, making a bar graph, and animating a bouncing ball.

`Chapter` 13, *Using MySQL Database*, considers how no real-time application is possible without storing information in a database. The information in a database needs to be managed as and when required. In this chapter, you will learn to display all the built-in tables in a default MySQL database. You will see how to store information in a MySQL database and search for the desired information in the database tables. Not only this; you will also learn to update information in the database tables and the procedure of deleting data from the database when no longer required anymore.

`Chapter` 14, *General-Purpose Utilities*, teaches you how to register a function that is called when a program exits, along with examinations of measuring clock ticks in the executing of a function, dynamic memory allocation, and handling signals.

`Chapter` 15, *Improving the Performance of Your Code*, focuses on using the register keyword, taking input faster, and applying loop unrolling for faster results.

`Chapter` 16, *Low-Level Programming*, looks at converting a binary number to decimal, multiplying and dividing two numbers using inline assembly language, and converting decimal values into binary using the bitwise operator and by masking certain bits of a register.

`Chapter` 17, *Embedded Software and IoT*, shows you how to toggle a port of a microcontroller in Embedded C, increment the value of a port, toggle voltage in Arduino, take input from the serial port, and how to detect and record temperatures using Arduino.

`Chapter 18`, *Applying Security in Coding*, demonstrates how to avoid buffer overflow, along with how to write secure code, avoid errors while string formatting, and avoid vulnerabilities while accessing files in C.

To get the most out of this book

You need to have some preliminary knowledge of C programming. You need to have basic knowledge of arrays, strings, functions, file handling, threads, and inter-process communication. Also, to handle databases, you will need to have basic knowledge of basic SQL commands.

Download the example code files

You can download the example code files for this book from your account at `www.packt.com`. If you purchased this book elsewhere, you can visit `www.packtpub.com/support` and register to have the files emailed directly to you.

You can download the code files by following these steps:

1. Log in or register at `www.packtpub.com`.
2. Select the **Support** tab.
3. Click on **Code Downloads**.
4. Enter the name of the book in the **Search** box and follow the onscreen instructions.

Once the file is downloaded, please make sure that you unzip or extract the folder using the latest version of:

- WinRAR/7-Zip for Windows
- Zipeg/iZip/UnRarX for Mac
- 7-Zip/PeaZip for Linux

The code bundle for the book is also hosted on GitHub at `https://github.com/PacktPublishing/Practical-C-Programming`. We also have other code bundles from our rich catalog of books and videos available at `https://github.com/PacktPublishing/`. Check them out!

Download the color images

We also provide a PDF file that has color images of the screenshots/diagrams used in this book. You can download it here: `https://static.packt-cdn.com/downloads/9781838641108_ColorImages.pdf`.

Conventions used

There are a number of text conventions used throughout this book.

`CodeInText`: Indicates code words in text, database table names, folder names, filenames, file extensions, path names, dummy URLs, user input, and Twitter handles. Here is an example: "In the figure, `1000` represents the memory address of the `i` variable."

A block of code is set as follows:

```
for(i=0;i<2;i++)
  {
    for(j=0;j<4;j++)
    {
      matR[i][j]=0;
      for(k=0;k<3;k++)
      {
        matR[i][j]=matR[i][j]+matA[i][k]*matB[k][j];
      }
    }
  }
```

When we wish to draw your attention to a particular part of a code block, the relevant lines or items are set in bold:

```
printf("How many elements are there? ");
scanf("%d", &n);
```

Any command-line input or output is written as follows:

```
D:\CBook>reversestring
Enter a string: manish
Reverse string is hsinam
```

Bold: Indicates a new term, an important word, or words that you see onscreen. For example, words in menus or dialog boxes appear in the text like this. Here is an example: "Simply click the **Next** button to continue."

 Warnings or important notes appear like this.

 Tips and tricks appear like this.

Sections

In this book, you will find several headings that appear frequently (*How to do it* and *How it works*).

To receive clear instructions on how to complete a recipe, use these sections as follows:

How to do it...

This section contains the steps required to follow the recipe.

How it works...

This section consists of a detailed explanation of the steps followed in the previous section.

There's more...

This section, when present, consists of additional information about the recipe in order to enhance your knowledge about the recipe.

See also

This section, when present, provides helpful links to other useful information for the recipe.

Get in touch

Feedback from our readers is always welcome.

General feedback: Email `feedback@packtpub.com` and mention the book title in the subject of your message. If you have questions about any aspect of this book, please email us at `questions@packtpub.com`.

Errata: Although we have taken every care to ensure the accuracy of our content, mistakes do happen. If you have found a mistake in this book, we would be grateful if you would report this to us. Please visit `www.packtpub.com/support/errata`, select your book, click on the Errata Submission Form link, and enter the details.

Piracy: If you come across any illegal copies of our works in any form on the internet, we would be grateful if you would provide us with the location address or website name. Please contact us at `copyright@packtpub.com` with a link to the material.

If you are interested in becoming an author: If there is a topic that you have expertise in and you are interested in either writing or contributing to a book, please visit `authors.packtpub.com`.

Reviews

Once you have read and used this book, why not leave a review on the site that you purchased it from? Potential readers can then see and use your unbiased opinion to make purchase decisions, we at Packt can understand what you think about our products, and our authors can see your feedback on their book. Thank you!

For more information about Packt, please visit `packtpub.com`.

Working with Arrays 1

Arrays are an important construct of any programming language. To keep data of a similar type together, we need arrays. Arrays are heavily used in applications where elements have to be accessed at random. Arrays are also a prime choice when you need to sort elements, look for desired data in a collection, and find common or unique data between two sets. Arrays are assigned contiguous memory locations and are a very popular structure for sorting and searching data collections because any element of an array can be accessed by simply specifying its subscript or index location. This chapter will cover recipes that include operations commonly applied to arrays.

In this chapter, we will learn how to make the following recipes using arrays:

- Inserting an element into a one-dimensional array
- Multiplying two matrices
- Finding the common elements in two arrays
- Finding the difference between two sets or arrays
- Finding the unique elements in an array
- Finding whether a matrix is sparse
- Merging two sorted arrays into one

Let's begin with the first recipe!

Inserting an element in an array

In this recipe, we will learn how to insert an element in-between an array. You can define the length of the array and also specify the location where you want the new value to be inserted. The program will display the array after the value has been inserted.

How to do it...

1. Let's assume that there is an array, **p**, with five elements, as follows:

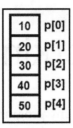

Figure 1.1

Now, suppose you want to enter a value, say **99**, at the third position. We will write a C program that will give the following output:

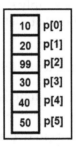

Figure 1.2

Here are the steps to follow to insert an element in an array:

1. Define a macro called `max` and initialize it to a value of `100`:

   ```
   #define max 100
   ```

2. Define an array `p` of size max elements:

   ```
   int p[max]
   ```

3. Enter the length of the array when prompted. The length you enter will be assigned to a variable `n`:

   ```
   printf("Enter length of array:");
   scanf("%d",&n);
   ```

4. A `for` loop will be executed prompting you to enter the elements of the array:

```
for(i=0;i<=n-1;i++ )
    scanf("%d",&p[i]);
```

5. Specify the position in the array where the new value has to be inserted:

```
printf("\nEnter position where to insert:");
scanf("%d",&k);
```

6. Because the arrays in C are zero-based, the position you enter is decremented by 1:

```
k--;
```

7. To create space for the new element at the specified index location, all the elements are shifted one position down:

```
for(j=n-1;j>=k;j--)
    p[j+1]=p[j];
```

8. Enter the new value which will be inserted at the vacated index location:

```
printf("\nEnter the value to insert:");
scanf("%d",&p[k]);
```

Here is the `insertintoarray.c` program for inserting an element in between an array:

```
#include<stdio.h>
#define max 100
void main()
{
    int p[max], n,i,k,j;
    printf("Enter length of array:");
    scanf("%d",&n);
    printf("Enter %d elements of array\n",n);
    for(i=0;i<=n-1;i++ )
        scanf("%d",&p[i]);
    printf("\nThe array is:\n");
    for(i = 0;i<=n-1;i++)
        printf("%d\n",p[i]);
    printf("\nEnter position where to insert:");
    scanf("%d",&k);
    k--;/*The position is always one value higher than the
```

```
    subscript, so it is decremented by one*/
        for(j=n-1;j>=k;j--)
            p[j+1]=p[j];
        /* Shifting all the elements of the array one position down
    from the location of insertion */
        printf("\nEnter the value to insert:");
        scanf("%d",&p[k]);
        printf("\nArray after insertion of element: \n");
        for(i=0;i<=n;i++)
            printf("%d\n",p[i]);
}
```

Now, let's go behind the scenes to understand the code better.

How it works...

Because we want to specify the length of the array, we will first define a macro called max and initialize it to a value of 100. I have defined the value of max as 100 because I assume that I will not need to enter more than 100 values in an array, but it can be any value as desired. An array, p, is defined of size max elements. You will be prompted to specify the length of the array. Let's specify the length of the array as 5. We will assign the value 5 to the variable n. Using a for loop, you will be asked to enter the elements of the array.

Let's say you enter the values in the array, as shown in *Figure 1.1* given earlier:

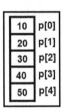

In the preceding diagram, the numbers, 0, 1, 2, and so on are known as index or subscript and are used for assigning and retrieving values from an array. Next, you will be asked to specify the position in the array where the new value has to be inserted. Suppose, you enter 3, which is assigned to the variable k. This means that you want to insert a new value at location 3 in the array.

Because the arrays in C are zero-based, position 3 means that you want to insert a new value at index location 2, which is **p[2]**. Hence, the position entered in k is decremented by 1.

To create space for the new element at index location **p[2]**, all the elements are shifted one position down. This means that the element at **p[4]** is moved to index location **p[5]**, the one at **p[3]** is moved to **p[4]**, and the element at **p[2]** is moved to **p[3]**, as follows:

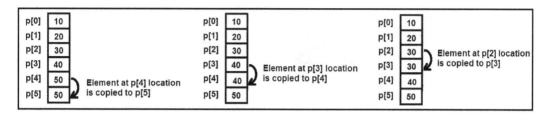

Figure 1.3

Once the element from the target index location is safely copied to the next location, you will be asked to enter the new value. Suppose you enter the new value as 99; that value will be inserted at index location **p[2]**, as shown in *Figure 1.2*, given earlier:

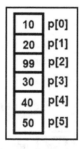

Let's use GCC to compile the `insertintoarray.c` program, as shown in this statement:

```
D:\CBook>gcc insertintoarray.c -o insertintoarray
```

Now, let's run the generated executable file, `insertintoarray.exe`, to see the program output:

```
D:\CBook>./insertintoarray
Enter length of array:5
Enter 5 elements of array
10
20
30
40
50
```

```
The array is:
10
20
30
40
50

Enter target position to insert:3
Enter the value to insert:99
Array after insertion of element:
10
20
99
30
40
50
```

Voilà! We've successfully inserted an element in an array.

There's more...

What if we want to delete an element from an array? The procedure is simply the reverse; in other words, all the elements from the bottom of the array will be copied one place up to replace the element that was deleted.

Let's assume array **p** has the following five elements (*Figure 1.1*):

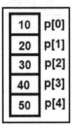

Suppose, we want to delete the third element, in other words, the one at **p[2]**, from this array. To do so, the element at **p[3]** will be copied to **p[2]**, the element at **p[4]** will be copied to **p[3]**, and the last element, which here is at **p[4]**, will stay as it is:

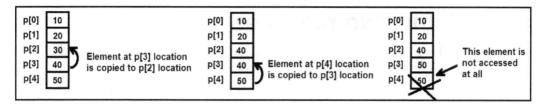

Figure 1.4

The `deletefromarray.c` program for deleting the array is as follows:

```
#include<stdio.h>
void main()
{
    int p[100],i,n,a;
    printf("Enter the length of the array: ");
    scanf("%d",&n);
    printf("Enter %d elements of the array \n",n);
    for(i=0;i<=n-1;i++)
        scanf("%d",&p[i]);
    printf("\nThe array is:\n");\
    for(i=0;i<=n-1;i++)
        printf("%d\n",p[i]);
    printf("Enter the position/location to delete: ");
    scanf("%d",&a);
    a--;
    for(i=a;i<=n-2;i++)
    {
        p[i]=p[i+1];
        /* All values from the bottom of the array are shifted up till
        the location of the element to be deleted */
    }
    p[n-1]=0;
    /* The vacant position created at the bottom of the array is set
to
    0 */
    printf("Array after deleting the element is\n");
    for(i=0;i<= n-2;i++)
        printf("%d\n",p[i]);
}
```

Now, let's move on to the next recipe!

Multiplying two matrices

A prerequisite for multiplying two matrices is that the number of columns in the first matrix must be equal to the number of rows in the second matrix.

How to do it...

1. Create two matrices of orders **2 x 3** and **3 x 4** each.
2. Before we make the matrix multiplication program, we need to understand how matrix multiplication is performed manually. To do so, let's assume that the two matrices to be multiplied have the following elements:

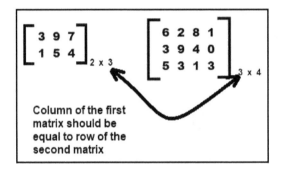

Figure 1.5

3. The resultant matrix will be of the order **2 x 4**, that is, the resultant matrix will have the same number of rows as the first matrix and the same number of columns as the second matrix:

$$\begin{bmatrix} 3 & 9 & 7 \\ 1 & 5 & 4 \end{bmatrix}_{2 \times 3} \mathbf{X} \begin{bmatrix} 6 & 2 & 8 & 1 \\ 3 & 9 & 4 & 0 \\ 5 & 3 & 1 & 3 \end{bmatrix}_{3 \times 4} = \begin{bmatrix} - & - & - & - \\ - & - & - & - \end{bmatrix}_{2 \times 4}$$

Figure 1.6

Essentially, the resultant matrix of the order **2 x 4** will have the following elements:

first row, first column	first row, second column	first row, third column	first row, fourth column
second row, first column	second row, second column	second row, third column	second row, fourth column

2 x 4

Figure 1.7

4. The element **first row, first column** in the resultant matrix is computed using the following formula:

   SUM(first element of the first row of the first matrix × first element of the first column of the second matrix), (second element of the first row... × second element of the first column...), (and so on...)

   For example, let's assume the elements of the two matrices are as shown in *Figure 1.5*. The elements in the first row and the first column of the resultant matrix will be computed as follows:

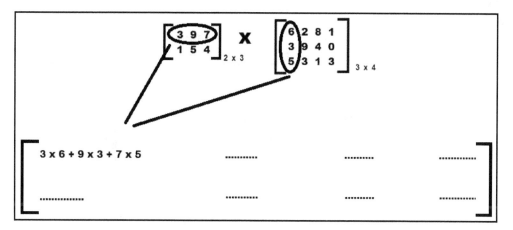

Figure 1.8

5. Hence, the element in **first row, first column** in the resultant matrix will be as follows:

$$(3×6)+(9×3)+(7×5)$$
$$=18 + 27 + 35$$
$$=80$$

Figure 1.9 explains how the rest of the elements are computed in the resultant matrix:

$$
\begin{bmatrix} 3 & 9 & 7 \\ 1 & 5 & 4 \end{bmatrix}_{2 \times 3}
\qquad
\begin{bmatrix} 6 & 2 & 8 & 1 \\ 3 & 9 & 4 & 0 \\ 5 & 3 & 1 & 3 \end{bmatrix}_{3 \times 4}
$$

$$
\begin{bmatrix}
3 \times 6 + 9 \times 3 + 7 \times 5 & 3 \times 2 + 9 \times 9 + 7 \times 3 & 3 \times 8 + 9 \times 4 + 7 \times 1 & 3 \times 1 + 9 \times 0 + 7 \times 3 \\
1 \times 6 + 5 \times 3 + 4 \times 5 & 1 \times 2 + 5 \times 9 + 4 \times 3 & 1 \times 8 + 5 \times 4 + 4 \times 1 & 1 \times 1 + 5 \times 0 + 4 \times 3
\end{bmatrix}
$$

$$
\begin{bmatrix}
18 + 27 + 35 & 6 + 81 + 21 & 24 + 36 + 7 & 3 + 0 + 21 \\
6 + 15 + 20 & 2 + 45 + 12 & 8 + 20 + 4 & 1 + 0 + 12
\end{bmatrix}
$$

$$
\begin{bmatrix}
80 & 108 & 67 & 24 \\
41 & 59 & 32 & 13
\end{bmatrix}
$$

Figure 1.9

The `matrixmulti.c` program for multiplying the two matrices is as follows:

```c
#include  <stdio.h>
int main()
{
   int matA[2][3], matB[3][4], matR[2][4];
   int i,j,k;
   printf("Enter elements of the first matrix of order 2 x 3 \n");
   for(i=0;i<2;i++)
   {
      for(j=0;j<3;j++)
      {
         scanf("%d",&matA[i][j]);
      }
   }
   printf("Enter elements of the second matrix of order 3 x 4 \n");
   for(i=0;i<3;i++)
   {
      for(j=0;j<4;j++)
      {
```

```
        scanf("%d",&matB[i][j]);
      }
   }
   for(i=0;i<2;i++)
   {
      for(j=0;j<4;j++)
      {
         matR[i][j]=0;
         for(k=0;k<3;k++)
         {
            matR[i][j]=matR[i][j]+matA[i][k]*matB[k][j];
         }
      }
   }
   printf("\nFirst Matrix is \n");
   for(i=0;i<2;i++)
   {
      for(j=0;j<3;j++)
      {
         printf("%d\t",matA[i][j]);
      }
      printf("\n");
   }
   printf("\nSecond Matrix is \n");
   for(i=0;i<3;i++)
   {
      for(j=0;j<4;j++)
      {
         printf("%d\t",matB[i][j]);
      }
      printf("\n");
   }
   printf("\nMatrix multiplication is \n");
   for(i=0;i<2;i++)
   {
      for(j=0;j<4;j++)
      {
         printf("%d\t",matR[i][j]);
      }
      printf("\n");
   }
   return 0;
}
```

Now, let's go behind the scenes to understand the code better.

How it works...

The two matrices are defined matA and matB of the orders 2 x 3 and 3 x 4, respectively, using the following statement:

```
int matA[2][3], matB[3][4]
```

You will be asked to enter the elements of the two matrices using the nested for loops. The elements in the matrix are entered in row-major order, in other words, all the elements of the first row are entered first, followed by all the elements of the second row, and so on.

In the nested loops, for i and for j, the outer loop, for i, represents the row and the inner loop, and for j represents the column.

While entering the elements of matrices matA and matB, the values entered in the two matrices will be assigned to the respective index locations of the two-dimensional arrays as follows:

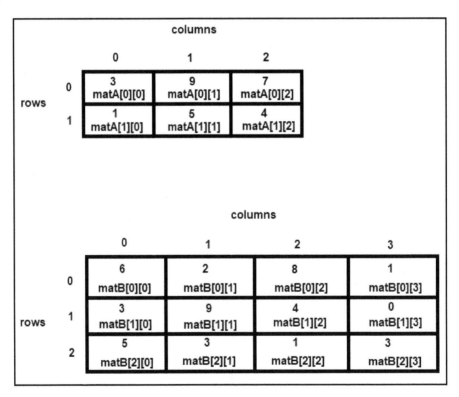

Figure 1.10

The nested loops that actually compute the matrix multiplication are as follows:

```
for(i=0;i<2;i++)
{
   for(j=0;j<4;j++)
   {
      matR[i][j]=0;
      for(k=0;k<3;k++)
      {
         matR[i][j]=matR[i][j]+matA[i][k]*matB[k][j];
      }
   }
}
```

The variable `i` represents the row of the resultant matrix, `j` represents the column of the resultant matrix, and `k` represents the common factor. The *common factor* here means the column of the first matrix and the row of the second matrix.

Recall that the prerequisite for matrix multiplication is that the column of the first matrix should have the same number of rows as the second matrix. Because the respective elements have to be added after multiplication, the element has to be initialized to 0 before addition.

The following statement initializes the elements of the resultant matrix:

```
matR[i][j]=0;
```

The `for k` loop inside the nested loops helps in selecting the elements in the rows of the first matrix and multiplying them by elements of the column of the second matrix:

```
matR[i][j]=matR[i][j]+matA[i][k]*matB[k][j];
```

Let's use GCC to compile the `matrixmulti.c` program as follows:

```
D:\CBook>gcc matrixmulti.c -o matrixmulti
```

Let's run the generated executable file, `matrixmulti.exe`, to see the output of the program:

```
D:\CBook\Chapters\1Arrays>./matrixmulti

Enter elements of the first matrix of order 2 x 3
3
9
7
1
5
```

```
4

Enter elements of the second matrix of order 3 x 4
6 2 8 1
3 9 4 0
5 3 1 3

First Matrix is
3 9 7
1 5 4

Second Matrix is
6 2 8 1
3 9 4 0
5 3 1 3

Matrix multiplication is
80 108 67 24
41 59 32 13
```

Voilà! We've successfully multiplied two matrices.

There's more...

One thing that you might notice while entering the elements of the matrix is that there are two ways of doing it.

1. The first method is that you press *Enter* after inputting each element as follows:

   ```
   3
   9
   7
   1
   5
   4
   ```

   The values will be automatically assigned to the matrix in row-major order, in other words, 3 will be assigned to matA[0][0], 9 will be assigned to matA[0][1], and so on.

2. The second method of entering elements in the matrix is as follows:

```
6  2  8  1
3  9  4  0
5  3  1  3
```

Here, 6 will be assigned to `matB[0][0]`, 2 will be assigned to `matB[0][1]`, and so on.

Now, let's move on to the next recipe!

Finding the common elements in two arrays

Finding the common elements in two arrays is akin to finding the intersection of two sets. Let's learn how to do it.

How to do it...

1. Define two arrays of a certain size and assign elements of your choice to both the arrays. Let's assume that we created two arrays called **p** and **q**, both of size four elements:

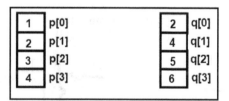

Figure 1.11

2. Define one more array. Let's call it array **r**, to be used for storing the elements that are common between the two arrays.

3. If an element in array **p** exists in the array **q**, it is added to array **r**. For instance, if the element at the first location in array **p**, which is at **p[0]**, does not appear in array **q**, it is discarded, and the next element, at **p[1]**, is picked up for comparison.

4. And if the element at **p[0]** is found anywhere in array **q**, it is added to array **r**, as follows:

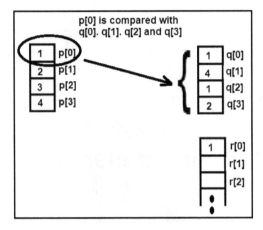

Figure 1.12

5. This procedure is repeated with other elements of array **q**. That is, **p[1]** is compared with **q[0]**, **q[1]**, **q[2]**, and **q[3]**. If **p[1]** is not found in array **q**, then before inserting it straightaway into array **r**, it is compared with the existing elements of array **r** to avoid repetitive elements.

6. Because the element at **p[1]** appears in array **q** and is not already present in array **r**, it is added to array **r** as follows:

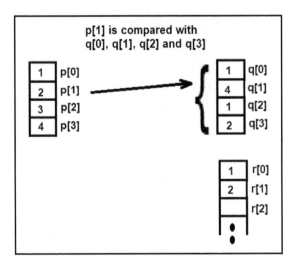

Figure 1.13

The `commoninarray.c` program for establishing common elements among the two arrays is as follows:

```c
#include<stdio.h>
#define max 100

int ifexists(int z[], int u, int v)
{
    int i;
    if (u==0) return 0;
    for (i=0; i<=u;i++)
        if (z[i]==v) return (1);
    return (0);
}
void main()
{
    int p[max], q[max], r[max];
    int m,n;
    int i,j,k;
    k=0;
    printf("Enter the length of the first array:");
    scanf("%d",&m);
    printf("Enter %d elements of the first array\n",m);
    for(i=0;i<m;i++ )
        scanf("%d",&p[i]);
    printf("\nEnter the length of the second array:");
    scanf("%d",&n);
    printf("Enter %d elements of the second array\n",n);
    for(i=0;i<n;i++ )
        scanf("%d",&q[i]);
    k=0;
    for (i=0;i<m;i++)
    {
        for (j=0;j<n;j++)
        {
            if (p[i]==q[j])
            {
                if(!ifexists(r,k,p[i]))
                {
                    r[k]=p[i];
                    k++;
                }
            }
        }
    }
    if(k>0)
    {
        printf("\nThe common elements in the two arrays are:\n");
```

```
            for(i = 0;i<k;i++)
                printf("%d\n",r[i]);
        }
        else
            printf("There are no common elements in the two
    arrays\n");
    }
```

Now, let's go behind the scenes to understand the code better.

How it works...

A macro, max, is defined of size 100. A function, ifexists(), is defined that simply returns true (1) or false (0). The function returns true if the supplied value exists in the specified array, and false if it doesn't.

Two arrays are defined, called p and q, of size max (in other words, 100 elements). You will be prompted to specify the length of the array, p, and then asked to enter the elements in that array. After that, you will be asked to specify the length of array q, followed by entering the elements in array q.

Thereafter, p[0], the first element in array p , is picked up, and by using the for loop, p[0] is compared with all the elements of array q. If p[0] is found in array q, then p[0] is added to the resulting array, r.

After a comparison of p[0], the second element in array p, p[1], is picked up and compared with all the elements of array q. The procedure is repeated until all the elements of array p are compared with all the elements of array q.

If any elements of array p are found in array q, then before adding that element to the resulting array, r, it is run through the ifexists() function to ensure that the element does not already exist in array r. This is because we don't want repetitive elements in array r.

Finally, all the elements in array r, which are the common elements of the two arrays, are displayed on the screen.

Let's use GCC to compile the commoninarray.c program as follows:

```
D:\CBook>gcc commoninarray.c -o commoninarray
```

Now, let's run the generated executable file, `commoninarray.exe`, to see the output of the program:

```
D:\CBook>./commoninarray
Enter the length of the first array:5
Enter 5 elements in the first array
1
2
3
4
5

Enter the length of the second array:4
Enter 4 elements in the second array
7
8
9
0

There are no common elements in the two arrays
```

Because there were no common elements between the two arrays entered previously, we can't quite say that we've truly tested the program. Let's run the program again, and this time, we will enter the array elements such that they have something in common.

```
D:\CBook>./commoninarray
Enter the length of the first array:4
Enter 4 elements in the first array
1
2
3
4

Enter the length of the second array:4
Enter 4 elements in the second array
1
4
1
2

The common elements in the two arrays are:
1
2
4
```

Voilà! We've successfully identified the common elements between two arrays.

Finding the difference between two sets or arrays

When we talk about the difference between two sets or arrays, we are referring to all the elements of the first array that don't appear in the second array. In essence, all the elements in the first array that are not common to the second array are referred to as the difference between the two sets. The difference in sets p and q, for example, will be denoted by p – q.

If array p, for example, has the elements {1, 2, 3, 4}, and array q has the elements {2, 4, 5, 6}, then the difference between the two arrays, p – q, will be {1,3}. Let's find out how this is done.

How to do it...

1. Define two arrays, say p and q, of a certain size and assign elements of your choice to both the arrays.
2. Define one more array, say r, to be used for storing the elements that represent the difference between the two arrays.
3. Pick one element from array p and compare it with all the elements of the array q.
4. If the element of array p exists in array q, discard that element and pick up the next element of array p and repeat from step 3.
5. If the element of array p does not exist in array q, add that element in array r. Before adding that element to array r, ensure that it does not already exist in array r.
6. Repeat steps 3 to 5 until all the elements of array p are compared.
7. Display all the elements in array r, as these are the elements that represent the difference between arrays p and q.

The differencearray.c program to establish the difference between two arrays is as follows:

```
#include<stdio.h>
#define max 100

int ifexists(int z[], int u, int v)
{
```

```
    int i;
    if (u==0) return 0;
    for (i=0;  i<=u;i++)
        if (z[i]==v) return (1);
    return (0);
}

void main()
{
    int p[max], q[max], r[max];
    int m,n;
    int i,j,k;
    printf("Enter length of first array:");
    scanf("%d",&m);
    printf("Enter %d elements of first array\n",m);
    for(i=0;i<m;i++ )
        scanf("%d",&p[i]);
    printf("\nEnter length of second array:");
    scanf("%d",&n);
    printf("Enter %d elements of second array\n",n);
    for(i=0;i<n;i++ )
scanf("%d",&q[i]);
    k=0;
    for (i=0;i<m;i++)
    {
        for (j=0;j<n;j++)
        {
            if (p[i]==q[j])
            {
break;
            }
        }
        if(j==n)
        {
            if(!ifexists(r,k,p[i]))
            {
                r[k]=p[i];
                k++;
            }
        }
    }
    printf("\nThe difference of the two array is:\n");
    for(i = 0;i<k;i++)
        printf("%d\n",r[i]);
}
```

Now, let's go behind the scenes to understand the code better.

How it works...

We defined two arrays called **p** and **q**. We don't want to fix the length of these arrays, so we should define a macro called `max` of value `100` and set the two arrays, **p** and **q**, to the size of `max`.

Thereafter, you will be prompted to specify the size of the first array and enter the elements in the first array, **p**. Similarly, you will be asked to specify the length of the second array, **q**, followed by entering the elements in the second array.

Let's assume you have specified the length of both arrays as 4 and have entered the following elements:

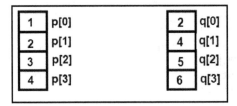

Figure 1.14

We need to pick up one element at a time from the first array and compare it with all the elements of the second array. If an element in array **p** does not appear in array **q**, it will be assigned to the third array we created, array **r**.

Array **r** will be used for storing the elements that define the difference between two arrays. As shown in *Figure 1.15*, the first element of array **p**, in other words, at **p[0]**, is compared with all the elements of array **q**, in other words, with **q[0]**, **q[1]**, **q[2]**, and **q[3]**.

Because the element at **p[0]**, which is **1**, does not appear in array **q**, it will be added to the array **r**, indicating the first element representing the difference between the two arrays:

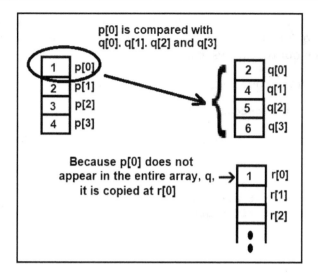

Figure 1.15

Because the element at **p[1]**, which is **2**, appears in array **q**, it is discarded, and the next element in array **p**, in other words, **p[2]**, is picked up and compared with all the elements in array **q**.

As the element at **p[2]** does not appear in array **q**, it is added to array **r** at the next available location, which is **r[1]** (see *Figure 1.16* as follows):

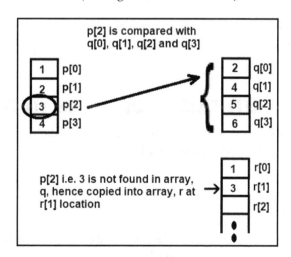

Figure 1.16

Continue the procedure until all the elements of array **p** are compared with all the elements of array **q**. Finally, we will have array **r**, with the elements showing the difference between our two arrays, **p** and **q**.

Let's use GCC to compile our program, `differencearray.c`, as follows:

```
D:\CBook>gcc differencearray.c -o differencearray
```

Now, let's run the generated executable file, `differencearray`, to see the output of the program:

```
D:\CBook>./differencearray
Enter length of first array:4
Enter 4 elements of first array
1
2
3
4
Enter length of second array:4
Enter 4 elements of second array
2
4
5
6
The difference of the two array is:
1
3
```

Voilà! We've successfully found the difference between two arrays. Now, let's move on to the next recipe!

Finding the unique elements in an array

In this recipe, we will learn how to find the unique elements in an array, such that the repetitive elements in the array will be displayed only once.

How to do it...

1. Define two arrays, **p** and **q**, of a certain size and assign elements only to array **p**. We will leave array **q** blank.
2. These will be our source and target arrays, respectively. The target array will contain the resulting unique elements of the source array.

3. After that, each of the elements in the source array will be compared with the existing elements in the target array.

4. If the element in the source array exists in the target array, then that element is discarded and the next element in the source array is picked up for comparison.

5. If the source array element does not exist in the target array, it is copied into the target array.

6. Let's assume that array **p** contains the following repetitive elements:

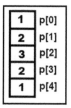

Figure 1.17

7. We will start by copying the first element of the source array, **p**, into the target array, **q**, in other words, **p[0]** into array **q[0]**, as follows:

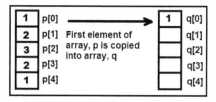

Figure 1.18

8. Next, the second array element of **p**, in other words, **p[1]**, is compared with all the existing elements of array **q**. That is, **p[1]** is compared with array **q** to check whether it already exists in array **q**, as follows:

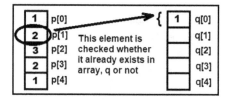

Figure 1.19

9. Because **p[1]** does not exist in array **q**, it is copied at **q[1]**, as shown in *Figure 1.20*:

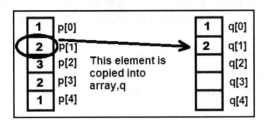

Figure 1.20

10. This procedure is repeated until all the elements of array **p** are compared with array q. In the end, we will have array **q**, which will contain the unique elements of array **p**.

Here is the `uniqueelements.c` program for finding the unique elements in the first array:

```c
#include<stdio.h>
#define max 100

int ifexists(int z[], int u, int v)
{
    int i;
    for (i=0; i<u;i++)
        if (z[i]==v) return (1);
    return (0);
}

void main()
{
    int p[max], q[max];
    int m;
    int i,k;
    k=0;
    printf("Enter length of the array:");
    scanf("%d",&m);
    printf("Enter %d elements of the array\n",m);
    for(i=0;i<m;i++ )
        scanf("%d",&p[i]);
    q[0]=p[0];
    k=1;
    for (i=1;i<m;i++)
    {
```

```
            if(!ifexists(q,k,p[i]))
            {
                q[k]=p[i];
                k++;
            }
    }
    printf("\nThe unique elements in the array are:\n");
    for(i = 0;i<k;i++)
        printf("%d\n",q[i]);
}
```

Now, let's go behind the scenes to understand the code better.

How it works...

We will define a macro called `max` of size `100`. Two arrays, `p` and `q`, are defined of size `max`. Array `p` will contain the original elements, and array `q` will contain the unique elements of array `p`. You will be prompted to enter the length of the array and, thereafter, using the `for` loop, the elements of the array will be accepted and assigned to array `p`.

The following statement will assign the first element of array `p` to the first index location of our blank array, which we will name array `q`:

```
q[0]=p[0]
```

A `for` loop is again used to access the rest of the elements of array `p`, one by one. First, the foremost element of array `p`, which is at `p[0]`, is copied to array `q` at `q[0]`.

Next, the second array `p` element, `p[1]`, is compared with all the existing elements of array `q`. That is, `p[1]` is checked against array `q` to confirm whether it is already present there.

Because there is only a single element in array `q`, `p[1]` is compared with `q[0]`. Because `p[1]` does not exist in array `q`, it is copied at `q[1]`.

This procedure is repeated for all elements in array `p`. Each of the accessed elements of array `p` is run through the `ifexists()` function to check whether any of them already exist in array `q`.

The function returns `1` if an element in array `p` already exists in array `q`. In that case, the element in array `p` is discarded and the next array element is picked up for comparison.

In case the `ifexists()` function returns 0, confirming that the element in array p does not exist in array q, the array p element is added to array q at the next available index/subscript location.

When all the elements of array p are checked and compared, array q will have only the unique elements of array p.

Let's use GCC to compile the `uniqueelements.c` program as follows:

```
D:\CBook>gcc uniqueelements.c -o uniqueelements
```

Now, let's run the generated executable file, `uniqueelements.exe`, to see the output of the program:

```
D:\CBook>./uniqueelements
Enter the length of the array:5
Enter 5 elements in the array
1
2
3
2
1

The unique elements in the array are:
1
2
3
```

Voilà! We've successfully identified the unique elements in an array. Now, let's move on to the next recipe!

Finding whether a matrix is sparse

A matrix is considered sparse when it has more zero values than non-zero values (and dense when it has more non-zero values). In this recipe, we will learn how to find out whether the specified matrix is sparse.

How to do it...

1. First, specify the order of the matrix. Then, you will be prompted to enter the elements in the matrix. Let's assume that you specified the order of the matrix as 4 x 4. After entering the elements in the matrix, it might appear like this:

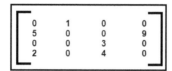

Figure 1.21

2. Once the elements of the matrix are entered, count the number of zeros in it. A counter for this purpose is initialized to **0**. Using nested loops, each of the matrix elements is scanned and, upon finding any zero elements, the value of the counter is incremented by 1.

3. Thereafter, the following formula is used for establishing whether the matrix is sparse.

   If counter > [(the number of rows x the number of columns)/2] = Sparse Matrix

4. Depending on the result of the preceding formula, one of the following messages will be displayed on the screen as follows:

   The given matrix is a sparse matrix

   or

   The given matrix is not a sparse matrix

The sparsematrix.c program for establishing whether the matrix is sparse is as follows:

```c
#include <stdio.h>
#define max 100

/*A sparse matrix has more zero elements than nonzero elements */
void main ()
{
    static int arr[max][max];
    int i,j,r,c;
```

```
int ctr=0;
printf("How many rows and columns are in this matrix? ");
scanf("%d %d", &r, &c);
printf("Enter the elements in the matrix :\n");
for(i=0;i<r;i++)
{
    for(j=0;j<c;j++)
    {
        scanf("%d",&arr[i][j]);
        if (arr[i][j]==0)
            ++ctr;
    }
}
if (ctr>((r*c)/2))
    printf ("The given matrix is a sparse matrix. \n");
else
    printf ("The given matrix is not a sparse matrix.\n");
printf ("There are %d number of zeros in the matrix.\n",ctr);
}
```

Now, let's go behind the scenes to understand the code better.

How it works...

Because we don't want to fix the size of the matrix, we will define a macro called `max` of value 100. A matrix, or a two-dimensional array called **arr**, is defined of the order max x max. You will be prompted to enter the order of the matrix, for which you can again enter any value up to 100.

Let's assume that you've specified the order of the matrix as 4 x 4. You will be prompted to enter elements in the matrix. The values entered in the matrix will be in row-major order. After entering the elements, the matrix **arr** should look like *Figure 1.22*, as follows:

	0	1	2	3
0	0 arr[0][0]	1 arr[0][1]	0 arr[0][2]	0 arr[0][3]
1	5 arr[1][0]	0 arr[1][1]	0 arr[1][2]	9 arr[1][3]
2	0 arr[2][0]	0 arr[2][1]	3 arr[2][2]	0 arr[2][3]
3	2 arr[3][0]	0 arr[3][1]	4 arr[3][2]	0 arr[3][3]

Figure 1.22

A counter called `ctr` is created and is initialized to `0`. Using nested loops, each element of matrix `arr` is checked and the value of `ctr` is incremented if any element is found to be 0. Thereafter, using the `if else` statement, we will check whether the count of zero values is more than non-zero values. If the count of zero values is more than non-zero values, then the message will be displayed on the screen as follows:

```
The given matrix is a sparse matrix
```

However, failing that, the message will be displayed on the screen as follows:

```
The given matrix is not a sparse matrix
```

Let's use GCC to compile the `sparsematrix.c` program as follows:

```
D:\CBook>gcc sparsematrix.c -o sparsematrix
```

Let's run the generated executable file, `sparsematrix.exe`, to see the output of the program:

```
D:\CBook>./sparsematrix
How many rows and columns are in this matrix? 4 4
Enter the elements in the matrix :
0 1 0 0
5 0 0 9
0 0 3 0
2 0 4 0
The given matrix is a sparse matrix.
There are 10 zeros in the matrix.
```

Okay. Let's run the program again to see the output when the count of non-zero values is higher:

```
D:\CBook>./sparsematrix
How many rows and columns are in this matrix? 4 4
Enter the elements in the matrix:
1 0 3 4
0 0 2 9
8 6 5 1
0 7 0 4
The given matrix is not a sparse matrix.
There are 5 zeros in the matrix.
```

Voilà! We've successfully identified a sparse and a non-sparse matrix.

There's more...

How about finding an identity matrix, in other words, finding out whether the matrix entered by the user is an identity matrix or not. Let me tell you—a matrix is said to be an identity matrix if it is a square matrix and all the elements of the principal diagonal are ones and all other elements are zeros. An identity matrix of the order **3 x 3** may appear as follows:

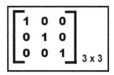

Figure 1.23

In the preceding diagram, you can see that the principal diagonal elements of the matrix are 1's and the rest of them are 0's. The index or subscript location of the principal diagonal elements will be `arr[0][0]`, `arr[1][1]`, and `arr[2][2]`, so the following procedure is followed to find out whether the matrix is an identity matrix or not:

- Checks that if the index location of the row and column is the same, in other words, if the row number is 0 and the column number, too, is 0, then at that index location, [0][0], the matrix element must be 1. Similarly, if the row number is 1 and the column number, too, is 1, that is, at the [1][1] index location, the matrix element must be 1.
- Verify that the matrix element is 0 at all the other index locations.

If both the preceding conditions are met, then the matrix is an identity matrix, or else it is not.

The `identitymatrix.c` program to establish whether the entered matrix is an identity matrix or not is given as follows:

```
        #include <stdio.h>
#define max 100
/* All the elements of the principal diagonal of the  Identity matrix
are ones and rest all are zero elements  */
void main ()
{
    static int arr[max][max];
    int i,j,r,c, bool;
    printf("How many rows and columns are in this matrix ? ");
    scanf("%d %d", &r, &c);
```

```
        if (r !=c)
        {
            printf("An identity matrix is a square matrix\n");
            printf("Because this matrix is not a square matrix, so it is
not an
                identity matrix\n");
        }
        else
        {
            printf("Enter elements in the matrix :\n");
            for(i=0;i<r;i++)
            {
                for(j=0;j<c;j++)
                {
                    scanf("%d",&arr[i][j]);
                }
            }
            printf("\nThe entered matrix is \n");
            for(i=0;i<r;i++)
            {
                for(j=0;j<c;j++)
                {
                    printf("%d\t",arr[i][j]);
                }
                printf("\n");
            }
            bool=1;
            for(i=0;i<r;i++)
            {
                for(j=0;j<c;j++)
                {
                    if(i==j)
                    {
                        if(arr[i][j] !=1)
                        {
                            bool=0;
                            break;
                        }
                    }
                    else
                    {
                        if(arr[i][j] !=0)
                        {
                            bool=0;
                            break;
                        }
                    }
                }
```

```
        }
        if(bool)
            printf("\nMatrix is an identity matrix\n");
        else
            printf("\nMatrix is not an identity matrix\n");
    }
}
```

Let's use GCC to compile the identitymatrix.c program as follows:

```
D:\CBook>gcc identitymatrix.c -o identitymatrix
```

No error is generated. This means the program is compiled perfectly and an executable file is generated. Let's run the generated executable file. First, we will enter a non-square matrix:

```
D:\CBook>./identitymatrix
How many rows and columns are in this matrix ? 3 4
An identity matrix is a square matrix
Because this matrix is not a square matrix, so it is not an identity
matrix
```

Now, let's run the program again; this time, we will enter a square matrix

```
D:\CBook>./identitymatrix
How many rows and columns are in this matrix ? 3 3
Enter elements in the matrix :
1 0 1
1 1 0
0 0 1

The entered matrix is
1        0        1
1        1        0
0        0        1

Matrix is not an identity matrix
```

Because a non-diagonal element in the preceding matrix is 1, it is not an identity matrix. Let's run the program again:

```
D:\CBook>./identitymatrix
How many rows and columns are in this matrix ? 3 3
Enter elements in the matrix :
1 0 0
0 1 0
0 0 1
The entered matrix is
```

```
1        0        0
0        1        0
0        0        1
Matrix is an identity matrix
```

Now, let's move on to the next recipe!

Merging two sorted arrays into a single array

In this recipe, we will learn to merge two sorted arrays into a single array so that the resulting merged array is also in sorted form.

How to do it...

1. Let's assume there are two arrays, **p** and **q**, of a certain length. The length of the two arrays can differ. Both have some sorted elements in them, as shown in *Figure 1.24*:

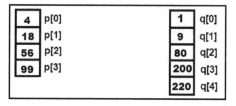

Figure 1.24

2. The merged array that will be created from the sorted elements of the preceding two arrays will be called array **r**. Three subscripts or index locations will be used to point to the respective elements of the three arrays.

3. Subscript i will be used to point to the index location of array p. Subscript j will be used to point to the index location of array q and subscript k will be used to point to the index location of array r. In the beginning, all three subscripts will be initialized to 0.

4. The following three formulas will be applied to get the merged sorted array:

> 1. The element at `p[i]` is compared with the element at `q[j]`. If `p[i]` is less than `q[j]`, then `p[i]` is assigned to array `r`, and the indices of arrays `p` and `r` are incremented so that the following element of array `p` is picked up for the next comparison as follows:

```
r[k]=p[i];
i++;
k++
```

> 2. If `q[j]` is less than `p[i]`, then `q[j]` is assigned to array `r`, and the indices of arrays `q` and `r` are incremented so that the following element of array `q` is picked up for the next comparison as follows:

```
r[k]=q[j];
i++;
k++
```

> 3. If `p[i]` is equal to `q[j]`, then both the elements are assigned to array `r`. `p[i]` is added to `r[k]`. The values of the `i` and `k` indices are incremented. `q[j]` is also added to `r[k]`, and the indices of the `q` and `r` arrays are incremented. Refer to the following code snippet:

```
r[k]=p[i];
i++;
k++
r[k]=q[j];
i++;
k++
```

5. The procedure will be repeated until either of the arrays gets over. If any of the arrays is over, the remainder of the elements of the other array will be simply appended to the array `r`.

The `mergetwosortedarrays.c` program for merging two sorted arrays is as follows:

```c
#include<stdio.h>
#define max 100

void main()
{
```

```c
int p[max], q[max], r[max];
int m,n;
int i,j,k;
printf("Enter length of first array:");
scanf("%d",&m);
printf("Enter %d elements of the first array in sorted order
\n",m);
for(i=0;i<m;i++)
    scanf("%d",&p[i]);
printf("\nEnter length of second array:");
scanf("%d",&n);
printf("Enter %d elements of the second array in sorted
order\n",n);
for(i=0;i<n;i++ )
    scanf("%d",&q[i]);
i=j=k=0;
while ((i<m) && (j <n))
{
    if(p[i] < q[j])
    {
        r[k]=p[i];
        i++;
        k++;
    }
    else
    {
        if(q[j]< p[i])
        {
            r[k]=q[j];
            k++;
            j++;
        }
        else
        {
            r[k]=p[i];
            k++;
            i++;
            r[k]=q[j];
            k++;
            j++;
        }
    }
}
while(i<m)
{
    r[k]=p[i];
    k++;
    i++;
```

```
    }
    while(j<n)
    {
        r[k]=q[j];
        k++;
        j++;
    }
    printf("\nThe combined sorted array is:\n");
    for(i = 0;i<k;i++)
        printf("%d\n",r[i]);
}
```

Now, let's go behind the scenes to understand the code better.

How it works...

A macro called max is defined of size 100. Three arrays, p, q, and r, are defined of size max. You will first be asked to enter the size of the first array, p, followed by the sorted elements for array p. The process is repeated for the second array q.

Three indices, i, j and k, are defined and initialized to 0. The three indices will point to the elements of the three arrays, p, q, and r, respectively.

The first elements of arrays **p** and **q**, in other words, **p[0]** and **q[0]**, are compared and the smaller one is assigned to array **r**.

Because **q[0]** is smaller than **p[0]**, **q[0]** is added to array **r**, and the indices of arrays **q** and **r** are incremented for the next comparison as follows:

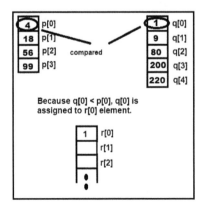

Figure 1.25

Next, **p[0]** will be compared with **q[1]**. Because **p[0]** is smaller than **q[1]**, the value at **p[0]** will be assigned to array **r** at **r[1]**:

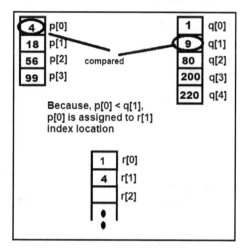

Figure 1.26

Then, **p[1]** will be compared with **q[1]**. Because **q[1]** is smaller than **p[1]**, **q[1]** will be assigned to array **r**, and the indices of the **q** and **r** arrays will be incremented for the next comparisons (refer to the following diagram):

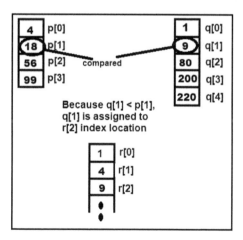

Figure 1.27

Let's use GCC to compile the `mergetwosortedarrays.c` program as follows:

```
D:\CBook>gcc mergetwosortedarrays.c -o mergetwosortedarrays
```

Now, let's run the generated executable file, `mergetwosortedarrays.exe`, in order to see the output of the program:

```
D:\CBook>./mergetwosortedarrays
Enter length of first array:4
Enter 4 elements of the first array in sorted order
4
18
56
99

Enter length of second array:5
Enter 5 elements of the second array in sorted order
1
9
80
200
220

The combined sorted array is:
1
4
9
18
56
80
99
200
220
```

Voilà! We've successfully merged two sorted arrays into one.

2
Managing Strings

Strings are nothing but arrays that store characters. Since strings are character arrays, they utilize less memory and lead to efficient object code, making programs run faster. Just like numerical arrays, strings are zero-based, that is, the first character is stored at index location 0. In C, strings are terminated by a null character, \0.

The recipes in this chapter will enhance your understanding of strings and will acquaint you with string manipulation. Strings play a major role in almost all applications. You will learn how to search strings (which is a very common task), replace a string with another string, search for a string that contains a specific pattern, and more.

In this chapter, you will learn how to create the following recipes using strings:

- Determining whether the string is a palindrome
- Finding the occurrence of the first repetitive character in a string
- Displaying the count of each character in a string
- Counting the vowels and consonants in a string
- Converting the vowels in a sentence to uppercase

Determining whether the string is a palindrome

A palindrome is a string that reads the same regardless of whether it is in a forward or backwards order. For example, the word *radar* is a palindrome because it reads the same way forwards and backwards.

How to do it...

1. Define two 80-character strings called `str` and `rev`(assuming your string will not exceed 79 characters). Your string can be of any length, but remember that the last position in the string is fixed for the null character `\0`:

```
char str[80],rev[80];
```

2. Enter characters that will be assigned to the `str` string:

```
printf("Enter a string: ");
scanf("%s",str);
```

3. Compute the length of the string using the `strlen` function and assign this to the n variable:

```
n=strlen(str);
```

4. Execute a `for` loop in reverse order to access the characters in the `str` string in reverse order, and then assign them to the `rev` string:

```
for(i=n-1;i >=0;  i--)
{
    rev[x]=str[i];
    x++;
}
rev[x]='\0';
```

5. Compare the two strings, `str` and `rev`, using `strcmp`:

```
if(strcmp(str,rev)==0)
```

6. If `str` and `rev` are the same, then the string is a palindrome.

 In C, the functionality of specific built-in functions is specified in the respective libraries, also known as header files. So, while writing C programs, whenever built-in functions are used, we need to use their respective header files in the program at the top. The header files usually have the extension `.h`. In the following program, I am using a built-in function called `strlen`, which finds out the length of a string. Therefore, I need to use its library, `string.h`, in the program.

The `palindrome.c` program for finding out whether the specified string is a palindrome is as follows:

```
#include<stdio.h>
#include<string.h>
void main()
{
    char str[80],rev[80];
    int n,i,x;
    printf("Enter a string: ");
    scanf("%s",str);
    n=strlen(str);
    x=0;
    for(i=n-1;i >=0;   i--)
    {
        rev[x]=str[i];
        x++;
    }
    rev[x]='\0';
    if(strcmp(str,rev)==0)
        printf("The %s is palindrome",str);
    else
        printf("The %s is not palindrome",str);
}
```

Now, let's go behind the scenes to understand the code better.

How it works...

To ensure that a string is a palindrome, we first need to ensure that the original string and its reverse form are of the same length.

Let's suppose that the original string is `sanjay` and it is assigned to a string variable, `str`. The string is a character array, where each character is stored individually as an array element and the last element in the string array is a null character. The null character is represented as `\0` and is always the last element in a string variable in C, as shown in the following diagram:

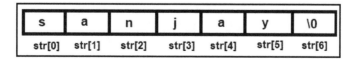

Figure 2.1

As you can see, the string uses zero-based indexing, that is, the first character is placed at index location **str[0]**, followed by the second character at **str[1]**, and so on. In regards to the last element, the null character is at **str[6]**.

Using the strlen library function, we will compute the length of the entered string and assign it to the n variable. By executing the for loop in reverse order, each of the characters of the str string is accessed in reverse order, that is, from n-1 to 0, and assigned to the rev string.

Finally, a null character, \0, is added to the rev string to make it a complete string. Therefore, rev will contain the characters of the str string, but in reverse order:

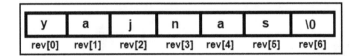

Figure 2.2

Next, we will run the strcmp function. If the function returns 0, it means that the content in the str and rev strings is exactly the same, which means that str is a palindrome. If the strcmp function returns a value other than 0, it means that the two strings are not the same; hence, str is not a palindrome.

Let's use GCC to compile the palindrome.c program, as follows:

```
D:\CBook>gcc palindrome.c -o palindrome
```

Now, let's run the generated executable file, palindrome.exe, to see the output of the program:

```
D:\CBook>./palindrome
Enter a string: sanjay
The sanjay is not palindrome
```

Now, suppose that str is assigned another character string, sanas. To ensure that the word in str is a palindrome, we will again reverse the character order in the string.

So, once more, we will compute the length of str, execute a for loop in reverse order, and access and assign each character in str to rev. The null character \0 will be assigned to the last location in rev, as follows:

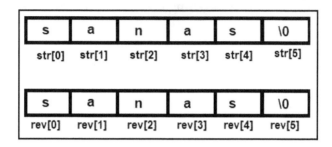

Figure 2.3

Finally, we will invoke the strcmp function again and supply both strings.

After compiling, let's run the program again with the new string:

```
D:\CBook>palindrome
Enter a string: sanas
The sanas is palindrome
```

Voilà! We have successfully identified whether our character strings are palindromes. Now, let's move on to the next recipe!

Finding the occurrence of the first repetitive character in a string

In this recipe, you will learn how to create a program that displays the first character to be repeated in a string. For example, if you enter the string racecar, the program should give the output as **The first repetitive character in the string racecar is c**. The program should display **No character is repeated in the string** if a string with no repetitive characters is entered.

How to do it...

1. Define two strings called `str1` and `str2`. Your strings can be of any length, but the last position in the string is fixed for the null character \0:

```
char str1[80],str2[80];
```

2. Enter characters to be assigned to `str1`. The characters will be assigned to the respective index locations of the string, beginning with `str1[0]`:

```
printf("Enter a string: ");
scanf("%s",str1);
```

3. Compute the length of `str1` using the `strlen` library function. Here, the first character of `str1` is assigned to `str2`:

```
n=strlen(str1);
str2[0]=str1[0];
```

4. Use a `for` loop to access all of the characters of `str1` one by one and pass them to the `ifexists` function to check whether that character already exists in `str2`. If the character is found in `str2`, this means it is the first repetitive character of the string, and so it is displayed on the screen:

```
for(i=1;i < n; i++)
{
    if(ifexists(str1[i], str2, x))
    {
        printf("The first repetitive character in %s is %c", str1,
            str1[i]);
        break;
    }
}
```

5. If the character of `str1` does not exist in `str2`, then it is simply added to `str2`:

```
else
{
    str2[x]=str1[i];
    x++;
}
```

The `repetitive.c` program for finding the occurrence of the first repetitive character in a string is as follows::

```c
#include<stdio.h>
#include<string.h>
int ifexists(char u, char z[],  int v)
{
    int i;
    for (i=0; i<v;i++)
        if (z[i]==u) return (1);
    return (0);
}

void main()
{
    char str1[80],str2[80];
    int n,i,x;
    printf("Enter a string: ");
    scanf("%s",str1);
    n=strlen(str1);
    str2[0]=str1[0];
    x=1;
    for(i=1;i < n;  i++)
    {
        if(ifexists(str1[i], str2, x))
        {
            printf("The first repetitive character in %s is %c", str1,
            str1[i]);
            break;
        }
        else
        {
            str2[x]=str1[i];
            x++;
        }
    }
    if(i==n)
        printf("There is no repetitive character in the string %s",
str1);
}
```

Now, let's go behind the scenes to understand the code better.

How it works...

Let's assume that we have defined a string, **str1**, of some length, and have entered the following characters—racecar.

Each of the characters of the string racecar will be assigned to the respective index locations of **str1**, that is, **r** will be assigned to **str1[0]**, **a** will be assigned to **str1[1]**, and so on. Because every string in C is terminated by a null character, **\0**, the last index location of **str1** will have the null character **\0**, as follows:

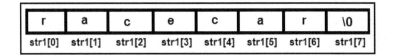

Figure 2.4

Using the library function strlen, the length of **str1** is computed and a for loop is used to access all of the characters of **str1**, one by one, except for the first character. The first character is already assigned to **str2**, as shown in the following diagram:

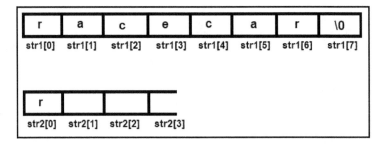

Figure 2.5

Each character that is accessed from **str1** is passed through the ifexists function. The ifexists function will check whether the supplied character already exists in **str2** and will return a Boolean value accordingly. The function returns 1, that is, true, if the supplied character is found in **str2**. The function returns 0, that is, false, if the supplied character is not found in **str2**.

If `ifexists` returns 1, this means that the character is found in **str2**, and hence, the first repetitive character of the string is displayed on the screen. If the `ifexists` function returns 0, this means that the character does not exist in **str2**, so it is simply added to **str2** instead.

Since the first character is already assigned, the second character of **str1** is picked up and checked to see if it already exists in **str2**. Because the second character of **str1** does not exist in **str2**, it is added to the latter string, as follows:

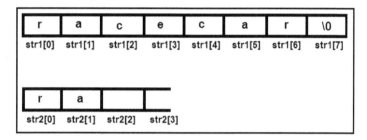

Figure 2.6

The procedure is repeated until all of the characters of **str1** are accessed. If all the characters of **str1** are accessed and none of them are found to exist in **str2**, this means that all of the characters in **str1** are unique and none of them are repeated.

The following diagram shows strings **str1** and **str2** after accessing the first four characters of **str1**. You can see that the four characters are added to **str2**, since none of them already exist in **str2**:

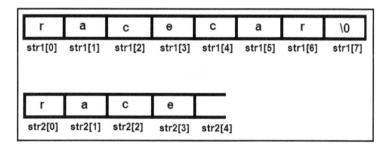

Figure 2.7

The next character to be accessed from **str1** is **c**. Before adding it to **str2**, it is compared with all the existing characters of **str2** to determine if it already exists there. Because the **c** character already exists in **str2**, it is not added to **str2** and is declared as the first repeating character in **str1**, as follows:

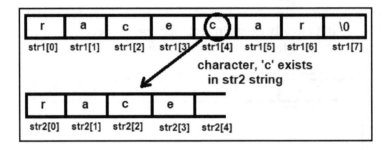

Figure 2.8

Let's use GCC to compile the `repetitive.c` program, as follows:

```
D:\CBook>gcc repetitive.c -o repetitive
```

Let's run the generated executable file, `repetitive.exe`, to see the output of the program:

```
D:\CBook>./repetitive
Enter a string: education
There is no repetitive character in the string education
```

Let's run the program again:

```
D:\CBook>repetitive
Enter a string: racecar
The first repetitive character in racecar is c
```

Voilà! We've successfully found the first repeating character in a string.

Now, let's move on to the next recipe!

Displaying the count of each character in a string

In this recipe, you will learn how to create a program that displays the count of each character in a string in a tabular form.

How to do it...

1. Create a string called `str`. The last element in the string will be a null character, `\0`.
2. Define another string called `chr` of matching length, to store the characters of `str`:

```
char str[80],chr[80];
```

3. Prompt the user to enter a string. The entered string will be assigned to the `str` string:

```
printf("Enter a string: ");
scanf("%s",str);
```

4. Compute the length of the string array, `str`, using `strlen`:

```
n=strlen(str);
```

5. Define an integer array called `count` to display the number of times the characters have occurred in `str`:

```
int count[80];
```

6. Execute `chr[0]=str[0]` to assign the first character of `str` to `chr` at index location `chr[0]`.
7. The count of the character that's assigned in the `chr[0]` location is represented by assigning 1 at the `count[0]` index location:

```
chr[0]=str[0];
count[0]=1;
```

8. Run a `for` loop to access each character in `str`:

```
for(i=1;i < n;   i++)
```

9. Run the `ifexists` function to find out whether the character of `str` exists in the `chr` string or not. If the character does not exist in the `chr` string, it is added to the `chr` string at the next index location and the respective index location in the `count` array is set to 1:

```
if(!ifexists(str[i], chr, x, count))
{
    x++;
    chr[x]=str[i];
    count[x]=1;
}
```

10. If the character exists in the `chr` string, the value in the respective index location in the `count` array is incremented by 1 in the `ifexists` function. The p and q arrays in the following snippet represent the `chr` and `count` arrays, respectively, since the `chr` and `count` arrays are passed and assigned to the p and q parameters in the `ifexists` function:

```
if (p[i]==u)
{
    q[i]++;
    return (1);
}
```

The `countofeach.c` program for counting each character in a string is as follows::

```
#include<stdio.h>
#include<string.h>
int ifexists(char u, char p[],  int v, int q[])
{
    int i;
    for (i=0; i<=v;i++)
    {
        if (p[i]==u)
        {
            q[i]++;
            return (1);
        }
    }
    if(i>v) return (0);
}
void main()
{
    char str[80],chr[80];
    int n,i,x,count[80];
    printf("Enter a string: ");
```

```
        scanf("%s",str);
        n=strlen(str);
        chr[0]=str[0];
        count[0]=1;
        x=0;
        for(i=1;i < n;   i++)
        {
             if(!ifexists(str[i], chr, x, count))
             {
                  x++;
                  chr[x]=str[i];
                  count[x]=1;
             }
        }
        printf("The count of each character in the string %s is \n", str);
        for (i=0;i<=x;i++)
             printf("%c\t%d\n",chr[i],count[i]);
}
```

Now, let's go behind the scenes to understand the code better.

How it works...

Let's assume that the two string variables you have defined, str and chr, are of the size 80 (you can always increase the size of the strings if you wish).

We will assign the character string racecar to the **str** string. Each of the characters will be assigned to the respective index locations of str, that is, **r** will be assigned to index location **str[0]**, **a** will be assigned to str[1], and so on. As always, the last element in the string will be a null character, as shown in the following diagram:

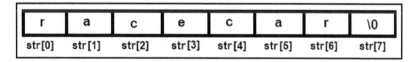

Figure 2.9

Using the strlen function, we will first compute the length of the string. Then, we will use the string array **chr** for storing characters of the **str** array individually at each index location. We will execute a for loop beginning from 1 until the end of the string to access each character of the string.

The integer array we defined earlier, that is, **count**, will represent the number of times the characters from **str** have occurred, which is represented by the index locations in the **chr** array. That is, if **r** is at index location **chr[0]**, then **count[0]** will contain an integer value (1, in this case) to represent the number of times the **r** character has occurred in the **str** string so far:

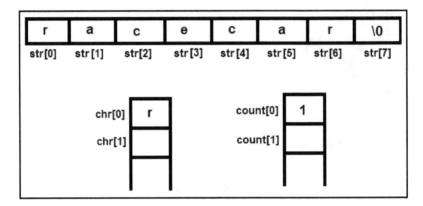

Figure 2.10

One of the following actions will be applied to every character that's accessed from the string:

- If the character exists in the **chr** array, the value in the respective index location in the **count** array is incremented by 1. For example, if the character of the string is found at the **chr[2]** index location, then the value in the **count[2]** index location is incremented by 1.
- If the character does not exist in the **chr** array, it is added to the **chr** array at the next index location, and the respective index location is found when the count array is set to **1**. For example, if the character **a** is not found in the **chr** array, it is added to the **chr** array at the next available index location. If the character **a** is added at the **chr[1]** location, then a value of **1** is assigned at the **count[1]** index location to indicate that the character shown in **chr[1]** has appeared once up until now.

When the `for` loop completes, that is when all of the characters in the string are accessed. The `chr` array will have individual characters of the string and the `count` array will have the count, or the number of times the characters represented by the `chr` array have occurred in the string. All of the elements in the `chr` and `count` arrays are displayed on the screen.

Let's use GCC to compile the `countofeach.c` program, as follows:

```
D:\CBook>gcc countofeach.c -o countofeach
```

Let's run the generated executable file, `countofeach.exe`, to see the output of the program:

```
D:\CBook>./countofeach
Enter a string: bintu
The count of each character in the string bintu is
b       1
i       1
n       1
t       1
u       1
```

Let's try another character string to test the results:

```
D:\CBook>./countofeach
Enter a string: racecar
The count of each character in the string racecar is
r       2
a       2
c       2
e       1
```

Voilà! We've successfully displayed the count of each character in a string.

Now, let's move on to the next recipe!

Counting vowels and consonants in a sentence

In this recipe, you will learn how to count the number of vowels and consonants in an entered sentence. The vowels are *a, e, i, o,* and *u,* and the rest of the letters are consonants. We will use ASCII values to identify the letters and their casing:

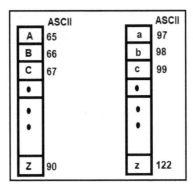

Figure 2.11

The blank spaces, numbers, special characters, and symbols will simply be ignored.

How to do it...

1. Create a string array called `str` to input your sentence. As usual, the last character will be a null character:

    ```
    char str[255];
    ```

2. Define two variables, `ctrV` and `ctrC`:

    ```
    int   ctrV,ctrC;
    ```

3. Prompt the user to enter a sentence of your choice:

    ```
    printf("Enter a sentence: ");
    ```

4. Execute the `gets` function to accept the sentence with blank spaces between the words:

    ```
    gets(str);
    ```

5. Initialize `ctrV` and `ctrC` to 0. The `ctrV` variable will count the number of vowels in the sentence, while the `ctrC` variable will count the number of consonants in the sentence:

```
ctrV=ctrC=0;
```

6. Execute a `while` loop to access each letter of the sentence one, by one until the null character in the sentence is reached.

7. Execute an `if` block to check whether the letters are uppercase or lowercase, using ASCII values. This also confirms that the accessed character is not a white space, special character or symbol, or number.

8. Once that's done, execute a nested `if` block to check whether the letter is a lowercase or uppercase vowel, and wait for the `while` loop to terminate:

```
while(str[i]!='\0')
{
    if((str[i] >=65 && str[i]<=90) || (str[i] >=97 &&
str[i]<=122))
    {
        if(str[i]=='A' ||str[i]=='E' ||str[i]=='I'
||str[i]=='O'
        ||str[i]=='U' ||str[i]=='a' ||str[i]=='e'
||str[i]=='i'
        ||str[i]=='o'||str[i]=='u')
            ctrV++;
        else
            ctrC++;
    }
    i++;
}
```

The `countvowelsandcons.c` program for counting vowels and consonants in a string is as follows:

```
#include <stdio.h>
void main()
{
    char str[255];
    int  ctrV,ctrC,i;
    printf("Enter a sentence: ");
    gets(str);
    ctrV=ctrC=i=0;
    while(str[i]!='\0')
    {
        if((str[i] >=65 && str[i]<=90) || (str[i] >=97 &&
str[i]<=122))
```

```
        {
            if(str[i]=='A' ||str[i]=='E' ||str[i]=='I' ||str[i]=='O'
            ||str[i]=='U' ||str[i]=='a' ||str[i]=='e' ||str[i]=='i'
            ||str[i]=='o'||str[i]=='u')
                ctrV++;
            else
                ctrC++;
        }
        i++;
    }
    printf("Number of vowels are : %d\nNumber of consonants are :
    %d\n",ctrV,ctrC);
}
```

Now, let's go behind the scenes to understand the code better.

How it works...

We are assuming that you will not enter a sentence longer than 255 characters, so we have defined our string variable accordingly. When prompted, enter a sentence that will be assigned to the str variable. Because a sentence may have blank spaces between the words, we will execute the gets function to accept the sentence.

The two variables that we've defined, that is, ctrV and ctrC, are initialized to 0. Because the last character in a string is always a null character, \0, a while loop is executed, which will access each character of the sentence one by one until the null character in the sentence is reached.

Every accessed letter from the sentence is checked to confirm that it is either an uppercase or lowercase character. That is, their ASCII values are compared, and if the ASCII value of the accessed character is a lowercase or uppercase character, only then it will execute the nested if block. Otherwise, the next character from the sentence will be accessed.

Once you have ensured that the accessed character is not a blank space, any special character or symbol, or a numerical value, then an if block will be executed, which checks whether the accessed character is a lowercase or uppercase vowel. If the accessed character is a vowel, then the value of the ctrV variable is incremented by 1. If the accessed character is not a vowel, then it is confirmed that it is a consonant, and so the value of the ctrC variable is incremented by 1.

Once all of the characters of the sentence have been accessed, that is, when the null character of the sentence is reached, the `while` loop terminates and the number of vowels and consonants stored in the `ctrV` and `ctrC` variables is displayed on the screen.

Let's use GCC to compile the `countvowelsandcons.c` program, as follows:

```
D:\CBook>gcc countvowelsandcons.c -o countvowelsandcons
```

Let's run the generated executable file, `countvowelsandcons.exe`, to see the output of the program:

```
D:\CBook>./countvowelsandcons
Enter a sentence: Today it might rain. Its a hot weather. I do like
rain
Number of vowels are : 18
Number of consonants are : 23
```

Voilà! We've successfully counted all of the vowels and consonants in our sentence.

Now, let's move on to the next recipe!

Converting the vowels in a sentence to uppercase

In this recipe, you will learn how to convert all of the lowercase vowels in a sentence to uppercase. The remaining characters in the sentence, including consonants, numbers, special symbols, and special characters, are simply ignored and will be left as they are.

Converting the casing of any letter is done by simply changing the ASCII value of that character, using the following formulas:

- Subtract 32 from the ASCII value of a lowercase character to convert it to uppercase
- Add 32 to the ASCII value of an uppercase character to convert it to lowercase

The following diagram shows the ASCII values of the uppercase and lowercase vowels:

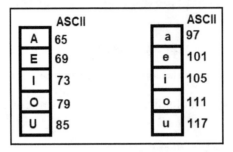

Figure 2.12

The ASCII value of the uppercase letters is lower than that of lowercase letters, and the difference between the values is 32.

How to do it...

1. Create a string called str to input your sentence. As usual, the last character will be a null character:

   ```
   char str[255];
   ```

2. Enter a sentence of your choice:

   ```
   printf("Enter a sentence: ");
   ```

3. Execute the gets function to accept the sentence with blank spaces between the words, and initialize the i variable to 0, since each character of the sentence will be accessed through i:

   ```
   gets(str);
   i=0
   ```

4. Execute a `while` loop to access each letter of the sentence one by one, until the null character in the sentence is reached:

```
while(str[i]!='\0')
{
     { ...
     }
}
i++;
```

5. Check each letter to verify whether it is a lowercase vowel. If the accessed character is a lowercase vowel, then the value 32 is subtracted from the ASCII value of that vowel to convert it to uppercase:

```
if(str[i]=='a' ||str[i]=='e' ||str[i]=='i' ||str[i]=='o'
||str[i]=='u')
     str[i]=str[i]-32;
```

6. When all of the letters of the sentence have been accessed, then simply display the entire sentence.

The `convertvowels.c` program for converting the lowercase vowels in a sentence to uppercase is as follows:

```
#include <stdio.h>
void main()
{
    char str[255];
    int  i;
    printf("Enter a sentence: ");
    gets(str);
    i=0;
    while(str[i]!='\0')
    {
        if(str[i]=='a' ||str[i]=='e' ||str[i]=='i' ||str[i]=='o'
        ||str[i]=='u')
            str [i] = str [i] -32;
        i++;
    }
    printf("The sentence after converting vowels into uppercase
is:\n");
    puts(str);
}
```

Now, let's go behind the scenes to understand the code better.

How it works...

Again, we will assume that you will not enter a sentence longer than 255 characters. Therefore, we have defined our string array, str , to be of the size 255. When prompted, enter a sentence to assign to the str array. Because a sentence may have blank spaces between the words, instead of scanf, we will use the gets function to accept the sentence.

To access each character of the sentence, we will execute a while loop that will run until the null character is reached in the sentence. After each character of the sentence, it is checked whether it is a lowercase vowel. If it is not a lowercase vowel, the character is ignored and the next character in the sentence is picked up for comparison.

If the character that's accessed is a lowercase vowel, then a value of 32 is subtracted from the ASCII value of the character to convert it to uppercase. Remember that the difference in the ASCII values of lowercase and uppercase letters is 32. That is, the ASCII value of lowercase a is 97 and that of uppercase A is 65. So, if you subtract 32 from 97, which is the ASCII value of lowercase a, the new ASCII value will become 65, which is the ASCII value of uppercase A.

The procedure of converting a lowercase vowel to an uppercase vowel is to first find the vowel in a sentence by using an if statement, and then subtract the value 32 from its ASCII value to convert it to uppercase.

Once all of the characters of the string are accessed and all of the lowercase vowels of the sentence are converted to uppercase, the entire sentence is displayed using the puts function.

Let's use GCC to compile the convertvowels.c program, as follows:

```
D:\CBook>gcc convertvowels.c -o convertvowels
```

Let's run the generated executable file, convertvowels.exe, to see the output of the program:

```
D:\CBook>./convertvowels
Enter a sentence: It is very hot today. Appears as if it might rain. I
like rain
The sentence after converting vowels into uppercase is:
It Is vEry hOt tOdAy. AppEArs As If It mIght rAIn. I lIkE rAIn
```

Voilà! We've successfully converted the lowercase vowels in a sentence to uppercase.

Exploring Functions

3

Whenever you need to create a large application, it is a wise decision to divide it into manageable chunks, called **functions**. Functions are small modules that represent tasks that can be executed independently. The code written inside a function can be invoked several times, which helps to avoid repetitive statements.

Functions help in the teamwork, debugging, and scaling of any application. Whenever you want to add more features to an application, simply add a few functions to it. When calling functions, the caller function may pass certain arguments, called **actual arguments**; these are then assigned to the parameters of the function. The parameters are also known as formal parameters.

The following recipes will help you understand how functions can be used to make complex applications easier and more manageable. Normally, a function can return only a single value. But in this chapter, we will learn a technique to return more than one value from a function. We will also learn how to apply recursion in functions.

In this chapter, we will cover the following recipes on strings:

- Determining whether a number is an Armstrong number
- Returning the maximum and minimum values of an array
- Finding GCD using recursion
- Converting a binary number into a hexadecimal number
- Determining whether a number is a palindrome

As I will be using a stack structure in the recipes in this chapter, let's have a quick introduction to stack.

What is a stack?

A Stack is a structure that can be implemented with arrays as well as linked lists. It is a sort of a bucket where the value you enter will be added at the bottom. The next item that you add to a stack will be kept just above the item that was added previously. The procedure of adding a value to the stack is called a push operation and the procedure of getting a value out of the stack is called a pop operation. The location where the value can be added or taken out of the stack is pointed at by a pointer called **top**. The value of the **top** pointer is **-1** when the stack is empty:

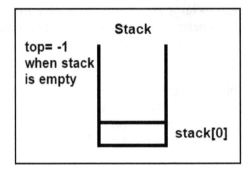

Figure 3.1

When the push operation is executed, the value of **top** is incremented by **1**, so that it can point to the location in the stack where the value can be pushed:

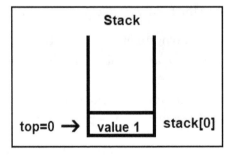

Figure 3.2

Now, the next value that will be pushed will be kept above value 1. More precisely, the value of the **top** pointer will be incremented by **1**, making its value 1, and the next value will be pushed to the **stack[1]** location, as follows:

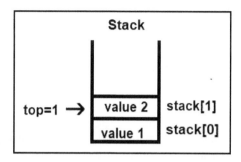

Figure 3.3

So, you can see that the stack is a **Last In First Out** (**LIFO**) structure; that is, the last value that was pushed sits at the top.

Now, when we execute a pop operation, the value at the top, that is, value **2**, will be popped out first, followed by the popping out of value **1**. Basically, in the pop operation, the value pointed at by the **top** pointer is taken out, and then the value of **top** is decremented by 1 so that it can point at the next value to be popped out.

Now, that we've understood stacks, let's begin with the first recipe.

Finding whether a number is an Armstrong number

An Armstrong number is a three-digit integer that is the sum of the cubes of its digits. This simply means that if $xyz = x^3+y^3+z^3$, it is an Armstrong number. For example, 153 is an Armstrong number because $1^3+5^3+3^3 = 153$.

Similarly, a number that comprises four digits is an Armstrong number if the sum of its digits raised to the power of four results in that number. For example, $pqrs = p^4+q^4+r^4+s^4$.

How to do it...

1. Enter a number to assign to the n variable:

    ```
    printf("Enter a number ");
    scanf("%d",&n);
    ```

2. Invoke the findarmstrong function. The value assigned to n will get passed to this function:

    ```
    findarmstrong(n)
    ```

3. In the function, the passed argument, n, is assigned to the numb parameter. Execute a while loop to separate out all the digits in the numb parameter:

    ```
    while(numb >0)
    ```

4. In the while loop, apply the mod 10 (%10) operator on the number assigned to the numb variable. The mod operator divides a number and returns the remainder:

    ```
    remainder=numb%10;
    ```

5. Push the remainder to the stack:

    ```
    push(remainder);
    ```

6. Remove the last digit of the number in the numb variable by dividing the numb variable by 10:

    ```
    numb=numb/10;
    ```

7. Repeat steps 4 to 6 until the number in the numb variable becomes 0. In addition, create a count counter to count the number of digits in the number. Initialize the counter to 0 and it will get incremented during the while loop:

    ```
    count++;
    ```

8. Pop all the digits from the stack and raise it to the given power. To pop all the digits from the stack, execute a while loop that will execute until top is greater than or equal to 0, that is, until the stack is empty:

    ```
    while(top >=0)
    ```

9. Inside the `while` loop, pop off a digit from the stack and raise it to the power of `count`, which is the count of the number of digits in the selected number. Then, add all the digits to the `value`:

```
j=pop();
value=value+pow(j,count);
```

10. Compare the number in the `value` variable with the number in the `numb` variable, and code it to return the value of `1` if both the compared numbers match:

```
if(value==numb)return 1;
```

If the numbers in the `numb` and `value` variables are the same, returning the Boolean value of `1`, that means the number is an Armstrong number.

Here is the `armstrong.c` program for finding out whether the specified number is an Armstrong number:

```c
/* Finding whether the entered number is an Armstrong number */
# include <stdio.h>
# include <math.h>

#define max 10

int top=-1;
int stack[max];
void push(int);
int pop();
int findarmstrong(int );
void main()
{
    int n;
    printf("Enter a number ");
    scanf("%d",&n);
    if (findarmstrong(n))
        printf("%d is an armstrong number",n);
    else printf("%d is not an armstrong number", n);
}
int findarmstrong(int numb)
{
    int j, remainder, temp,count,value;
    temp=numb;
    count=0;
    while(numb >0)
    {
        remainder=numb%10;
```

```
        push(remainder);
        count++;
        numb=numb/10;
    }
    numb=temp;
    value=0;
    while(top >=0)
    {
        j=pop();
        value=value+pow(j,count);
    }
    if(value==numb) return 1;
    else return 0;
}
void push(int m)
{
    top++;
    stack[top]=m;
}
int pop()
{
    int j;
    if(top==-1) return(top);
    else
    {
        j=stack[top];
        top--;
        return(j);
    }
}
```

Now, let's go behind the scenes.

How it works...

First, we will apply the mod **10** operator to separate our digits. Assuming the number entered by us is **153**, you can see that **153** is divided by **10** and the remaining **3** is pushed to the stack:

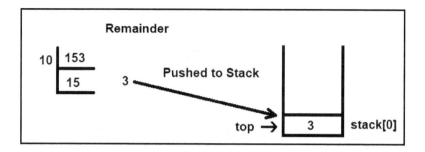

Figure 3.4

The value in the stack is pushed at the index location indicated by **top**. Initially, the value of **top** is -1. It is so because before the push operation, the value of **top** is incremented by 1, and the array is zero-based, that is, the first element in the array is placed at the 0 index location. Consequently, the value of **top** has to be initialized to -1. As mentioned, the value of **top** is incremented by 1 before pushing, that is, the value of **top** will become **0**, and the remainder of **3** is pushed to **stack[0]**.

In the stack, the value of top is incremented by 1 to indicate the location in the stack where the value will be pushed.

We will again apply the mod **10** operator to the **15** quotient. The remainder that we will get is **5**, which will be pushed to the stack. Again, before pushing to the stack, the value of **top**, which was 0, is incremented to 1. At **stack[1]**, the remainder is pushed:

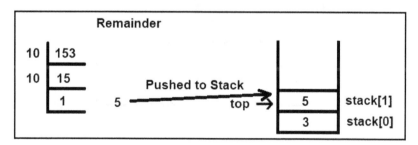

Figure 3.5

To the **1** quotient, we will again apply the mod **10** operator. But because 1 is not divisible by **10**, **1** itself will be considered as the remainder and will be pushed to the stack. The value of **top** will again be incremented by 1 and **1** will be pushed to **stack[2]**:

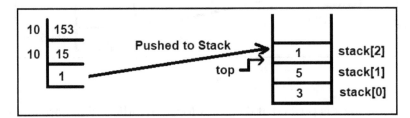

Figure 3.6

Once all the digits are separated and placed in the stack, we will pop them out one by one. Then, we will raise each digit to the power equal to the count of the digits. Because the number **153** consists of three digits, each digit is raised to the power of **3**.

While popping values out of the stack, the value indicated by the **top** pointer is popped out. The value of **top** is **2**, hence the value at **stack[2]**, that is, **1**, is popped out and raised to the power of **3**, as follows:

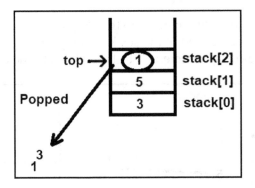

Figure 3.7

After the pop operation, the value of **top** will be decremented to 1 to indicate the next location to be popped out. Next, the value at **stack[1]** will be popped out and raised to the power of **3**. We will then add this value to our previous popped-out one:

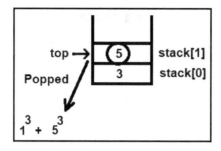

Figure 3.8

After the popping-out operation, the value of **top** is decremented by 1, now making its value **0**. So, the value at **stack[0]** is popped out and raised to the power of **3**. The result is added to our earlier computation:

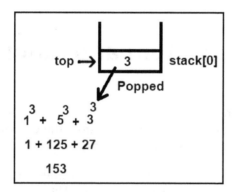

Figure 3.9

The result after computing $1^3 + 5^3 + 3^3$ is **153**, which is the same as the original number. This proves that **153** is an Armstrong number.

Let's use GCC to compile the `armstrong.c` program, as follows:

```
D:\CBook>gcc armstrong.c -o armstrong
```

Let's check whether `127` is an Armstrong number:

```
D:\CBook>./armstrong
Enter a number 127
127 is not an armstrong number
```

Let's check whether `153` is an Armstrong number:

```
D:\CBook>./armstrong
Enter a number 153
153 is an armstrong number
```

Let's check whether `1634` is an Armstrong number:

```
D:\CBook>./armstrong
Enter a number 1634
1634 is an armstrong number
```

Voilà! We've successfully made a function to find whether a specified number is an Armstrong number or not.

Now, let's move on to the next recipe!

Returning maximum and minimum values in an array

C functions cannot return more than one value. But what if you want a function to return more than one value? The solution is to store the values to be returned in an array and make the function return the array instead.

In this recipe, we will make a function return two values, the maximum and minimum values, and store them in another array. Thereafter, the array containing the maximum and minimum values will be returned from the function.

How to do it...

1. The size of the array whose maximum and minimum values have to be found out is not fixed, hence we will define a macro called `max` of size `100`:

   ```
   #define max 100
   ```

2. We will define an `arr` array of the max size, that is, `100` elements:

   ```
   int arr[max];
   ```

3. You will be prompted to specify the number of elements in the array; the length you enter will be assigned to the n variable:

```
printf("How many values? ");
scanf("%d",&n);
```

4. Execute a for loop for n number of times to accept n values for the arr array:

```
for(i=0;i<n;i++)
    scanf("%d",&arr[i]);
```

5. Invoke the maxmin function to pass the arr array and its length, n, to it. The array that will be returned by the maxmin function will be assigned to the integer pointer, *p:

```
p=maxmin(arr,n);
```

6. When you look at the function definition, int *maxmin(int ar[], int v) { }, the arr and n arguments passed to the maxmin function are assigned to the ar and v parameters, respectively. In the maxmin function, define an mm array of two elements:

```
static int mm[2];
```

7. To compare it with the rest of the elements, the first element of ar array is stored at mm[0] and mm[1]. A loop is executed from the 1 value till the end of the length of the array and within the loop, the following two formulas are applied:

- We will use mm[0] to store the minimum value of the arr array. The value in mm[0] is compared with the rest of the elements. If the value in mm[0] is greater than any of the array elements, we will assign the smaller element to mm[0]:

```
if(mm[0] > ar[i])
    mm[0]=ar[i];
```

- We will use mm[1] to store the maximum value of the arr array. If the value at mm[1] is found to be smaller than any of the rest of the array element, we will assign the larger array element to mm[1]:

```
if(mm[1]< ar[i])
    mm[1]= ar[i];
```

8. After the execution of the for loop, the mm array will have the minimum and maximum values of the arr array at mm[0] and mm[1], respectively. We will return this mm array to the main function where the *p pointer is set to point at the returned array, mm:

```
return mm;
```

9. The *p pointer will first point to the memory address of the first index location, that is, mm[0]. Then, the content of that memory address, that is, the minimum value of the array, is displayed. After that, the value of the *p pointer is incremented by 1 to make it point to the memory address of the next element in the array, that is, the mm[1] location:

```
printf("Minimum value is %d\n",*p++);
```

10. The mm[1] index location contains the maximum value of the array. Finally, the maximum value pointed to by the *p pointer is displayed on the screen:

```
printf("Maximum value is %d\n",*p);
```

The returnarray.c program explains how an array can be returned from a function. Basically, the program returns the minimum and maximum values of an array:

```
/* Find out the maximum and minimum values using a function returning
an array */
# include <stdio.h>
#define max 100
int *maxmin(int ar[], int v);
void main()
{
    int   arr[max];
    int n,i, *p;
    printf("How many values? ");
    scanf("%d",&n);
    printf("Enter %d values\n", n);
    for(i=0;i<n;i++)
        scanf("%d",&arr[i]);
    p=maxmin(arr,n);
    printf("Minimum value is %d\n",*p++);
    printf("Maximum value is %d\n",*p);
}
int *maxmin(int ar[], int v)
{
    int i;
```

```
        static int mm[2];
        mm[0]=ar[0];
        mm[1]=ar[0];
        for (i=1;i<v;i++)
        {
            if(mm[0] > ar[i])
                mm[0]=ar[i];
            if(mm[1]< ar[i])
                mm[1]= ar[i];
        }
        return mm;
    }
```

Now, let's go behind the scenes.

How it works...

We will use two arrays in this recipe. The first array will contain the values from which the maximum and minimum values have to be found. The second array will be used to store the minimum and maximum values of the first array.

Let's call the first array **arr** and define it to contain five elements with the following values:

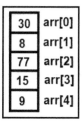

Figure 3.10

Let's call our second array **mm**. The first location, **mm[0]**, of the **mm** array will be used for storing the minimum value and the second location, **mm[1]**, for storing the maximum value of the **arr** array. To enable comparison of the elements of the **mm** array with the elements of the **arr** array, copy the first element of the **arr** array at **arr[0]** to both **mm[0]** and **mm[1]**:

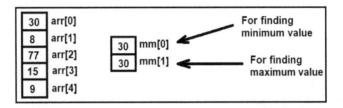

Figure 3.11

Now, we will compare the rest of the elements of the **arr** array with **mm[0]** and **mm[1]**. To keep the minimum value at **mm[0]**, any element smaller than the value at **mm[0]** will be assigned to **mm[0]**. Values larger than **mm[0]** are simply ignored. For example, the value at **arr[1]** is smaller than that at **mm[0]**, that is, 8 < 30. So, the smaller value will be assigned to **mm[0]**:

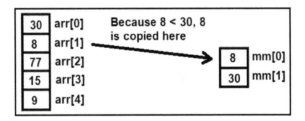

Figure 3.12

We will apply reverse logic to the element at **mm[1]**. Because we want the maximum value of the **arr** array at **mm[1]**, any element found larger than the value at **mm[1]** will be assigned to **mm[1]**. All smaller values will be simply ignored.

We will continue this process with the next element in the **arr** array, which is **arr[2]**. Because 77 > 8, it will be ignored when compared with **mm[0]**. But 77 > 30, so it will be assigned to **mm[1]**:

Figure 3.13

We will repeat this procedure with the rest of the elements of the **arr** array. Once all the elements of the **arr** array are compared with both the elements of the **mm** array, we will have the minimum and maximum values at **mm[0]** and **mm[1]**, respectively:

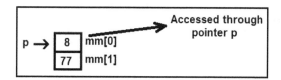

Figure 3.14

Let's use GCC to compile the `returnarray.c` program, as follows:

```
D:\CBook>gcc returnarray.c -o returnarray
```

Here is the output of the program:

```
D:\CBook>./returnarray
How many values? 5
Enter 5 values
30
8
77
15
9
Minimum value is 8
Maximum value is 77
```

Voilà! We've successfully returned the maximum and minimum values in an array.

Now, let's move on to the next recipe!

Finding the greatest common divisor using recursion

In this recipe, we will use recursive functions to find the **greatest common divisor (GCD)**, also known as the highest common factor) of two or more integers. The GCD is the largest positive integer that divides each of the integers. For example, the GCD of 8 and 12 is 4, and the GCD of 9 and 18 is 9.

How to do it...

The `int gcd(int x, int y)` recursive function finds the GCD of two integers, x and y, using the following three rules:

- If y=0, the GCD of x and y is x.
- If x mod y is 0, the GCD of x and y is y.
- Otherwise, the GCD of x and y is `gcd(y, (x mod y))`.

Follow the given steps to find the GCD of two integers recursively:

1. You will be prompted to enter two integers. Assign the integers entered to two variables, u and v:

   ```
   printf("Enter two numbers: ");
   scanf("%d %d",&x,&y);
   ```

2. Invoke the gcd function and pass the x and y values to it. The x and y values will be assigned to the a and b parameters, respectively. Assign the GCD value returned by the gcd function to the g variable:

   ```
   g=gcd(x,y);
   ```

3. In the gcd function, a % b is executed. The % (mod) operator divides the number and returns the remainder:

   ```
   m=a%b;
   ```

4. If the remainder is non-zero, call the gcd function again, but this time the arguments will be `gcd(b,a % b)`, that is, `gcd(b,m)`, where m stands for the mod operation:

   ```
   gcd(b,m);
   ```

5. If this again results in a non-zero remainder, that is, if `b % m` is non-zero, repeat the `gcd` function with the new values obtained from the previous execution:

```
gcd(b,m);
```

6. If the result of `b % m` is zero, `b` is the GCD of the supplied arguments and is returned back to the `main` function:

```
return(b);
```

7. The result, `b`, that is returned back to the `main` function is assigned to the `g` variable, which is then displayed on the screen:

```
printf("Greatest Common Divisor of %d and %d is %d",x,y,g);
```

The `gcd.c` program explains how the greatest common divisor of two integers is computed through the recursive function:

```c
#include <stdio.h>
int gcd(int p, int q);
void main()
{
    int x,y,g;
    printf("Enter two numbers: ");
    scanf("%d %d",&x,&y);
    g=gcd(x,y);
    printf("Greatest Common Divisor of %d and %d is %d",x,y,g);
}
int gcd(int a, int b)
{
    int m;
    m=a%b;
    if(m==0)
        return(b);
    else
        gcd(b,m);
}
```

Now, let's go behind the scenes.

How it works...

Let's assume we want to find the GCD of two integers, **18** and **24**. To do so, we will invoke the gcd(x,y) function, which in this case is gcd(18,24). Because **24**, that is, y, is not zero, Rule 1 is not applicable here. Next, we will use Rule 2 to check whether 18%24 (x % y) is equal to **0**. Because **18** cannot be divided by **24**, **18** will be the remainder:

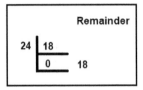

Figure 3.15

Since the parameters of Rule 2 were also not met, we will use Rule 3. We will invoke the gcd function with the gcd(b,m) argument, which is gcd(24,18%24). Now, m stands for the mod operation. At this stage, we will again apply Rule 2 and collect the remainder:

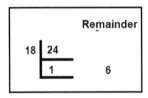

Figure 3.16

Because the result of 24%18 is a non-zero value, we will invoke the gcd function again with the gcd(b, m) argument, which is now gcd(18, 24%18), since we were left with **18** and **6** from the previous execution. We will again apply Rule 2 to this execution. When **18** is divided by **6**, the remainder is **0**:

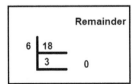

Figure 3.17

At this stage, we have finally fulfilled the requirements of one of the rules, Rule 2. If you recall, Rule 2 says that if x mod y is **0**, the GCD is y. Because the result of **18** mod **6** is **0**, the GCD of **18** and **24** is **6**.

Let's use GCC to compile the gcd.c program, as follows:

```
D:\CBook>gcc gcd.c -o gcd
```

Here is the output of the program:

```
D:\CBook>./gcd
Enter two numbers: 18 24
Greatest Common Divisor of 18 and 24 is 6
D:\CBook>./gcd
Enter two numbers: 9 27
Greatest Common Divisor of 9 and 27 is 9
```

Voilà! We've successfully found the GCD using recursion.

Now, let's move on to the next recipe!

Converting a binary number into a hexadecimal number

In this recipe, we will learn how to convert a binary number into a hexadecimal number. A binary number comprises two bits, 0 and 1. To convert a binary number into a hexadecimal number, we first need to convert the binary number into a decimal number and then convert the resulting decimal number to hexadecimal.

How to do it...

1. Enter a binary number and assign it to the b variable:

```
printf("Enter a number in binary number ");
scanf("%d",&b);
```

2. Invoke the `intodecimal` function to convert the binary number into a decimal number, and pass the b variable to it as an argument. Assign the decimal number returned by the `intodecimal` function to the d variable:

```
d=intodecimal(b);
```

3. On looking at the `intodecimal` definition, int intodecimal(int bin) { }, we can see that the b argument is assigned to the bin parameter of the `intodecimal` function.

4. Separate all the binary digits and multiply them by 2 raised to the power of their position in the binary number. Sum the results to get the decimal equivalent. To separate each binary digit, we need to execute a while loop until the binary number is greater than 0:

```
while(bin >0)
```

5. Within the while loop, apply the mod 10 operator on the binary number and push the remainder to the stack:

```
remainder=bin%10;
push(remainder);
```

6. Execute another while loop to get the decimal number of all the binary digits from the stack. The while loop will execute until the stack becomes empty (that is, until the value of top is greater than or equal to 0):

```
while(top >=0)
```

7. In the while loop, pop off all the binary digits from the stack and multiply each one by 2 raised to the power of top. Sum the results to get the decimal equivalent of the entered binary number:

```
j=pop();
deci=deci+j*pow(2,exp);
```

8. Invoke the `intohexa` function and pass the binary number and the decimal number to it to get the hexadecimal number:

```
void intohexa(int bin, int deci)
```

9. Apply the mod `16` operator in the `intohexa` function on the decimal number to get its hexadecimal. Push the remainder that you get to the stack. Apply mod `16` to the quotient again and repeat the process until the quotient becomes smaller than `16`:

```
remainder=deci%16;
push(remainder);
```

10. Pop off the remainders that are pushed to the stack to display the hexadecimal number:

```
j=pop();
```

If the remainder that is popped off from the stack is less than 10, it is displayed as such. Otherwise, it is converted to its equivalent letter, as mentioned in the following table, and the resulting letter is displayed:

Decimal	Hexadecimal
10	A
11	B
12	C
13	D
14	E
15	F

```
if(j<10)printf("%d",j);
else printf("%c",prnhexa(j));
```

The `binarytohexa.c` program explains how a binary number can be converted into a hexadecimal number:

```
//Converting binary to hex
# include <stdio.h>
#include   <math.h>
#define max 10
int top=-1;
int stack[max];
void push();
int pop();
char prnhexa(int);
int intodecimal(int);
void intohexa(int, int);
void main()
{
    int b,d;
```

```
        printf("Enter a number in binary number ");
        scanf("%d",&b);
        d=intodecimal(b);
        printf("The decimal of binary number %d is %d\n", b, d);
        intohexa(b,d);
}
int intodecimal(int bin)
{
        int deci, remainder,exp,j;
        while(bin >0)
        {
            remainder=bin%10;
            push(remainder);
            bin=bin/10;
        }
        deci=0;
        exp=top;
        while(top >=0)
        {
            j=pop();
            deci=deci+j*pow(2,exp);
            exp--;
        }
        return (deci);
}
void intohexa(int bin, int deci)
{
        int remainder,j;
        while(deci >0)
        {
            remainder=deci%16;
            push(remainder);
            deci=deci/16;
        }
        printf("The hexa decimal format of binary number %d is ",bin);
        while(top >=0)
        {
            j=pop();
            if(j<10)printf("%d",j);
            else printf("%c",prnhexa(j));
        }
}
void push(int m)
{
        top++;
        stack[top]=m;
}
int pop()
```

```
{
    int j;
    if(top==-1)return(top);
    j=stack[top];
    top--;
    return(j);
}
char prnhexa(int v)
{
    switch(v)
    {
        case 10: return ('A');
                break;
        case 11: return ('B');
                break;
        case 12: return ('C');
                break;
        case 13: return ('D');
                break;
        case 14: return ('E');
                break;
        case 15: return ('F');
                break;
    }
}
```

Now, let's go behind the scenes.

How it works...

The first step is to convert the binary number into a decimal number. To do so, we will separate all the binary digits and multiply each by **2** raised to the power of their position in the binary number. We will then apply the mod **10** operator in order to separate the binary number into individual digits. Every time mod **10** is applied to the binary number, its last digit is separated and then pushed to the stack.

Let's assume that the binary number that we need to convert into a hexadecimal format is **110001**. We will apply the mod **10** operator to this binary number. The mod operator divides the number and returns the remainder. On application of the mod **10** operator, the last binary digit—in other words the rightmost digit will be returned as the remainder (as is the case with all divisions by **10**).

The operation is pushed in the stack at the location indicated by the **top** pointer. The value of **top** is initially -1. Before pushing to the stack, the value of **top** is incremented by 1. So, the value of **top** increments to 0 and the binary digit that appeared as the remainder (in this case, 1) is pushed to **stack[0]** (see *Figure 3.18*), and **11000** is returned as the quotient:

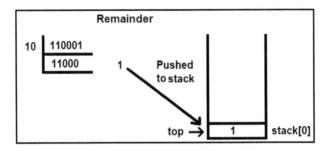

Figure 3.18

We will again apply the mod **10** operator to the quotient to separate the last digit of the present binary number. This time, **0** will be returned as the remainder and **1100** as the quotient on the application of the mod **10** operator. The remainder is again pushed to the stack. As mentioned before, the value of **top** is incremented before applying the push operation. As the value of **top** was 0, it is incremented to **1** and our new remainder, **0**, is pushed to **stack[1]**:

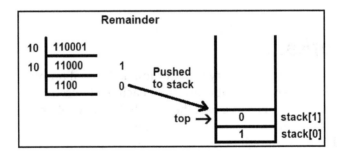

Figure 3.19

We will repeat this procedure until all the digits of the binary number are separated and pushed to the stack, as follows:

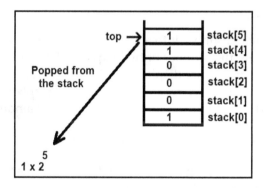

Figure 3.20

Once that's done, the next step is to pop the digits out one by one and multiply every digit by **2** raised to the power of **top**. For example, **2** raised to the power of top means **2** will be raised to the value of the index location from where the binary digit was popped off. The value from the stack is popped out from the location indicated by **top**.

The value of **top** is currently **5**, hence the element at **stack[5]** will be popped out and multiplied by **2** raised to the power **5**, as follows:

Figure 3.21

After popping a value from the stack, the value of **top** is decremented by 1 to point at the next element to be popped out. The procedure is repeated until every digit is popped out and multiplied by **2** raised to the power of its top location value. *Figure 3.19* shows how all the binary digits are popped from the stack and multiplied by **2** raised to the power of **top**:

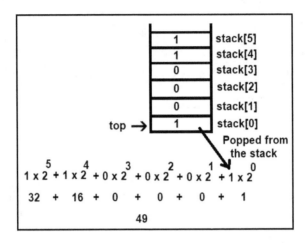

Figure 3.22

The resulting number we get is the decimal equivalent of the binary number that was entered by the user.

Now, to convert a decimal number into a hexadecimal format, we will divide it by 16. We need to keep dividing the number until the quotient becomes smaller than 16. The remainders of the division are displayed in LIFO order. If the remainder is below 10, it is displayed as is; otherwise, its equivalent letter is displayed. You can use the preceding table to find the equivalent letter if you get a remainder between 10 and 15.

In the following figure, you can see that the decimal number **49** is divided by **16**. The remainders are displayed in LIFO order to display the hexadecimal, hence 31 is the hexadecimal of the binary number **110001**. You don't need to apply the preceding table as both the remainders are less than 10:

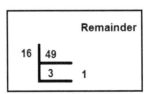

Figure 3.23

Let's use GCC to compile the `binaryintohexa.c` program, as follows:

```
D:\CBook>gcc binaryintohexa.c -o binaryintohexa
```

Here is one output of the program:

```
D:\CBook>./binaryintohexa
Enter a number in binary number 110001
The decimal of binary number 110001 is 49
The hexa decimal format of binary number 110001 is 31
```

Here is another output of the program:

```
D:\CBook>./binaryintohexa
Enter a number in binary number 11100
The decimal of binary number 11100 is 28
The hexa decimal format of binary number 11100 is 1C
```

Voilà! We've successfully converted a binary number into a hexadecimal number.

Now, let's move on to the next recipe!

Finding whether a number is a palindrome

A palindrome number is one that appears the same when read forward and backward. For example, 123 is not a palindrome but 737 is. To find out whether a number is a palindrome, we need to split it into separate digits and convert the unit of the original number to hundred and the hundred to unit.

For example, a `pqr` number will be called a **palindrome number** if `pqr=rqp`. And `pqr` will be equal to `rqp` only if the following is true:

$$p \times 100 + q \times 10 + r = r \times 100 + q \times 10 + p$$

In other words, we will have to multiply the digit in the unit place by 10^2 to convert it into the hundreds and convert the digit in the hundreds place to unit by multiplying it by 1. If the result matches the original number, it is a palindrome.

How to do it...

1. Enter a number to assign to the n variable:

```
printf("Enter a number ");
scanf("%d",&n);
```

2. Invoke the findpalindrome function and pass the number in the n variable to it as an argument:

```
findpalindrome(n)
```

3. The n argument is assigned to the numb parameter in the findpalindrome function. We need to separate each digit of the number; to do so, we will execute a while loop for the time the value in the numb variable is greater than 0:

```
while(numb >0)
```

4. Within the while loop, we will apply mod 10 on the number. On application of the mod 10 operator, we will get the remainder, which is basically the last digit of the number:

```
remainder=numb%10;
```

5. Push that remainder to the stack:

```
push(remainder);
```

6. Because the last digit of the number is separated, we need to remove the last digit from the existing number. That is done by dividing the number by 10 and truncating the fraction. The while loop will terminate when the number is individually divided into separate digits and all the digits are pushed to the stack:

```
numb=numb/10;
```

7. The number at the top of the stack will be the hundred and the one at the bottom of the stack will be the unit of the original number. Recall that we need to convert the hundred of the original number to the unit and vice versa. Pop all the digits out from the stack one by one and multiply each of them by 10 raised to a power. The power will be 0 for the first digit that is popped off. The power will be incremented with every value that is popped off. After being multiplied by 10 raised to the respective power, the digits are added into a separate variable, called `value`:

```
j=pop();
value=value+j*pow(10,count);
count++;
```

8. If the numbers in the `numb` and `value` variables match, that means the number is a palindrome. If the number is a palindrome, the `findpalindrome` function will return a value of 1, otherwise it will return a value of 0:

```
if(numb==value) return (1);
else return (0);
```

The `findpalindrome.c` program determines whether the entered number is a palindrome number:

```
//Find out whether the entered number is a palindrome or not
# include <stdio.h>
#include <math.h>
#define max 10
int top=-1;
int stack[max];
void push();
int pop();
int findpalindrome(int);
void main()
{
    int n;
    printf("Enter a number ");
    scanf("%d",&n);
    if(findpalindrome(n))
        printf("%d is a palindrome number",n);
    else
        printf("%d is not a palindrome number", n);
}
int findpalindrome(int numb)
{
    int j, value, remainder, temp,count;
```

```
        temp=numb;
        while(numb >0)
        {
            remainder=numb%10;
            push(remainder);
            numb=numb/10;
        }
        numb=temp;
        count=0;
        value=0;
        while(top >=0)
        {
            j=pop();
            value=value+j*pow(10,count);
            count++;
        }
        if(numb==value) return (1);
        else return (0);
}
void push(int m)
{
    top++;
    stack[top]=m;
}
int pop()
{
    int j;
    if(top==-1)return(top);
    else
    {
        j=stack[top];
        top--;
        return(j);
    }
}
```

Now, let's go behind the scenes.

How it works...

Let's assume that the number we entered is **737**. Now, we want to know whether **737** is a palindrome. We will start by applying the mod **10** operator on **737**. On application, we will receive the remainder, **7**, and the quotient, **73**. The remainder, **7**, will be pushed to the stack. Before pushing to the stack, however, the value of the **top** pointer is incremented by 1. The value of **top** is -1 initially; it is incremented to **0** and the remainder of **7** is pushed to **stack[0]** (see *Figure 3.21*).

The mod **10** operator returns the last digit of the number as the remainder. The quotient that we get on the application of the mod **10** operator is the original number with its last digit removed. That is, the quotient that we will get on the application of mod **10** operator on **737** is **73**:

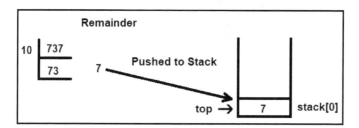

Figure 3.24

To the quotient, **73**, we will apply the mod **10** operator again. The remainder will be the last digit, which is **3**, and the quotient will be **7**. The value of **top** is incremented by 1, making its value 1, and the remainder is pushed to **stack[1]**. To the quotient, **7**, we will again apply the mod **10** operator. Because **7** cannot be divided by **10**, **7** itself is returned and is pushed to the stack. Again, before the push operation, the value of **top** is incremented by 1, making its value **2**. The value of **7** will be pushed to **stack[2]**:

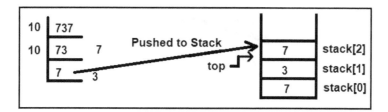

Figure 3.25

After separating the number into individual digits, we need to pop each digit from the stack one by one and multiply each one by **10** raised to a power. The power will be **0** for the topmost digit on the stack and will increment by 1 after every pop operation. The digit that will be popped from the stack will be the one indicated to by the top pointer. The value of **top** is **2**, so the digit on **stack[2]** is popped out and is multiplied by **10** raised to power of **0**:

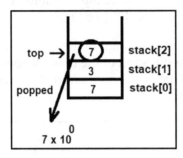

Figure 3.26

After every pop operation, the value of **top** is decremented by 1 and the value of the power is incremented by 1. The next digit that will be popped out from the stack is the one on **stack[1]**. That is, **3** will be popped out and multiplied by **10** raised to the power of **1**. Thereafter, the value of **top** will be decremented by 1, that is, the value of **top** will become **0**, and the value of the power will be incremented by 1, that is, the value of the power that was **1** will be incremented to **2**. The digit on **stack[0]** will be popped out and multiplied by **10** raised to the power of **2**:

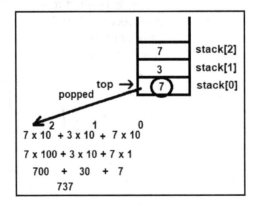

Figure 3.27

All the digits that are multiplied by **10** raised to the respective power are then summed. Because the result of the computation matches the original number, **737** is a palindrome.

Let's use GCC to compile the `findpalindrome.c` program, as shown in the following statement:

```
D:\CBook>gcc findpalindrome.c -o findpalindrome
```

Let's check whether `123` is a palindrome number:

```
D:\CBook>./findpalindrome
Enter a number 123
123 is not a palindrome number
```

Let's check whether `737` is a palindrome number:

```
D:\CBook>./findpalindrome
Enter a number 737
737 is a palindrome number
```

Voilà! We've successfully determined whether a number was a palindrome.

4
Preprocessing and Compilation

There are several preprocessor statements that can help you determine which source code needs to be compiled and which needs to be excluded from being compiled. That is, a condition can be applied and the desired statements will be compiled only if the specified condition is true. These directives can be nested for more precise branching. There are numerous preprocessor statements, such as `#if`, `#ifdef`, `#ifndef`, `#else`, `#elif`, and `#endif`, that can be used to collect statements into blocks that we want to be compiled when the specified condition is true.

Some of the advantages of using macros are as follows:

- The execution speed of the program increases as the value or code of the macro is substituted by the name of the macro. So, the time involved in invoking or calling the functions by the compiler is saved.
- Macros reduce the length of the program.

The main disadvantage of using a macro is that the size of the program increases prior to the compilation of the program, as all the macros are substituted by their code. In this chapter, we will learn how to apply conditional compilation using preprocessor directives.

We will also learn how to implement validation in the program by making use of assertions. Assertions are a sort of validation check for different critical statements of the program. If those assertions or expressions don't validate or return false, then an error is displayed and the program is aborted. The main difference between this and usual error handling is that assertions can be disabled at runtime.

 If the `#define NDEBUG` macro is defined near the `#include <assert.h>` directive, it will disable the assert function.

Besides the normal asserts, there are also asserts that are referred to as static or compile-time asserts, which are used to catch errors at the time of compilation. Such asserts can be used to do compile-time validations.

In addition to this, we will learn how to use stringize and token-pasting operators using the example of a pizza parlor.

In this chapter, we will learn how to make the following recipes:

- Performing conditional compilation with directives
- Applying assertions for validation
- Using assertions to ensure a pointer is not pointing to NULL
- Catching errors early with compile-time assertions
- Applying stringize and token-pasting operators

Let's start with the first recipe.

Performing conditional compilation with directives

In this recipe, we will learn how to apply conditional compilation. We will define certain macros, and then, by applying the #if, #ifdef, #ifndef, #else, #elif, #endif, and #undef preprocessor directives, we will direct the compiler to compile the desired code. Considering the example of a bookstore, let's assume that a user is asked to enter the price of the book. The program will apply different discounts, festival offers, a discount coupon, and Kindle options on the basis of the Qty macro, which represents the quantity or number of books purchased by the user. The program also defines other macros that determine different offers that are applicable.

How to do it...

Follow these steps to perform conditional compilation with preprocessor directives:

1. Define a Qty macro and assign it an initial value:

```
#define Qty 10
```

2. The user will be prompted to enter the price of a book:

```
printf("Enter price of a book ");
scanf("%f", &price);
```

3. The total number of books is computed using the `Qty*price` formula:

```
totalAmount=Qty*price;
```

4. On the basis of the `Qty` macro, the `#if`, `#elif`, `#else`, and `#endif` directives are used to determine the discount on the total number.

5. Once the discount percentage is determined, the amount after deducting the discount is computed and is assigned to the `afterDisc` variable:

```
afterDisc=totalAmount - (totalAmount*discount)/100;
```

6. The festival discount is also computed on the basis of the `FestivalOffer` macro. That is, the `#ifdef`, `#else`, and `#endif` directives are used to confirm whether the `FestivalOffer` macro is defined and, accordingly, the amount that the customer has to pay after deducting the festival discount is computed:

```
#ifdef FestivalOffer
 afterFDisc=afterDisc-(totalAmount*FestivalOffer)/100;
 #else
 afterFDisc=afterDisc;
 #endif
```

7. The `#if defined` directive is used to confirm whether the `DiscountCoupon` macro is defined in the program or not. And, accordingly, the user is informed whether they are eligible for the discount coupon:

```
#if defined (DiscountCoupon)
 printf("You are also eligible for a discount coupon of $
%d\n", DiscountCoupon);
 #endif
```

8. The preprocessor directives, `#ifndef` and `#endif`, are used to determine whether the `Kindle` macro is defined or not. If the `Kindle` macro is not yet defined, it is defined and its value is set. Accordingly, the user is informed of how many months they will be eligible for the `Kindle` version of the book:

```
#ifndef Kindle
 #define Kindle 1
 #endif
 printf("You can use the Kindle version of the book for %d
         month(s)\n", Kindle);
```

The program for performing conditional compilation with preprocessor directives is shown in the following code snippet:

```c
// condcompile.c
#include <stdio.h>
#define Qty 10
#define FestivalOffer 2
#define DiscountCoupon 5
#define Kindle 2

int main()
{
    int discount;
    float price, totalAmount, afterDisc, afterFDisc;
    printf("Enter price of a book ");
    scanf("%f", &price);
#if Qty >= 10
        discount=15;
#elif Qty >=5
        discount=10;
#else
        discount=5;
#endif
    totalAmount=Qty*price;
    afterDisc=totalAmount - (totalAmount*discount)/100;
#ifdef FestivalOffer
        afterFDisc=afterDisc-(totalAmount*FestivalOffer)/100;
#else
        afterFDisc=afterDisc;
#endif
    printf("Quantity = %d, Price is $ %.2f, total amount for the
            books is $ %.2f\n", Qty, price, totalAmount);
    printf("Discount is %d%% and the total amount after
            discount is $ %.2f\n", discount, afterDisc);
#ifdef FestivalOffer
```

```
        printf("Festival discount is %d%%, the total amount
                after festival discount is $ %.2f\n",
                FestivalOffer, afterFDisc);
    #endif
    #if defined (DiscountCoupon)
        printf("You are also eligible for a discount
                coupon of $ %d\n", DiscountCoupon);
    #endif
    #ifndef Kindle
        #define Kindle 1
    #endif
    printf("You can use the Kindle version of the book
            for %d month(s)\n", Kindle);
    return 0;
}
```

Now, let's go behind the scenes to understand the code better.

How it works...

Four macros, called Qty, FestivalOffer, DiscountCoupon, and Kindle, are defined with the values of 10, 2, 5, and 2, respectively. The user is prompted to enter the price of a book. The value entered by the user is assigned to the variable price. The #if, #elif, #else, and #endif conditional directives are then used to determine the amount of discount to be applied to the books depending on the value of the Qty macro. Because, the current value of the Qty macro is 10, the value of the discount variable will be set to 15 through the preprocessor directives. The value of the discount variable can be changed at any time simply by changing the value of the Qty macro. The total number of the books is computed by multiplying the values of Qty by the price, and the resultant value is assigned to the totalAmount variable. Because the user is given some kind of discount on the basis of the Qty value, the amount that the user has to pay after deducting the discount is computed and the resulting amount is assigned to the afterDisc variable.

Again, because the FestivalOffer macro is defined, the #ifdef, #else, and #endif preprocessor directives are used to compute the amount that the customer has to pay after deducting a festival discount of 2%. We can always comment out the #define FestivalOffer statement to undefine the macro; in this case, no festival discount will be given to the customer.

The total amount is displayed on the screen as well as the amount after deducting the discount. And if the festival offer is applied, the amount after deducting the festival offer is also displayed on the screen.

The `#if defined` directive is used to confirm whether the `DiscountCoupon` macro is defined or not. Because currently in the program the `DiscountCoupon` macro is defined and is assigned the value of 5, a message is displayed informing that they are eligible for an additional discount coupon of $5 too. You can always comment out the `DiscountCoupon` macro if you want to avoid giving any discount coupons. The Kindle version of the book has to be given to the customer for at least a month. Because the `Kindle` macro is defined in the program and is assigned the value of 2, a message is displayed on the screen informing the user that they are allowed to use the Kindle version of the book for 2 months. However, if you comment out the `Kindle` macro, the `#ifndef` and `#endif` preprocessor directives are used to set the value of the `Kindle` macro to 1 if the `Kindle` macro is not defined in the program. Therefore, if the `Kindle` macro is not defined in the program, a message will be displayed informing the user that they are allowed to use the Kindle version of the book for 1 month.

The program is compiled using GCC, as shown in the following screenshot. Because no error appears during compilation, this means that the `condcompile.c` program is successfully compiled into a `.exe` file: `condcompile.exe`. On executing the file, the user will be prompted to enter the price of the book and, according to the defined macros, the total amount and the discounted amount will be displayed, as shown in the following screenshot:

```
D:\CAdvBook>gcc condcompile.c -o condcompile

D:\CAdvBook>condcompile
Enter price of a book 40
Quantity = 10, Price is $ 40.00, total amount for the books is $ 400.00
Discount is 15% and the total amount after discount is $ 340.00
Festival discount is 2%, the total amount after festival discount is $ 332.00
You are also eligible for a discount coupan of $ 5
You can use the Kindle version of the book for 2 month(s)
```

Figure 4.1

Next, keeping the value of the Qty macro to 10 and try commenting out the following two macros:

```
#define FestivalOffer 2
#define Kindle 2
```

The preceding program will show the following output:

```
D:\CAdvBook>gcc condcompile.c -o condcompile

D:\CAdvBook>condcompile
Enter price of a book 40
Quantity = 10, Price is $ 40.00, total amount for the books is $ 400.00
Discount is 15% and the total amount after discount is $ 340.00
You are also eligible for a discount coupan of $ 5
You can use the Kindle version of the book for 1 month(s)
```

Figure 4.2

You can see in the output that because the value of the Qty macro is still 10, the customer will continue to get a discount of 15% as shown in the preceding screenshot. Additionally, the festival discount is not given to the customer at all. Because DiscountCoupon macro is still defined, the customer will continue to get discount coupon of $5 and the Kindle version is reduced to 1 month.

As we mentioned earlier, the #undef directive removes the current definition of the macro. The following code snippet uses the defined macro and then undefines it after using it:

```c
#include <stdio.h>
#define qty 10

int main()
{
    #ifdef qty
        amount =qty * rate;
        #undef qty
    #endif
  return 0;
}
```

You can see that the qty macro is used and then undefined after usage. Now, let's move on to the next recipe!

Applying assertions for validation

In this recipe, we will learn how to implement validation using assertion. The program will ask the user to enter the information of the passengers that are flying from one place to another. Using assertions, we can ensure that the number of passengers entered is a positive number. If the number of passengers entered is zero or a negative value, the program will abort.

How to do it...

Follow these steps to create a validation check using assertion. The recipe will not allow the program to run if the value of the number of passengers is zero or negative:

1. The user is prompted to enter how many passengers are flying:

```
printf("How many passengers ? ");
scanf("%d",&noOfPassengers);
```

2. An `assert` instance is defined to ensure that the value of the number of passengers should not be 0 or negative. If the user enters a value of 0 or negative for the number of passengers, an error message will be displayed showing the line number, and the program will abort:

```
assert(noOfPassengers > 0 && "Number of passengers should
          be a positive integer");
```

3. If the value for the number of passengers entered is a positive value, the user is asked to supply other information such as where the flight is going from, where the flight is going to, and the date of the journey:

```
printf("Flight from: ");
while((c= getchar()) != '\n' && c != EOF);
gets(fl_from);
printf("Flight to: ");
gets(fl_to);
printf("Date of journey ");
scanf("%s", dateofJourney);
```

4. The entered information of the passengers is then displayed on the screen:

```
printf("Number of passengers %d\n", noOfPassengers);
printf("Flight from: %s\n", fl_from);
printf("Flight to: %s\n", fl_to);
printf("Date of journey: %s\n", dateofJourney);
```

The program for implementing a validation check using assertions is shown in the following code snippet:

```c
// assertdemoprog.c
#include <stdio.h>
#include <assert.h>

int main(void)
{
    int c, noOfPassengers;
    char fl_from[30], fl_to[30], dateofJourney[12];
    printf("How many passengers ? ");
    scanf("%d",&noOfPassengers);
    assert(noOfPassengers > 0 && "Number of passengers should
                                be a positive integer");
    printf("Flight from: ");
    while((c= getchar()) != '\n' && c != EOF);
        gets(fl_from);
        printf("Flight to: ");
        gets(fl_to);
        printf("Date of journey ");
        scanf("%s", dateofJourney);
        printf("The information entered is:\n");
        printf("Number of passengers %d\n", noOfPassengers);
        printf("Flight from: %s\n", fl_from);
        printf("Flight to: %s\n", fl_to);
        printf("Date of journey: %s\n", dateofJourney);
        return 0;
}
```

Now, let's go behind the scenes to understand the code better.

How it works...

The program prompts the user to enter the information of the passengers that are flying from one place to another on a specific date. In order to ensure that the value of the number of passengers is not zero or negative, an assertion is used. The `assert` expression validates the value assigned to the `noOfPassengers` variable. It checks whether the value of the `noOfPassengers` variable is greater than 0 or not. If it is, the program will continue to execute the rest of the statements; otherwise, the filename and the line number are sent to the standard error and the program is aborted.

If the assert statement is validated, that is, if the value assigned to `noOfPassengers` is more than 0, then the user is asked to enter the other details of the passengers such as where the flight is going from, where the flight is going to, and the date of the journey. The entered information is then displayed on the screen.

The program is compiled using GCC, as shown in the following screenshot. Because no error appears during compilation, this means the `assertdemoprog.c` program is successfully compiled into a `.exe` file: `assertdemoprog.exe`. On executing the file, the user is prompted to enter the number of passengers flying. If the number of passengers entered is a positive value, the program will run perfectly, as shown in the following screenshot:

```
D:\CAdvBook>gcc assertdemoprog.c -o assertdemoprog

D:\CAdvBook>assertdemoprog
How many passengers ? 1
Flight from: New Delhi
Flight to: Sydney
Date of journey 10/12/2019
The information entered is:
Number of passengers 1
Flight from: New Delhi
Flight to: Sydney
Date of journey: 10/12/2019
```

Figure 4.3

While executing the program for the second time, if the value entered is negative or zero for the `noOfPassengers` variable, an error will be displayed showing the program name and line number, and the program is aborted. The specified error message, `"Number of passengers should be a positive integer"`, will be displayed:

```
D:\CAdvBook>assertdemoprog
How many passengers ? 0
assertion "noOfPassengers > 0 && "Number of passengers should be a positive
 integer"" failed: file "assertdemoprog.c", line 10, function: main
  0 [main] assertdemoprog 1347 cygwin_exception::open_stackdumpfile: Dumpin
g stack trace to assertdemoprog.exe.stackdump
```

Figure 4.4

Voilà! We have successfully applied assertions to validate our data.

Using assertions to ensure a pointer is not pointing to NULL

Let's perform one more recipe on assertions. Let's apply assertions to ensure that a pointer is not pointing to NULL and is instead pointing to a memory address that is to be accessed. Essentially, in this recipe, we will learn to compute the average of a few numbers, where the numbers are stored in an array, and the array elements are accessed through a pointer.

How to do it...

Follow these steps to ensure that the pointer is not NULL and is pointing to a memory address by making use of assertions:

1. Define an array containing a number of integers whose average is to be computed:

   ```
   int arr[]={3,9,1,6,2};
   ```

2. Set a pointer to point to the array:

   ```
   ptr=arr;
   ```

3. Define a function for calculating the average of the array elements. A pointer to an array and the count of the number of values in the array are both passed to this function:

   ```
   average=findaverage(ptr, count);
   ```

4. In the function, define an assert expression that ensures that the pointer is not NULL. If the pointer is NULL, the program will display an error and will be aborted:

   ```
   assert(Ptr != NULL && "Pointer is not pointing to any array");
   ```

5. If the pointer is not `NULL`, the array elements will be accessed through the pointer and their average will be computed and displayed on the screen:

```
for(i=0;i<Count;i++)
  {
    sum+=*Ptr;
    Ptr++;
  }
Average=(float)sum/Count;
```

The program for implementing a validation that ensures the pointer is not `NULL` and is pointing to a memory address is shown as follows:

```
// assertprog.c
#include <stdio.h>
#include <assert.h>

float findaverage(int *Ptr, int Count);

int main()
{
    int arr[]={3,9,1,6,2};
    float average;
    int *ptr=NULL,count;
    ptr=arr;
    count=5;
    average=findaverage(ptr, count);
    printf("Average of values is %f\n", average);
    return(0);
}

float findaverage(int *Ptr, int Count)
{
    int sum,i;
    float Average;
    assert(Ptr != NULL && "Pointer is not pointing to any array");
    sum=0;
    for(i=0;i<Count;i++)
    {
        sum+=*Ptr;
        Ptr++;
    }
    Average=(float)sum/Count;
    return(Average);
}
```

Now, let's go behind the scenes to understand the code better.

How it works...

In this program, the average of several integers is computed via an array. That is, a number of integers whose average is supposed to be computed are assigned to an array and an integer pointer is used to access the array elements. A function named `findaverage` is defined, to which the integer pointer and the count of the numbers are passed. In the function, an assert is used that ensures that the pointer is not NULL. If the pointer is not NULL, the array elements are accessed through the pointer and their addition is done. After the addition of the numbers, their average is computed. The computed average is then returned to the `main` function where the average is displayed on the screen. If the pointer is not pointing to the array and is instead pointing to NULL, the program will display an error and will be aborted.

The program is compiled using GCC, as shown in the following screenshot. Because no error appears during compilation, this means the `assertprog.c` program is successfully compiled into a `.exe` file: `assertprog.exe`. Because the pointer is pointing to the array while executing the file, we get the average of the numerical values specified in the array, as shown in the following screenshot:

```
D:\CAdvBook>gcc assertprog.c -o assertprog

D:\CAdvBook>assertprog
Average of values is 4.200000
```

Figure 4.5

Next, comment out the following line in which the pointer is pointing to the array:

```
ptr=arr;
```

The `ptr` pointer now is pointing to NULL. Hence, on running the program, it will display an error, as shown in the following screenshot:

```
D:\CAdvBook>gcc assertprog.c -o assertprog

D:\CAdvBook>assertprog
assertion "Ptr != NULL && "Pointer is not pointing to any array"" failed:
  file "assertprog.c", line 22, function: findaverage
      0 [main] assertprog 1335 cygwin_exception::open_stackdumpfile: Dump
ing stack trace to assertprog.exe.stackdump
```

Figure 4.6

Voilà! We have successfully used assertions to ensure that our pointer is not pointing to NULL.

Now, let's move on to the next recipe!

Catching errors early with compile-time assertions

In this recipe, we will make use of assertions to detect errors at the time of compilation. Essentially, we will create a structure and will make a compile-time assertion that ensures the size of the structure is of some specific bytes. The program will abort if the size of the structure is not equal to the specified value. This constraint will help in determining the capacity of storage and also in the easy maintenance of records, that is, for deletes and updates.

How to do it...

Follow these steps to create a compile-time assert expression that ensures that the user-defined structure is a specified number of bytes:

1. Define a structure with a few members:

```
struct customers
{
int orderid;
char customer_name[20];
float amount;
};
```

2. Define a compile-time assert that puts a constraint on the size of the structure. The program will compile only when the assert is validated, that is, the size of the structure is exactly equal to the bytes mentioned in the assert expression:

```
static_assert(sizeof(struct customers) == 28, "The structure
is consuming unexpected number of bytes");
```

3. In the main body of the program, you can write any executable code. This code will compile and execute only when the `assert` expression is validated:

```
static_assert(sizeof(struct customers) == 28, "The structure
is consuming unexpected number of bytes");
```

The program for implementing compile-time validation to ensure that the size of a structure is exactly equal to a specific number of bytes is shown in the following code snippet:

```
// compileassert.c
#include <stdio.h>
#include <assert.h>

struct customers
{
    int orderid;
    char customer_name[20];
    float amount;
};

static_assert(sizeof(struct customers) == 28, "The structure is
consuming unexpected number of bytes");

int main(void)
{
    printf("sizeof(int) %d\n",sizeof(int));
    printf("sizeof(float) %d\n",sizeof(float));
    printf("sizeof(char) %d\n",sizeof(char));
    printf("sizeof(struct customers) %d\n",sizeof(struct customers));
    return 0;
}
```

Now, let's go behind the scenes to understand the code better.

How it works...

A structure is defined by the name customers, which consists of a few members. The members of the structure are of different data types. A compile-time assert is defined that places a constraint on the size of the customers structure to be of 28 bytes exactly. That means the program will not be compiled if the size of the structure is less than or greater than 28 bytes. The main function simply displays the size of different data types such as int, float, and char. The program also displays the size of the complete customers structure.

The program is compiled using GCC, as shown in the following screenshot. Because the size of the customers structure is exactly the same as that specified in the compile-time assert, the program compiles perfectly and the compileassert.c program is successfully compiled into a .exe file: compileassert.exe. On executing the file, we get the output showing the size of different data types and that of the customers structure, as shown in the following screenshot:

```
D:\CAdvBook>gcc compileassert.c -o compileassert

D:\CAdvBook>compileassert
sizeof(int) 4
sizeof(float) 4
sizeof(char) 1
sizeof(struct customers) 28
```

Figure 4.7

After changing the value in the assert function, that is, if the size of the structure does not match the value mentioned in the compile-time assert, we get a compilation error as follows:

```
D:\CAdvBook>gcc compileassert.c -o compileassert
In file included from compileassert.c:2:0:
compileassert.c:11:1: error: static assertion failed: "The structure is
consuming unexpected number of bytes"
 static_assert(sizeof(struct customers) == 24, "The structure is consumi
ng unexpected number of bytes");
 ^
```

Figure 4.8

Voilà! We have successfully implemented compile-time assertions to be able to catch errors early in the system. Now, let's move on to the next recipe!

Applying stringize and token-pasting operators

The stringize or hash symbol (#) can be used in a macro definition to convert the macro parameter into a string constant. You can imagine that the parameter is enclosed in double quotes and returned. It is also known as a token-concatenation operator.

The token-pasting operator (##) combines two parameters when used in a macro definition. That is, the two parameters on either side of each ## operator are joined into a single string. More precisely, it performs string concatenation on the two parameters to form a new string.

In this recipe, we will learn how to apply stringize and token-pasting operators in computing. The user is asked to specify a certain pizza size and their desired toppings and, accordingly, the price of the pizza is displayed.

How to do it...

Following these steps to create a recipe that uses stringize and token-pasting operators:

1. Define a macro with the name `pizzaprice` using a token-pasting operator:

   ```
   #define pizzaprice(a, b) a##b
   ```

2. Define one more macro with the name `convertIntoStr` using a stringize operator:

   ```
   #define convertIntoStr(str) #str
   ```

3. Define a few variables such as `smallnormal`, `mediumnormal`, `largenormal`, and `smallextra` that represent the price for a pizza of different pizza sizes and toppings:

   ```
   float smallnormal=5;
    float mediumnormal=7;
   ```

```
float largenormal=10;
float smallextra=7;
float mediumextra=9;
float largeextra=12;
char pizzasize[30];
char topping[20];
```

4. The user is asked to enter the pizza size desired by the customer and the size entered is assigned to the `pizzasize` variable:

```
printf("What size pizza you want? small/medium/large: ");
scanf("%s", pizzasize);
```

5. Then, the user is asked to specify whether the pizza is desired with normal cheese or extra cheese, and the choice entered by the user is assigned to the `topping` variable:

```
printf("Normal or with extra cheese? normal/extra: ");
scanf("%s",topping);
```

6. Next, branching is done on the basis of the value of the `topping` variable:

```
if(strcmp(topping, "normal")==0)
{...........
}
if(strcmp(topping, "extra")==0)
{...................
}
```

7. Additionally, the size entered in the `pizzasize` variable is compared to check whether the pizza size is small, medium, or large and, accordingly, the arguments are passed to the `pizzaprice` macro:

```
if(strcmp(pizzasize, "small")==0)
.........
else
if(strcmp(pizzasize, "medium")==0)
............
else
..................
```

8. The `pizzaprice` macro joins the `pizzasize` and `topping` arguments together and expands them into a concatenated variable:

```
pizzaprice(small, extra));
```

Here, small can be replaced by medium or large depending on the size chosen by the user. Additionally, extra can be replaced by normal if the user wants a pizza with normal cheese.

9. The value of the concatenated variable is displayed as the price of the specified pizza with the desired toppings:

```
printf("The prize for %s size pizza with %s toppings is $%.2f
\n", pizzasize, topping, pizzaprice(small, extra));
```

The program for applying stringize and token-pasting operators is shown in the following code:

```
// preconcat.c
#include <stdio.h>
#include <string.h>

#define pizzaprice(a, b) a##b
#define convertIntoStr(str) #str

int main()
{
    float smallnormal=5;
    float mediumnormal=7;
    float largenormal=10;
    float smallextra=7;
    float mediumextra=9;
    float largeextra=12;
    char pizzasize[30];
    char topping[20];

    printf("What size pizza you want? small/medium/large: ");
    scanf("%s", pizzasize);
    printf("Normal or with extra cheese? normal/extra: ");
    scanf("%s",topping);
    if(strcmp(topping, "normal")==0)
    {
        if(strcmp(pizzasize, "small")==0)
            printf("The prize for %s size pizza with %s toppings is
                    $%.2f \n", pizzasize, topping,
                    pizzaprice(small, normal));
        else
            if(strcmp(pizzasize, "medium")==0)
                printf("The prize for %s size pizza with %s
                        toppings is $%.2f \n", pizzasize, topping,
                        pizzaprice(medium, normal));
            else
```

```
                printf("The prize for %s size pizza with %s
                    toppings is $%.2f \n", pizzasize, topping,
                    pizzaprice(large, normal));
    }
    if(strcmp(topping, "extra")==0)
    {
        if(strcmp(pizzasize, "small")==0)
            printf("The prize for %s size pizza with %s toppings
                is $%.2f \n", pizzasize, topping,
                pizzaprice(small, extra));
        else
            if(strcmp(pizzasize, "medium")==0)
                printf("The prize for %s size pizza with %s toppings
                    is $%.2f \n", pizzasize, topping,
                    pizzaprice(medium, extra));
            else
                printf("The prize for %s size pizza with %s toppings
                    is $%.2f \n", pizzasize, topping,
                    pizzaprice(large, extra));
    }
    printf(convertIntoStr(Thanks for visiting us));
    return 0;
}
```

Now, let's go behind the scenes to understand the code better.

How it works...

A token-pasting operator is used to define a macro with the name pizzaprice. This macro concatenates the two a and b parameters into a single string. In addition to this, a stringize operator is used to define a macro with the name convertIntoStr, which converts the str parameter into a string. A number of variables are defined, such as smallnormal, mediumnormal, largenormal, and smallextra. These variables represent the price of a small-sized normal pizza, a medium-sized normal pizza, a large-sized normal pizza, and a small-sized pizza with extra cheese, respectively. The normal suffix declares that this is the price of a pizza with a regular amount of cheese. The extra suffix indicates that this variable represents the price of a pizza with extra cheese.

The user is prompted to enter what pizza size the customer is ordering. The size entered is assigned to the pizzasize variable. After that, the user is asked whether the pizza is desired with normal cheese or extra cheese and the choice that is entered is assigned to the topping variable.

Next, branching is done on the basis of the value in the `topping` variable. If the topping is normal, the string in `pizzasize` is compared to check whether the pizza size is small, medium, or large and, accordingly, the arguments are passed to the `pizzaprice` macro. For example, if the user has entered small as the pizza size and the topping as extra, the `pizzaprice` macro is invoked with two parameters (small and extra). The `pizzaprice` macro, being a token-pasting operator, will concatenate the small and extra strings into `smallextra`, and hence the value of the `smallextra` variable will be displayed as the price of the small-sized pizza with extra cheese as a topping.

The `pizzasize` and `topping` variables are combined into a concatenated string, and hence will access the value in the respective variable. Finally, the `convertIntoStr` macro is invoked, which includes a stringize operator to display a `Thanks for visiting us` string at the end of the bill.

The program is compiled using GCC, as shown in the following screenshot. Because no error appears during compilation, the `preconcat.c` program is successfully compiled into a `.exe` file: `preconcat.exe`. On executing the file, the user will be asked to enter the desired pizza size and toppings and, accordingly, the program will display the price of the pizza, as shown in the following screenshot:

```
D:\CAdvBook>gcc preconcat.c -o preconcat

D:\CAdvBook>preconcat
What size pizza you want? small/medium/large: small
Normal or with extra cheeze? normal/extra: extra
The prize for small size pizza with extra toppings is $7.00
Thanks for visiting us

D:\CAdvBook>preconcat
What size pizza you want? small/medium/large: large
Normal or with extra cheeze? normal/extra: normal
The prize for large size pizza with normal toppings is $10.00
Thanks for visiting us
```

Figure 4.9

Voilà! We have successfully applied the stringize and token-pasting operators and created custom pizza orders.

Deep Dive into Pointers

5

Pointers have been the popular choice among programmers when it comes to using memory in an optimized way. Pointers have made it possible to access the content of any variable, array, or data type. You can use pointers for low-level access to any content and improve the overall performance of an application.

In this chapter, we will look at the following recipes on pointers:

- Reversing a string using pointers
- Finding the largest value in an array using pointers
- Sorting a singly linked list
- Finding the transpose of a matrix using pointers
- Accessing a structure using a pointer

Before we start with the recipes, I would like to discuss a few things related to how pointers work.

What is a pointer?

A pointer is a variable that contains the memory address of another variable, array, or string. When a pointer contains the address of something, it is said to be pointing at that thing. When a pointer points at something, it receives the right to access the content of that memory address. The question now is—why do we need pointers at all?

We need them because they do the following:

- Facilitate the dynamic allocation of memory
- Provide an alternative way to access a data type (apart from variable names, you can access the content of a variable through pointers)
- Make it possible to return more than one value from a function

For example, consider an i integer variable:

```
int i;
```

When you define an integer variable, two bytes will be allocated to it in memory. This set of two bytes can be accessed by a memory address. The value assigned to the variable is stored inside that memory location, as shown in the following diagram:

Figure 5.1

In the preceding diagram, **1000** represents the memory address of the **i** variable. Though, in reality, memory address is quite big and is in hex format, for the sake of simplicity, I am taking a small integer number, **1000**. The value of **10** is stored inside the memory address, **1000**.

Now, a j integer pointer can be defined as follows:

```
int *j;
```

This j integer pointer can point to the i integer through the following statement:

```
j=&i;
```

The & (ampersand) symbol represents the address, and the address of **i** will be assigned to the **j** pointer, as shown in the following diagram. The **2000** address is assumed to be the address of the **j** pointer and the address of the **i** pointer, that is, **1000**, is stored inside the memory location assigned to the **j** pointer, as shown in the following diagram:

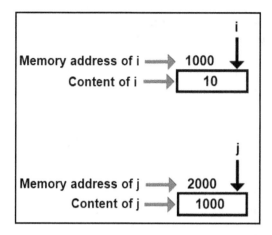

Figure 5.2

The address of the i integer can be displayed by the following statements:

```
printf("Address of i is %d\n", &i);
printf("Address of i is %d\n", j);
```

To display the contents of i, we can use the following statements:

```
printf("Value of i is %d\n", i);
printf("Value of i is %d\n", *j);
```

 In the case of pointers, & (ampersand) represents the memory address and * (asterisk) represents content in the memory address.

We can also define a pointer to an integer pointer by means of the following statement:

```
int **k;
```

This pointer to a k integer pointer can point to a j integer pointer using the following statement:

```
k=&j;
```

Through the previous statement, the address of the **j** pointer will be assigned to the pointer to a **k** integer pointer, as shown in the following diagram. The value of **3000** is assumed to be the memory address of **k**:

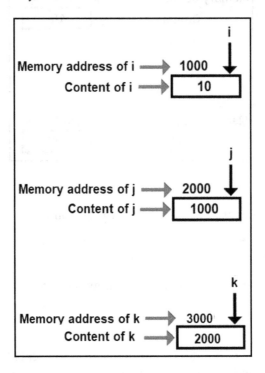

Figure 5.3

Now, when you display the value of k, it will display the address of j:

```
printf("Address of j =%d %d \n",&j,k);
```

To display the address of i through k, we need to use *k, because *k means that it will display the contents of the memory address pointed at by k. Now, k is pointing at j and the content in j is the address of i:

```
printf("Address of i = %d %d %d\n",&i,j,*k);
```

Similarly, to display the value of i through k, **k has to be used as follows:

```
printf("Value of i is %d %d %d %d \n",i,*(&i),*j,**k);
```

Using pointers enables us to access content precisely from desired memory locations. But allocating memory through pointers and not releasing it when the job is done may lead to a problem called **memory leak**. A memory leak is a sort of resource leak. A memory leak can allow unauthorized access of the memory content to hackers and may also block some content from being accessed even though it is present.

Now, let's begin with the first recipe of this chapter.

Reversing a string using pointers

In this recipe, we will learn to reverse a string using pointers. The best part is that we will not reverse the string and copy it onto another string, but we will reverse the original string itself.

How to do it...

1. Enter a string to assign to the str string variable as follows:

```
printf("Enter a string: ");
scanf("%s", str);
```

2. Set a pointer to point at the string, as demonstrated in the following code. The pointer will point at the memory address of the string's first character:

```
ptr1=str;
```

3. Find the length of the string by initializing an n variable to 1. Set a while loop to execute when the pointer reaches the null character of the string as follows:

```
n=1;
while(*ptr1 !='\0')
{
```

4. Inside the while loop, the following actions will be performed:

   - The pointer is moved one character forward.
   - The value of the n variable is incremented by 1:

```
ptr1++;
n++;
```

5. The pointer will be at the null character, so move the pointer one step back to make it point at the last character of the string as follows:

```
ptr1--;
```

6. Set another pointer to point at the beginning of the string as follows:

```
ptr2=str;
```

7. Exchange the characters equal to half the length of the string. To do that, set a `while` loop to execute for `n/2` times, as demonstrated in the following code snippet:

```
m=1;
while(m<=n/2)
```

8. Within the `while` loop, the first exchange operations take place; that is, the characters pointed at by our pointers are exchanged:

```
temp=*ptr1;
*ptr1=*ptr2;
*ptr2=temp;
```

9. After the character exchange, set the second pointer to move forward to point at its next character, that is, at the second character of the string, and move the first pointer backward to make it point at the second to last character as follows:

```
ptr1--;
ptr2++;
```

10. Repeat this procedure for n/2 times, where `n` is the length of the string. When the `while` loop is finished, we will have the reverse form of the original string displayed on the screen:

```
printf("Reverse string is %s", str);
```

The `reversestring.c` program for reversing a string using pointers is as follows:

```c
#include <stdio.h>
void main()
{
    char str[255], *ptr1, *ptr2, temp ;
    int n,m;
    printf("Enter a string: ");
    scanf("%s", str);
    ptr1=str;
```

```
      n=1;
      while(*ptr1 !='\0')
      {
          ptr1++;
          n++;
      }
      ptr1--;
      ptr2=str;
      m=1;
      while(m<=n/2)
      {
          temp=*ptr1;
          *ptr1=*ptr2;
          *ptr2=temp;
          ptr1--;
          ptr2++;;
          m++;
      }
      printf("Reverse string is %s", str);
}
```

Now, let's go behind the scenes.

How it works...

We will be prompted to enter a string that will be assigned to the str variable. A string is nothing but a character array. Assuming we enter the name manish, each character of the name will be assigned to a location in the array one by one (see *Figure 5.4*). We can see that the first character of the string, the letter **m**, is assigned to the **str[0]** location, followed by the second string character being assigned to the **str[1]** location, and so on. The null character, as usual, is at the end of the string, as shown in the following diagram:

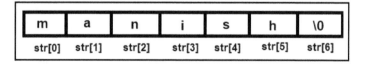

Figure 5.4

To reverse the string, we will seek the help of two pointers: one will be set to point at the first character of the string, and the other at the final character of the string. So, the first **ptr1** pointer is set to point at the first character of the string as follows:

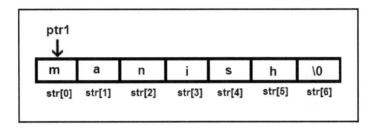

Figure 5.5

The exchanging of the characters has to be executed equal to half the length of the string; therefore, the next step will be to find the length of the string. After finding the string's length, the **ptr1** pointer will be set to move to the final character of the string.

In addition, another **ptr2** pointer is set to point at **m**, the first character of the string, as shown in the following diagram:

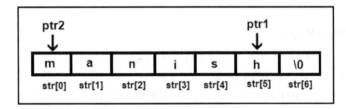

Figure 5.6

The next step is to interchange the first and last characters of the string that are being pointed at by the **ptr1** and **ptr2** pointers (see *Figure 5.7 (a)*). After interchanging the characters pointed at by the **ptr1** and **ptr2** pointers, the string will appear as shown in *Figure 5.7 (b)*:

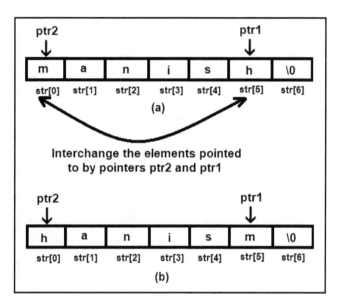

Figure 5.7

After interchanging the first and last characters, we will interchange the second and the second to last characters of the string. To do so, the **ptr2** pointer will be moved forward and set to point at the next character in line, and the **ptr1** pointer will be moved backward and set to point at the second to last character.

You can see in the following *Figure 5.8 (a)* that the **ptr2** and **ptr1** pointers are set to point at the **a** and **s** characters. Once this is done, another interchanging of the characters pointed at by **ptr2** and **ptr1** will take place. The string will appear as follows (*Figure 5.8 (b)*) after the interchanging of the **a** and **s** characters:

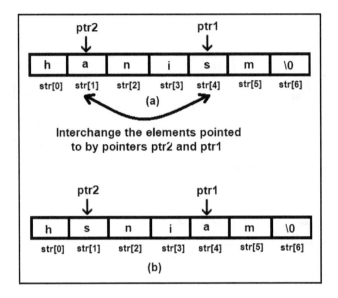

Figure 5.8

The only task now left in reversing the string is to interchange the third and the third to last character. So, we will repeat the relocation process of the **ptr2** and **ptr1** pointers. Upon interchanging the **n** and **i** characters of the string, the original **str** string will have been reversed, as follows:

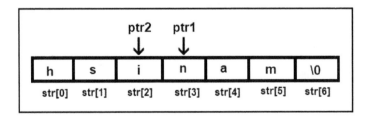

Figure 5.9

After applying the preceding steps, if we print the **str** string, it will appear in reverse.

Let's use GCC to compile the `reversestring.c` program as follows:

```
D:\CBook>gcc reversestring.c -o reversestring
```

If you get no errors or warnings, that means the `reversestring.c` program has been compiled into an executable file, called `reversestring.exe`. Let's run this executable file as follows:

```
D:\CBook>./reversestring
Enter a string: manish
Reverse string is hsinam
```

Voilà! We've successfully reversed a string using pointers. Now, let's move on to the next recipe!

Finding the largest value in an array using pointers

In this recipe, all the elements of the array will be scanned using pointers.

How to do it...

1. Define a macro by the name `max` with a size of `100` as follows:

   ```
   #define max 100
   ```

2. Define a `p` integer array of a `max` size, as demonstrated in the following code:

   ```
   int p[max]
   ```

3. Specify the number of elements in the array as follows:

   ```
   printf("How many elements are there? ");
   scanf("%d", &n);
   ```

4. Enter the elements for the array as follows:

   ```
   for(i=0;i<n;i++)
       scanf("%d",&p[i]);
   ```

5. Define two `mx` and `ptr` pointers to point at the first element of the array as follows:

```
mx=p;
ptr=p;
```

6. The `mx` pointer will always point at the maximum value of the array, whereas the `ptr` pointer will be used for comparing the remainder of the values of the array. If the value pointed to by the `mx` pointer is smaller than the value pointed at by the `ptr` pointer, the `mx` pointer is set to point at the value pointed at by `ptr`. The `ptr` pointer will then move to point at the next array element as follows:

```
if (*mx < *ptr)
    mx=ptr;
```

7. If the value pointed at by the `mx` pointer is larger than the value pointed to by the `ptr` pointer, the `mx` pointer is undisturbed and is left to keep pointing at the same value and the `ptr` pointer is moved further to point at the next array element for the following comparison:

```
ptr++;
```

8. This procedure is repeated until all the elements of the array (pointed to by the `ptr` pointer) are compared with the element pointed to by the `mx` pointer. Finally, the `mx` pointer will be left pointing at the maximum value in the array. To display the maximum value of the array, simply display the array element pointed to by the `mx` pointer as follows:

```
printf("Largest value is %d\n", *mx);
```

The `largestinarray.c` program for finding out the largest value in an array using pointers is as follows:

```
#include <stdio.h>
#define max 100
void main()
{
    int p[max], i, n, *ptr, *mx;
    printf("How many elements are there? ");
    scanf("%d", &n);
    printf("Enter %d elements \n", n);
    for(i=0;i<n;i++)
        scanf("%d",&p[i]);
    mx=p;
```

```
    ptr=p;
    for(i=1;i<n;i++)
    {
        if (*mx < *ptr)
            mx=ptr;
        ptr++;
    }
    printf("Largest value is %d\n", *mx);
}
```

Now, let's go behind the scenes.

How it works...

Define an array of a certain size and enter a few elements in it. These will be the values among which we want to find the largest value. After entering a few elements, the array might appear as follows:

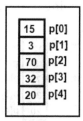

Figure 5.10

We will use two pointers for finding the largest value in the array. Let's name the two pointers **mx** and **ptr**, where the **mx** pointer will be used to point at the maximum value of the array, and the **ptr** pointer will be used for comparing the rest of the array elements with the value pointed at by the **mx** pointer. Initially, both the pointers are set to point at the first element of the array, **p[0]**, as shown in the following diagram:

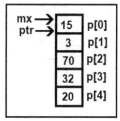

Figure 5.11

The **ptr** pointer is then moved to point at the next element of the array, **p[1]**. Then, the values pointed at by the **mx** and **ptr** pointers are compared. This process continues until all the elements of the array have been compared as follows:

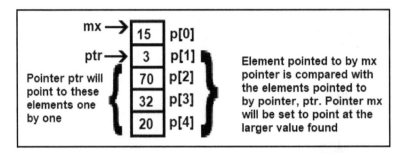

Figure 5.12

Recall that we want the **mx** pointer to keep pointing at the larger value. Since 15 is greater than 3 (see *Figure 5.13*), the position of the **mx** pointer will be left undisturbed, and the **ptr** pointer will be moved to point at the next element, **p[2]**, as follows:

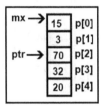

Figure 5.13

Again, the values pointed at by the **mx** and **ptr** pointers, which are the values 15 and 70 respectively, will be compared. Now, the value pointed at by the **mx** pointer is smaller than the value pointed at by the **ptr** pointer. So, the **mx** pointer will be set to point at the same array element as **ptr** as follows:

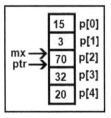

Figure 5.14

The comparison of the array elements will continue. The idea is to keep the **mx** pointer pointing at the largest element in the array, as shown in the following diagram:

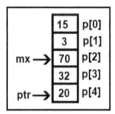

Figure 5.15

As shown in *Figure 5.15*, **70** is greater than **20**, so the **mx** pointer will remain at **p[2]**, and the **ptr** pointer will move to the next element, **p[4]**. Now, the **ptr** pointer is pointing at the last array element. So, the program will terminate, displaying the last value pointed at by the **mx** pointer, which also happens to be the largest value in the array.

Let's use GCC to compile the `largestinarray.c` program as the following statement:

```
D:\CBook>gcc largestinarray.c -o largestinarray
```

If you get no errors or warnings, that means that the `largestinarray.c` program has been compiled into an executable file, `largestinarray.exe`. Let's now run this executable file as follows:

```
D:\CBook>./largestinarray
How many elements are there? 5
Enter 5 elements
15
3
70
35
20
Largest value is 70
You can see that the program displays the maximum value in the array
```

Voilà! We've successfully found the largest value in an array using pointers. Now, let's move on to the next recipe!

Sorting a singly linked list

In this recipe, we will learn how to create a singly linked list comprising integer elements, and then we will learn how to sort this linked list in ascending order.

A singly linked list consists of several nodes that are connected through pointers. A node of a singly linked list might appear as follows:

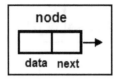

Figure 5.16

As you can see, a node of a singly linked list is a structure composed of two parts:

- **Data:** This can be one or more variables (also called members) of integer, float, string, or any data type. To keep the program simple, we will take **data** as a single variable of the integer type.
- **Pointer:** This will point to the structure of the type node. Let's call this pointer **next** in this program, though it can be under any name.

We will use bubble sort for sorting the linked list. Bubble sort is a sequential sorting technique that sorts by comparing adjacent elements. It compares the first element with the second element, the second element with the third element, and so on. The elements are interchanged if they are not in the preferred order. For example, if you are sorting elements into ascending order and the first element is larger than the second element, their values will be interchanged. Similarly, if the second element is larger than the third element, their values will be interchanged too.

This way, you will find that, by the end of the first iteration, the largest value will *bubble* down towards the end of the list. After the second iteration, the second largest value will be *bubbled* down to the end of the list. In all, n-1 iterations will be required to sort the n elements using bubble sort algorithm.

Let's understand the steps in creating and sorting a singly linked list.

How to do it...

1. Define a node comprising two members—data and next. The data member is for storing integer values and the next member is a pointer to link the nodes as follows:

```
struct node
{
   int data;
   struct node *next;
};
```

2. Specify the number of elements in the linked list. The value entered will be assigned to the n variable as follows:

```
printf("How many elements are there in the linked list ?");
scanf("%d",&n);
```

3. Execute a for loop for n number of times. Within the for loop, a node is created by the name newNode. When asked, enter an integer value to be assigned to the data member of newNode as follows:

```
newNode=(struct node *)malloc(sizeof(struct node));
scanf("%d",&newNode->data);
```

4. Two pointers, startList and temp1, are set to point at the first node. The startList pointer will keep pointing at the first node of the linked list. The temp1 pointer will be used to link the nodes as follows:

```
startList = newNode;
temp1=startList;
```

5. To connect the newly created nodes, the following two tasks are performed:

   - The next member of temp1 is set to point at the newly created node.
   - The temp1 pointer is shifted to point at the newly created node as follows:

```
temp1->next = newNode;
temp1=newNode;
```

6. When the `for` loop gets over, we will have a singly linked list with its first node pointed at by `startList`, and the next pointer of the last node pointing at NULL. This linked list is ready to undergo the sorting procedure. Set a `for` loop to execute from 0 until $n-2$ that is equal to n-1 iterations as follows:

```
for(i=n-2;i>=0;i--)
```

7. Within the `for` loop, to compare values, use two pointers, `temp1` and `temp2`. Initially, `temp1` and `temp2` will be set to point at the first two nodes of the linked list, as shown in the following code snippet:

```
temp1=startList;
temp2=temp1->next;
```

8. Compare the nodes pointed at by `temp1` and `temp2` in the following code:

```
if(temp1->data > temp2->data)
```

9. After comparing the first two nodes, the `temp1` and `temp2` pointers will be set to point at the second and third nodes, and so on:

```
temp1=temp2;
temp2=temp2->next;
```

10. The linked list has to be arranged in ascending order, so the data member of `temp1` must be smaller than the data member of `temp2`. In case the data member of `temp1` is larger than the data member of `temp2`, the interchanging of the values of the data members will be done with the help of a temporary variable, k, as follows:

```
k=temp1->data;
temp1->data=temp2->data;
temp2->data=k;
```

11. After n-1 performing iterations of comparing and interchanging consecutive values, if the first value in the pair is larger than the second, all the nodes in the linked list will be arranged in ascending order. To traverse the linked list and to display the values in ascending order, a temporary t pointer is set to point at the node pointed at by `startList`, that is, at the first node of the linked list, as follows:

```
t=startList;
```

12. A `while` loop is executed until the `t` pointer reaches `NULL`. Recall that the next pointer of the last node is set to NULL, so the `while` loop will execute until all the nodes of the linked list are traversed as follows:

```
while(t!=NULL)
```

13. Within the `while` loop, the following two tasks will be performed:

- The data member of the node pointed to by the `t` pointer is displayed.
- The `t` pointer is moved further to point at its next node:

```
printf("%d\t",t->data);
t=t->next;
```

The `sortlinkedlist.c` program for creating a singly linked list, followed by sorting it in ascending order, is as follows:

```
/* Sort the linked list by bubble sort */
#include<stdio.h>
#include <stdlib.h>
struct node
{
  int data;
  struct node *next;
};
void main()
{
    struct node *temp1,*temp2, *t,*newNode, *startList;
    int n,k,i,j;
    startList=NULL;
    printf("How many elements are there in the linked list ?");
    scanf("%d",&n);
    printf("Enter elements in the linked list\n");
    for(i=1;i<=n;i++)
    {
        if(startList==NULL)
        {
            newNode=(struct node *)malloc(sizeof(struct node));
            scanf("%d",&newNode->data);
            newNode->next=NULL;
            startList = newNode;
            temp1=startList;
        }
        else
        {
            newNode=(struct node *)malloc(sizeof(struct node));
            scanf("%d",&newNode->data);
```

```
                    newNode->next=NULL;
                    temp1->next = newNode;
                    temp1=newNode;
            }
    }
    for(i=n-2;i>=0;i--)
    {
        temp1=startList;
        temp2=temp1->next;
        for(j=0;j<=i;j++)
        {
            if(temp1->data > temp2->data)
            {
                k=temp1->data;
                temp1->data=temp2->data;
                temp2->data=k;
            }
            temp1=temp2;
            temp2=temp2->next;
        }
    }
    printf("Sorted order is: \n");
    t=startList;
    while(t!=NULL)
    {
        printf("%d\t",t->data);
        t=t->next;
    }
}
```

Now, let's go behind the scenes.

How it works...

This program is performed in two parts—the first part is the creation of a singly linked list, and the second part is the sorting of the linked list.

Let's start with the first part.

Creating a singly linked list

We will start by creating a new node by the name of **newNode**. When prompted, we will enter the value for its data member and then set the next **newNode** pointer to **NULL** (as shown in *Figure 5.17*). This next pointer will be used for connecting with other nodes (as we will see shortly):

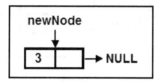

Figure 5.17

After the first node is created, we will make the following two pointers point at it as follows:

- **startList**: To traverse the singly linked list, we will need a pointer that points at the first node of the list. So, we will define a pointer called **startList** and set it to point at the first node of the list.
- **temp1**: In order to connect with the next node, we will need one more pointer. We will call this pointer **temp1**, and set it to point at the **newNode** (see *Figure 5.18*):

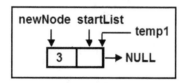

Figure 5.18

We will now create another node for the linked list and call that **newNode** as well. The pointer can point to only one structure at a time. So, the moment we create a new node, the **newNode** pointer that was pointing at the first node will now point at the recently created node. We will be prompted to enter a value for the data member of the new node, and its next pointer will be set to **NULL**.

You can see in the following diagram that the two pointers, **startList** and **temp1**, are pointing at the first node and the **newNode** pointer is pointing at the newly created node. As stated earlier, **startList** will be used for traversing the linked list and **temp1** will be used for connecting with the newly created node as follows:

Figure 5.19

To connect the first node with **newNode**, the next pointer of **temp1** will be set to point at **newNode** (see *Figure 5.20 (a)*). After connecting with **newNode**, the temp1 pointer will be moved further and set to point at **newNode** (see *Figure 5.20 (b)*) so that it can be used again for connecting with any new nodes that may be added to the linked list in future:

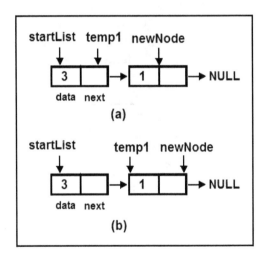

Figure 5.20

Steps three and four will be repeated for the rest of the nodes of the linked list. Finally, the singly linked list will be ready and will look something like this:

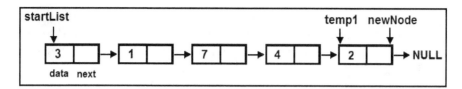

Figure 5.21

Now that we have created the singly linked list, the next step is to sort the linked list in ascending order.

Sorting the singly linked list

We will use the bubble sort algorithm for sorting the linked list. In the bubble sort technique, the first value is compared with the second value, the second is compared with the third value, and so on. If we want to sort our list in ascending order, then we will need to keep the smaller values toward the top when comparing the values.

Therefore, while comparing the first and second values, if the first value is larger than the second value, then their places will be interchanged. If the first value is smaller than the second value, then no interchanging will happen, and the second and third values will be picked up for comparison.

There will be n-1 iterations of such comparisons, meaning if there are five values, then there will be four iterations of such comparisons; and after every iteration, the last value will be left out—that is, it will not be compared as it reaches its destination. The destination here means the location where the value must be kept when arranged in ascending order.

The first iteration

To sort the linked list, we will employ the services of two pointers—**temp1** and **temp2**. The **temp1** pointer is set to point at the first node, and **temp2** is set to point at the next node as follows:

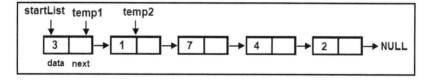

Figure 5.22

We will be sorting the linked list in ascending order, so we will keep the smaller values toward the beginning of the list. The data members of **temp1** and **temp2** will be compared. Because `temp1->data` is greater than `temp2->data`, that is, the data member of **temp1** is larger than the data member of **temp2**, their places will be interchanged (see the following diagram). After interchanging the data members of the nodes pointed at by **temp1** and **temp2**, the linked list will appear as follows:

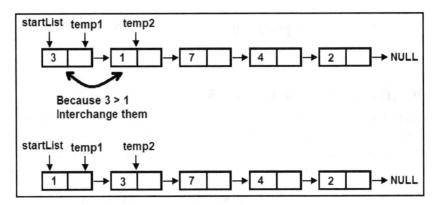

Figure 5.23

After this, the two pointers will shift further, that is, the **temp1** pointer will be set to point at **temp2**, and the **temp2** pointer will be set to point at its next node. We can see in *Figure 5.24 (a)* that the **temp1** and **temp2** pointers are pointing at the nodes with the values 3 and 7, respectively. We can also see that `temp1->data` is less than `temp2->data`, that is, 3 < 7. Since the data member of **temp1** is already smaller than the data member of **temp2**, no interchanging of values will take place and the two pointers will simply move one step further (see *Figure 5.24 (b)*).

Now, because 7 > 4, their places will be interchanged. The values of data members pointed at by **temp1** and **temp2** will interchange as follows (*Figure 5.24 (c)*):

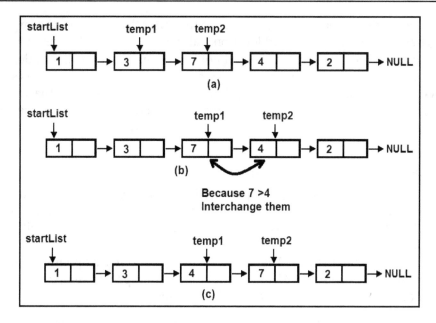

Figure 5.24

After that, the **temp1** and **temp2** pointer will be shifted one step further, that is, **temp1** will point at **temp2**, and **temp2** will move onto its next node. We can see in the following *Figure 5.25 (a)* that **temp1** and **temp2** are pointing at the nodes with the values 7 and 2, respectively. Again, the data members of **temp1** and **temp2** will be compared. Because temp1->data is greater than temp2->data, their places will be interchanged. *Figure 5.25 (b)* shows the linked list after interchanging values of the data members:

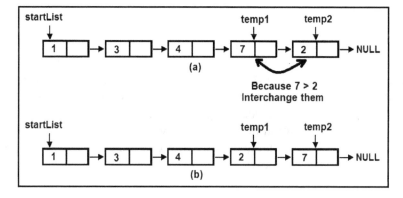

Figure 5.25

This was the first iteration, and you can notice that after this iteration, the largest value, 7, has been set to our desired location—at the end of the linked list. This also means that in the second iteration, we will not have to compare the last node. Similarly, after the second iteration, the second highest value will reach or is set to its actual location. The second highest value in the linked list is 4, so after the second iteration, the four node will just reach the seven node. How? Let's look at the second iteration of bubble sort.

The second iteration

We will begin the comparison by comparing first two nodes, so the **temp1** and **temp2** pointers will be set to point at the first and second nodes of the linked list, respectively (see *Figure 5.26 (a)*). The data members of **temp1** and **temp2** will be compared. As is clear, temp1->data is less than temp2->data (that is, 1 < 7), so their places will not be interchanged. Thereafter, the **temp1** and **temp2** pointers will shift one step further. We can see in *Figure 5.26 (b)* that the **temp1** and **temp2** pointers are set to point at nodes of the values 3 and 4, respectively:

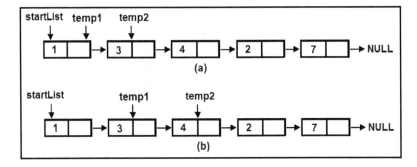

Figure 5.26

Once again, the data members of the **temp1** and **temp2** pointers will be compared. Because temp1->data is less than temp2->data, that is, 3 < 4 , their places will again not be interchanged and the **temp1** and **temp2** pointers will, again, shift one step further. That is, the **temp1** pointer will be set to point at **temp2**, and **temp2** will be set to point at its next node. You can see in *Figure 5.27 (a)* that the **temp1** and **temp2** pointers are set to point at nodes with the values 4 and 2, respectively. Because 4 > 2, their places will be interchanged. After interchanging the place of these values, the linked list will appear as follows in *Figure 5.27 (b)*:

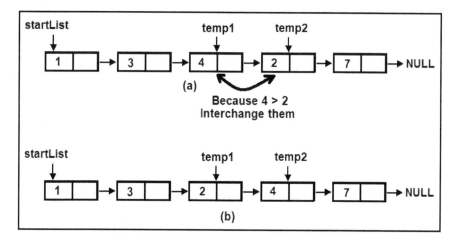

Figure 5.27

This is the end of the second iteration, and we can see that the second largest value, four, is set to our desired location as per ascending order. So, with every iteration, one value is being set at the required location. Accordingly, the next iteration will require one comparison less.

The third and fourth iterations

In the third iteration, we will only need to do the following comparisons:

1. Compare the first and second nodes
2. Compare the second and third nodes

After the third iteration, the third largest value, that is, three, will be set at our desired location, that is, just before node four.

In the fourth, and final, iteration, only the first and second nodes will be compared. The linked list will be sorted in ascending order as follows after the fourth iteration:

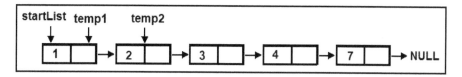

Figure 5.28

Let's use GCC to compile the `sortlinkedlist.c` program as follows:

```
D:\CBook>gcc sortlinkedlist.c -o sortlinkedlist
```

If you get no errors or warnings, that means that the `sortlinkedlist.c` program has been compiled into an executable file, `sortlinkedlist.exe`. Let's run this executable file as follows:

```
D:\CBook>./sortlinkedlist
How many elements are there in the linked list ?5
Enter elements in the linked list
3
1
7
4
2
Sorted order is:
1       2       3       4       7
```

Voilà! We've successfully created and sorted a singly linked list. Now, let's move on to the next recipe!

Finding the transpose of a matrix using pointers

The best part of this recipe is that we will not only display the transpose of the matrix using pointers, but we will also create the matrix itself using pointers.

The transpose of a matrix is a new matrix that has rows equal to the number of columns of the original matrix and columns equal to the number of rows. The following diagram shows you a matrix of order **2 x 3** and its transpose, of order **3 x 2**:

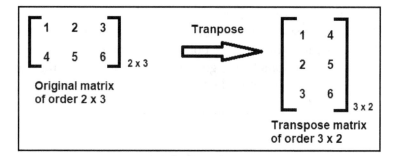

Figure 5.29

Basically, we can say that, upon converting the rows into columns and columns into rows of a matrix, you get its transpose.

How to do it...

1. Define a matrix of 10 rows and 10 columns as follows (you can have a bigger matrix if you wish):

```
int a[10][10]
```

2. Enter the size of the rows and columns as follows:

```
printf("Enter rows and columns of matrix: ");
scanf("%d %d", &r, &c);
```

3. Allocate memory locations equal to `r *c` quantity for keeping the matrix elements as follows:

```
ptr = (int *)malloc(r * c * sizeof(int));
```

4. Enter elements of the matrix that will be assigned sequentially to each allocated memory as follows:

```
for(i=0; i<r; ++i)
{
    for(j=0; j<c; ++j)
    {
        scanf("%d", &m);
        *(ptr+ i*c + j)=m;
    }
}
```

5. In order to access this matrix via a pointer, set a `ptr` pointer to point at the first memory location of the allocated memory block, as shown in *Figure 5.30*. The moment that the `ptr` pointer is set to point at the first memory location, it will automatically get the address of the first memory location, so `1000` will be assigned to the `ptr` pointer:

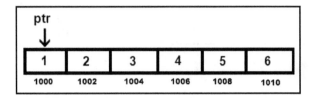

Figure 5.30

6. To access these memory locations and display their content, use the `* (ptr +i*c + j)` formula within the nested loop, as shown in this code snippet:

```
for(i=0; i<r; ++i)
{
    for(j=0; j<c; ++j)
    {
        printf("%d\t",*(ptr +i*c + j));
    }
    printf("\n");
}
```

7. The value of the `r` row is assumed to be two, and that of column `c` is assumed to be three. With values of `i=0` and `j=0`, the formula will compute as follows:

```
*(ptr +i*c + j);
*(1000+0*3+0)
*1000
```

It will display the content of the memory address, `1000`.

When the value of `i=0` and `j=1`, the formula will compute as follows:

```
*(ptr +i*c + j);
*(1000+0*3+1)
*(1000+1)
*(1002)
```

We will first get *(1000+1), because the ptr pointer is an integer pointer, and it will jump two bytes every time we add the value 1 to it at every memory location, from which we will get *(1002), and it will display the content of the memory location 1002.

Similarly, the value of i=0 and j=2 will lead to *(1004); that is, the content of the memory location 1004 will be displayed. Using this formula, the value of i=1 and j=0 will lead to *(1006); the value of i=1 and j=1 will lead to *(1008); and the value of i=1 and j=2 will lead to *(1010). So, when the aforementioned formula is applied within the nested loops, the original matrix will be displayed as follows:

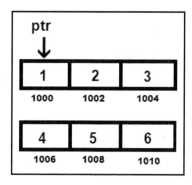

Figure 5.31

8. To display the transpose of a matrix, apply the following formula within the nested loops:

```
*(ptr +j*c + i))
```

Again, assuming the values of row (r=2) and column (c=3), the following content of memory locations will be displayed:

i	j	Memory address
0	0	1000
0	1	1006
1	0	1002
1	1	1008
2	0	1004
2	1	1010

So, upon applying the preceding formula, the content of the following memory address will be displayed as the following in *Figure 5.32*. And the content of these memory addresses will comprise the transpose of the matrix:

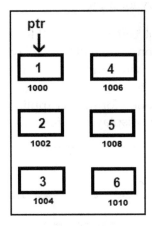

Figure 5.32

Let's see how this formula is applied in a program.

The transposemat.c program for displaying the transpose of a matrix using pointers is as follows:

```c
#include <stdio.h>
#include <stdlib.h>
void main()
{
    int a[10][10],  r, c, i, j, *ptr,m;
    printf("Enter rows and columns of matrix: ");
    scanf("%d %d", &r, &c);
    ptr = (int *)malloc(r * c * sizeof(int));
    printf("\nEnter elements of matrix:\n");
    for(i=0; i<r; ++i)
    {
        for(j=0; j<c; ++j)
        {
            scanf("%d", &m);
            *(ptr+ i*c + j)=m;
        }
    }
    printf("\nMatrix using pointer is: \n");
    for(i=0; i<r; ++i)
    {
        for(j=0; j<c; ++j)
```

```
        {
            printf("%d\t",*(ptr +i*c + j));
        }
        printf("\n");
    }
    printf("\nTranspose of Matrix:\n");
    for(i=0; i<c; ++i)
    {
        for(j=0; j<r; ++j)
        {
            printf("%d\t",*(ptr +j*c + i));
        }
        printf("\n");
    }
}
```

Now, let's go behind the scenes.

How it works...

Whenever an array is defined, the memory allocated to it internally is a sequential memory. Now let's define a matrix of size 2 x 3, as shown in the following diagram. In that case, the matrix will be assigned six consecutive memory locations of two bytes each (see *Figure 5.33*). Why two bytes each? This is because an integer takes two bytes. This also means that if we define a matrix of the float type that takes four bytes, each allocated memory location would consist of four bytes:

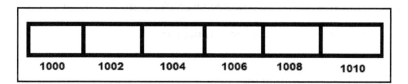

Figure 5.33

In reality, the memory address is long and is in hex format; but for simplicity, we will take the memory addresses of integer type and take easy-to-remember numbers, such as **1000**, as memory addresses. After memory address **1000**, the next memory address is **1002** (because an integer takes two bytes).

Now, to display the original matrix elements in row-major form using a pointer, we will need to display the elements of memory locations, **1000**, **1002**, **1004**, and so on:

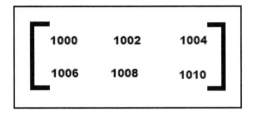

Figure 5.34

Similarly, in order to display the transpose of the matrix using a pointer, we will need to display the elements of memory locations; **1000**, **1006**, **1002**, **1008**, **1004**, and **1010**:

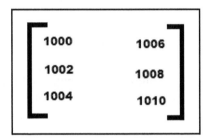

Figure 5.35

Let's use GCC to compile the `transposemat.c` program as follows:

```
D:\CBook>gcc transposemat.c -o transposemat
```

If you get no errors or warnings, that means that the `transposemat.c` program has been compiled into an executable file, `transposemat.exe`. Let's run this executable file with the following code snippet:

```
D:\CBook>./transposemat
Enter rows and columns of matrix: 2 3

Enter elements of matrix:
1
2
3
4
5
6
```

```
Matrix using pointer is:
1        2        3
4        5        6

Transpose of Matrix:
1        4
2        5
3        6
```

Voilà! We've successfully found the transpose of a matrix using pointers. Now, let's move on to the next recipe!

Accessing a structure using a pointer

In this recipe, we will make a structure that stores the information of an order placed by a specific customer. A structure is a user-defined data type that can store several members of different data types within it. The structure will have members for storing the order number, email address, and password of the customer:

```
struct cart
{
    int orderno;
    char emailaddress[30];
    char password[30];
};
```

The preceding structure is named cart, and comprises three members – orderno of the int type for storing the order number of the order placed by the customer, and emailaddress and password of the string type for storing the email address and password of the customer, respectively. Let's begin!

How to do it...

1. Define a cart structure by the name mycart. Also, define two pointers to structure of the cart structure, ptrcart and ptrcust, as shown in the following code snippet:

```
struct cart mycart;
struct cart *ptrcart, *ptrcust;
```

2. Enter the order number, email address, and password of the customer, and these values will be accepted using the `mycart` structure variable. As mentioned previously, the dot operator (`.`) will be used for accessing the structure members, `orderno`, `emailaddress`, and `password`, through a structure variable as follows:

```
printf("Enter order number: ");
scanf("%d",&mycart.orderno);
printf("Enter email address: ");
scanf("%s",mycart.emailaddress);
printf("Enter password: ");
scanf("%s",mycart.password);
```

3. Set the pointer to the `ptrcart` structure to point at the `mycart` structure using the `ptrcart=&mycart` statement. Consequently, the pointer to the `ptrcart` structure will be able to access the members of the `mycart` structure by using the arrow (`->`) operator. By using `ptrcart->orderno`, `ptrcart->emailaddress`, and `ptrcart->password`, the values assigned to the `orderno`, `emailaddress`, and `password` structure members are accessed and displayed:

```
printf("\nDetails of the customer are as follows:\n");
printf("Order number : %d\n", ptrcart->orderno);
printf("Email address : %s\n", ptrcart->emailaddress);
printf("Password : %s\n", ptrcart->password);
```

4. We will also modify the email address and password of the customer by asking them to enter a new email address and password and accept the new details via the pointer to the `ptrcart` structure as follows. Because `ptrcart` is pointing to the `mycart` structure, the new email address and password will overwrite the existing values that were assigned to the structure members of `mycart`:

```
printf("\nEnter new email address: ");
scanf("%s",ptrcart->emailaddress);
printf("Enter new password: ");
scanf("%s",ptrcart->password);
/*The new modified values of orderno, emailaddress and
password members are displayed using structure variable,
mycart using dot operator (.).*/
printf("\nModified customer's information is:\n");
printf("Order number: %d\n", mycart.orderno);
printf("Email address: %s\n", mycart.emailaddress);
printf("Password: %s\n", mycart.password);
```

5. Then, define a pointer to the `*ptrcust` structure. Using the following `malloc` function, allocate memory for it. The `sizeof` function will find out the number of bytes consumed by each of the structure members and return the total number of bytes consumed by the structure as a whole:

```
ptrcust=(struct cart *)malloc(sizeof(struct cart));
```

6. Enter the order number, email address, and password of the customer, and all the values will be assigned to the respective structure members using a pointer to a structure as follows. Obviously, the arrow operator (->) will be used for accessing the structure members through a pointer to a structure:

```
printf("Enter order number: ");
scanf("%d",&ptrcust->orderno);
printf("Enter email address: ");
scanf("%s",ptrcust->emailaddress);
printf("Enter password: ");
scanf("%s",ptrcust->password);
```

7. The values entered by the user are then displayed through the pointer to the `ptrcust` structure again as follows:

```
printf("\nDetails of the second customer are as follows:\n");
printf("Order number : %d\n", ptrcust->orderno);
printf("Email address : %s\n", ptrcust->emailaddress);
printf("Password : %s\n", ptrcust->password);
```

The following `pointertostruct.c` program explains how to access a structure by using a pointer:

```
#include <stdio.h>
#include <stdlib.h>

struct cart
{
    int orderno;
    char emailaddress[30];
    char password[30];
};

void main()
{
    struct cart mycart;
    struct cart *ptrcart, *ptrcust;
    ptrcart = &mycart;
    printf("Enter order number: ");
```

```
        scanf("%d",&mycart.orderno);
        printf("Enter email address: ");
        scanf("%s",mycart.emailaddress);
        printf("Enter password: ");
        scanf("%s",mycart.password);
        printf("\nDetails of the customer are as follows:\n");
        printf("Order number : %d\n", ptrcart->orderno);
        printf("Email address : %s\n", ptrcart->emailaddress);
        printf("Password : %s\n", ptrcart->password);

        printf("\nEnter new email address: ");
        scanf("%s",ptrcart->emailaddress);
        printf("Enter new password: ");
        scanf("%s",ptrcart->password);
        printf("\nModified customer's information is:\n");
        printf("Order number: %d\n", mycart.orderno);
        printf("Email address: %s\n", mycart.emailaddress);
        printf("Password: %s\n", mycart.password);

        ptrcust=(struct cart *)malloc(sizeof(struct cart));
        printf("\nEnter information of another customer:\n");
        printf("Enter order number: ");
        scanf("%d",&ptrcust->orderno);
        printf("Enter email address: ");
        scanf("%s",ptrcust->emailaddress);
        printf("Enter password: ");
        scanf("%s",ptrcust->password);
        printf("\nDetails of the second customer are as follows:\n");
        printf("Order number : %d\n", ptrcust->orderno);
        printf("Email address : %s\n", ptrcust->emailaddress);
        printf("Password : %s\n", ptrcust->password);
    }
```

Now, let's go behind the scenes.

How it works...

When you define a variable of the type structure, that variable can access members of the structure in the following format:

```
structurevariable.structuremember
```

You can see a period (.) between the structure variable and the structure member. This period (.) is also known as a dot operator, or member access operator. The following example will make it clearer:

```
struct cart mycart;
mycart.orderno
```

In the preceding code, you can see that `mycart` is defined as a structure variable of the `cart` structure. Now, the `mycart` structure variable can access the `orderno` member by making the member access operator (.).

You can also define a pointer to a structure. The following statement defines `ptrcart` as a pointer to the `cart` structure.

```
struct cart *ptrcart;
```

When the pointer to a structure points to a structure variable, it can access the structure members of the structure variable. In the following statement, the pointer to the `ptrcart` structure points at the address of the `mycart` structure variable:

```
ptrcart = &mycart;
```

Now, `ptrcart` can access the structure members, but instead of the dot operator (.), the arrow operator (->) will be used. The following statement accesses the `orderno` member of the structure using the pointer to a structure:

```
ptrcart->orderno
```

If you don't want a pointer to a structure to point at the structure variable, then memory needs to be allocated for a pointer to a structure to access structure members. The following statement defines a pointer to a structure by allocating memory for it:

```
ptrcust=(struct cart *)malloc(sizeof(struct cart));
```

The preceding code allocates memory equal to the size of a `cart` structure, typecasts that memory to be used by a pointer to a `cart` structure, and assigns that allocated memory to `ptrcust`. In other words, `ptrcust` is defined as a pointer to a structure, and it does not need to point to any structure variable, but can directly access the structure members.

Let's use GCC to compile the `pointertostruct.c` program as follows:

```
D:\CBook>gcc pointertostruct.c -o pointertostruct
```

If you get no errors or warnings, that means that the `pointertostruct.c` program has been compiled into an executable file, `pointertostruct.exe`. Let's run this executable file as follows:

```
D:\CBook>./pointertostruct
Enter order number: 1001
Enter email address: bmharwani@yahoo.com
Enter password: gold

Details of the customer are as follows:
Order number : 1001
Email address : bmharwani@yahoo.com
Password : gold

Enter new email address: harwanibm@gmail.com
Enter new password: diamond

Modified customer's information is:
Order number: 1001
Email address: harwanibm@gmail.com
Password: diamond

Enter information of another customer:
Enter order number: 1002
Enter email address: bintu@yahoo.com
Enter password: platinum

Details of the second customer are as follows:
Order number : 1002
Email address : bintu@yahoo.com
Password : platinum
```

Voilà! We've successfully accessed a structure using a pointer.

6
File Handling

Data storage is a mandatory feature in all applications. When we enter any data while running a program, that data is stored as RAM, which means that it is temporary in nature. We will not get that data back when running the program the next time. But what if we want the data to stay there so we can refer to it again when we need it? In this case, we have to store the data.

Basically, we want our data to be stored and to be accessible and available for reuse whenever required. In C, data storage can be done through traditional file handling techniques and through the database system. The following are the two types of file handling available in C:

- **Sequential file handling**: Data is written in a simple text format and can be read and written sequentially. To read the nth line, we have to first read n-1 lines.
- **Random file handling**: Data is written as bytes and can be read or written randomly. We can read or write any line randomly by positioning the file pointer at the desired location.

In this chapter, we will go through the following recipes using file handling:

- Reading a text file and converting all characters after a period into uppercase
- Displaying the contents of a random file in reverse order
- Counting the number of vowels in a file
- Replacing a word in a file with another word
- Encrypting a file

Before we start with the recipes, let's review some of the functions we will be using to create our recipes.

Functions used in file handling

I've divided this section into two parts. In the first part, we will look at the functions specific to the sequential file handling method. In the second, we will look at the functions used for random files.

Functions commonly used in sequential file handling

The following are some of the functions that are used to open, close, read, and write in a sequential file.

fopen()

The `fopen()` function is used for opening a file for reading, writing, and doing other operations. Here is its syntax:

```
FILE *fopen (const char *file_name, const char *mode)
```

Here, `file_name` represents the file that we want to work on and `mode` states the purpose for which we want to open the file. It can be any of the following:

- `r`: This opens the file in read mode and sets the file pointer at the first character of the file.
- `w`: This opens the file in write mode. If the file exists, it will be overwritten.
- `a`: Opens the file in append mode. Newly entered data will be added at the end of the file.
- `r+`: This opens the file in read and write mode. The file pointer is set to point at the beginning of the file. The file content will not be deleted if it already exists. It will not create a file if it does not already exist.
- `w+`: This also opens the file in read and write mode. The file pointer is set to point at the beginning of the file. The file content will be deleted if it already exists, but the file will be created if it does not already exist.
- `a+`: This opens a file for reading as well as for appending new content.

The `fopen` function returns a file descriptor that points to the file for performing different operations.

fclose()

The `fclose()` function is used for closing the file. Here is its syntax:

```
int fclose(FILE *file_pointer)
```

Here, `file_pointer` represents the file pointer that is pointing at the open file.

The function returns a `0` value if the file is successfully closed.

fgets()

The `fgets()` function is used for reading a string from the specified file. Here is its syntax:

```
char *fgets(char *string, int length, FILE *file_pointer)
```

This function has the following features:

- `string`: This represents the character array to which the data that is read from the file will be assigned.
- `length`: This represents the maximum number of characters that can be read from the file. The *length-1* number of characters will be read from the file. The reading of data from the file will stop either at *length-1* location or at the new line character, \n, whichever comes first.
- `file_pointer`: This represents the file pointer that is pointing at the file.

fputs()

The `fputs()` function is used for writing into the file. Here is its syntax:

```
int fputs (const char *string, FILE *file_pointer)
```

Here, `string` represents the character array containing the data to be written into the file. The `file_pointer` phrase represents the file pointer that is pointing at the file.

Functions commonly used in random files

The following functions are used to set the file pointer at a specified location in the random file, indicate the location where the file pointer is pointing currently, and rewind the file pointer to the beginning of the random file.

fseek()

The fseek() function is used for setting the file pointer at the specific position in the file. Here is its syntax:

```
fseek(FILE *file_pointer, long int offset, int location);
```

This function has the following features:

- file_pointer: This represents the file pointer that points at the file.
- offset: This represents the number of bytes that the file pointer needs to be moved from the position specified by the location parameter. If the value of offset is positive, the file pointer will move forward in the file, and if it is negative, the file pointer will move backward from the given position.
- location: This is the value that defines the position from which the file pointer needs to be moved. That is, the file pointer will be moved equal to the number of bytes specified by the offset parameter from the position specified by the location parameter. Its value can be 0, 1, or 2, as shown in the following table:

Value	Meaning
0	The file pointer will be moved from the beginning of the file
1	The file pointer will be moved from the current position
2	The file pointer will be moved from the end of the file

Let's look at the following example. Here, the file pointer will be moved 5 bytes forward from the beginning of the file:

```
fseek(fp,5L,0)
```

In the following example, the file pointer will be moved 5 bytes backward from the end of the file:

```
fseek(fp,-5L,2)
```

ftell()

The `ftell()` function returns the byte location where `file_pointer` is currently pointing at the file. Here is its syntax:

```
long int ftell(FILE *file_pointer)
```

Here, `file_pointer` is a file pointer pointing at the file.

rewind()

The `rewind()` function is used for moving the file pointer back to the beginning of the specified file. Here is its syntax:

```
void rewind(FILE *file_pointer)
```

Here, `file_pointer` is a file pointer pointing at the file.

In this chapter, we will learn to use both types of file handling using recipes that make real-time applications.

Reading a text file and converting all characters after the period into uppercase

Say we have a file that contains some text. We think that there is an anomaly in the text—every first character after the period is in lowercase when it should be in uppercase. In this recipe, we will read that text file and convert each character after the period (.) that is, in lowercase into uppercase.

 In this recipe, I assume that you know how to create a text file and how to read a text file. If you don't know how to perform these actions, you will find programs for both of them in *Appendix A*.

How to do it...

1. Open the sequential file in read-only mode using the following code:

```
fp = fopen (argv [1],"r");
```

2. If the file does not exist or does not have enough permissions, an error message will be displayed and the program will terminate. Set this up using the following code:

```
if (fp == NULL) {
    printf("%s file does not exist\n", argv[1]);
    exit(1);
}
```

3. One line is read from the file, as shown in the following code:

```
fgets(buffer, BUFFSIZE, fp);
```

4. Each character of the line is accessed and checked for the presence of periods, as shown in the following code:

```
for(i=0;i<n;i++)
    if(buffer[i]=='.')
```

5. If a period is found, the character following the period is checked to confirm whether it is in uppercase, as shown in the following code:

```
if(buffer[i] >=97 && buffer[i] <=122)
```

6. If the character following the period is in lowercase, a value of 32 is subtracted from the ASCII value of the lowercase character to convert it into uppercase, as shown in the following code:

```
buffer[i]=buffer[i]-32;
```

7. If the line is not yet over, then the sequence from step 4 onward is repeated till step 6; otherwise, the updated line is displayed on the screen, as shown in the following code:

```
puts(buffer);
```

8. Check whether the end of file has been reached using the following code. If the file is not over, repeat the sequence from step 3:

```
while (!feof(fp))
```

The preceding steps are pictorially explained in the following diagram (*Figure 6.1*):

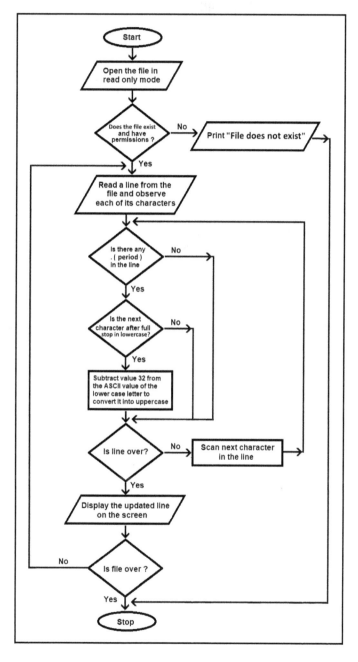

Figure 6.1

The `convertcase.c` program for converting a lowercase character found after a period in a file into uppercase is as follows:

```c
#include <stdio.h>
#include <string.h>
#include <stdlib.h>

#define BUFFSIZE 255

void main (int argc, char* argv[])
{
    FILE *fp;
    char buffer[BUFFSIZE];
    int i,n;

    fp = fopen (argv [1],"r");
    if (fp == NULL) {
        printf("%s file does not exist\n", argv[1]);
        exit(1);
    }
    while (!feof(fp))
    {
        fgets(buffer, BUFFSIZE, fp);
        n=strlen(buffer);
        for(i=0;i<n;i++)
        {
            if(buffer[i]=='.')
            {
                i++;
                while(buffer[i]==' ')
                {
                    i++;
                }
                if(buffer[i] >=97 && buffer[i] <=122)
                {
                    buffer[i]=buffer[i]-32;
                }
            }
        }
        puts(buffer);
    }
    fclose(fp);
}
```

Now, let's go behind the scenes.

How it works...

The file whose name is supplied as a command-line argument is opened in read-only mode and is pointed to by the file pointer, `fp`. This recipe is focused on reading a file and changing its case, so if the file does not exist or does not have read permission, an error will be displayed and the program will terminate.

A `while` loop will be set to execute until `feof` (the end of file) is reached. Within the `while` loop, each line of the file will be read one by one and assigned to the string named `buffer`. The `fgets()` function will be used to read one line at a time from the file. A number of characters will be read from the file until the newline character, `\n`, is reached, to a maximum of 254.

The following steps will be performed on each of the lines assigned to the string buffer:

1. The length of the buffer string will be computed and a `for` loop will be executed to access each of the characters in the string buffer.
2. The string buffer will be checked to see whether there are any periods in it.
3. If one is found, the character following it will be checked to see whether it is into lowercase. ASCII values will be used to then convert the lowercase characters into uppercase (refer to `Chapter 2`, *Managing Strings*, for more information on the ASCII values that correspond to the letters of the alphabet). If the character following the period is in lowercase, a value of 32 will be deducted from the ASCII value of the lowercase character to convert it into uppercase. Remember, the ASCII value of uppercase characters is lower by a value of 32 than their corresponding lowercase characters.
4. The updated string `buffer` with the character following the period converted into uppercase will be displayed on the screen.

When all the lines of the file are read and displayed, the file pointed to by the `fp` pointer will be closed.

Let's use GCC to compile the `convertcase.c` program as follows:

```
D:\CBook>gcc convertcase.c -o convertcase
```

If you get no errors or warnings, this means that the `convertcase.c` program has been compiled into an executable file, `convertcase.exe`.

Let's say that I have created a file called `textfile.txt` with the following content:

```
D:\CBook>type textfile.txt
I am trying to create a sequential file. it is through C programming.
It is very hot today. I have a cat. do you like animals? It might
rain. Thank you. Bye
```

 The preceding command is executed in Windows' Command Prompt.

Let's run the executable file, `convertcase.exe`, and then pass the `textfile.txt` file to it, as shown in the following code:

```
D:\CBook>./convertcase textfile.txt
I am trying to create a sequential file. It is through C programming.
It is very hot today. I have a cat. Do you like animals? It might
rain. Thank you. Bye
```

You can see in the preceding output that the characters that were in lowercase after the period are now converted into uppercase.

Let's move on to the next recipe!

Displaying the contents of a random file in reverse order

Let's say that we have a random file that contains some lines of text. Let's find out how to reverse the contents of this file.

 This program will not give the correct output if a random file does not exist. Please read *Appendix A* to learn how to create a random file.

How to do it...

1. Open the random file in read-only mode using the following code:

```
fp = fopen (argv[1], "rb");
```

2. If the file does not exist or does not have enough permissions, an error message will be displayed and the program will terminate, as shown in the following code:

```
if (fp == NULL) {
    perror ("An error occurred in opening the file\n");
    exit(1);
}
```

3. To read the random file in reverse order, execute a loop equal to the number of lines in the file. Every iteration of the loop will read one line beginning from the bottom of the file. The following formula will be used to find out the number of lines in the file:

total number of bytes used in the file/size of one line in bytes

The code for doing this is as follows:

```
fseek(fp, 0L, SEEK_END);
n = ftell(fp);
nol=n/sizeof(struct data);
```

4. Because the file has to be read in reverse order, the file pointer will be positioned at the bottom of the file, as shown in the following code:

```
fseek(fp, -sizeof(struct data)*i, SEEK_END);
```

5. Set a loop to execute that equals the number of lines in the file computed in step 3, as shown in the following code:

```
for (i=1;i<=nol;i++)
```

6. Within the loop, the file pointer will be positioned as follows:

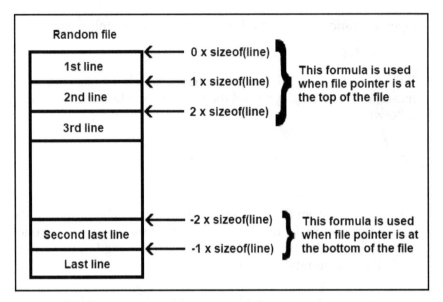

Figure 6.2

7. To read the last line, the file pointer will be positioned at the byte location where the last line begins, at the **-1 x sizeof(line)** byte location. The last line will be read and displayed on the screen, as shown in the following code:

```
fread(&line,sizeof(struct data),1,fp);
puts(line.str);
```

8. Next, the file pointer will be positioned at the byte location from where the second last line begins, at the **-2 x sizeof(line)** byte location. Again, the second last line will be read and displayed on the screen.

9. The procedure will be repeated until all of the lines in the file have been read and displayed on the screen.

The `readrandominreverse.c` program for reading the random file in reverse order is as follows:

```c
#include <string.h>
#include <stdio.h>
#include <stdlib.h>

struct data{
    char str[ 255 ];
};

void main (int argc, char* argv[])
{
    FILE *fp;
    struct data line;
    int n,nol,i;
    fp = fopen (argv[1], "rb");
    if (fp == NULL) {
        perror ("An error occurred in opening the file\n");
        exit(1);
    }
    fseek(fp, 0L, SEEK_END);
    n = ftell(fp);
    nol=n/sizeof(struct data);
    printf("The content of random file in reverse order is :\n");
    for (i=1;i<=nol;i++)
    {
        fseek(fp, -sizeof(struct data)*i, SEEK_END);
        fread(&line,sizeof(struct data),1,fp);
        puts(line.str);
    }
    fclose(fp);
}
```

Now, let's go behind the scenes.

How it works...

We will open the chosen file in read-only mode. If the file opens successfully, it will be pointed at by the file pointer `fp`. Next, we will find out the total number of lines in the file using the following formula:

total number of bytes used by the file/number of bytes used by one line

To know the total number of bytes used by the file, the file pointer will be positioned at the bottom of the file and we will invoke the `ftell` function. The `ftell` function finds the current location of the file pointer. Because the file pointer is at the end of the file, using this function will tell us the total number of bytes used by the file. To find the number of bytes used by one line, we will use the `sizeof` function. We will apply the preceding formula to compute the total number of lines in the file; this will be assigned to the variable, `nol`.

We will set a `for` loop to execute for `nol` number of times. Within the `for` loop, the file pointer will be positioned at the end of the last line so that all of the lines from the file can be accessed in reverse order. So, the file pointer is first set at the (-1 * size of one line) location at the bottom of the file. Once the file pointer is positioned at this location, we will use the `fread` function to read the last line of the file and assign it to the structure variable line. The string in line will then be displayed on the screen.

After displaying the last line on the screen, the file pointer will be set at the byte position of the second last line at (-2 * size of one line). We will again use the `fread` function to read the second last line and display it on the screen.

This procedure will be executed for the number of times that the `for` loop executes, and the `for` loop will execute the same number of times as there are lines in the file. Then the file will be closed.

Let's use GCC to compile the `readrandominreverse.c` program, as follows:

```
D:\CBook>gcc readrandominreverse.c -o readrandominreverse
```

If you get no errors or warnings, this means that the `readrandominreverse.c` program has been compiled into an executable file, `readrandominreverse.exe`.

Let's assume that we have a random file, `random.data`, with the following text:

```
This is a random file. I am checking if the code is working
perfectly well. Random file helps in fast accessing of
desired data. Also you can access any content in any order.
```

Let's run the executable file, `readrandominreverse.exe`, to display the random file, `random.data`, in reverse order using the following code:

```
D:\CBook>./readrandominreverse random.data
The content of random file in reverse order is :
desired data. Also you can access any content in any order.
perfectly well. Random file helps in fast accessing of
This is a random file. I am checking if the code is working
```

By comparing the original file with the preceding output, you can see that the file content is displayed in reverse order.

Now, let's move on to the next recipe!

Counting the number of vowels in a file

In this recipe, we will open a sequential text file and count the number of vowels (both uppercase and lowercase) that it contains.

 In this recipe, I will assume that a sequential file already exists. Please read *Appendix A* to learn how to create a sequential file.

How to do it...

1. Open the sequential file in read-only mode using the following code:

```
fp = fopen (argv [1],"r");
```

2. If the file does not exist or does not have enough permissions, an error message will be displayed and the program will terminate, as shown in the following code:

```
if (fp == NULL) {
    printf("%s file does not exist\n", argv[1]);
    exit(1);
}
```

3. Initialize the counter that will count the number of vowels in the file to 0, as shown in the following code:

```
count=0;
```

4. One line is read from the file, as shown in the following code:

```
fgets(buffer, BUFFSIZE, fp);
```

5. Each character of the line is accessed and checked for any lowercase or uppercase vowels, as shown in the following code:

```
if(buffer[i]=='a' || buffer[i]=='e' || buffer[i]=='i' ||
buffer[i]=='o' || buffer[i]=='u' || buffer[i]=='A' ||
buffer[i]=='E' || buffer[i]=='I' || buffer[i]=='O' ||
buffer[i]=='U')
```

6. If any vowel is found, the value of the counter is incremented by 1, as shown in the following code:

```
count++;
```

7. Step 5 will be repeated until the end of the line has been reached. Check whether the end of the file has been reached. Repeat from step 4 until the end of the file, as shown in the following code:

```
while (!feof(fp))
```

8. Display the count of the number of vowels in the file by printing the value in the counter variable on the screen, as shown in the following code:

```
printf("The number of vowels are %d\n",count);
```

The preceding steps are shown in the following diagram:

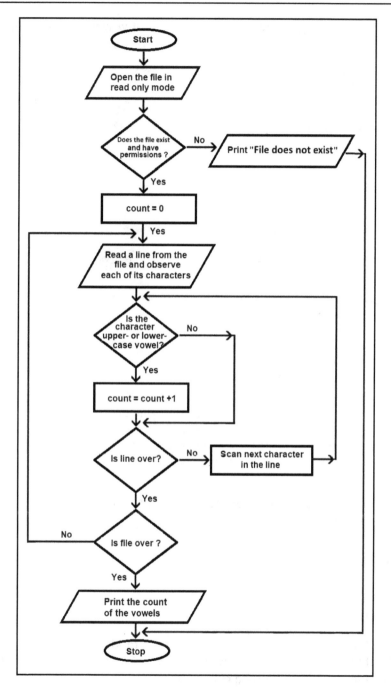

Figure 6.3

The `countvowels.c` program to count the number of vowels in a sequential text file is as follows:

```c
#include <stdio.h>
#include <stdlib.h>
#include <string.h>

#define BUFFSIZE 255

void main (int argc, char* argv[])
{
    FILE *fp;
    char buffer[BUFFSIZE];
    int n, i, count=0;
    fp = fopen (argv [1],"r");
    if (fp == NULL) {
        printf("%s file does not exist\n", argv[1]);
        exit(1);
    }
    printf("The file content is :\n");
    while (!feof(fp))
    {
        fgets(buffer, BUFFSIZE, fp);
        puts(buffer);
        n=strlen(buffer);
        for(i=0;i<n;i++)
        {
            if(buffer[i]=='a' || buffer[i]=='e' || buffer[i]=='i' ||
            buffer[i]=='o' || buffer[i]=='u' || buffer[i]=='A' ||
            buffer[i]=='E' || buffer[i]=='I' || buffer[i]=='O' ||
            buffer[i]=='U') count++;
        }
    }
    printf("The number of vowels are %d\n",count);
    fclose(fp);
}
```

Now, let's go behind the scenes.

How it works...

We will open the chosen sequential file in read-only mode. If the file opens successfully, it will be pointed at by the file pointer, `fp`. To count the number of vowels in the file, we will initialize a counter from 0.

We will set a `while` loop to execute until the file pointer, `fp`, reaches the end of the file. Within the `while` loop, each line in the file will be read using the `fgets` function. The `fgets` function will read the `BUFFSIZE` number of characters from the file. The value of the `BUFFSIZE` variable is `255`, so `fgets` will read either `254` characters from the file or will read characters until the newline character, `\n`, is reached, whichever comes first.

The line read from the file is assigned to the `buffer` string. To display the file contents along with the count of the vowels, the content in the `buffer` string is displayed on the screen. The length of the `buffer` string will be computed and a `for` loop will be set to execute equaling the length of the string.

Each of the characters in the buffer string will be checked in the `for` loop. If any lowercase or uppercase vowels appear in the line, the value of the counter variable will be incremented by `1`. When the `while` loop ends, the counter variable will have the total count of the vowels present in the file. Finally, the value in the counter variable will be displayed on the screen.

Let's use GCC to compile the `countvowels.c` program as follows:

```
D:\CBook>gcc countvowels.c -o countvowels
```

If you get no errors or warnings, then this means that the `countvowels.c` program has been compiled into an executable file called `countvowels.exe`.

Let's assume that we have a text file called `textfile.txt` with some content. We will run the executable file, `countvowels.exe`, and supply the `textfile.txt` file to it to count the number of vowels in it, as shown in the following code:

```
D:\CBook>./countvowels textfile.txt
The file content is :
I am trying to create a sequential file. it is through C programming.
It is very hot today. I have a cat. do you like animals? It might
rain. Thank you. bye
The number of vowels are 49
```

You can see from the output of the program that the program not only displays the count of the vowels, but also the complete content of the file.

Now, let's move on to the next recipe!

Replacing a word in a file with another word

Let's say that you want to replace all occurrences of the word is with the word was in one of your files. Let's find out how to do this.

 In this recipe, I will assume that a sequential file already exists. Please read *Appendix A* to learn how to create a sequential file.

How to do it...

1. Open the file in read-only mode using the following code:

```
fp = fopen (argv [1],"r");
```

2. If the file does not exist or does not have enough permissions, an error message will be displayed and the program will terminate, as shown in the following code:

```
if (fp == NULL) {
    printf("%s file does not exist\n", argv[1]);
    exit(1);
}
```

3. Enter the word to be replaced using the following code:

```
printf("Enter a string to be replaced: ");
scanf("%s", str1);
```

4. Enter the new word that will replace the old word using the following code:

```
printf("Enter the new string ");
scanf("%s", str2);
```

5. Read a line from the file using the following code:

```
fgets(line, 255, fp);
```

6. Check whether the word to be replaced appears anywhere in the line using the following code:

```
if(line[i]==str1[w])
{
    oldi=i;
    while(w<ls1)
    {
        if(line[i] != str1[w])
            break;
        else
        {
            i++;
            w++;
        }
    }
}
```

7. If the word appears in the line, then simply replace it with the new word using the following code:

```
if(w==ls1)
{
    i=oldi;
    for (k=0;k<ls2;k++)
    {
        nline[x]=str2[k];
        x++;
    }
    i=i+ls1-1;
}
```

8. If the word does not appear anywhere in the line, then move on to the next step. Print the line with the replaced word using the following code:

```
puts(nline);
```

9. Check whether the end of the file has been reached using the following code:

```
while (!feof(fp))
```

10. If the end of the file has not yet been reached, go to step 4. Close the file using the following code:

```
fclose(fp);
```

The `replaceword.c` program replaces the specified word in a file with another word and displays the modified content on the screen:

```c
#include <stdio.h>
#include <string.h>
#include <stdlib.h>

void main (int argc, char* argv[])
{
    FILE *fp;
    char line[255], nline[300], str1[80], str2[80];
    int i,ll, ls1,ls2, x,k, w, oldi;

    fp = fopen (argv [1],"r");
    if (fp == NULL) {
        printf("%s file does not exist\n", argv[1]);
        exit(1);
    }
    printf("Enter a string to be replaced: ");
    scanf("%s", str1);
    printf("Enter the new string ");
    scanf("%s", str2);
    ls1=strlen(str1);
    ls2=strlen(str2);
    x=0;
    while (!feof(fp))
    {
        fgets(line, 255, fp);
        ll=strlen(line);
        for(i=0;i<ll;i++)
        {
            w=0;
            if(line[i]==str1[w])
            {
                oldi=i;
                while(w<ls1)
                {
                    if(line[i] != str1[w])
                        break;
                    else
                    {
                        i++;
                        w++;
                    }
                }
                if(w==ls1)
                {
                    i=oldi;
```

```
                    for (k=0;k<ls2;k++)
                    {
                            nline[x]=str2[k];
                            x++;
                    }
                    i=i+ls1-1;
                }
                else
                {
                        i=oldi;
                        nline[x]=line[i];
                        x++;
                }
            }
            else
            {
                    nline[x]=line[i];
                    x++;
            }
        }
        nline[x]='\0';
        puts(nline);
    }
    fclose(fp);
}
```

Now, let's go behind the scenes.

How it works...

Open the chosen file in read-only mode. If the file opens successfully, then the file pointer, fp, will be set to point at it. Enter the word to be replaced and assign it to the string variable, str1. Similarly, enter the new string that will be assigned to another string variable, str2. The length of the two strings, str1 and str2, will be computed and assigned to the variables, ls1 and ls2, respectively.

Set a while loop to execute until the file pointed at by fp pointer gets over. Within the while loop, one line from the file will be read using the fgets function. The fgets function reads the file until the maximum length that is specified or the new line character, \n, is reached, whichever comes first. Because strings are terminated with a mandatory null character, \0, a maximum of 254 characters will be read from the file.

The string that is read from the file will be assigned to the `line` variable. The length of the `line` string will be computed and assigned to the `ll` variable. Using a `for` loop, each of the characters in the line variable will be accessed to check whether they match with `str1[0]`—that is, with the first character of the string to be replaced. The characters in the `line` variable that don't match with the string to be replaced will be assigned to another string, called `nline`. The `nline` string will contain the desired content—that is, all of the characters of the `line` variable and the new string. If it exists in `line`, then the string will be replaced with the new string and the entire modified content will be assigned to the new string, `nline`.

If the first character of the string to be replaced matches with any of the characters in `line`, then the `while` loop will be used to match all of the successive characters of the string that is to be replaced with the successive characters in `line`. If all of the characters of the string that is to be replaced match with successive characters in `line`, then all of the characters of the string to be replaced are replaced with the new string and assigned to the new string, `nline`. That way, the `while` loop will read one line of text at a time from the file, searching for occurrences of the string to be replaced. If it is found, it replaces it with the new string and assigns the modified line of text to another string, `nline`. The null character, `\0`, is added to the modified string, `nline`, and is displayed on the screen. Finally, the file pointed to by the file pointer, `fp`, is closed.

In this recipe, I am replacing the desired word and another string and displaying the updated content on the screen. If you want the updated content to be written into another file, then you can always open another file in write mode and execute the `fputs` function to write the updated content in it.

Let's use GCC to compile the `replaceword.c` program, as follows:

```
D:\CBook>gcc replaceword.c -o replaceword
```

If you get no errors or warnings, then this means that the `replaceword.c` program has been compiled into an executable file, `replaceword.exe`. Let's run the executable file, `replaceword.exe`, and supply a text file to it. We will assume that a text file called `textfile.txt` exists and has the following content:

```
I am trying to create a sequential file. it is through C programming.
It is very hot today. I have a cat. do you like animals? It might
rain. Thank you. bye
```

Now, let's use this file to replace one of its words with another word using the following code:

```
D:\CBook>./replaceword textfile.txt
Enter a string to be replaced: is
Enter the new string was
I am trying to create a sequential file. it was through C programming.
It was very hot today. I have a cat. do you like animals? It might
rain. Thank you. Bye
```

You can see that all occurrences of the word `is` are replaced by `was` in `textfile.txt`, and the modified content is displayed on the screen. We've successfully replaced the words of our choice.

Now, let's move on to the next recipe!

Encrypting a file

Encryption means converting content into a coded format so that unauthorized persons will be unable to see or access the original content of the file. A text file can be encrypted by applying a formula to the ASCII value of the content.

The formula or code can be of your choosing, and it can be as simple or complex as you want. For example, let's say that you have chosen to replace the current ASCII value of all letters by moving them forward 15 values. In this case, if the letter is a lowercase *a* that has the ASCII value of 97, then the forward shift of the ASCII values by 15 will make the *encrypted* letter a lowercase *p*, which has the ASCII value of 112 (97 + 15 = 112).

> In this recipe, I assume that a sequential file that you want to encrypt already exists. Please read *Appendix A* to learn how to create a sequential file. You can also refer to *Appendix A* if you want to know how an encrypted file is decrypted.

How to do it...

1. Open the source file in read-only mode using the following code:

```
fp = fopen (argv [1],"r");
```

2. If the file does not exist or does not have enough permissions, an error message will be displayed and the program will terminate, as shown in the following code:

```
if (fp == NULL) {
    printf("%s file does not exist\n", argv[1]);
    exit(1);
}
```

3. Open the destination file, the file where the encrypted text will be written, in write-only mode using the following code:

```
fq = fopen (argv[2], "w");
```

4. Read a line from the file and access each of its characters using the following code:

```
fgets(buffer, BUFFSIZE, fp);
```

5. Using the following code, subtract a value of 45 from the ASCII value of each of the characters in the line to encrypt that character:

```
for(i=0;i<n;i++)
    buffer[i]=buffer[i]-45;
```

6. Repeat step 5 until the line is over. Once all of the characters in the line are encrypted, write the encrypted line into the destination file using the following code:

```
fputs(buffer,fq);
```

7. Check whether the end of the file has been reached using the following code:

```
while (!feof(fp))
```

8. Close the two files using the following code:

```
fclose (fp);
fclose (fq);
```

The preceding steps are shown in the following diagram:

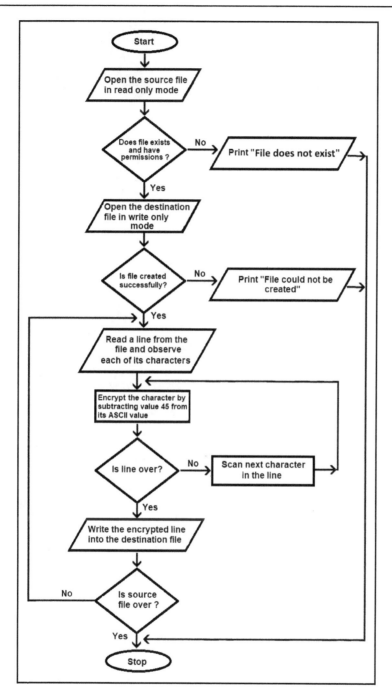

Figure 6.4

The `encryptfile.c` program to encrypt a file is as follows:

```c
#include <stdio.h>
#include <stdlib.h>
#include <string.h>

#define BUFFSIZE 255
void main (int argc, char* argv[])
{
    FILE *fp,*fq;
    int   i,n;
    char buffer[BUFFSIZE];

    /* Open the source file in read mode */
    fp = fopen (argv [1],"r");
    if (fp == NULL) {
        printf("%s file does not exist\n", argv[1]);
        exit(1);
    }
    /* Create the destination file.  */
    fq = fopen (argv[2], "w");
    if (fq == NULL) {
        perror ("An error occurred in creating the file\n");
        exit(1);
    }
    while (!feof(fp))
    {
        fgets(buffer, BUFFSIZE, fp);
        n=strlen(buffer);
        for(i=0;i<n;i++)
            buffer[i]=buffer[i]-45;
        fputs(buffer,fq);
    }
    fclose (fp);
    fclose (fq);
}
```

Now, let's go behind the scenes.

How it works...

The first file name that is passed through the command-line arguments is opened in read-only mode. The second file name that is passed through the command-line arguments is opened in write-only mode. If both files are opened correctly, then the `fp` and `fq` pointers , respectively, will point at the read-only and write-only files.

We will set a `while` loop to execute until it reaches the end of the source file. Within the loop, one line from the source file will be read using the `fgets` function. The `fgets` function reads the specified number of bytes from the file or until the new line character, \n, is reached. If the new line character does not appear in the file, then the `BUFFSIZE` constant limits the bytes to be read from the file to `254`.

The line read from the file is assigned to the `buffer` string . The length of the string `buffer` is computed and assigned to the variable, n. We will then set a `for` loop to execute until it reaches the end of the length of the `buffer` string, and within the loop, the ASCII value of each character will be changed.

To encrypt the file, we will subtract a value of `45` from the ASCII value of each of the characters, although we can apply any formula we like. Just ensure that you remember the formula, as we will need to reverse it in order to decrypt the file.

After applying the formula to all of the characters, the encrypted line will be written into the target file. In addition, to display the encrypted version on the screen, the encrypted line will be displayed on the screen.

When the `while` loop is finished, all of the lines from the source file will be written into the target file after they are encrypted. Finally, the two files will be closed.

Let's use GCC to compile the `encryptfile.c` program, as follows:

```
D:\CBook>gcc encryptfile.c -o encryptfile
```

If you get no errors or warnings, this means that the `encryptfile.c` program has been compiled into an executable file, `encryptfile.exe`. Let's run this executable file.

Before running the executable file, though, let's take a look at the text file, `textfile.txt`, which will be encrypted using this program. The contents of this text file are as follows:

```
I am trying to create a sequential file. it is through C programming.
It is very hot today. I have a cat. do you like animals? It might
rain. Thank you. bye
```

Let's run the executable file, `encryptfile.exe`, on `textfile.txt` and put the encrypted content into another file named `encrypted.txt` using the following code:

```
D:\CBook>./encryptfile textfile.txt encrypted.txt
```

The normal content in `textfile.txt` is encrypted and the encrypted content is written into another file named `encrypted.txt`. The encrypted content will appear as follows:

```
D:\CBook>type encrypted.txt
≤4@≤GEL<A:≤GB≤6E84G8≤4≤F8DH8AG<4?≤9<?8≤<G≤<F≤G;EBH:;≤≤CEB:E4@@<A:≤≤≤G≤<
F≤I8EL≤;BG≤GB74L≤;4I8≤4≤64G≤≤7B≤LBH≤?<>8≤4A<@4?F≤≤≤≤G≤@<:;G≤E4<A';4A>≤L
BH≤5L8
```

The preceding command is executed in Windows' Command Prompt.

Voila! We've successfully encrypted the file!

See also

To learn how to create and read content in sequential file, random file and decrypting a file visit *Appendix C* found on this link: `https://github.com/PacktPublishing/Practical-C-Programming/blob/master/Appendix%20C.pdf`.

Implementing Concurrency

7

Multitasking is a key feature in almost all operating systems; it increases the efficiency of the CPU and utilizes resources in a better manner. Threads are the best way to implement multitasking. A process can contain more than one thread to implement multitasking.

In this chapter, we will cover the following recipes involving threads:

- Performing a task with a single thread
- Performing multiple tasks with multiple threads
- Using `mutex` to share data between two threads
- Understanding how a deadlock is created
- Avoiding a deadlock

The terms process and thread can be confusing, so first, we'll make sure that you understand them.

What are processes and threads?

Whenever we run a program, the moment that it is loaded from the hard disk (or any other storage) into the memory, it becomes a process. A **process** is executed by a processor, and for its execution, it requires a **program counter (PC)** to keep track of the next instruction to be executed, the CPU registers, the signals, and so on.

A **thread** refers to a set of instructions within a program that can be executed independently. A thread has its own PC and set of registers, among other things. In that way, a process is comprised of several threads. Two or more threads can share their code, data, and other resources, but special care must be taken when sharing resources among threads, as it might lead to ambiguity and deadlock. An operating system also manages a thread pool.

A **thread pool** contains a collection of threads that are waiting for tasks to be allocated to them for concurrent execution. Using threads from the thread pool instead of instantiating new threads helps to avoid the delay that is caused by creating and destroying new threads; hence, it increases the overall performance of the application.

Basically, threads enhance the efficiency of an application through parallelism, that is, by running two or more independent sets of code simultaneously. This is called **multithreading**.

Multithreading is not supported by C, so to implement it, POSIX threads (Pthreads) are used. GCC allows for the implementation of a pthread.

While using a pthread, a variable of the type pthread_t is defined to store the thread identifier. A **thread identifier** is a unique integer, that is ,assigned to a thread in the system.

You must be wondering which function is used for creating a thread. The pthread_create function is invoked to create a thread. The following four arguments are passed to the pthread_create function:

- A pointer to the thread identifier, which is set by this function
- The attributes of the thread; usually, NULL is provided for this argument to use the default attributes
- The name of the function to execute for the creation of the thread
- The arguments to be passed to the thread, set to NULL if no arguments need to be passed to the thread

When two or more threads operate on the same data, that is, when they share the same resources, certain check measures must be applied so that only one thread is allowed to manipulate the shared resource at a time; other threads' access must be blocked. One of the methods that helps to avoid ambiguity when a resource is shared among threads is mutual exclusion.

Mutual exclusion

To avoid ambiguity when two or more threads access the same resource, **mutual exclusion** implements serializing access to the shared resources. When one thread is using a resource, no other thread is allowed to access the same resource. All of the other threads are blocked from accessing the same resource until the resource is free again.

A `mutex` is basically a lock that is associated with the shared resource. To read or modify the shared resource, a thread must first acquire the lock for that resource. Once a thread acquires a lock (or `mutex`) for that resource, it can go ahead with processing that resource. All of the other threads that wish to work on it will be compelled to wait until the resource is unlocked. When the thread finishes its processing on the shared resource, it unlocks the `mutex`, enabling the other waiting threads to acquire a `mutex` for that resource. Aside from `mutex`, a semaphore is also used in process synchronization.

A **semaphore** is a concept that is used to avoid two or more processes from accessing a common resource in a concurrent system. It is basically a variable that is manipulated to only allow one process to have access to a common resource and implement process synchronization. A semaphore uses the signaling mechanism, that is, it invokes `wait` and `signal` functions, respectively, to inform that the common resource has been acquired or released. A `mutex`, on the other hand, uses the locking mechanism—the process has to acquire the lock on the `mutex` object before working on the common resource.

Although `mutex` helps to manage shared resources among threads, there is a problem. An application of `mutex` in the wrong order may lead to a deadlock. A deadlock occurs in a situation when a thread that has `lock X` tries to acquire `lock Y` to complete its processing, while another thread that has `lock Y` tries to acquire `lock X` to finish its execution. In such a situation, a deadlock will occur, as both of the threads will keep waiting indefinitely for the other thread to release its lock. As no thread will be able to finish its execution, no thread will be able to free up its locks, either. One solution to avoid a deadlock is to let threads acquire locks in a specific order.

The following functions are used to create and manage threads:

- `pthread_join`: This function makes the thread wait for the completion of all its spawned threads. If it is not used, the thread will exit as soon as it completes its task, ignoring the states of its spawned threads. In other words, `pthread_join` blocks the calling thread until the thread specified in this function terminates.
- `pthread_mutex_init`: This function initializes the `mutex` object with the specified attributes. If `NULL` is used for the attributes, the default `mutex` attributes are used for initializing the `mutex` object. When the `mutex` is initialized, it is in an unlocked state.

- `pthread_mutex_lock`: This function locks the specified `mutex` object. If the `mutex` is already locked by some other thread, the calling thread will get suspended, that is, it will be asked to wait until the `mutex` gets unlocked. This function returns the `mutex` object in a locked state. The thread that locks the `mutex` becomes its owner and remains the owner until it unlocks the `mutex`.

- `pthread_mutex_unlock`: This function releases the specified `mutex` object. The thread that has invoked the `pthread_mutex_lock` function and is waiting for the `mutex` to get unlocked will become unblocked and acquire the `mutex` object, that is, the waiting thread will be able to access and lock the `mutex` object. If there are no threads waiting for the `mutex`, the `mutex` will remain in the unlocked state without any owner thread.

- `pthread_mutex_destroy`: This function destroys a `mutex` object and frees up the resources allocated to it. The `mutex` must be in an unlocked state before invoking this method.

> Depending on the operating system, a lock may be a **spinlock**. If any thread tries to acquire a lock but the lock is not free, a spinlock will make the thread wait in a loop until the lock becomes free. Such locks keep the thread busy while it's waiting for the lock to free up. They are efficient, as they avoid the consumption of time and resources in process rescheduling or context switching.

That is enough theory. Now, let's start with some practical examples!

Performing a task with a single thread

In this recipe, we will be creating a thread to perform a task. In this task, we will display the sequence numbers from 1 to 5. The focus of this recipe is to learn how a thread is created and how the main thread is asked to wait until the thread finishes its task.

How to do it...

1. Define a variable of the type `pthread_t` to store the thread identifier:

   ```
   pthread_t tid;
   ```

2. Create a thread and pass the identifier that was created in the preceding step to the `pthread_create` function. The thread is created with the default attributes. Also, specify a function that needs to be executed to create the thread:

   ```
   pthread_create(&tid, NULL, runThread, NULL);
   ```

3. In the function, you will be displaying a text message to indicate that the thread has been created and is running:

   ```
   printf("Running Thread \n");
   ```

4. Invoke a `for` loop to display the sequence of numbers from 1 to 5 through the running thread:

   ```
   for(i=1;i<=5;i++) printf("%d\n",i);
   ```

5. Invoke the `pthread_join` method in the main function to make the `main` method wait until the thread completes its task:

   ```
   pthread_join(tid, NULL);
   ```

The `createthread.c` program for creating a thread and making it perform a task is as follows:

```c
#include <stdio.h>
#include <stdlib.h>
#include <pthread.h>

void *runThread(void *arg)
{
    int i;
    printf("Running Thread \n");
    for(i=1;i<=5;i++) printf("%d\n",i);
    return NULL;
}

int main()
{
    pthread_t tid;
```

```
        printf("In main function\n");
        pthread_create(&tid, NULL, runThread, NULL);
        pthread_join(tid, NULL);
        printf("Thread over\n");
        return 0;
}
```

Now, let's go behind the scenes.

How it works...

We will define a variable called `tid` of the type `pthread_t` to store the thread identifier. A **thread identifier** is a unique integer, that is, assigned to a thread in the system. Before creating a thread, the message `In main function` is displayed on the screen. We will create a thread and pass the identifier `tid` to the `pthread_create` function. The thread is created with the default attributes, and the `runThread` function is set to execute to create the thread.

In the `runThread` function, we will display the text message `Running Thread` to indicate that the thread was created and is running. We will invoke a `for` loop to display the sequence of numbers from 1 to 5 through the running thread. By invoking the `pthread_join` method, we will make the `main` method wait until the thread completes its task. It is essential to invoke the `pthread_join` here; otherwise, the `main` method will exit without waiting for the completion of the thread.

Let's use GCC to compile the `createthread.c` program, as follows:

```
D:\CBook>gcc createthread.c -o createthread
```

If you get no errors or warnings, that means the `createthread.c` program has been compiled into an executable file, `createthread.exe`. Let's run this executable file:

Figure 7.1

Voila! We've successfully completed a task with a single thread. Now, let's move on to the next recipe!

Performing multiple tasks with multiple threads

In this recipe, you will learn how to multitask by executing two threads in parallel. Both of the threads will do their tasks independently. As the two threads will not be sharing a resource, there will not be a situation of race condition or ambiguity. The CPU will execute any thread randomly at a time, but finally, both of the threads will finish the assigned task. The task that the two threads will perform is displaying the sequence of numbers from 1 to 5.

How to do it...

1. Define two variables of the type `pthread_t` to store two thread identifiers:

   ```
   pthread_t tid1, tid2;
   ```

2. Invoke the `pthread_create` function twice to create two threads, and assign the identifiers that we created in the previous step. The two threads are created with the default attributes. Specify two respective functions that need to be executed for the two threads:

   ```
   pthread_create(&tid1,NULL,runThread1,NULL);
   pthread_create(&tid2,NULL,runThread2,NULL);
   ```

3. In the function of the first thread, display a text message to indicate that the first thread was created and is running:

   ```
   printf("Running Thread 1\n");
   ```

4. To indicate the execution of the first thread, execute a `for` loop in the first function to display the sequence of numbers from 1 to 5. To distinguish from the second thread, the sequence of numbers that were generated by the first thread are prefixed by `Thread 1`:

   ```
   for(i=1;i<=5;i++)
       printf("Thread 1 - %d\n",i);
   ```

5. Similarly, in the second thread, display a text message to inform that the second thread has also been created and is running:

```
printf("Running Thread 2\n");
```

6. Again, in the second function, execute a `for` loop to display the sequence of numbers from 1 to 5. To differentiate these numbers from the ones generated by `thread1`, this sequence of numbers will be preceded by the text `Thread 2`:

```
for(i=1;i<=5;i++)
    printf("Thread 2 - %d\n",i);
```

7. Invoke the `pthread_join` twice, and pass the thread identifiers we created in step 1 to it. `pthread_join` will make the two threads, and the `main` method will wait until both of the threads have completed their tasks:

```
pthread_join(tid1,NULL);
pthread_join(tid2,NULL);
```

8. When both of the threads are finished, a text message will be displayed to confirm this:

```
printf("Both threads are over\n");
```

The `twothreads.c` program for creating two threads and making them work on independent resources is as follows:

```
#include<pthread.h>
#include<stdio.h>

void *runThread1(void *arg){
    int i;
    printf("Running Thread 1\n");
    for(i=1;i<=5;i++)
        printf("Thread 1 - %d\n",i);
}

void *runThread2(void *arg){
    int i;
    printf("Running Thread 2\n");
    for(i=1;i<=5;i++)
        printf("Thread 2 - %d\n",i);
}

int main(){
    pthread_t tid1, tid2;
```

```
      pthread_create(&tid1,NULL,runThread1,NULL);
      pthread_create(&tid2,NULL,runThread2,NULL);
      pthread_join(tid1,NULL);
      pthread_join(tid2,NULL);
      printf("Both threads are over\n");
      return 0;
   }
```

Now, let's go behind the scenes.

How it works...

We will define two variables of the type pthread_t, by the names tid1 and tid2, to store two thread identifiers. These thread identifiers uniquely represent the threads in the system. We will invoke the pthread_create function twice to create two threads and assign their identifiers to the two variables tid1 and tid2, whose addresses are passed to the pthread_create function.

The two threads are created with the default attributes. We will execute the function runThread1 to create the first thread, and then the runThread2 function to create the second thread.

In the runThread1 function, we will display the message Running Thread 1 to indicate that the first thread was created and is running. In addition, we will invoke a for loop to display the sequence of numbers from 1 to 5 through the running thread. The sequence of numbers that are generated by the first thread will be prefixed by Thread 1.

Similarly, in the runThread2 function, we will display the message Running Thread 2 to inform that the second thread was also created and is running. Again, we will invoke a for loop to display the sequence of numbers from 1 to 5. To differentiate these numbers from the ones generated by thread1, these numbers are preceded by the text Thread 2.

We will then invoke the pthread_join method twice and pass our two thread identifiers, tid1 and tid2, to it. The pthread_join is invoked to make the two threads, and the main method waits until both of the threads have completed their respective tasks. When both of the threads are over, that is, when the functions runThread1 and runThread2 are over, a message saying that Both threads are over will be displayed in the main function.

Let's use GCC to compile the `twothreads.c` program, as follows:

```
D:\CBook>gcc twothreads.c -o twothreads
```

If you get no errors or warnings, that means the `twothreads.c` program has been compiled into an executable file, `twothreads.exe`. Let's run this executable file:

Figure 7.2

You may not get exactly the same output, as it depends on the CPU, but it is certain that both threads will exit simultaneously.

Voila! We've successfully completed multiple tasks with multiple threads. Now, let's move on to the next recipe!

Using mutex to share data between two threads

Running two or more threads independently, where each accesses its own resources, is quite convenient. However, sometimes, we want the threads to share and process the same resource simultaneously so that we can finish a task faster. Sharing a common resource may lead to problems, as one thread might read the data before the other thread writes the updated data, leading to an ambiguous situation. To avoid such a situation, `mutex` is used. In this recipe, you will learn how to share common resources between two threads.

How to do it...

1. Define two variables of the `pthread_t` type to store two thread identifiers. Also, define a `mutex` object:

   ```
   pthread_t tid1,tid2;
   pthread_mutex_t lock;
   ```

2. Invoke the `pthread_mutex_init` method to initialize the `mutex` object with the default `mutex` attributes:

   ```
   pthread_mutex_init(&lock, NULL)
   ```

3. Invoke the `pthread_create` function twice to create two threads, and assign the identifiers that we created in step 1. Execute a function for creating the two threads:

   ```
   pthread_create(&tid1, NULL, &runThread, NULL);
   pthread_create(&tid2, NULL, &runThread, NULL);
   ```

4. In the function, the `pthread_mutex_lock` method is invoked and the `mutex` object is passed to it to lock it:

   ```
   pthread_mutex_lock(&lock);
   ```

5. Invoke the `pthread_self` method and assign the ID of the calling thread to a variable of the `pthread_t` type. Invoke the `pthread_equal` method and compare it with the variable to find out which thread is currently executing. If the first thread is being executed, display the message `First thread is running` on the screen:

   ```
   pthread_t id = pthread_self();
   if(pthread_equal(id,tid1))
       printf("First thread is running\n");
   ```

6. To indicate that the thread is executing a common resource, display the text message `Processing the common resource` on the screen:

   ```
   printf("Processing the common resource\n");
   ```

7. Invoke the `sleep` method to make the first thread sleep for 5 seconds:

   ```
   sleep(5);
   ```

8. After a duration of 5 seconds, display the message `First thread is over` on the screen:

```
printf("First thread is over\n\n");
```

9. The `pthread_mutex_unlock` function will be invoked, and the `mutex` object that we created in the first step will be passed to it to unlock it:

```
pthread_mutex_unlock(&lock);
```

10. The `thread` function will be invoked by the second thread. Lock the `mutex` object again:

```
pthread_mutex_lock(&lock);
```

11. To indicate that the second thread is running at the moment, display the message `Second thread is running` on the screen:

```
printf("Second thread is running\n");
```

12. Again, to indicate that the common resource is being accessed by the thread, display the message `Processing the common resource` on the screen:

```
printf("Processing the common resource\n");
```

13. Introduce a delay of 5 seconds. Then, display the message `second thread is over` on the screen:

```
sleep(5);
printf("Second thread is over\n\n");
```

14. Unlock the `mutex` object:

```
pthread_mutex_unlock(&lock);
```

15. Invoke the `pthread_join` method twice and pass the thread identifiers to it:

```
pthread_join(tid1, NULL);
pthread_join(tid2, NULL);
```

16. Invoke the `pthread_mutex_destroy` method to destroy the `mutex` object:

```
pthread_mutex_destroy(&lock);
```

The twothreadsmutex.c program for creating two threads that share common resources is as follows:

```c
#include<stdio.h>
#include<pthread.h>
#include<unistd.h>
pthread_t tid1,tid2;
pthread_mutex_t lock;

void* runThread(void *arg)
{
    pthread_mutex_lock(&lock);
    pthread_t id = pthread_self();
    if(pthread_equal(id,tid1))
        printf("First thread is running\n");
    else
        printf("Second thread is running\n");
    printf("Processing the common resource\n");
    sleep(5);
    if(pthread_equal(id,tid1))
        printf("First thread is over\n\n");
    else
        printf("Second thread is over\n\n");
    pthread_mutex_unlock(&lock);
    return NULL;
}

int main(void)
{
    if (pthread_mutex_init(&lock, NULL) != 0)
        printf("\n mutex init has failed\n");
    pthread_create(&tid1, NULL, &runThread, NULL);
    pthread_create(&tid2, NULL, &runThread, NULL);
    pthread_join(tid1, NULL);
    pthread_join(tid2, NULL);
    pthread_mutex_destroy(&lock);
    return 0;
}
```

Now, let's go behind the scenes.

How it works...

We will first define a mutex object by the name lock. Recall that a mutex is basically a lock associated with a shared resource. To read or modify the shared resource, a thread needs to first acquire the lock for that resource. We will define two variables of the pthread_t type , with the names tid1 and tid2, to store two thread identifiers.

We will invoke the pthread_mutex_init method that initializes the lock object with the default mutex attributes. When it's initialized, the lock object is in an unlocked state. We then invoke the pthread_create function twice to create two threads and assign their identifiers to the two variables tid1 and tid2, whose addresses are passed to the pthread_create function. The two threads are created with the default attributes.

Next, we will execute the runThread function to create the two threads. In the runThread function, we will invoke the pthread_mutex_lock method and pass the mutex object lock to it to lock it. Now, the rest of the threads (if any) will be asked to wait until the mutex object lock is unlocked. We will invoke the pthread_self method and assign the ID of the calling thread to the variable id of the pthread_t type. We will then invoke the pthread_equal method to ensure that if the calling thread is the one with the identifier assigned to the tid1 variable, then the message First thread is running will display on the screen.

Next, the message Processing the common resource is displayed on the screen. We will invoke the sleep method to make the first thread sleep for 5 seconds. After a duration of 5 seconds, the message First thread is over will be displayed on the screen to indicate that the first thread is over. We will then invoke pthread_mutex_unlock and pass the mutex object lock to it to unlock it. Unlocking the mutex object is an indication to the other threads that the common resource can be used by other threads, too.

The runThread method will be invoked by the second thread, with the identifier tid2. Again, the mutex object lock is locked, and the id of the calling thread, that is, the second thread, is assigned to the variable id. The message Second thread is running is displayed on the screen, followed by the message Processing the common resource.

We will introduce a delay of 5 seconds to indicate that the second thread is processing the common resource. Then, the message `second thread is over` will be displayed on the screen. The `mutex` object `lock` is now unlocked. We will invoke the `pthread_join` method twice and pass the `tid1` and `tid2` thread identifiers to it. `pthread_join` is invoked to make the two threads and the `main` method wait until both of the threads have completed their tasks.

When both of the threads are over, we will invoke the `pthread_mutex_destroy` method to destroy the `mutex` object `lock` and free up the resources allocated to it.

Let's use GCC to compile the `twothreadsmutex.c` program, as follows:

```
D:\CBook>gcc twothreadsmutex.c -o twothreadsmutex
```

If you get no errors or warnings, that means the `twothreadsmutex.c` program has been compiled into an executable file, `twothreadsmutex.exe`. Let's run this executable file:

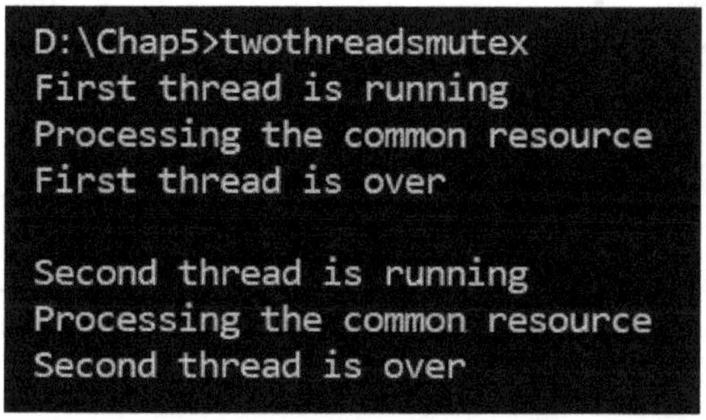

```
D:\Chap5>twothreadsmutex
First thread is running
Processing the common resource
First thread is over

Second thread is running
Processing the common resource
Second thread is over
```

Figure 7.3

Voila! We've successfully used `mutex` to share data between two threads. Now, let's move on to the next recipe!

Understanding how a deadlock is created

Locking a resource helps in non-ambiguous results, but locking can also lead to a deadlock. A **deadlock** is a situation wherein a thread has acquired the lock for one resource and wants to acquire the lock for a second resource. However, at the same time, another thread has acquired the lock for the second resource, but wants the lock for the first resource. Because the first thread will keep waiting for the second resource lock to be free and the second thread will keep waiting for the first resource lock to be free, the threads will not be able to proceed further, and the application will hang (as the following diagram illustrates):

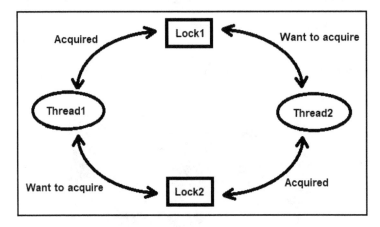

Figure 7.4

In this recipe, we will use a stack. A stack requires two operations—push and pop. To make only one thread execute a push or pop operation at a time, we will use two mutex objects—pop_mutex and push_mutex. The thread needs to acquire locks on both of the objects to operate on the stack. To create a situation of deadlock, we will make a thread acquire one lock and ask it to acquire another lock, which was already acquired by another thread.

How to do it...

1. Define a macro of the value 10, and define an array of an equal size:

```
#define max 10
int stack[max];
```

2. Define two `mutex` objects; one will be used while popping from the stack (pop_mutex), and the other will be used while pushing a value to the stack (push_mutex):

```
pthread_mutex_t pop_mutex;
pthread_mutex_t push_mutex;
```

3. To use the `stack`, initialize the value of `top` to −1:

```
int top=-1;
```

4. Define two variables of the type `pthread_t` to store two thread identifiers:

```
pthread_t tid1,tid2;
```

5. Invoke the `pthread_create` function to create the first thread; the thread will be created with the default attributes. Execute the `push` function to create this thread:

```
pthread_create(&tid1,NULL,&push,NULL);
```

6. Invoke the `pthread_create` function again to create the second thread; this thread will also be created with the default attributes. Execute the `pop` function to create this thread:

```
pthread_create(&tid2,NULL,&pop,NULL);
```

7. In the `push` function, invoke the `pthread_mutex_lock` method and pass the `mutex` object for the `push` operation (push_mutex) to lock it:

```
pthread_mutex_lock(&push_mutex);
```

8. Then, the `mutex` object for the `pop` operation (pop_mutex) will be locked by the first thread:

```
pthread_mutex_lock(&pop_mutex);
```

9. The user is asked to enter the value to be pushed to the `stack`:

```
printf("Enter the value to push: ");
scanf("%d",&n);
```

10. The value of `top` is incremented to `0`. The value that was entered in the previous step is pushed to the location `stack[0]`:

```
top++;
stack[top]=n;
```

11. Invoke `pthread_mutex_unlock` and unlock the `mutex` objects meant for the pop (`pop_mutex`) and push operations (`push_mutex`):

```
pthread_mutex_unlock(&pop_mutex);
pthread_mutex_unlock(&push_mutex);
```

12. At the bottom of the `push` function, display a text message indicating that the value is pushed to the stack:

```
printf("Value is pushed to stack \n");
```

13. In the `pop` function, invoke the `pthread_mutex_lock` function to lock the `mutex` object `pop_mutex`. It will lead to a deadlock:

```
pthread_mutex_lock(&pop_mutex);
```

14. Again, try to lock the `push_mutex` object, too (although it is not possible, as it is always acquired by the first thread):

```
sleep(5);
pthread_mutex_lock(&push_mutex);
```

15. The value in the stack, that is, pointed to by the `top` pointer is popped:

```
k=stack[top];
```

16. Thereafter, the value of `top` is decremented by 1 to make it -1 again. The value, that, is, popped from the stack is displayed on the screen:

```
top--;
printf("Value popped is %d \n",k);
```

17. Then, unlock the `mutex` object `push_mutex` and the `pop_mutex` object:

```
pthread_mutex_unlock(&push_mutex);
pthread_mutex_unlock(&pop_mutex);
```

18. In the `main` function, invoke the `pthread_join` method and pass the thread identifiers that were created in step 1 to it:

```
pthread_join(tid1,NULL);
pthread_join(tid2,NULL);
```

The `deadlockstate.c` program for creating two threads and understanding how a deadlock occurs while acquiring locks is as follows:

```
#include <stdio.h>
#include <pthread.h>
#include <unistd.h>
#include <stdlib.h>

#define max 10
pthread_mutex_t pop_mutex;
pthread_mutex_t push_mutex;
int stack[max];
int top=-1;

void * push(void *arg) {
    int n;
    pthread_mutex_lock(&push_mutex);
    pthread_mutex_lock(&pop_mutex);
    printf("Enter the value to push: ");
    scanf("%d",&n);
    top++;
    stack[top]=n;
    pthread_mutex_unlock(&pop_mutex);
    pthread_mutex_unlock(&push_mutex);
    printf("Value is pushed to stack \n");
}
void * pop(void *arg) {
    int k;
    pthread_mutex_lock(&pop_mutex);
    pthread_mutex_lock(&push_mutex);
    k=stack[top];
    top--;
    printf("Value popped is %d \n",k);
    pthread_mutex_unlock(&push_mutex);
    pthread_mutex_unlock(&pop_mutex);
}

int main() {
    pthread_t tid1,tid2;
    pthread_create(&tid1,NULL,&push,NULL);
    pthread_create(&tid2,NULL,&pop,NULL);
    printf("Both threads are created\n");
```

```
        pthread_join(tid1,NULL);
        pthread_join(tid2,NULL);
        return 0;
    }
```

Now, let's go behind the scenes.

How it works...

We will first define a macro called `max` of the value `10`, along with an array stack of the size `max`. Then, we will define two `mutex` objects with the names `pop_mutex` and `push_mutex`. To use the `stack`, we will initialize the value of `top` to `-1`. We will also define two variables of the type `pthread_t`, with the names `tid1` and `tid2`, to store two thread identifiers.

We will invoke the `pthread_create` function to create the first thread, and we will assign the identifier returned by the function to the variable `tid1`. The thread will be created with the default attributes, and we will execute the `push` function to create this thread.

We will invoke the `pthread_create` function again to create the second thread, and we will assign the identifier returned by the function to the variable `tid2`. This thread is also created with the default attributes, and we will execute the `pop` function to create this thread. On the screen, we will display the message `Both threads are created`.

In the `push` function, we will invoke the `pthread_mutex_lock` method and pass the `mutex` object `push_mutex` to it to lock it. Now, if any other thread asks for the `push_mutex` object, it will need to wait until the object is unlocked.

Then, the `mutex` object `pop_mutex` will be locked by the first thread. We will be asked to enter the value to be pushed to the stack. The entered value will be assigned to the variable `n`. The value of `top` will be incremented to `0`. The value that we enter will be pushed to the location `stack[0]`.

Next, we will invoke the `pthread_mutex_unlock` and pass the `mutex` object `pop_mutex` to it to unlock it. Also, the `mutex` object `push_mutex` will be unlocked. At the bottom of the `push` function, we will display the message `Value is pushed to stack`.

In the `pop` function, the `mutex` object `pop_mutex` will be locked, and then it will try to lock the `push_mutex` object that is already locked by first thread. The value in the stack, that is, pointed at by the pointer `top` will be popped. Because the value of `top` is 0, the value at the `stack[0]` location will be picked up and assigned to the variable `k`. Thereafter, the value of `top` will decrement by 1 to make it −1 again. The value, that is, popped from the stack will be displayed on the screen. Then, the `mutex` object `push_mutex` will be unlocked, followed by unlocking the `pop_mutex` object.

In the `main` function, we will invoke the `pthread_join` method twice and pass the `tid1` and `tid2` thread identifiers to it. The reason that we invoke the `pthread_join` method is to make the two threads and the `main` method wait until both of the threads have completed their tasks.

In this program, a deadlock has occurred because in the `push` function, the first thread locked the `push_mutex` object and tried to get the lock of the `pop_mutex` object, which was already locked by the second thread in the `pop` function. In the `pop` function, the thread locked the `mutex` object `pop_mutex` and tried to lock the `push_mutex` object, which was already locked by the first thread. So, neither of the threads will be able to finish, and they will keep waiting indefinitely for the other thread to release its `mutex` object.

Let's use GCC to compile the `deadlockstate.c` program, as follows:

```
D:\CBook>gcc deadlockstate.c -o deadlockstate
```

If you get no errors or warnings, that means the `deadlockstate.c` program is compiled into an executable file, `deadlockstate.exe`. Let's run this executable file:

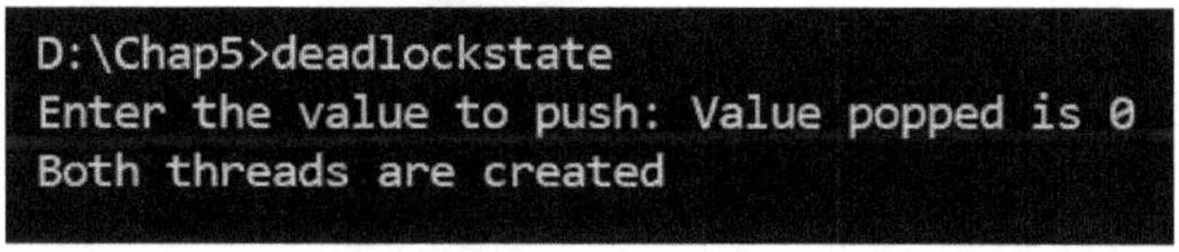

```
D:\Chap5>deadlockstate
Enter the value to push: Value popped is 0
Both threads are created
```

Figure 7.5

You've now seen how a deadlock can occur. Now, let's move on to the next recipe!

Avoiding a deadlock

A deadlock can be avoided if the threads are allowed to acquire the locks in a sequence. Let's suppose that a thread acquires the lock for a resource and wants to acquire the lock for a second resource. Any other thread that tries to acquire the first lock will be asked to wait, as it was already acquired by the first thread. Therefore, the second thread will not be able to acquire the lock for the second resource either, since it can only acquire locks in a sequence. However, our first thread will be allowed to acquire the lock to the second resource without waiting.

Applying a sequence to the locking of resources is the same as allowing only one thread to acquire resources at a time. The other threads will only be able to acquire the resources after the previous thread is over. This way, we will not have a deadlock on our hands.

How to do it...

1. Define an array of 10 elements:

   ```
   #define max 10
   int stack[max];
   ```

2. Define two `mutex` objects—one to indicate the `pop` operation of the stack (`pop_mutex`), and another to represent the `push` operation of the stack (`push_mutex`):

   ```
   pthread_mutex_t pop_mutex;
   pthread_mutex_t push_mutex;
   ```

3. To use the `stack`, the value of `top` is initialized to −1:

   ```
   int top=-1;
   ```

4. Define two variables of the type `pthread_t`, to store two thread identifiers:

   ```
   pthread_t tid1,tid2;
   ```

5. Invoke the `pthread_create` function to create the first thread. The thread is created with the default attributes, and the `push` function is executed to create the thread:

   ```
   pthread_create(&tid1,NULL,&push,NULL);
   ```

6. Invoke the `pthread_create` function again to create the second thread. The thread is created with the default attributes, and the `pop` function is executed to create this thread:

```
pthread_create(&tid2,NULL,&pop,NULL);
```

7. To indicate that the two threads were created, display the message `Both threads are created`:

```
printf("Both threads are created\n");
```

8. In the `push` function, invoke the `pthread_mutex_lock` method and pass the `mutex` object `push_mutex`, related to the `push` operation, to it, in order to lock it:

```
pthread_mutex_lock(&push_mutex);
```

9. After a sleep of 2 seconds, the `mutex` object, that is, meant to invoke the `pop` operation `pop_mutex` will be locked by the first thread:

```
sleep(2);
pthread_mutex_lock(&pop_mutex);
```

10. Enter the value to be pushed to the stack:

```
printf("Enter the value to push: ");
scanf("%d",&n);
```

11. The value of `top` is incremented to 0. To `stack[0]` location, the value, that is, entered by the user is pushed:

```
top++;
stack[top]=n;
```

12. Invoke `pthread_mutex_unlock` and pass the `mutex` object `pop_mutex` to it to unlock it. Also, the `mutex` object `push_mutex` will be unlocked:

```
pthread_mutex_unlock(&pop_mutex);
pthread_mutex_unlock(&push_mutex);
```

13. At the bottom of the `push` function, display the message `Value is pushed to stack`:

```
printf("Value is pushed to stack \n");
```

14. In the `pop` function, the `pthread_mutex_lock` function is invoked to lock the `mutex` object `push_mutex`:

    ```
    pthread_mutex_lock(&push_mutex);
    ```

15. After a sleep (or delay) of 5 seconds, the `pop` function will try to lock the `pop_mutex` object, too. However, the `pthread_mutex_lock` function will not be invoked, as the thread is kept waiting for the `push_mutex` object to be unlocked:

    ```
    sleep(5);
    pthread_mutex_lock(&pop_mutex);
    ```

16. The value in the stack pointed to by the pointer `top` is popped. Because the value of `top` is 0, the value at the location `stack[0]` is picked up:

    ```
    k=stack[top];
    ```

17. Thereafter, the value of `top` will be decremented by 1 to make it −1 again. The value, that is, popped from the stack will be displayed on the screen:

    ```
    top--;
    printf("Value popped is %d \n",k);
    ```

18. Then, the `mutex` object `pop_mutex` will be unlocked, followed by the `push_mutex` object:

    ```
    pthread_mutex_unlock(&pop_mutex);
    pthread_mutex_unlock(&push_mutex);
    ```

19. In the `main` function, invoke the `pthread_join` method twice and pass the thread identifiers that were created in step 1 to it:

    ```
    pthread_join(tid1,NULL);
    pthread_join(tid2,NULL);
    ```

The `avoiddeadlockst.c` program for creating two threads and understanding how a deadlock can be avoided while acquiring locks is as follows:

```
#include <stdio.h>
#include <pthread.h>
#include<unistd.h>
#include <stdlib.h>

#define max 10
pthread_mutex_t pop_mutex;
```

```
pthread_mutex_t push_mutex;
int stack[max];
int top=-1;

void * push(void *arg) {
    int n;
    pthread_mutex_lock(&push_mutex);
    sleep(2);
    pthread_mutex_lock(&pop_mutex);
    printf("Enter the value to push: ");
    scanf("%d",&n);
    top++;
    stack[top]=n;
    pthread_mutex_unlock(&pop_mutex);
    pthread_mutex_unlock(&push_mutex);
    printf("Value is pushed to stack \n");
}

void * pop(void *arg) {
    int k;
    pthread_mutex_lock(&push_mutex);
    sleep(5);
    pthread_mutex_lock(&pop_mutex);
    k=stack[top];
    top--;
    printf("Value popped from stack is %d \n",k);
    pthread_mutex_unlock(&pop_mutex);
    pthread_mutex_unlock(&push_mutex);
}

int main() {
    pthread_t tid1,tid2;
    pthread_create(&tid1,NULL,&push,NULL);
    pthread_create(&tid2,NULL,&pop,NULL);
    printf("Both threads are created\n");
    pthread_join(tid1,NULL);
    pthread_join(tid2,NULL);
    return 0;
}
```

Now, let's go behind the scenes.

How it works...

We will start by defining a macro called `max` of the value `10`. Then, we will define an array `stack` of the size `max`. We will define two `mutex` objects with the names `pop_mutex` and `push_mutex`.

To use the stack, the value of `top` will be initialized to `-1`. We will define two variables of the type `pthread_t`, with the names `tid1` and `tid2`, to store two thread identifiers.

We will invoke the `pthread_create` function to create the first thread and assign the identifier returned by the function to the variable `tid1`. The thread will be created with the default attributes, and the `push` function will be executed to create this thread.

We will invoke the `pthread_create` function a second time to create the second thread, and we'll assign the identifier returned by the function to the variable `tid2`. The thread will be created with the default attributes and the `pop` function will be executed to create this thread. On the screen, we will display the message `Both threads are created`.

In the `push` function, the `pthread_mutex_lock` method is invoked, and the `mutex` object `push_mutex` is passed to it to lock it. Now, if any other thread asks for the `pop_mutex` object, it will need to wait until the object is unlocked. After a sleep of `2` seconds, the `mutex` object `pop_mutex` is locked by the first thread.

We will be prompted to enter the value to be pushed to the stack. The entered value will be assigned to the variable n. The value of `top` will increment to `0`. The value that we enter will be pushed to the location `stack[0]`. Now, the `pthread_mutex_unlock` will be invoked, and the `mutex` object `pop_mutex` will be passed to it to unlock it. Also, the `mutex` object `push_mutex` will be unlocked. At the bottom of the `push` function, the message `Value is pushed to stack` will be displayed.

In the `pop` function, it will try to lock the `mutex` object `push_mutex`, but because it is already locked by the first thread, this thread will be asked to wait. After a sleep or delay of `5` seconds, it will also try to lock the `pop_mutex` object. The value in the stack, that is, pointed at by the pointer `top` will be popped. Because the value of top is `0`, the value at `stack[0]` is picked up and assigned to the variable k.

Thereafter, the value of `top` will decrement by 1 to make it −1 again. The value, that is, popped from the stack will be displayed on the screen. Then, the `mutex` object `pop_mutex` will be unlocked, followed by the `push_mutex` object.

In the `main` function, the `pthread_join` method is invoked twice, and the `tid1` and `tid2` thread identifiers are passed to it. The `pthread_join` is invoked to make the two threads and the `main` method wait until both of the threads have completed their tasks.

Here, we avoided a deadlock because the locking and unlocking of the `mutex` objects was done in a sequence. In the `push` function, the first thread locked the `push_mutex` object and tried to get a lock on the `pop_mutex` object. The `pop_mutex` was kept free because the second thread in the `pop` function first tried to lock the `push_mutex` object, followed by the `pop_mutex` object. Since the first thread had already locked the `push_mutex` object, the second thread was asked to wait. Consequently, both of the `mutex` objects, `push_mutex` and `pop_mutex`, were in an unlocked state, and the first thread was able to easily lock both of the `mutex` objects and use the common resource. After finishing its task, the first thread will unlock both of the `mutex` objects, enabling the second thread to lock both of the `mutex` objects and access the common resource thread.

Let's use GCC to compile the `avoiddeadlockst.c` program, as follows:

```
D:\CBook>gcc avoiddeadlockst.c -o avoiddeadlockst
```

If you get no errors or warnings, that means the `avoiddeadlockst.c` program has been compiled into an executable file, `avoiddeadlockst.exe`. Let's run this executable file:

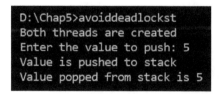

Figure 7.6

Voila! We've successfully avoided a deadlock.

8

Networking and Inter-Process Communication

Processes run individually and work independently in their respective address spaces. However, they sometimes need to communicate with each other to pass on information. For processes to cooperate, they need to be able to communicate with each other as well as synchronize their actions. Here are the types of communication that take place between processes:

- **Synchronous communication**: Such communication doesn't allow the process to continue with any other work until the communication is over
- **Asynchronous communication**: In this communication, the process can continue doing other tasks, and so it supports multitasking and results in better efficiency
- **Remote Procedure Call** (**RPC**): This is a protocol that uses client service techniques for communication where the client cannot do anything, that is, it is suspended until it gets a response from the server

These communications can be unidirectional or bidirectional. To enable any form of communication between processes, the following popular **interprocess communication** (**IPC**) mechanisms are used: pipes, FIFOs (named pipes), sockets, message queues, and shared memory. Pipes and FIFO enable unidirectional communication, whereas sockets, message queues, and shared memory enable bidirectional communication.

In this chapter, we will learn how to make the following recipes so that we can establish communication between processes:

- Communicating between processes using pipes
- Communicating between processes using FIFO
- Communicating between the client and server using socket programming
- Communicating between processes using a UDP socket
- Passing a message from one process to another using the message queue
- Communicating between processes using shared memory

Let's begin with the first recipe!

Communicating between processes using pipes

In this recipe, we will learn how to write data into a pipe from its writing end and then how to read that data from its reading end. This can happen in two ways:

- One process, both writing and reading from the pipe
- One process writing and another process reading from the pipe

Before we begin with the recipes, let's quickly review the functions, structures, and terms that are used in successful interprocess communication.

Creating and to connecting processes

The most commonly used functions and terms for communication between processes are `pipe`, `mkfifo`, `write`, `read`, `perror`, and `fork`.

pipe()

A pipe is used for connecting two processes. The output from one process can be sent as an input to another process. The flow is unidirectional, that is, one process can write to the pipe and another process can read from the pipe. Writing and reading are done in an area of main memory, which is also known as a virtual file. Pipes have a **First in First out** (**FIFO**) or a queue structure, that is, what is written first will be read first.

A process should not try to read from the pipe before something is written into it, otherwise it will suspend until something is written into the pipe.

Here is its syntax:

```
int pipe(int arr[2]);
```

Here, `arr[0]` is the file descriptor for the read end of the pipe, and `arr[1]` is the file descriptor for the write end of the pipe.

The function returns 0 on success and –1 on error.

mkfifo()

This function creates a new FIFO special file. Here is its syntax:

```
int mkfifo(const char *filename, mode_t permission);
```

Here, `filename` represents the filename, along with its complete path, and `permission` represents the permission bits of the new FIFO file. The default permissions are read and write permission for the owner, group, and others, that is, (0666).

The function returns 0 on successful completion; otherwise, it returns –1.

write()

This function is used for writing into the specified file or pipe whose descriptor is supplied. Here is its syntax:

```
write(int fp, const void *buf, size_t n);
```

It writes the *n* number of bytes into the file that's being pointed to by the file pointer, `fp`, from the buffer, `buf`.

read()

This function reads from the specified file or pipe whose descriptor is supplied in the method. Here is its syntax:

```
read(int fp, void *buf, size_t n);
```

It tries to read up to *n* number of bytes from a file that's being pointed to by a descriptor, `fp`. The bytes that are read are then assigned to the buffer, `buf`.

perror()

This displays an error message indicating the error that might have occurred while invoking a function or system call. The error message is displayed to `stderr`, that is, the standard error output stream. This is basically the console.

Here is its syntax:

```
void perror ( const char * str );
```

The error message that is displayed is optionally preceded by the message that's represented by `str`.

fork()

This is used for creating a new process. The newly created process is called the child process, and it runs concurrently with the parent process. After executing the `fork` function, the execution of the program continues and the instruction following the `fork` function is executed by the parent as well as the child process. If the system call is successful, it will return a process ID of the child process and returns a `0` to the newly created child process. The function returns a negative value if the child process is not created.

Now, let's start with the first recipe for enabling communication between processes using pipes.

One process, both writing and reading from the pipe

Here, we will learn how writing and reading from the pipe are done by a single process.

How to do it...

1. Define an array of size 2 and pass it as an argument to the pipe function.
2. Invoke the write function and write your chosen string into the pipe through the write end of the array. Repeat the procedure for the second message.
3. Invoke the read function to read the first message from the pipe. Invoke the read function again to read the second message.

The readwritepipe.c program for writing into the pipe and reading from it thereafter is as follows:

```c
#include <stdio.h>
#include <unistd.h>
#include <stdlib.h>

#define max 50

int main()
{
    char str[max];
    int pp[2];

    if (pipe(pp) < 0)
        exit(1);
    printf("Enter first message to write into pipe: ");
    gets(str);
    write(pp[1], str, max);
    printf("Enter second message to write into pipe: ");
    gets(str);
    write(pp[1], str, max);
    printf("Messages read from the pipe are as follows:\n");
    read(pp[0], str, max);
    printf("%s\n", str);
    read(pp[0], str, max);
    printf("%s\n", str);
    return 0;
}
```

Let's go behind the scenes.

How it works...

We defined a macro, max, of size of 50, a string, str, of size max, and an array, pp, with size 2 . We will invoke the pipe function to connect two processes and pass the pp array to it. The index location, pp[0], will get the file descriptor for the reading end of the pipe and pp[1] will get the file descriptor for the write end of the pipe. The program will exit if the pipe function does not execute successfully.

You will be prompted to enter the first message to be written into the pipe. The text that's entered by you will be assigned to the string variable, str. Invoke the write function and the string in str will be written into the pipe, pp. Repeat the procedure for the second message. The second text that's entered by you will also be written into the pipe.

Obviously, the second text will be written behind the first text in the pipe. Now, invoke the read function to read from the pipe. The text that was entered first in the pipe will be read and assigned to the string variable, str, and is consequently displayed on the screen. Again, invoke the read function and the second text message in the pipe will be read from its read end and assigned to the string variable, str, and then displayed on the screen.

Let's use GCC to compile the readwritepipe.c program, as follows:

```
$ gcc readwritepipe.c -o readwritepipe
```

If you get no errors or warnings, this means that the readwritepipe.c program has been compiled into an executable file, readwritepipe.exe. Let's run this executable file:

```
$ ./readwritepipe

Enter the first message to write into pipe: This is the first message
for the pipe
Enter the second message to write into pipe: Second message for the
pipe
Messages read from the pipe are as follows:
This is the first message for the pipe
Second message for the pipe
```

In the preceding program, the main thread does the job of writing and reading from the pipe. But what if we want one process to write into the pipe and another process to read from the pipe? Let's find out how we can make that happen.

One process writing into the pipe and another process reading from the pipe

In this recipe, we will use the fork system call to create a child process. Then, we will write into the pipe using the child process and read from the pipe through the parent process, thereby establishing communication between two processes.

How to do it...

1. Define an array of size 2.
2. Invoke the `pipe` function to connect the two processes and pass the array we defined previously to it.
3. Invoke the `fork` function to create a new child process.
4. Enter the message that is going to be written into the pipe. Invoke the `write` function using the newly created child process.
5. The parent process invokes the `read` function to read the text that's been written into the pipe.

The `pipedemo.c` program for writing into the pipe through a child process and reading from the pipe through the parent process is as follows:

```c
#include <stdio.h>
#include <stdlib.h>
#include <string.h>
#include <unistd.h>

#define max   50

int main()
{
    char wstr[max];
    char rstr[max];
    int pp[2];
    pid_t p;
    if(pipe(pp) < 0)
    {
        perror("pipe");
    }
    p = fork();
    if(p >= 0)
    {
        if(p == 0)
```

```
            {
                printf ("Enter the string : ");
                gets(wstr);
                write (pp[1] , wstr , strlen(wstr));
                exit(0);
            }
            else
            {
                read (pp[0] , rstr , sizeof(rstr));
                printf("Entered message : %s\n " , rstr);
                exit(0);
            }
        }
        else
        {
            perror("fork");
            exit(2);
        }
        return 0;
    }
```

Let's go behind the scenes.

How it works...

Define a macro max, of size 50 and two string variables, wstr and rstr, of size max. The wstr string will be used for writing into the pipe and rstr will be used for reading from the pipe. Define an array, pp, of size 2, which will be used for storing the file descriptors of the read and write ends of the pipe. Define a variable, p, of the pid_t data type, which will be used for storing a process ID.

We will invoke the pipe function to connect the two processes and pass the pp array to it. The index location pp[0] will get the file descriptor for the reading end of the pipe, while pp[1] will get the file descriptor for the write end of the pipe. The program will exit if the pipe function does not execute successfully.

Then, we will invoke the fork function to create a new child process. You will be prompted to enter the message to be written into the pipe. The text you enter will be assigned to the string variable wstr. When we invoke the write function using the newly created child process, the string in the wstr variable will be written into the pipe, pp. Thereafter, the parent process will invoke the read function to read the text that's been written into the pipe. The text that's read from the pipe will be assigned to the string variable rstr and will consequently be displayed on the screen.

Let's use GCC to compile the `pipedemo.c` program, as follows:

```
$ gcc pipedemo.c -o pipedemo
```

If you get no errors or warnings, this means that the `pipedemo.c` program has been compiled into an executable file, `pipedemo.exe`. Let's run this executable file:

```
$ ./pipedemo
Enter the string : This is a message from the pipe
Entered message : This is a message from the pipe
```

Voila! We've successfully communicated between processes using pipes. Now, let's move on to the next recipe!

Communicating between processes using FIFO

In this recipe, we will learn how two processes communicate using a named pipe, also known as FIFO. This recipe is divided into the following two parts:

- Demonstrating how data is written into a FIFO
- Demonstrating how data is read from a FIFO

The functions and terms we learned in the previous recipe will also be applicable here.

Writing data into a FIFO

As the name suggests, we will learn how data is written into a FIFO in this recipe.

How to do it...

1. Invoke the `mkfifo` function to create a new FIFO special file.
2. Open the FIFO special file in write-only mode by invoking the `open` function.
3. Enter the text to be written into the FIFO special file.
4. Close the FIFO special file.

The `writefifo.c` program for writing into a FIFO is as follows:

```
#include <stdio.h>
#include <sys/stat.h>
#include <fcntl.h>
#include <unistd.h>

int main()
{
    int fw;
    char str[255];
    mkfifo("FIFOPipe", 0666);
    fw = open("FIFOPipe", O_WRONLY);
    printf("Enter text: ");
    gets(str);
    write(fw,str, sizeof(str));
    close(fw);
    return 0;
}
```

Let's go behind the scenes.

How it works...

Let's assume we have defined a string called `str` of size `255`. We will invoke the `mkfifo` function to create a new FIFO special file. We will create the FIFO special file with the name `FIFOPipe` with read and write permissions for owner, group, and others.

We will open this FIFO special file in write-only mode by invoking the `open` function. Then, we will assign the file descriptor of the opened FIFO special file to the `fw` variable. You will be prompted to enter the text that is going to be written into the file. The text you enter will be assigned to the `str` variable, which in turn will be written into the special FIFO file when you invoke the `write` function. Finally, close the FIFO special file. Let's use GCC to compile the `writefifo.c` program, as follows:

```
$ gcc writefifo.c -o writefifo
```

If you get no errors or warnings, this means that the `writefifo.c` program has compiled into an executable file, `writefifo.exe`. Let's run this executable file:

```
$ ./writefifo
Enter text: This is a named pipe demo example called FIFO
```

If your program does not prompts for the string that means it is waiting for the other end of the FIFO to open. That is, you need to run the next recipe, *Reading data from a FIFO,* on the second Terminal screen. Please press *Alt+F2* on Cygwin to open the next terminal screen.

Now, let's check out the other part of this recipe.

Reading data from a FIFO

In this recipe, we will see how we can read data from a FIFO.

How to do it...

1. Open the FIFO special file in read-only mode by invoking the open function.
2. Read the text from the FIFO special file using the read function.
3. Close the FIFO special file.

The readfifo.c program for reading from the named pipe (FIFO) is as follows:

```
#include <fcntl.h>
#include <stdio.h>
#include <sys/stat.h>
#include <unistd.h>

#define BUFFSIZE 255

int main()
{
    int fr;
    char str[BUFFSIZE];
    fr = open("FIFOPipe", O_RDONLY);
    read(fr, str, BUFFSIZE);
    printf("Read from the FIFO Pipe: %s\n", str);
    close(fr);
    return 0;
}
```

Let's go behind the scenes.

How it works...

We will start by defining a macro called BUFFSIZE of size 255 and a string called str of size BUFFSIZE, that is, 255 characters. We will open the FIFO special file named FIFOPipe in read-only mode by invoking the open function. The file descriptor of the opened FIFO special file will be assigned to the fr variable.

Using the read function, the text from the FIFO special file will be read and assigned to the str string variable. The text that's read from the FIFO special file will then be displayed on the screen. Finally, the FIFO special file will be closed.

Now, press *Alt + F2* to open a second Terminal window. In the second Terminal window, let's use GCC to compile the readfifo.c program, as follows:

```
$ gcc readfifo.c -o readfifo
```

If you get no errors or warnings, this means that the readfifo.c program has compiled into an executable file, readfifo.exe. Let's run this executable file:

```
$ ./readfifo
Read from the FIFO Pipe: This is a named pipe demo example called FIFO
```

The moment you run the readfifo.exe file, you will find, that on the previous Terminal screen where writefifo.c program was run will prompt you to enter a string. The moment you enter a string on that Terminal and press *Enter* key, you will get the output from the readfifo.c program.

Voila! We've successfully communicated between processes using a FIFO. Now, let's move on to the next recipe!

Communicating between the client and server using socket programming

In this recipe, we will learn how data from the server process is sent to the client process. This recipe is divided into the following parts:

- Sending data to the client
- Reading data that's been sent from the server

Before we begin with the recipes, let's quickly review the functions, structures, and terms that are used in successful client-server communication.

Client-server model

Different models are used for IPC, but the most popular one is the client-server model. In this model, whenever the client needs some information, it connects to another process called the server. But before establishing the connection, the client needs to know whether the server already exists, and it should know the address of the server.

On the other hand, the server is meant to serve the needs of the client and does not need to know the address of the client prior to the connection. To establish a connection, a basic construct called a socket is required, and both the connecting processes must establish their own sockets. The client and the server need to follow certain procedures to establish their sockets.

To establish a socket on the client side, a socket is created with the `socket` function system call. Thereafter, that socket is connected to the server's address using the `connect` function system call, followed by sending and receiving data by invoking the `read` function and `write` function system calls.

To establish a socket on the server side, again, a socket is created with the `socket` function system call and then the socket is bonded to an address using the `bind` function system call. Thereafter, the `listen` function system call is invoked to listen for the connections. Finally, the connection is accepted by invoking the `accept` function system call.

struct sockaddr_in structure

This structure references the socket's elements that are used for keeping addresses. The following are the built-in members of this structure:

```
struct sockaddr_in {
  short int sin_family;
  unsigned short int sin_port;
  struct in_addr sin_addr;
  unsigned char sin_zero[8];
};
```

Here, we have the following:

- `sin_family`: Represents an address family. The valid options are `AF_INET`, `AF_UNIX`, `AF_NS`, and `AF_IMPLINK`. In most applications, the address family that's used is `AF_INET`.
- `sin_port`: Represents the 16-bit service port number.
- `sin_addr`: Represents a 32-bit IP address.
- `sin_zero`: This is not used and is usually set to `NULL`.

`struct in_addr` comprise one member, as follows:

```
struct in_addr {
    unsigned long s_addr;
};
```

Here, `s_addr` is used to represent the address in network byte order.

socket()

This function creates an endpoint for communication. To establish communication, every process needs a socket at the end of the communication line. Also, the two communicating processes must have the same socket type and both should be in the same domain. Here is the syntax for creating a socket:

```
int socket(int domain, int type, int protocol);
```

Here, `domain` represents the communication domain in which a socket is to be created. Basically, the `address family` or `protocol family` is specified, which will be used in the communication.

A few of the popular `address family` are listed as follows:

- `AF_LOCAL`: This is used for local communication.
- `AF_INET`: This is used for IPv4 internet protocols.
- `AF_INET6`: This is used for IPv6 internet protocols.
- `AF_IPX`: This is used for protocols that use standard **IPX** (short for **Internetwork Packet Exchange**) socket addressing.
- `AF_PACKET`: This is used for packet interface.

- `type`: Represents the type of socket to be created. The following are the popular socket types:
  - `SOCK_STREAM`: Stream sockets communicate as a continuous stream of characters using a **Transmission Control Protocol (TCP)**. TCP is a reliable stream-oriented protocol. So, the `SOCK_STREAM` type provides reliable, bidirectional, and connection-based byte streams.
    - `SOCK_DGRAM`: Datagram sockets read the entire messages at once using a **User Datagram Protocol (UDP)**. UDP is an unreliable, connectionless, and message-oriented protocol. These messages are of a fixed maximum length.
  - `SOCK_SEQPACKET`: Provides reliable, bidirectional, and connection-based transmission paths for datagrams.
- `protocol`: Represents the protocol to be used with the socket. A `0` value is specified so that you can use the default protocol that's suitable for the requested socket type.

 You can replace the `AF_` prefix in the preceding list with `PF_` for `protocol family`.

On successful execution, the `socket` function returns a file descriptor that can be used to manage sockets.

memset()

This is used to fill a block of memory with the specified value. Here is its syntax:

```
void *memset(void *ptr, int v, size_t n);
```

Here, `ptr` points at the memory address to be filled, `v` is the value to be filled in the memory block, and `n` is the number of bytes to be filled, starting at the location of the pointer.

htons()

This is used to convert the unsigned short integer from host to network byte order.

bind()

A socket that is created with the `socket` function remains in the assigned address family. To enable the socket to receive connections, an address needs to be assigned to it. The `bind` function assigns the address to the specified socket. Here is its syntax:

```
int bind(int fdsock, const struct sockaddr *structaddr, socklen_t
    lenaddr);
```

Here, `fdsock` represents the file descriptor of the socket, `structaddr` represents the `sockaddr` structure that contains the address to be assigned to the socket, and `lenaddr` represents the size of the address structure that's pointed to by `structaddr`.

listen()

It listens for connections on a socket in order to accept incoming connection requests. Here is its syntax:

```
int listen(int sockfd, int lenque);
```

Here, `sockfd` represents the file descriptor of the socket, and `lenque` represents the maximum length of the queue of pending connections for the given socket. An error will be generated if the queue is full.

If the function is successful it returns zero, otherwise it returns -1.

accept()

It accepts a new connection on the listening socket, that is, the first connection from the queue of pending connections is picked up. Actually, a new socket is created with the same socket type protocol and address family as the specified socket, and a new file descriptor is allocated for that socket. Here is its syntax:

```
int accept(int socket, struct sockaddr *address, socklen_t *len);
```

Here, we need to address the following:

- `socket`: Represents the file descriptor of the socket waiting for the new connection. This is the socket that is created when the `socket` function is bound to an address with the `bind` function, and has invoked the `listen` function successfully.

- `address`: The address of the connecting socket is returned through this parameter. It is a pointer to a `sockaddr` structure, through which the address of the connecting socket is returned.
- `len`: Represents the length of the supplied `sockaddr` structure. When returned, this parameter contains the length of the address returned in bytes.

send()

This is used for sending the specified message to another socket. The socket needs to be in a connected state before you can invoke this function. Here is its syntax:

```
ssize_t send(int fdsock, const void *buf, size_t length, int flags);
```

Here, `fdsock` represents the file descriptor of the socket through which a message is to be sent, `buf` points to the buffer that contains the message to be sent, `length` represents the length of the message to be sent in bytes, and `flags` specifies the type of message to be sent. Usually, its value is kept at `0`.

connect()

This initiates a connection on a socket. Here is its syntax:

```
int connect(int fdsock, const struct sockaddr *addr,  socklen_t len);
```

Here, `fdsock` represents the file descriptor of the socket onto which the connection is desired, `addr` represents the structure that contains the address of the socket, and `len` represents the size of the structure `addr` that contains the address.

recv()

This is used to receive a message from the connected socket. The socket may be in connection mode or connectionless mode. Here is its syntax:

```
ssize_t recv(int fdsock, void *buf, size_t len, int flags);
```

Here, `fdsock` represents the file descriptor of the socket from which the message has to be fetched, `buf` represents the buffer where the message that is received is stored, `len` specifies the length in bytes of the buffer that's pointed to by the `buf` argument, and `flags` specifies the type of message being received. Usually, its value is kept at `0`.

We can now begin with the first part of this recipe – how to send data to the client.

Sending data to the client

In this part of the recipe, we will learn how a server sends desired data to the client.

How to do it...

1. Define a variable of type `sockaddr_in`.
2. Invoke the `socket` function to create a socket. The port number that's specified for the socket is `2000`.
3. Call the `bind` function to assign an IP address to it.
4. Invoke the `listen` function.
5. Invoke the `accept` function.
6. Invoke the `send` function to send the message that was entered by the user to the socket.
7. The socket at the client end will receive the message.

The server program, `serverprog.c`, for sending a message to the client is as follows:

```
#include <stdio.h>
#include <sys/socket.h>
#include <netinet/in.h>
#include <string.h>
#include <arpa/inet.h>

int main(){
    int serverSocket, toSend;
    char str[255];
    struct sockaddr_in server_Address;
    serverSocket = socket(AF_INET, SOCK_STREAM, 0);
    server_Address.sin_family = AF_INET;
    server_Address.sin_port = htons(2000);
    server_Address.sin_addr.s_addr = inet_addr("127.0.0.1");
    memset(server_Address.sin_zero, '\0', sizeof
    server_Address.sin_zero);
```

```
    bind(serverSocket, (struct sockaddr *) &server_Address,
    sizeof(server_Address));
    if(listen(serverSocket,5)==-1)
    {
        printf("Not able to listen\n");
        return -1;
    }
    printf("Enter text to send to the client: ");
    gets(str);
    toSend = accept(serverSocket, (struct sockaddr *) NULL, NULL);
    send(toSend,str, strlen(str),0);
    return 0;
}
```

Let's go behind the scenes.

How it works...

We will start by defining a string of size `255`, and a `server_Address` variable of type `sockaddr_in`. This structure references the socket's elements. Then, we will invoke the `socket` function to create a socket by the name of `serverSocket`. A socket is an endpoint for communication. The address family that's supplied for the socket is `AF_INET`, and the socket type selected is the stream socket type, since the communication that we want is of a continuous stream of characters.

The address family that's specified for the socket is `AF_INET`, and is used for IPv4 internet protocols. The port number that's specified for the socket is `2000`. Using the `htons` function, the short integer `2000` is converted into the network byte order before being applied as a port number. The fourth parameter, `sin_zero`, of the `server_Address` structure is set to `NULL` by invoking the `memset` function.

To enable the created `serverSocket` to receive connections, call the `bind` function to assign an address to it. Using the `sin_addr` member of the `server_Address` structure, a 32-bit IP address will be applied to the socket. Because we are working on the local machine, the localhost address `127.0.0.1` will be assigned to the socket. Now, the socket can receive the connections. We will invoke the `listen` function to enable the `serverSocket` to accept incoming connection requests. The maximum pending connections that the socket can have is 5.

You will be prompted to enter the text that is to be sent to the client. The text you enter will be assigned to the `str` string variable. By invoking the `accept` function, we will enable the `serverSocket` to accept a new connection.

The address of the connection socket will be returned through the structure of type `sockaddr_in`. The socket that is returned and that is ready to accept a connection is named `toSend`. We will invoke the `send` function to send the message that's entered by you. The socket at the client end will receive the message.

Let's use GCC to compile the `serverprog.c` program, as follows:

```
$ gcc serverprog.c -o serverprog
```

If you get no errors or warnings, this means that the `serverprog.c` program has compiled into an executable file, `serverprog.exe`. Let's run this executable file:

```
$ ./serverprog
Enter text to send to the client: thanks and good bye
```

Now, let's look at the other part of this recipe.

Reading data that's been sent from the server

In this part of the recipe, we will learn how data that's been sent from the server is received and displayed on the screen.

How to do it...

1. Define a variable of type `sockaddr_i`.
2. Invoke the `socket` function to create a socket. The port number that's specified for the socket is `2000`.
3. Invoke the `connect` function to initiate a connection to the socket.
4. Because we are working on the local machine, the localhost address `127.0.0.1` is assigned to the socket.
5. Invoke the `recv` function to receive the message from the connected socket. The message that's read from the socket is then displayed on the screen.

The client program, `clientprog.c`, for reading a message that's sent from the server is as follows:

```
#include <stdio.h>
#include <sys/socket.h>
#include <netinet/in.h>
#include <string.h>
#include <arpa/inet.h>

int main(){
    int clientSocket;
    char str[255];
    struct sockaddr_in client_Address;
    socklen_t address_size;
    clientSocket = socket(AF_INET, SOCK_STREAM, 0);
    client _Address.sin_family = AF_INET;
    client _Address.sin_port = htons(2000);
    client _Address.sin_addr.s_addr = inet_addr("127.0.0.1");
    memset(client _Address.sin_zero, '\0', sizeof
client_Address.sin_zero);
    address_size = sizeof server_Address;
    connect(clientSocket, (struct sockaddr *) &client_Address,
address_size);
    recv(clientSocket, str, 255, 0);
    printf("Data received from server: %s", str);
    return 0;
}
```

Let's go behind the scenes.

How it works...

So, we have defined a string of size `255` and a variable called `client_Address` of type `sockaddr_in`. We will invoke the `socket` function to create a socket by the name of `clientSocket`.

The address family that's supplied for the socket is `AF_INET` and is used for IPv4 internet protocols, and the socket type that's selected is stream socket type. The port number that's specified for the socket is `2000`. By using the `htons` function, the short integer `2000` is converted into the network byte order before being applied as a port number.

We will set the fourth parameter, `sin_zero`, of the `client_Address` structure to `NULL` by invoking the `memset` function. We will initiate the connection to the `clientSocket` by invoking the connect function. By using the `sin_addr` member of the `client_Address` structure, a 32-bit IP address is applied to the socket. Because we are working on the local machine, the localhost address `127.0.0.1` is assigned to the socket. Finally, we will invoke the `recv` function to receive the message from the connected `clientSocket`. The message that's read from the socket will be assigned to the `str` string variable, which will then be displayed on the screen.

Now, press *Alt + F2* to open a second Terminal window. Here, let's use GCC to compile the `clientprog.c` program, as follows:

```
$ gcc clientprog.c -o clientprog
```

If you get no errors or warnings, this means that the `clientprog.c` program has compiled into an executable file, `clientprog.exe`. Let's run this executable file:

```
$ ./clientprog
Data received from server: thanks and good bye
```

Voila! We've successfully communicated between the client and server using socket programming. Now, let's move on to the next recipe!

Communicating between processes using a UDP socket

In this recipe, we will learn how two-way communication is implemented between a client and a server using a UDP socket. This recipe is divided into the following parts:

- Awaiting a message from the client and sending a reply using a UDP socket
- Sending a message to the server and receiving the reply from the server using the UDP socket

Before we begin with these recipes, let's quickly review the functions, structures, and terms that are used in successful interprocess communication using a UDP socket.

Using a UDP socket for server-client communication

In the case of communication with UDP, the client does not establish a connection with the server but simply sends a datagram. The server does not have to accept a connection; it simply waits for datagrams to be sent from the client. Every datagram contains the address of the sender, enabling the server to identify the client on the basis of where the datagram is sent from.

For communication, the UDP server first creates a UDP socket and binds it to the server address. Then, the server waits until the datagram packet arrives from the client. Once it has arrived, the server processes the datagram packet and sends a reply to the client. This procedure keeps on repeating.

On the other hand, the UDP client, for communication, creates a UDP socket, sends a message to the server, and waits for the server's response. The client will keep repeating the procedure if they want to send more messages to the server, otherwise the socket descriptor will close.

bzero()

This places *n* zero-valued bytes in the specified area. Here it its syntax:

```
void bzero(void *r, size_t n);
```

Here, r is the area that's pointed to by r and n is the n number of zero values bytes that are placed in the area that was pointed to by r.

INADDR_ANY

This is an IP address that is used when we don't want to bind a socket to any specific IP. Basically, while implementing communication, we need to bind our socket to an IP address. When we don't know the IP address of our machine, we can use the special IP address INADDR_ANY. It allows our server to receive packets that have been targeted by any of the interfaces.

sendto()

This is used to send a message on the specified socket. The message can be sent in connection mode as well as in connectionless mode. In the case of connectionless mode, the message is sent to the specified address. Here it its syntax:

```
ssize_t sendto(int fdsock, const void *buff, size_t len, int flags,
const struct sockaddr *recv_addr, socklen_t recv_len);
```

Here, we need to address the following:

- `fdsock`: Specifies the file descriptor of the socket.
- `buff`: Points to a buffer that contains the message to be sent.
- `len`: Specifies the length of the message in bytes.
- `flags`: Specifies the type of the message that is being transmitted. Usually, its value is kept as 0.
- `recv_addr`: Points to the `sockaddr` structure that contains the receiver's address. The length and format of the address depends on the address family that's been assigned to the socket.
- `recv_len`: Specifies the length of the `sockaddr` structure that's pointed to by the `recv_addr` argument.

On successful execution, the function returns the number of bytes sent, otherwise it returns −1.

recvfrom()

This is used to receive a message from a connection-mode or connectionless-mode socket. Here it its syntax:

```
ssize_t recvfrom(int fdsock, void *buffer, size_t length, int flags,
struct sockaddr *address, socklen_t *address_len);
```

Here, we need to address the following:

- `fdsock`: Represents the file descriptor of the socket.
- `buffer`: Represents the buffer where the message is stored.
- `length`: Represents the number of bytes of the buffer that are pointed to by the `buffer` parameter.

- `flags`: Represents the type of message that's received.
- `address`: Represents the `sockaddr` structure in which the sending address is stored. The length and format of the address depend on the address family of the socket.
- `address_len`: Represents the length of the `sockaddr` structure that's pointed to by the address parameter.

The function returns the length of the message that's written to the buffer, which is pointed to by the buffer argument.

Now, we can begin with the first part of this recipe: preparing a server to wait for and reply to a message from the client using a UDP socket.

Await a message from the client and sending a reply using a UDP socket

In this part of the recipe, we will learn how a server waits for the message from the client and how, on receiving a message from the client, it replies to the client.

How to do it...

1. Define two variables of type `sockaddr_in`. Invoke the `bzero` function to initialize the structure.
2. Invoke the `socket` function to create a socket. The address family that's supplied for the socket is `AF_INET`, and the socket type that's selected is datagram type.
3. Initialize the members of the `sockaddr_in` structure to configure the socket. The port number that's specified for the socket is `2000`. Use `INADDR_ANY`, a special IP address, to assign an IP address to the socket.
4. Call the `bind` function to assign the address to it.
5. Call the `recvfrom` function to receive the message from the UDP socket, that is, from the client machine. A null character, `\0`, is added to the message that's read from the client machine and is displayed on the screen. Enter the reply that is to be sent to the client.
6. Invoke the `sendto` function to send the reply to the client.

The server program, `udps.c`, for waiting for a message from the client and sending a reply to it using a UDP socket is as follows:

```c
#include <stdio.h>
#include <strings.h>
#include <sys/types.h>
#include <arpa/inet.h>
#include <sys/socket.h>
#include<netinet/in.h>
#include <stdlib.h>

int main()
{
    char msgReceived[255];
    char msgforclient[255];
    int UDPSocket, len;
    struct sockaddr_in server_Address, client_Address;
    bzero(&server_Address, sizeof(server_Address));
    printf("Waiting for the message from the client\n");
    if ( (UDPSocket = socket(AF_INET, SOCK_DGRAM, 0)) < 0 ) {
        perror("Socket could not be created");
        exit(1);
    }
    server_Address.sin_addr.s_addr = htonl(INADDR_ANY);
    server_Address.sin_port = htons(2000);
    server_Address.sin_family = AF_INET;
    if ( bind(UDPSocket, (const struct sockaddr *)&server_Address,
    sizeof(server_Address)) < 0 )
    {
        perror("Binding could not be done");
        exit(1);
    }
    len = sizeof(client_Address);
    int n = recvfrom(UDPSocket, msgReceived, sizeof(msgReceived),  0,
    (struct sockaddr*)&client_Address,&len);
    msgReceived[n] = '\0';
    printf("Message received from the client: ");
    puts(msgReceived);
    printf("Enter the reply to be sent to the client: ");
    gets(msgforclient);
    sendto(UDPSocket, msgforclient, 255, 0, (struct
    sockaddr*)&client_Address, sizeof(client_Address));
    printf("Reply to the client sent \n");
}
```

Let's go behind the scenes.

How it works...

We start by defining two strings by the names of `msgReceived` and `msgforclient`, both of which are of size `255`. These two strings will be used to receive the message from and send a message to the client, respectively. Then, we will define two variables, `server_Address` and `client_Address`, of type `sockaddr_in`. These structures will reference the socket's elements and store the server's and client's addresses, respectively. We will invoke the `bzero` function to initialize the `server_Address` structure, that is, zeros will be filled in for all of the members of the `server_Address` structure.

The server, as expected, waits for the datagram from the client. So, the following text message is displayed on the screen: `Waiting for the message from the client`. We invoke the `socket` function to create a socket by the name of `UDPSocket`. The address family that's supplied for the socket is `AF_INET`, and the socket type that's selected is datagram. The members of the `server_Address` structure are initialized to configure the socket.

Using the `sin_family` member, the address family that's specified for the socket is `AF_INET`, which is used for IPv4 internet protocols. The port number that's specified for the socket is `2000`. Using the `htons` function, the short integer `2000` is converted into the network byte order before being applied as a port number. Then, we use a special IP address, `INADDR_ANY`, to assign an IP address to the socket. Using the `htonl` function, the `INADDR_ANY` will be converted into the network byte order before being applied as the address to the socket.

To enable the created socket, `UDPSocket`, to receive connections, we will call the `bind` function to assign the address to it. We will call the `recvfrom` function to receive the message from the UDP socket, that is, from the client machine. The message that's read from the client machine is assigned to the `msgReceived` string, which is supplied in the `recvfrom` function. A null character, `\0`, is added to the `msgReceived` string and is displayed on the screen. Thereafter, you will be prompted to enter the reply to be sent to the client. The reply that's entered is assigned to `msgforclient`. By invoking the `sendto` function, the reply is sent to the client. After sending the message, the following message is displayed to the screen: `Reply to the client sent`.

Now, let's look at the other part of this recipe.

Sending a message to the server and receiving the reply from the server using the UDP socket

As the name suggests, in this recipe we will show you how the client sends a message to the server and then receives a reply from the server using the UDP socket.

How to do it...

1. Execute the first three steps from the previous part of this recipe. Assign the localhost IP address, 127.0.0.1, as the address to the socket.
2. Enter the message to be sent to the server. Invoke the sendto function to send the message to the server.
3. Invoke the recvfrom function to get the message from the server. The message that's received from the server is then displayed on the screen.
4. Close the descriptor of the socket.

The client program, udpc.c, to send a message to the server and to receive the reply using a UDP socket is as follows:

```c
#include <stdio.h>
#include <strings.h>
#include <sys/types.h>
#include <arpa/inet.h>
#include <sys/socket.h>
#include<netinet/in.h>
#include<unistd.h>
#include<stdlib.h>

int main()
{
    char msgReceived[255];
    char msgforserver[255];
    int UDPSocket, n;
    struct sockaddr_in client_Address;
    printf("Enter the message to send to the server: ");
    gets(msgforserver);
    bzero(&client_Address, sizeof(client_Address));
    client_Address.sin_addr.s_addr = inet_addr("127.0.0.1");
    client_Address.sin_port = htons(2000);
    client_Address.sin_family = AF_INET;
    if ( (UDPSocket = socket(AF_INET, SOCK_DGRAM, 0)) < 0 ) {
```

```
        perror("Socket could not be created");
        exit(1);
    }
    if(connect(UDPSocket, (struct sockaddr *)&client_Address,
    sizeof(client_Address)) < 0)
    {
        printf("\n Error : Connect Failed \n");
        exit(0);
    }
    sendto(UDPSocket, msgforserver, 255, 0, (struct sockaddr*)NULL,
    sizeof(client_Address));
    printf("Message to the server sent. \n");
    recvfrom(UDPSocket, msgReceived, sizeof(msgReceived), 0, (struct
    sockaddr*)NULL, NULL);
    printf("Received from the server: ");
    puts(msgReceived);
    close(UDPSocket);
}
```

Now, let's go behind the scenes.

How it works...

In the first part of this recipe, we have already defined two strings by the names of
`msgReceived` and `msgforclient`, both of which are of size `255`. We have also
defined two variables, `server_Address` and `client_Address`, of type
`sockaddr_in`.

Now, you will be prompted to enter a message that is to be sent to the server. The
message you enter will be assigned to the `msgforserver` string. Then, we will invoke
the `bzero` function to initialize the `client_Address` structure, that is, zeros will be
filled in for all the members of the `client_Address` structure.

Next, we will initialize the members of the `client_Address` structure to configure
the socket. Using the `sin_family` member, the address family that's specified for the
socket is `AF_INET`, which is used for IPv4 internet protocols. The port number that's
specified for the socket is `2000`. By using the `htons` function, the short integer, `2000`,
is converted into the network byte order before being applied as a port number. Then,
we will assign the localhost IP address, `127.0.0.1`, as the address to the socket. We
will invoke the `inet_addr` function on the localhost address to convert the string
containing the address in standard IPv4 dotted decimal notation into an integer value
(suitable to be used as an internet address) before is it applied to the `sin_addr`
member of the `client_Address` structure.

We will invoke the `socket` function to create a socket by the name of `UDPSocket`. The address family that's supplied for the socket is `AF_INET`, and the socket type that's selected is datagram.

Next, we will invoke the `sendto` function to send the message that's been assigned to the `msgforserver` string to the server. Similarly, we will invoke the `recvfrom` function to get the message from the server. The message that's received from the server is assigned to the `msgReceived` string, which is then displayed on the screen. Finally, the descriptor of the socket is closed.

Let's use GCC to compile the `udps.c` program, as follows:

```
$ gcc udps.c -o udps
```

If you get no errors or warnings, this means that the `udps.c` program has compiled into an executable file, `udps.exe`. Let's run this executable file:

```
$ ./udps
Waiting for the message from the client
```

Now, press *Alt + F2* to open a second Terminal window. Here, let's use GCC again to compile the `udpc.c` program, as follows:

```
$ gcc udpc.c -o udpc
```

If you get no errors or warnings, this means that the `udpc.c` program has compiled into an executable file, `udpc.exe`. Let's run this executable file:

```
$ ./udpc
Enter the message to send to the server: Will it rain today?
Message to the server sent.
```

The output on the server will give us the following output:

```
Message received from the client: Will it rain today?
Enter the reply to be sent to the client: It might
Reply to the client sent
```

Once the reply is sent from the server, on the client window, you will get the following output:

```
Received from the server: It might
```

To run the recipes that demonstrate IPC using shared memory and message queue, we need to run Cygserver. If you are running these programs on Linux, then you can skip this section. Let's see how Cygserver is run.

Running Cygserver

Before executing the command to run the Cygwin server, we need to configure Cygserver and install it as a service. To do so, you need to run the `cygserver.conf` script on the Terminal. The following is the output you get by running the script:

```
$ ./bin/cygserver-config
Generating /etc/cygserver.conf file
Warning: The following function requires administrator privileges!
Do you want to install cygserver as service? yes

The service has been installed under LocalSystem account.
To start it, call `net start cygserver' or `cygrunsrv -S cygserver'.

Further configuration options are available by editing the
configuration
file /etc/cygserver.conf. Please read the inline information in that
file carefully. The best option for the start is to just leave it
alone.

Basic Cygserver configuration finished. Have fun!
```

Now, Cygserver will have been configured and installed as a service. The next step is to run the server. To run Cygserver, you need to use the following command:

```
$ net start cygserver
The CYGWIN cygserver service is starting.
The CYGWIN cygserver service was started successfully.
```

Now that Cygserver is running, we can make a recipe to demonstrate IPC using shared memory and message queues.

Passing a message from one process to another using the message queue

In this recipe, we will learn how communication between two processes is established using the message queue. This recipe is divided into the following parts:

- Writing a message into the message queue
- Reading a message from the message queue

Before we begin with these recipes, let's quickly review the functions, structures, and terms that are used in successful interprocess communication using shared memory and message queues.

Functions used in IPC using shared memory and message queues

The most commonly used functions and terms for IPC using shared memory and message queues are `ftok`, `shmget`, `shmat`, `shmdt`, `shmctl`, `msgget`, `msgrcv`, and `msgsnd`.

ftok()

This generates an IPC key on the basis of the supplied filename and ID. The filename can be provided along with its complete path. The filename must refer to an existing file. Here is the syntax:

```
key_t ftok(const char *filename, int id);
```

The `ftok` function will generate the same key value if the same filename (with same path) and the same ID is supplied. Upon successful completion, `ftok` will return a key, otherwise it will return −1.

shmget()

This allocates a shared memory segment and returns the shared memory identifier that's associated with the key. Here is its syntax:

```
int shmget(key_t key, size_t size, int shmflg);
```

Here, we need to address the following:

- `key`: This is (usually) the value that is returned by invoking the `ftok` function. You can also set the value of the key as `IPC_PRIVATE` if you don't want the shared memory to be accessed by other processes.
- `size`: Represents the size of the desired shared memory segment.

- `shmflg`: This can be any of the following constants:
    - `IPC_CREAT`: This creates a new segment if no shared memory identifier exists for the specified key. If this flag is not used, the function returns the shared memory segment associated with the key.
    - `IPC_EXCL`: This makes the `shmget` function fail if the segment already exists with the specified key.

On successful execution, the function returns the shared memory identifier in the form of a non-negative integer, otherwise it returns -1.

shmat()

This is used to attach a shared memory segment to the given address space. That is, the shared memory identifier that's received by invoking the `shmgt` function needs to be associated with the address space of a process. Here is its syntax:

```
void *shmat(int shidtfr, const void *addr, int flag);
```

Here, we need to address the following:

- `shidtfr`: Represents the memory identifier of the shared memory segment.
- `addr`: Represents the address space where the segment needs to be attached. If `shmaddr` is a null pointer, the segment is attached at the first available address or selected by the system.
- `flag`: This is attached as a read-only memory if the flag is `SHM_RDONLY`; otherwise, it is readable and writable.

If successfully executed, the function attaches the shared memory segment and returns the segment's start address, otherwise it returns -1.

shmdt()

This detaches the shared memory segment. Here is its syntax:

```
int shmdt(const void *addr);
```

Here, `addr` represents the address at which the shared memory segment is located.

shmctl()

This is used for performing certain control operations on the specified shared memory segment. Here is its syntax:

```
int shmctl(int shidtr, int cmd, struct shmid_ds *buf);
```

Here, we have to address the following:

- shidtr: Represents the identifier of the shared memory segment.
- cmd: This can have any of the following constants:
    - IPC_STAT: This copies the content of the shmid_ds data structure associated with the shared memory segment represented by shidtr into the structure that's pointed to by buf
    - IPC_SET: This writes the content of the structure that's pointed to by buf into the shmid_ds data structure, which is associated with the memory segment that's represented by shidtr
    - IPC_RMID: This removes the shared memory identifier that's specified by shidtr from the system and destroys the shared memory segment and shmid_ds data structure associated with it
- buf: This is a pointer to a shmid_ds structure.

If successfully executed, the function returns 0, otherwise it returns -1.

msgget()

This is used for creating a new message queue, and for accessing an existing queue that is related to the specified key. If this is executed successfully, the function returns the identifier of the message queue:

```
int msgget(key_t key, int flag);
```

Here, we have to address the following:

- key: This is a unique key value that is retrieved by invoking the ftok function.
- flag: This can be any of the following constants:
  - IPC_CREAT: Creates the message queue if it doesn't already exist and returns the message queue identifier for the newly created message queue. If the message queue already exists with the supplied key value, it returns its identifier.
  - IPC_EXCL: If both IPC_CREAT and IPC_EXCL are specified and the message queue does not exist, then it is created. However, if it already exists, then the function will fail.

msgrcv()

This is used for reading a message from a specified message queue whose identifier is supplied. Here is its syntax:

```
int msgrcv(int msqid, void *msgstruc, int msgsize, long typemsg, int
flag);
```

Here, we have to address the following:

- msqid: Represents the message queue identifier of the queue from which the message needs to be read.
- msgstruc: This is the user-defined structure into which the read message is placed. The user-defined structure must contain two members. One is usually named mtype, which must be of type long int that specifies the type of the message, and the second is usually called mesg, which should be of char type to store the message.
- msgsize: Represents the size of text to be read from the message queue in terms of bytes. If the message that is read is larger than msgsize, then it will be truncated to msgsize bytes.
- typemsg: Specifies which message on the queue needs to be received:
  - If typemsg is 0, the first message on the queue is received
  - If typemsg is greater than 0, the first message whose mtype field is equal to typemsg is received
  - If typemsg is less than 0, a message whose mtype field is less than or equal to typemsg is received

- `flag`: Determines the action to be taken if the desired message is not found in the queue. It keeps its value of 0 if you don't want to specify the `flag`. The `flag` can have any of the following values:
  - `IPC_NOWAIT`: This makes the `msgrcv` function fail if there is no desired message in the queue, that is, it will not make the caller wait for the appropriate message on the queue. If `flag` is not set to `IPC_NOWAIT,` it will make the caller wait for an appropriate message on the queue instead of failing the function.
  - `MSG_NOERROR`: This allows you to receive text that is larger than the size that's specified in the `msgsize` argument. It simply truncates the text and receives it. If this `flag` is not set, on receiving the larger text, the function will not receive it and will fail the function.

If the function is executed successfully, the function returns the number of bytes that were actually placed into the text field of the structure that is pointed to by `msgstruc`. On failure, the function returns a value of −1.

msgsnd()

This is used for sending or delivering a message to the queue. Here is its syntax:

```
int msgsnd ( int msqid, struct msgbuf *msgstruc, int msgsize, int
flag );
```

Here, we have to address the following:

- `msqid`: Represents the queue identifier of the message that we want to send. The queue identifier is usually retrieved by invoking the `msgget` function.
- `msgstruc`: This is a pointer to the user-defined structure. It is the `mesg` member that contains the message that we want to send to the queue.

- `msgsize`: Represents the size of the message in bytes.
- `flag`: Determines the action to be taken on the message. If the `flag` value is set to `IPC_NOWAIT` and if the message queue is full, the message will not be written to the queue, and the control is returned to the calling process. But if `flag` is not set and the message queue is full, then the calling process will suspend until a space becomes available in the queue. Usually, the value of `flag` is set to 0.

If this is executed successfully, the function returns 0, otherwise it returns −1.

We will now begin with the first part of this recipe: writing a message into the queue.

Writing a message into the message queue

In this part of the recipe, we will learn how a server writes a desired message into the message queue.

How to do it...

1. Generate an IPC key by invoking the `ftok` function. A filename and ID are supplied while creating the IPC key.
2. Invoke the `msgget` function to create a new message queue. The message queue is associated with the IPC key that was created in step 1.
3. Define a structure with two members, `mtype` and `mesg`. Set the value of the `mtype` member to 1.
4. Enter the message that's going to be added to the message queue. The string that's entered is assigned to the `mesg` member of the structure that we defined in step 3.
5. Invoke the `msgsnd` function to send the entered message into the message queue.

The `messageqsend.c` program for writing the message to the message queue is as follows:

```
#include <sys/types.h>
#include <sys/ipc.h>
#include <sys/msg.h>
#include <stdio.h>
#include <string.h>
#include <stdlib.h>
```

```
#define MSGSIZE     255

struct msgstruc {
    long mtype;
    char mesg[MSGSIZE];
};

int main()
{
    int msqid, msglen;
    key_t key;
    struct msgstruc msgbuf;
    system("touch messagefile");
    if ((key = ftok("messagefile", 'a')) == -1) {
        perror("ftok");
        exit(1);
    }
    if ((msqid = msgget(key, 0666 | IPC_CREAT)) == -1) {
        perror("msgget");
        exit(1);
    }
    msgbuf.mtype = 1;
    printf("Enter a message to add to message queue : ");
    scanf("%s",msgbuf.mesg);
    msglen = strlen(msgbuf.mesg);
    if (msgsnd(msqid, &msgbuf, msglen, IPC_NOWAIT) < 0)
        perror("msgsnd");
    printf("The message sent is %s\n", msgbuf.mesg);
    return 0;
}
```

Let's go behind the scenes.

How it works...

We will start by generating an IPC key by invoking the `ftok` function. The filename and ID are supplied while creating the IPC key are `messagefile` and a, respectively. The generated key is assigned to the key variable. Thereafter, we will invoke the `msgget` function to create a new message queue. The message queue is associated with the IPC key we just created using the `ftok` function.

Next, we will define a structure by the name of `msgstruc` with two members, `mtype` and `mesg`. The `mtype` member helps in determining the sequence number of the message that is going to be sent or received from the message queue. The `mesg` member contains the message that is going to be read or written into the message queue. We will define a variable called `msgbuf` of the `msgstruc` structure type. The value of the `mtype` member is set to `1`.

You will be prompted to enter the message that is going to be added to the message queue. The string you enter is assigned to the `mesg` member of the `msgbuf` structure. The `msgsnd` function is invoked to send the message you entered into the message queue. Once the message is written into the message queue, a text message is displayed on the screen as confirmation.

Now, let's move on to the other part of this recipe.

Reading a message from the message queue

In this part of the recipe, we will learn how the message that was written into the message queue is read and displayed on the screen.

How to do it...

1. Invoke the `ftok` function to generate an IPC key. The filename and ID are supplied while creating the IPC key. These must be the same as what were applied while generating the key for writing the message in the message queue.
2. Invoke the `msgget` function to access the message queue that is associated with the IPC key. The message queue that's associated with this key already contains a message that we wrote through the previous program.
3. Define a structure with two members, `mtype` and `mesg`.
4. Invoke the `msgrcv` function to read the message from the associated message queue. The structure that was defined in Step 3 is passed to this function.
5. The read message is then displayed on the screen.

The `messageqrecv.c` program for reading a message from the message queue is as follows:

```
#include <sys/types.h>
#include <sys/ipc.h>
#include <sys/msg.h>
#include <stdio.h>
#include <stdlib.h>
#define MSGSIZE      255

struct msgstruc {
    long mtype;
    char mesg[MSGSIZE];
};

int main()
{
    int msqid;
    key_t key;
    struct msgstruc rcvbuffer;

    if ((key = ftok("messagefile", 'a')) == -1) {
        perror("ftok");
        exit(1);
    }
    if ((msqid = msgget(key, 0666)) < 0)
    {
        perror("msgget");
        exit(1);
    }
    if (msgrcv(msqid, &rcvbuffer, MSGSIZE, 1, 0) < 0)
    {
        perror("msgrcv");
        exit(1);
    }
    printf("The message received is %s\n", rcvbuffer.mesg);
    return 0;
}
```

Let's go behind the scenes.

How it works...

First, we will invoke the `ftok` function to generate an IPC key. The filename and ID that are supplied while creating the IPC key are `messagefile` and `a`, respectively. These filenames and ID must be the same as the ones that were applied while generating the key for writing the message in the message queue. The generated key is assigned to the key variable.

Thereafter, we will invoke the `msgget` function to access the message queue that is associated with the IPC key. The identifier of the accessed message queue is assigned to the `msqid` variable. The message queue that's associated with this key already contains the message that we wrote in the previous program.

Then, we will define a structure by the name `msgstruc` with two members, `mtype` and `mesg`. The `mtype` member is for determining the sequence number of the message to be read from the message queue. The `mesg` member will be used for storing the message that is read from the message queue. We will then define a variable called `rcvbuffer` of the `msgstruc` structure type. We will invoke the `msgrcv` function to read the message from the associated message queue.

The message identifier, `msqid`, is passed to the function, along with the `rcvbuffer` – the structure whose `mesg` member will store the read message. After successful execution of the `msgrcv` function, the `mesg` member of the `rcvbuffer` containing the message from the message queue will be displayed on screen.

Let's use GCC to compile the `messageqsend.c` program, as follows:

```
$ gcc messageqsend.c -o messageqsend
```

If you get no errors or warnings, this means that the `messageqsend.c` program has compiled into an executable file, `messageqsend.exe`. Let's run this executable file:

```
$ ./messageqsend
Enter a message to add to message queue : GoodBye
The message sent is GoodBye
```

Now, press *Alt* + *F2* to open a second Terminal screen. On this screen, you can compile and run the script for reading the message from the message queue.

Let's use GCC to compile the `messageqrecv.c` program, as follows:

```
$ gcc messageqrecv.c -o messageqrecv
```

If you get no errors or warnings, this means that the `messageqrecv.c` program has compiled into an executable file, `messageqrecv.exe`. Let's run this executable file:

```
$ ./messageqrecv
The message received is GoodBye
```

Voila! We've successfully passed a message from one process to another using the message queue. Let's move on to the next recipe!

Communicating between processes using shared memory

In this recipe, we will learn how communication between two processes is established using shared memory. This recipe is divided into the following parts:

- Writing a message into shared memory
- Reading a message from shared memory

We will start with the first one, that is, *Writing a message into shared memory*. The functions we learned in the previous recipe will also be applicable here.

Writing a message into shared memory

In this part of this recipe, we will learn how a message is written into shared memory.

How to do it...

1. Invoke the `ftok` function to generate an IPC key by supplying a filename and an ID.
2. Invoke the `shmget` function to allocate a shared memory segment that is associated with the key that was generated in step 1.
3. The size that's specified for the desired memory segment is `1024`. Create a new memory segment with read and write permissions.
4. Attach the shared memory segment to the first available address in the system.
5. Enter a string that is then assigned to the shared memory segment.
6. The attached memory segment will be detached from the address space.

The `writememory.c` program for writing data into the shared memory is as follows:

```c
#include <stdio.h>
#include <sys/ipc.h>
#include <sys/shm.h>
#include <stdio.h>
#include <stdlib.h>

int main()
{
    char *str;
    int shmid;

    key_t key = ftok("sharedmem",'a');
    if ((shmid = shmget(key, 1024,0666|IPC_CREAT)) < 0) {
        perror("shmget");
        exit(1);
    }
    if ((str = shmat(shmid, NULL, 0)) == (char *) -1) {
        perror("shmat");
        exit(1);
    }
    printf("Enter the string to be written in memory : ");
    gets(str);
    printf("String written in memory: %s\n",str);
    shmdt(str);
    return 0;
}
```

Let's go behind the scenes.

How it works...

By invoking the `ftok` function, we generate an IPC key with the filename `sharedmem` (you can change this) and an ID of `a`. The generated key is assigned to the key variable. Thereafter, invoke the `shmget` function to allocate a shared memory segment that is associated with the supplied key generated using the `ftok` function.

The size that's specified for the desired memory segment is `1024`. Create a new memory segment with read and write permissions and assign the shared memory identifier to the `shmid` variable. Then, attach the shared memory segment to the first available address in the system.

Once the memory segment is attached to the address space, the segment's start address is assigned to the `str` variable. You will be asked to enter a string. The string you enter will be assigned to the shared memory segment through the `str` variable. Finally, the attached memory segment is detached from the address space.

Let's move on to the next part of this recipe, *Reading a message from shared memory*.

Reading a message from shared memory

In this part of the recipe, we will learn how the message that was written into shared memory is read and displayed on screen.

How to do it...

1. Invoke the `ftok` function to generate an IPC key. The filename and ID that are supplied should be the same as those in the program for writing content into shared memory.
2. Invoke the `shmget` function to allocate a shared memory segment. The size that's specified for the allocated memory segment is `1024` and is associated with the IPC key that was generated in step 1. Create the memory segment with read and write permissions.
3. Attach the shared memory segment to the first available address in the system.
4. The content from the shared memory segment is read and displayed on screen.
5. The attached memory segment is detached from the address space.
6. The shared memory identifier is removed from the system, followed by destroying the shared memory segment.

The `readmemory.c` program for reading data from shared memory is as follows:

```c
#include <stdio.h>
#include <sys/ipc.h>
#include <sys/shm.h>
#include <stdio.h>
#include <stdlib.h>

int main()
{
    int shmid;
```

```
    char * str;
    key_t key = ftok("sharedmem",'a');
    if ((shmid = shmget(key, 1024,0666|IPC_CREAT)) < 0) {
        perror("shmget");
        exit(1);
    }
    if ((str = shmat(shmid, NULL, 0)) == (char *) -1) {
        perror("shmat");
        exit(1);
    }
    printf("Data read from memory: %s\n",str);
    shmdt(str);
    shmctl(shmid,IPC_RMID,NULL);
    return 0;
}
```

Let's go behind the scenes.

How it works...

We will invoke the `ftok` function to generate an IPC key. The filename and ID that are supplied for generating the key are `sharedmem` (any name) and `a`, respectively. The generated key is assigned to the `key` variable. Thereafter, we will invoke the `shmget` function to allocate a shared memory segment. The size that's specified for the allocated memory segment is `1024` and is associated with the IPC key that was generated earlier.

We will create the new memory segment with read and write permissions and assign the fetched shared memory identifier to the `shmid` variable. The shared memory segment is then attached to the first available address in the system. This is done so that we can access the text that was written in the shared memory segment through the previous program.

So, after the memory segment is attached to the address space, the segment's start address is assigned to the `str` variable. Now, we can read the content that's been written in the shared memory through the previous program in the current program. The content from the shared memory segment is read through the `str` string and displayed on screen.

Thereafter, the attached memory segment is detached from the address space. Finally, the shared memory identifier `shmid` is removed from the system and the shared memory segment is destroyed.

Let's use GCC to compile the `writememory.c` program, as follows:

```
$ gcc writememory.c -o writememory
```

If you get no errors or warnings, this means that the `writememory.c` program has compiled into an executable file, `writememory.exe`. Let's run this executable file:

```
$ ./writememory
Enter the string to be written in memory : Today it might rain
String written in memory: Today it might rain
```

Now, press *Alt* + *F2* to open a second Terminal window. In this window, let's use GCC to compile the `readmemory.c` program, as follows:

```
$ gcc readmemory.c -o readmemory
```

If you get no errors or warnings, this means that the `readmemory.c` program has compiled into an executable file, `readmemory.exe`. Let's run this executable file:

```
$ ./readmemory
 Data read from memory: Today it might rain
```

Voila! We've successfully communicated between processes using shared memory.

Sorting and Searching

9

Searching, as the name suggests, is the process of locating a specific element in a group of elements. Searching can be broadly classified as one of the following two types:

- **Linear searching**: Where each element in the list is sequentially searched to find the desired item.
- **Binary search**: Where the list is assumed to already be sorted, and the middle value of the list is compared with the item to be searched to determine which half of the list needs to be considered for searching the item. The process of dividing the list continues until the item is found.

Sorting, on the other hand, is the procedure of arranging certain elements in a certain order. The order can be ascending, descending, or in another specific order. Not only can the individual numerals and strings be sorted, but even records can be sorted. Records are sorted on the basis of some key that is unique to every record. These are the two main categories of sorting:

- **Internal sorting**: Where all the elements that are being sorted are uploaded together in the primary memory
- **External sorting**: Where some elements to be sorted are uploaded to the primary memory, and the rest are kept in auxiliary memory, such as on a hard disk or pen drive

To be able to conduct effective searches, we need to know how to sort data. Sorting is essential because it makes the task of searching quite easy and fast.

In this chapter, you will learn the following recipes:

- Searching for an item using binary search
- Arranging numbers in ascending order using bubble sort

- Arranging numbers in ascending order using insertion sort
- Arranging numbers in ascending order using quick sort
- Arranging numbers in descending order using heap sort

Let's begin with the first recipe!

Searching for an item using binary search

Binary search uses the *divide and conquer* approach. The item to be searched for is compared with the middle item in an array or file. This helps in determining which half of the array or file might contain the item being searched for. After that, the middle value of the half that was considered is compared with the item being searched for to determine which quarter part of the array or file might contain the item being searched for. The process continues until either the item being searched for is found, or no more divisions of the array or file are possible, in which case, it is understood that the item being searched for is not present in the file or array.

How to do it...

Consider an array is arr of size len elements. We want to search for a number, numb, in this array, arr. Here are the steps to search for numb in the arr array using binary search:

1. Initialize two variables, lower and upper.
2. Calculate the middle location of the array.
3. If the value to search, numb, is found at location arr[mid] then display Value found and exit (that is, jump to *step 8*).
4. If your search value is larger than the array's middle value, confine the search to the lower half of the array. So, set the lower limit of the array to the array's middle value.
5. If your search value is smaller than the array's middle value, confine the search to the upper half of the array. So, set the upper limit of the array to the array's middle value.
6. Repeat *steps 3* through *5* as long as upper>=lower.

7. The execution will proceed with this step only if the value is not found. Then display `Value not found` and exit.
8. Exit.

The program for searching for an element in a sorted array using the binary search technique is as follows:

```c
//binarysearch.c

#include <stdio.h>

#define max 20
int binary_search(int[], int, int);

int main() {
  int len, found, numb, arr[max], i;
  printf("Enter the length of an array: ");
  scanf("%d", & len);
  printf("Enter %d values in sorted order \n", len);
  for (i = 0; i < len; i++)
    scanf("%d", & arr[i]);
  printf("Enter the value to search ");
  scanf("%d", & numb);
  found = binary_search(arr, numb, len);
  if (found == numb)
    printf("Value %d is found in the list\n", numb);
  else
    printf("Value %d is not found in the list \n", numb);
  return 0;
}

int binary_search(int arr[], int pnumb, int plen) {
  int lindex = 0, mid, uindex = plen - 1, nfound;
  while (uindex >= lindex) {
    mid = (uindex + lindex) / 2;
    if (pnumb == arr[mid]) {
      nfound = arr[mid];
      break;
    } else {
      if (pnumb > arr[mid])
        lindex = mid + 1;
      else
        uindex = mid - 1;
    }
  }
  return (nfound);
}
```

Now, let's go behind the scenes to understand the code better.

How it works...

Let's define a macro called `max` of size 20 and an array, `arr`, of size `max`, that is, 20 elements (you can increase the value of the `max` macro to any larger value as desired). Next, we will specify the length of the array. Let's say that the length you entered is 8, which is then assigned to the `len` variable. When prompted, enter the specified number of sorted elements. The sorted elements you enter will be assigned to the `arr` array, as follows:

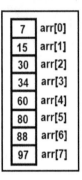

Figure 9.1

Then, you will be prompted to enter the number you want to search for in the sorted array. Let's say you picked 45; this number will be assigned to the `numb` variable. We will invoke the `binary_search` function and all three items – the `arr` array, the `numb` variable containing the number to search for, and the length of the array in `len` – are passed to the function. The `arr`, `numb`, and `len` arguments will be assigned to the `arr`, `pnumb`, and `plen` parameters respectively.

In the `binary_search` function, we will initialize two variables: `lindex` to 0 and `uindex` to 7, that is, equal to the length of the array; these two indexes represent the lower and upper index locations of the array respectively. Because arrays are zero-based, the eighth element of the array will be found at index location 7. We'll set a `while` loop to execute for as long as the value of `uindex` is greater than or equal to the value of `lindex`.

To compare the search value with the middle value of the array, we will first compute the middle value; sum the values of `lindex` and `uindex`, and divide the result by 2. The output of (0+7)/2 is 3. Then, compare the value of the `numb` variable, that is, 45, with the value at location `arr[3]`, derived from your computation, that is, with 34 (see *Figure 9.2*):

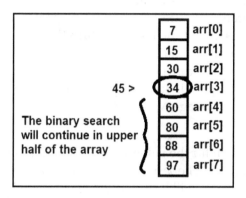

Figure 9.2

Because 45 is greater than 34, we will have to continue our search in the lower half of the array. However, since our list is sorted in ascending order, we can now concentrate our search in the lower half of the array.

Now, the value of `lindex` is set equal to `mid+1`, that is, 4. Again, execute the `while` loop because `uindex`, that is, 7, is still greater than `lindex`. We will now compute the middle value of the upper half of the array: (4+7)/2 = 5. The search value 45 will be compared with `arr[5]`, that is, with 80. Because 45 is smaller than 80, we will continue our search in the lower half of the array, as follows:

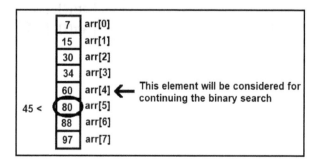

Figure 9.3

Next, the value of `uindex` is set equal to `mid-1`, that is, equal to 4. And the value of `lindex` from our previous computation is also 4. We will again execute the `while` loop because 4=4. The middle value of the array will be computed as (4+4)/2, that is, the search value 45 will be compared with `arr[4]`, which is 60.

Because 45 < 60, the value of `uindex` will be set to `mid-1`, that is, equal to 3. The `while` loop will exit because our `uindex` (3) is not greater than our `lindex` (4) any more. The `binary_search` function will return the `nfound` variable to the `main` function. The `nfound` variable contains some garbage value, which is then assigned to the `found` variable in the `main` function. In the `main` function, the values in the `found` and `numb` variables are compared. Because the garbage value is not equal to the value in the `numb` variable, 45, a message, `Value 45 is not found in the list` will be displayed on the screen.

Suppose you want to search for the value 15 now. The values of `lindex` and `uindex` will again be 0 and 7 initially. The `while` loop will execute and the middle value will be computed as (0+7)/2, which will be 3. The value of 15 will be compared with the corresponding location, `arr[3]`, that is, with 34. The value of 15 is smaller than 34, so the upper half of the array will be considered to continue the binary search, as shown in the following figure:

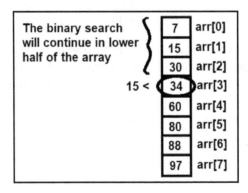

Figure 9.4

The value of the uindex variable is set equal to mid−1, that is, 2. Because uindex is still greater than lindex, that is, 2 >=0, the while loop will execute again. Again, the middle value is computed as (0+2)/2, which is 1. This means that 15 is compared with the arr[1] element.

The value at the arr[1] location is 15 only; hence, the nfound variable is set to 15 in the binary_search function and the nfound variable is returned to the main function. In the main function, the value of the nfound variable will be assigned to the found variable. Because the value in the found and numb variables are the same, the message Value 15 is found in the list will be displayed onscreen.

The program is compiled using GCC, as shown in the following screenshot. Because no error appears on compilation, that means the binarysearch.c program has successfully been compiled into an EXE file, that is, to the binarysearch.exe file. On executing the executable file, if we try searching for a value that is not found in the list, we get the following output:

```
D:\CAdvBook>gcc binarysearch.c -o binarysearch

D:\CAdvBook>binarysearch
Enter the length of an array: 8
Enter 8 values in sorted order
7
15
30
34
60
80
88
97
Enter the value to search 45
Value 45 is not found in the list
```

Figure 9.5

If we run the executable file again and enter a number that exists in the array, we may get the following output:

```
D:\CAdvBook>binarysearch
Enter the length of an array: 8
Enter 8 values in sorted order
7
15
30
34
60
80
88
97
Enter the value to search 15
Value 15 is found in the list
```

Figure 9.6

Voilà! We've successfully used binary search to locate an item in a sorted array. Now let's move on to the next recipe!

Arranging numbers in ascending order using bubble sort

In this recipe, we will learn how to arrange some integers in ascending order using the bubble sort technique. In this technique, the first element is compared with the second, the second is compared with the third, the third with the fourth, and so on.

How to do it...

Consider an array, arr, of size len elements. We want to arrange elements of the arr array in ascending order. Here are the steps to do so:

1. Initialize a variable, say i, to len −2.
2. Follow and repeat *steps 3* through *5* as long as i >=1. The value of i will be decremented by 1 after every iteration, that is, i=len−2, len−3, len−4, ...1.

3. Initialize another variable, j, to 0.

4. Repeat *step 5* to j<=i. The value of j will increase after every iteration, that is, j=1, 2 . . . i.

5. If arr[j] > arr[j+1], then interchange the two values.

6. Exit the search.

The program for sorting elements of an integer array using the bubble sort technique is as follows:

```
//bubblesort.c

#include <stdio.h>

#define max 20
int main() {
  int arr[max], temp, len, i, j;
  printf("How many values are there? ");
  scanf("%d", & len);
  printf("Enter %d values to sort\n", len);
  for (i = 0; i < len; i++)
    scanf("%d", & arr[i]);
  for (i = len - 2; i >= 1; i--) {
    for (j = 0; j <= i; j++) {
      if (arr[j] > arr[j + 1]) {
        temp = arr[j];
        arr[j] = arr[j + 1];
        arr[j + 1] = temp;
      }
    }
  }
  printf("The sorted array is:\n");
  for (i = 0; i < len; i++)
    printf("%d\n", arr[i]);
  return 0;
}
```

Now, let's go behind the scenes to understand the code better.

How it works...

We will start by defining a macro, max, of value 20. You can always increase the value of max as required. Then, we will define an array, arr, of size max, that is, of size 20. You will be asked how many values you want to sort. Assuming that you want to sort seven elements, the value you entered will be assigned to the len variable. You will be prompted to enter the values to be sorted, which will then be assigned to the arr array. The seven values to be sorted in the arr array might appear as follows:

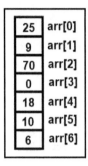

Figure 9.7

Now, we will run two nested for loops: the outer for loop will execute from len-2, that is, from value 5 to 1 in descending order, and the inner for loop will execute for the value from 0 to i. That means, in the first iteration, the value of i will be 5, so the inner for j loop will execute from 0 to 5. Within the inner for loop, the first value of arr will be compared with the second, the second value with the third, and so on:

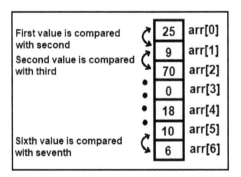

Figure 9.8

The tendency is to keep the value at the lower index smaller than the value at the higher index. If the first value is larger than the second, they will change places; and if the first value is already smaller than the second value, then the next two values in line, that is, the second and third values, are taken for consideration. Similarly, if the second value is larger than the third, they too will swap places; if not, then the next set of values, that is, the third and fourth values, will be compared. The process will continue until the last pair, that is, the sixth and seventh values in our case, are compared.

The entire first iteration of comparisons is illustrated as follows:

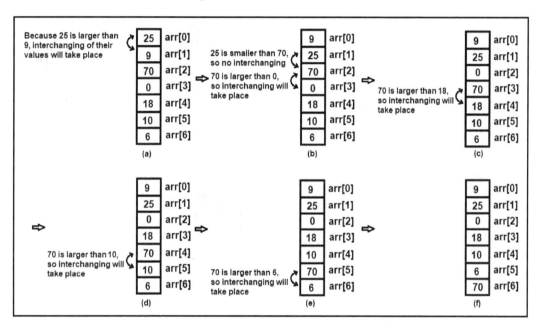

Figure 9.9

You can see that after the first iteration, the largest value has bubbled down to the bottom of the list. Now, the value of the outer loop, that is, the value of i will be decremented by 1, making it 4. Consequently, the value of j in the inner loop will make the for loop run from value 0 to 4. It also means that now, the first value will be compared with the second, the second with the third, and so on. Finally, the fifth value (that is, the value at index location 4) will be compared with the sixth value (that is, the value at index location 5). The last element at index location 6 will not be compared as it is already at its correct destination:

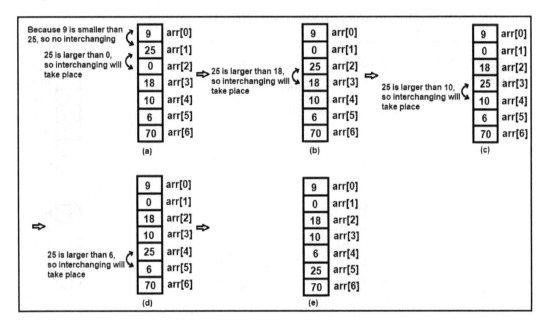

Figure 9.10

Again, after the second iteration, the value of the outer loop will be decremented by 1, making it 3. As a result, the value of j in the inner loop will make the for loop run from value 0 to 3. In the last, the fourth value, that is, the value at index location 3, will be compared with the fifth value. The last two elements at index location 5 and 6 are not compared as both are at their correct destination:

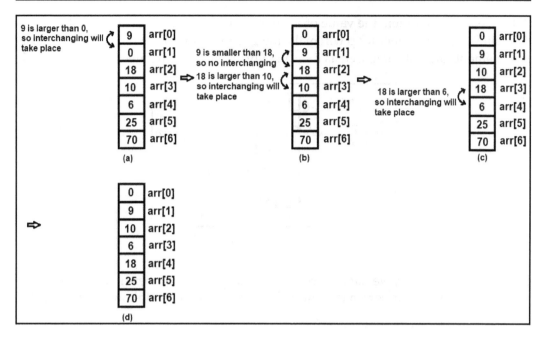

Figure 9.11

After the third iteration, the value of i will be decremented by 1, making it 2. Hence, the value of j will make the for loop run from value 0 to 2. The last three elements at index location 4, 5, and 6 are not compared as they already are at their correct destination:

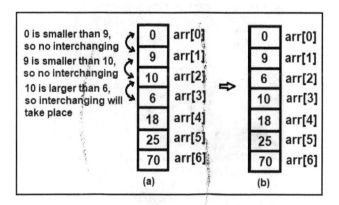

Figure 9.12

After the fourth iteration, the value of i will be decremented again, making it 1. So, the value of j in the inner loop will make the for loop run from value 0 to 1. The last four elements are not compared as they already are at their final destination:

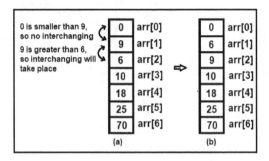

Figure 9.13

So, after five iterations, we have successfully arranged the numbers in our array in ascending order. The program is compiled using GCC with the following statement:

```
gcc bubblesort.c -o bubblesort
```

Because no error appears on compilation, that means the bubblesort.c program has successfully been compiled into the bubblesort.exe file. On executing this file, it will ask us to specify how many numbers there are to be sorted. Then the program will prompt us to enter the numbers to be sorted. After entering the numbers, they will appear sorted in ascending order, as shown in the following screenshot:

```
D:\CAdvBook>gcc bubblesort.c -o bubblesort

D:\CAdvBook>bubblesort
How many values are there? 7
Enter 7 values to sort
25
9
70
0
18
10
6
The sorted array is:
0
6
9
10
18
25
70
```

Figure 9.14

Voilà! We've successfully used the bubble sort technique to arrange numbers in ascending order.

Now let's move on to the next recipe!

Arranging numbers in ascending order using insertion sort

In this sorting technique, a region of the array, which might be the lower or upper part, is considered as sorted. An element outside the sorted region is picked up and its appropriate place is searched for in the sorted region (so that even after the insertion of this element, the region remains sorted) and the element is inserted there, hence the name insertion sort.

How to do it...

We will create a function for insertion sort called InsertionSort, which we will invoke as follows, where arr is the array to be sorted and consists of n number of elements.

Here are the steps that are followed in the InsertionSort method:

1. Initialize a variable, say i, to 1.
2. Repeat steps 2 to 5 n-1 times, that is, while i >= n 1. The value of i is incremented by 1 after every iteration, i=1,2,3 .... n-1.
3. Initialize a variable, j, to the value of i.
4. Repeat the following step 5 for j=i to j >=0. The value of j is decremented by 1 after every iteration, that is, j=i, i-1, i-2, ...0.
5. If arr[j] <arr[j-1], then interchange the values.

The program for sorting the elements of an integer array using the insertion sort technique is as follows:

```c
//insertionsort.c

#include <stdio.h>

#define max 20

int main() {
  int arr[max], i, j, temp, len;
  printf("How many numbers are there ? ");
  scanf("%d", & len);
  printf("Enter %d values to sort\n", len);
  for (i = 0; i < len; i++)
    scanf("%d", & arr[i]);
  for (i = 1; i < len; i++) {
    for (j = i; j > 0; j--) {
      if (arr[j] < arr[j - 1]) {
        temp = arr[j];
        arr[j] = arr[j - 1];
        arr[j - 1] = temp;
      }
    }
  }
  printf("\nThe ascending order of the values entered is:\n");
  for (i = 0; i < len; i++)
    printf("%d\n", arr[i]);
  return 0;
}
```

Now, let's go behind the scenes to understand the code better.

How it works...

Let's assume that the numbers that we need to sort are not greater than 20; so we will define a macro of size 20. You can always assign any value to this macro. Next, we will define an integer array, arr, of size max. You will be prompted to enter how many numbers you wanted to sort. Let's say we want to sort eight values; so the value 8 entered by us will be assigned to a variable, len. Thereafter, you will be asked to enter the eight values that need to be sorted. So, let's say we entered the following values, which were assigned to the arr array:

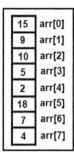

Figure 9.15

In this sorting method, we will take the help of a nested loop, where the outer loop, i, runs from 1 to 7 and the inner loop, j, runs from the value beginning from i to its value is more than 0. So, in the first iteration of the nested loop, the inner loop will execute only once where the value of i will be 1. The value at the arr[1] index location is compared with that at arr[0]. The tendency is to keep the lower value at the top, so if the value at arr[1] is greater than that at arr[0], the place of the two values will be interchanged. Because 15 is greater than 9 (on the left side of *Figure 9.16*), the values in the two index locations will be interchanged (on the right side of *Figure 9.16*) as follows:

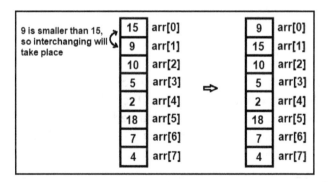

Figure 9.16

After the first iteration, the value of i will be incremented to 2 and the inner loop, j, will run from the value of 2 to 1, that is, the inner loop will execute twice: once with the value of j equal to 2 and then when the value of j is decremented to 1. Within the inner loop, the value at arr[2] will be compared with that at arr[1]. In addition, the value at arr[1] will be compared with that at arr[0]. If arr[2] < arr[1], then interchanging of the values will take place. Similarly, if arr[1] < arr[0], interchanging of their values will take place.

The value at arr[2] that is 10 is less than the value at arr[1], that is, 15; so these values will interchange places (see *Figure 9.17*). After interchanging the values, we find that the value at arr[1] is greater than the value at arr[0]. So, no interchanging will take place now. *Figure 9.17* shows the procedure of the second iteration:

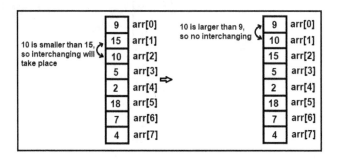

Figure 9.17

After the second iteration, the value of i will be incremented to 3 and the value of j will run from the values of 3 to 1. Hence, the interchanging of values will take place if the following conditions are met:

- If arr[3] < arr[2]
- If arr[2] < arr[1]
- If arr[1] < arr[0]

You can see in *Figure 9.18(a)* that arr[3], that is, 5, is smaller than arr[2], that is, 15, so their values will be interchanged. Similarly, the values at arr[2] and arr[1], and then arr[1] and arr[0], will also be interchanged (see *Figure 9.18(b)* and *(c)*, respectively). *Figure 9.18(d)* shows the array after all the interchanges have been performed:

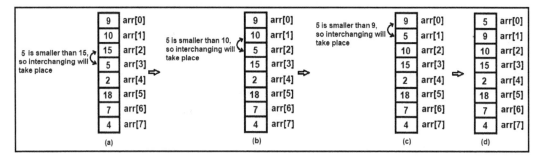

Figure 9.18

After the third iteration, the value of `i` will be incremented to 4 and the value of `j` will run from the values of 4 to 1. So interchanging of values will take place if the following conditions are met:

- If `arr[4] < arr[3]`
- If `arr[3] < arr[2]`
- If `arr[2] < arr[1]`
- If `arr[1] < arr[0]`

You can see in *Figure 9.19* that the main tendency of all these comparisons is to bring the lower values above the larger values in the array:

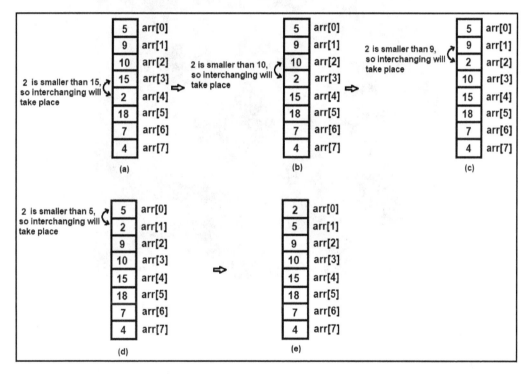

Figure 9.19

The same procedure will be followed for the rest of the elements in the array.

The program is compiled using GCC with the following statement:

```
gcc insertionsort.c -o insertionsort
```

Because no error appears on compilation, that means the `insertionsort.c` program has successfully been compiled into the `insertionsort.exe` file. On execution, it will ask you to specify how many numbers have to be sorted. Following this, the program will prompt us to enter the numbers to be sorted. After entering the numbers, they will appear sorted in ascending order, as shown in the following screenshot:

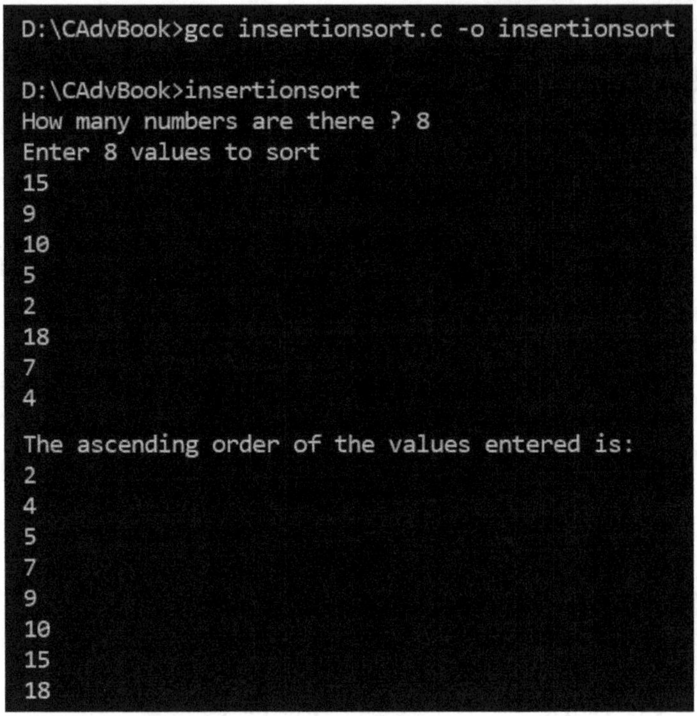

```
D:\CAdvBook>gcc insertionsort.c -o insertionsort

D:\CAdvBook>insertionsort
How many numbers are there ? 8
Enter 8 values to sort
15
9
10
5
2
18
7
4

The ascending order of the values entered is:
2
4
5
7
9
10
15
18
```

Figure 9.20

Voilà! We've successfully used insertion sort to arrange numbers in ascending order.

Now let's move on to the next recipe!

Arranging numbers in ascending order using quick sort

Quick sort is a divide-and-conquer algorithm. It divides an array on the basis of a pivot, where the pivot is an element in the array, in order that all the elements smaller than the pivot are placed before the pivot and all the larger ones are placed after it.

So, at the location of the pivot, the array is divided into two subarrays. The process of finding the pivot is repeated on both the arrays. The two arrays are further subdivided on the basis of the pivot.

Hence, quick sort is a recursive procedure and the procedure of dividing the arrays into subarrays continues recursively until the subarray has only one element.

How to do it...

The quick sort process comprises the following important tasks:

- Finding the pivot
- Splitting the array at the location of the pivot

We will be using two methods: `QuickSort` and `FindingPivot`.

Quick sort

This method takes an array or subarray into consideration. It invokes the method to find the pivot of the array or subarray and splits the array or subarray on the basis of the pivot. Here is its syntax:

```
Quick Sort (arr,n)
```

Here, `arr` is the array consisting of n elements.

This is how we use this method:

1. Let `l=1` and `u=n`, where `l` and `u` represent the lower and upper index location, respectively, of the array.
2. Push `l` into `stack1`.
3. Push `u` into `stack2`.

4. While `stack1` or `stack2` is not empty, repeat steps 5 through 10.

5. Pop the lower index location of the array from `stack1` into variable s, that is, s becomes the lower index location of the array to be sorted.

6. Pop the upper index location from `stack2` into the variable e, that is, the e variable will get the upper index location of the array.

7. Find out the pivot by invoking the `FindingPivot` method as follows:

```
pivot=FindingPivot(arr,s,e)
```

Recall that a pivot point is an index location in the array where the elements smaller than the pivot are before it and elements larger than the pivot are after it. The array is split at the pivot point and the quick sort method is recursively applied on the two halves individually.

8. Once the pivot is known, divide the array into two halves. One array will have values from s (the lower index location) to `pivot-1`, and another array with the elements ranges from `pivot+1` to e (the upper index location).

9. For the first half of the array, push s into `stack1` and `pivot-1` into `stack2`.

10. For the second half of the array, push `pivot+1` into `stack1` and e into `stack2`.

FindingPivot

This method finds the pivot of the array or subarray. Here is its syntax:

```
FindingPivot (arr,start,end)
```

Here, `arr` represents the array of n elements, `start` represents the starting index location of the array, and `end` represents the ending index location of the array.

This is how we use this method:

1. Repeat *steps 2* through *8* of the `QuickSort` method.

2. Store the value of the `start` variable in another variable, say, `lower`.

3. Start from the right index location and move to the left. Initially, the first element is the pivot. The tendency is to keep the elements larger than the pivot on the right-hand side of the pivot and the elements smaller than the pivot on the left-hand side.

4. If `lower=end`, that means, we found the pivot. The pivot is equal to the value of lower. Return `lower` as the location of the pivot element.

5. If `arr[lower] > arr[end]`, then interchange the values' places. Now, move from left to right comparing each value with the pivot, and move up until we get the value lower than the value of pivot.

6. While `arr[start] <= arr[lower]` and `lower != start`, repeat:

    `start=start+1`

7. If `lower=start` then pivot is lower. Return `lower` as the location of the pivot element.

8. If `arr[start] > arr[lower]`, then interchange the values' places.

The program for sorting elements of an integer array using the quick sort technique is as follows:

```
//quick sort.c

# include<stdio.h>
# define stacksize 10
#define arrsize 20
int top1 = -1, top2 = -1;
int stack1[stacksize];
int stack2[stacksize];
int arr[arrsize];

int quick(int, int);
void pushstk1(int);
void pushstk2(int);
int popstk1();
int popstk2();

int main() {
  int sindex, eindex, lindex, uindex, k, pivot, i, len;
  printf("How many numerical to sort? ");
  scanf("%d", & len);
  printf("Enter %d numerical:\n", len);
  for (i = 0; i <= len - 1; i++)
    scanf("%d", & arr[i]);
  lindex = 0;
  uindex = len - 1;
  pushstk1(lindex);
  pushstk2(uindex);
  while (top1 != -1) {
    sindex = popstk1();
    eindex = popstk2();
```

```
      pivot = quick(sindex, eindex);
      if (sindex < pivot - 1) {
        pushstk1(sindex);
        pushstk2(pivot - 1);
      }
      if (pivot + 1 < eindex) {
        pushstk1(pivot + 1);
        pushstk2(eindex);
      }
    }
    printf("\nAscending order using Quick Sort is:\n");
    for (i = 0; i <= len - 1; i++)
      printf("%d\n", arr[i]);
    return 0;
  }

int quick(int si, int ei) {
  int li, temp;
  li = si;
  while (1) {
    while (arr[ei] >= arr[li] && li != ei)
      ei--;
    if (li == ei) return (li);
    if (arr[li] > arr[ei]) {
      temp = arr[li];
      arr[li] = arr[ei];
      arr[ei] = temp;
      li = ei;
    }
    while (arr[si] <= arr[li] && li != si)
      si++;
    if (li == si) return (li);
    if (arr[si] > arr[li]) {
      temp = arr[si];
      arr[si] = arr[li];
      arr[li] = temp;
      li = si;
    }
  }
  return 0;
}
void pushstk1(int s) {
  top1++;
  stack1[top1] = s;
}
void pushstk2(int e) {
  top2++;
  stack2[top2] = e;
```

```
}
int popstk1() {
    return (stack1[top1--]);
}
int popstk2() {
    return (stack2[top2--]);
}
```

Now, let's go behind the scenes to understand the code better.

How it works...

You will be asked to specify how many numbers you require to be sorted. Suppose we want to sort 8 numbers; the value 8 entered by the user will be assigned to the len variable. A for loop is executed enabling us to enter the number to be sorted. The values we enter will be assigned to the arr array as shown in *Figure 9.21*.

Two variables, lindex and uindex, are initialized to represent the desired first and last index of the array, that is 0 and 7, respectively. The lindex and uindex locations are supposed to keep the smallest and largest values in the array. The values of lindex and uindex, that is, 0 and 7, will be pushed to the stack. In the pushstk1 function, the value of the top index, whose default value is -1, is incremented to 0 and the value of lindex is assigned to the stack1 array at the [0] index location. Similarly, in the pushstk2 function, the value of the top2 index is also incremented to 0, and the value of uindex is assigned to the stack2 array at the [0] location.

A while loop is set to execute for as long as the value of top1 is not equal to 1. That means, until stack1 is empty, the program will keep executing. Within the while loop, the values pushed in stack1 and stack2 are popped and assigned to the two variables of sindex and eindex, respectively. These variables represent the starting and ending index locations of the array or the part of the array that we want to sort using quick sort.

stack1 and stack2 contain the values of 0 and 7, respectively, which are popped and assigned to sindex and eindex, respectively. The quick function is invoked and the values in sindex and eindex are passed to an argument. In the quick functions, the values of sindex and eindex arguments are assigned to the two parameters of si and ei, respectively.

Within the quick function, the value of `si`, that is 0, is assigned to another variable, `li`. A while loop is executed in an infinite loop. Within the while loop, another while loop is set to execute that will make `ei` move toward the left, that is, it will make the value of `ei` decrement until the element at the `arr[ei]` location is greater than the `arr[li]` location:

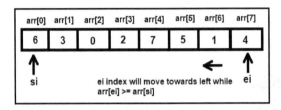

Figure 9.21

Because `arr[ei] < arr[si]`, interchanging of their values will take place (see *Figure 9.22(a)*). After interchanging the values at `arr[ei]` and `arr[si]`, the `arr` array will appear as shown in *Figure 9.22(b)*:

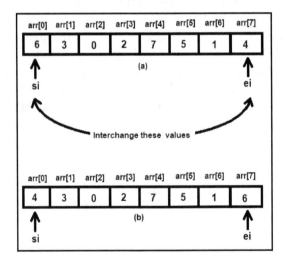

Figure 9.22

After interchanging of values, the index location number of `ei`, that is 7, will be assigned to `li`. Another while loop is set to execute while `arr[si]` is smaller than `arr[li]`, where `li` represents the `ei` index currently; and within the `while` loop, the location of the `si` index pointer is incremented. That is, the `si` index pointer is moved right to `arr[si] < arr[li]`:

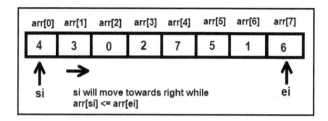

Figure 9.23

Now, the following things will happen:

- Because `arr[si] < arr[ei]` (that is, 4 < 6), `si` will move right by one location to `arr[1]`
- Because `arr[si] < arr[ei]` (that is, now 3 < 6), `si` will again move right by one location to `arr[2]`
- Because `arr[si] < arr[ei]` (that is, now 0 < 6), `si` will again move right by one location to `arr[3]`
- Because `arr[si] < arr[ei]` (that is, now 2 < 6), `si` will again move right by one location to `arr[4]`
- Because `arr[si] > arr[ei]` (that is, now 7 > 6), interchanging of their values will take place (see *Figure 9.24*):

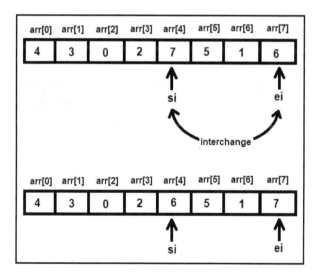

Figure 9.24

After interchanging of values at arr[ei] and arr[si], the location number of arr[si], that is, 4, will be assigned to li. The process is repeated; that is, again a while loop is set to execute while arr[ei] > arr[si]. Within the while loop, the location of ei is decremented, or it moves to the left:

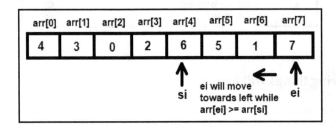

Figure 9.25

While comparing arr[ei] and arr[si], we will find that arr[ei] > arr[si] (7 > 6), so ei will be decremented to value 6 (see *Figure 9.26(a)*). Again, because arr[ei] < arr[si] (1 < 6), interchanging of values of these index locations will take place (see *Figure 9.26(b)*). The location number of ei, 6 now, will be assigned to variable li.

Another while loop is set to execute while arr[si] < arr[ei] (remember the location number of ei is assigned to li). The following things will happen in this while loop:

- Because arr[si] < arr[ei] (that is, 1 < 6), si will move right to arr[5]
- Because still arr[si] < arr[ei] (that is, 5 < 6), si will move right to arr[6]
- Because now the location of ei and si are the same, the quick function will terminate returning the number 6 to the main function (see *Figure 9.26(c)*). So, the number 6 will become the pivot of the arr array.

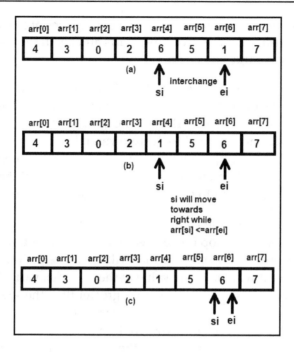

Figure 9.26

Two `if` statements are executed and the array is split into two parts: the first part ranges from `arr[0]` to `arr[5]` and the other part from `arr[7]` to `arr[7]`, that is, of a single element. The first and last index values of the two parts of the array are pushed to the stack.

The first and last index locations of the second part of the array, that is, 7, will be pushed to both `stack1` and `stack2`. The first and last index locations of the first part of array, that is, 0 and 5, will also be pushed to `stack1` and `stack2`, respectively (see *Figure 9.27*).

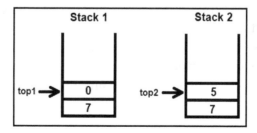

Figure 9.27

The complete quick sort technique is applied on both halves of the array. Again, the two halves will be partitioned into two more parts and again the quick sort technique is applied on those two parts, and so on.

The outer while loop repeats and the popstk1() and popstk2() functions will be invoked to pop off the values in the stack1 and stack2 arrays. The values of the top1 and top2 indices are 1, so the values at the stack1[1] and stack2[1] index locations are picked up and assigned to the two variables, sindex and eindex, respectively. Again, the quick() function is invoked and the two variables, sindex and eindex, are passed to it. In the quick function, the values of the sindex and eindex arguments are assigned to the si and ei parameters respectively

Within the quick() function, the value of the si variable, that is, 0, is assigned to another variable, li. A while loop is executed in an infinite loop. Within the while loop, another while loop is set to execute that will make the ei index location to move toward the left, that is, it will make the value of the ei index variable decrement for the time the element at the arr[ei] location is greater than the arr[si] location (see *Figure 9.28(a)*). Because arr[ei] > arr[si], the value of the ei variable will be decremented to 4 (see *Figure 9.28(b)*). Now, we find that arr[ei], that is, 1 is less than arr[si], that is, 4, so interchanging of their values will take place. After interchanging the values at that arr[ei] and arr[si] index locations, the arr array will appear as shown in *Figure 9.28(c)*.

After interchanging the values, the value of the ei variable is assigned to the li variable, that is, 4, is assigned to the li variable. Another while loop is set to execute while the arr[si] element is smaller than arr[li], where li represents the si index currently; and within the while loop, the value of the si index pointer is incremented. The following things will happen:

- Because arr[si], that is, 1, is less than arr[ei], that is, 4, si will be incremented to a value of 1.
- Because arr[si], that is, 3, is less than arr[ei], that is, 4, si will be incremented to a value of 2.
- Because arr[si], that is, 0, is less than arr[ei], that is, 4, si will be incremented to a value of 3.
- Because arr[si], that is, 2, is less than arr[ei], that is, 6, si will be incremented to a value of 4.

Because the values of the `ei` and `si` variables have become the same, the `quick()` function will terminate, returning the value 4 to the `main` function (see *Figure 9.28(d)*):

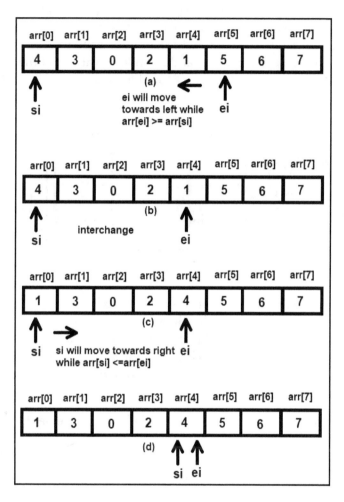

Figure 9.28

On returning to the main function, two if statements are executed and the array is split into two parts: the first part ranges from the arr[0] to the arr[3] index locations, and the other part will range from the arr[5] to the arr[5] index locations, that is, of a single element. The starting and ending index values of the two parts of the array are pushed to the stack. The starting and ending index locations of the second part of the array (that is, 5 and 5) will be pushed to stack1 and stack2, respectively. Similarly, the starting and ending index locations of the first part of the array (that is, 0 and 3) are pushed to stack1 and stack2, respectively (see *Figure 9.29*).

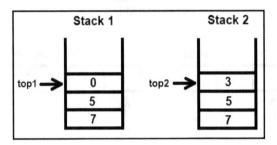

Figure 9.29

The whole quick sort technique is applied on all the partitions of the array until the stacks are empty. That is, the outer while loop repeats and the popstk1() and popstk2() functions will be invoked to pop off the values in the stack1 and stack2 arrays. Again, the quick() function is invoked and the two variables, sindex and eindex, that are popped from the stack are passed to it. The procedure continues until the whole array is sorted.

The program is compiled using GCC using the following statement:

```
gcc quick sort.c -o quick sort
```

Because no error appears on compilation, that means the quick sort.c program has successfully been compiled into the quick sort.exe file. On executing the file, it will ask you to specify how many numbers there are to be sorted. Following this, the program will prompt you to enter the numbers to be sorted. After entering the numbers, they will appear sorted in ascending order, as shown in the following screenshot:

```
D:\CAdvBook>gcc quicksort.c -o quicksort

D:\CAdvBook>quicksort
How many numerical to sort? 8
Enter 8 numericals:
6
3
0
2
7
5
1
4

Ascending order using Quick Sort is:
0
1
2
3
4
5
6
7
```

Figure 9.30

Voilà! We have successfully arranged the numbers in our array using quick sort. Now let's move on to the next recipe!

Arranging numbers in descending order using heap sort

In this recipe, we will learn to arrange some integers in descending order using the heap sort technique.

How to do it...

The heap sort method is divided into the following two tasks:

1. Creating a max-heap
2. Deleting the max-heap

Let's start with creating a max-heap.

Creating a max-heap

The following steps are followed for creating a max-heap:

1. The user is asked to enter a number. The number is used to create a heap. The number entered by the user is assigned to an array heap at index location x, where x begins with a value of 0 and increments after every insertion.
2. The newly inserted number is compared with the element of its parent node. Because we are making use of a max-heap, we need to maintain a rule: the value of the parent node should be always larger than its child node. The location of the parent node is computed using the formula `parent=(x-1)/2`, where x represents the index location where the new node is inserted.
3. Check if the value of the new node is greater than the value of its parent. Interchange the values of `heap[parent]` and `heap[x]` with the help of an extra variable.
4. Recursively check the value of the parent of the parent node to see whether the property of the max-heap is maintained or not.

Once the heap is made, the second task of deleting the max-heap will begin. Every time a node is deleted from a max-heap, the deleted node is kept in another array, say `arr`, that will contain the sorted elements. The task of deleting the max-heap is repeated as many times as the number of elements present in the max-heap.

Deleting the max-heap

Three variables, `leftchild`, `rightchild`, and `root`, are initialized as follows:

```
leftchild=0
rightchild=0
root=1
```

The following steps are performed to delete a max-heap:

1. The element at the root node is temporarily assigned to the n variable.
2. The last element of the heap is placed at the root node.
3. If the value of the last index location is 1 or 2, that is, if the heap has only 1 or 2 elements left, then return to the caller with the n variable.
4. Since the last element is placed at the root node, reduce the size of the heap by 1.
5. To maintain the max-heap property, repeat *steps 6* through *9* while rightchild <=last. Recall, the property of the max-heap is that the value of the parent node should be always larger than its children node.
6. Calculate the leftchild and rightchild locations.
7. If heap[root] > heap[leftchild] && heap[root] > heap[rightchild], return n and exit.
8. If the value of the left child is greater than the value of the right child, then interchange the value of the root and that of the left child. The root will come down at the left child to check whether the max-heap property is maintained or not.
9. If the value of the right child is greater than the value of the left child, then interchange the value of the root and that of the right child. The root will come down at the right child to check whether the max-heap property is maintained or not.
10. When all the elements of the max-heap are over, that means the arr array will have all the sorted elements. So, the final step is to print the arr array, which contains the sorted elements.

The program for sorting elements of an integer array using the heap sort technique is as follows:

```
//heapsort.c

# include <stdio.h>
#define max 20
int heap[max], len;

void insheap(int h);
int delsheap(int j);

int main() {
  int arr[max], numb, i, j;
  printf("How many elements to sort? ");
  scanf("%d", & len);
```

```
    printf("Enter %d values \n", len);
    for (i = 0; i < len; i++) {
        scanf("%d", & numb);
        insheap(numb);
    }
    j = len - 1;
    for (i = 0; i < len; i++) {
        arr[i] = delsheap(j);
        j--;
    }
    printf("\nThe Descending order is: \n");
    for (i = 0; i < len; i++)
        printf("%d\n", arr[i]);
    return 0;
}

void insheap(int value) {
    static int x;
    int par, cur, temp;
    if (x == 0) {
        heap[x] = value;\
        x++;
    } else {
        heap[x] = value;
        par = (x - 1) / 2;
        cur = x;
        do {
            if (heap[cur] > heap[par]) {
                temp = heap[cur];
                heap[cur] = heap[par];
                heap[par] = temp;
                cur = par;
                par = (cur - 1) / 2;
            } else break;
        } while (cur != 0);
        x++;
    }
}

int delsheap(int j) {
    int loc, n = 0, pos, lc = 0, rc = 0, temp = 0;
    loc = j;
    pos = 0;
    n = heap[pos];
    heap[pos] = heap[loc];
    if (loc == 0 || loc == 1) return (n);
    loc--;
    lc = 2 * pos + 1;
```

```
    rc = 2 * pos + 2;
    while (rc <= loc) {
      if ((heap[pos] > heap[lc] && heap[pos] > heap[rc]))
        return (n);
      else {
        if (heap[lc] > heap[rc]) {
          temp = heap[lc];
          heap[lc] = heap[pos];
          heap[pos] = temp;
          pos = lc;
        } else {
          temp = heap[rc];
          heap[rc] = heap[pos];
          heap[pos] = temp;
          pos = rc;
        }
        lc = 2 * pos + 1;
        rc = 2 * pos + 2;
      }
    }
  }
  if (lc == loc) {
    if (heap[pos] < heap[lc]) {
      temp = heap[pos];
      heap[pos] = heap[lc];
      heap[lc] = temp;
      pos = lc;
    }
  }
  return (n);
}
```

Now, let's go behind the scenes to understand the code better.

How it works...

A heap is a complete binary tree that can be either a max-heap or a min-heap. The max-heap has the property that the key value of any node must be greater than or equal to the key values of its children. In the min-heap, the key value of any node must be lower than or equal to the values of its children.

In this recipe, we will learn to create a max-heap of the following list of integers:

5	2	9	3	1	4	6

In this heap sort method, the binary tree is constructed in the form of an array. In heap sort, the values in the array are added one by one, keeping the max-heap property true (that is, the key value of any node should be larger than or equal to its children). While adding the elements of the array, we keep track of the key value of the parent node with $(x-1)/2$, where x is the element whose parent is to be found. If the element inserted in the heap is larger than the key value of its parent, then interchanging takes place. For example, suppose the first key value entered is 5 (it is considered as the root); it is stored as the first element of the array, that is, heap[0]:

heap[0]	heap[1]	heap[2]	heap[3]	heap[4]	heap[5]	heap[6]	
5							(5)

Figure 9.31

Then 2 is added to it as a left child. The first child will always be added to the left. When another value is entered, it is entered at the location of heap[1]. After insertion, its parent node location is computed with $(x-1)/2$, where x is 1. So, the parent comes out to be location 0. So, heap[1] is compared with its parent element, heap[0]. If the key element of the parent element, heap[0], is larger than heap[1], then we move further; else, we interchange their key values. In our example, the second element is 2, so no interchanging is required:

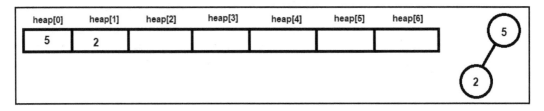

Figure 9.32

Now, we move to enter the third element. The third element is 9, and it is added as a right child of node 5 (see *Figure 9.33 (a)*). In the array, it is stored at the location of heap[2]. Again, its parent element location is computed by $(x-1)/2$, which again comes out to be 0. In keeping the property of max-heap (that the value of the parent node should be larger than or equal to its children), we compare the key values of the heap[0] and heap[2] elements. Because heap[0] is less than heap[2], it is violating the max-heap property. Thus, the key values of heap[0] and heap[2] will be interchanged, as shown in *Figure 9.33(b)*:

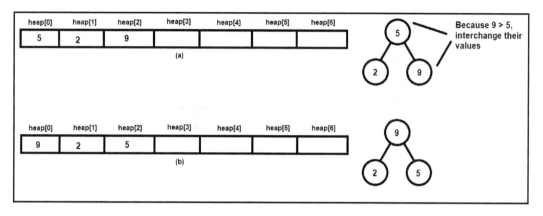

Figure 9.33

Then 3 is added as a left child of node 2, as shown in *Figure 9.34(a)*. In the array, the new value is inserted at the index location of `heap[3]`. Again, its parent element location is computed using the formula `(x-1)/2`, where x represents the index location where new value is inserted, that is, 3. The parent element location is computed as 1. In keeping with the property of max-heap, `heap[1]` must be larger than or equal to `heap[3]`. But because `heap[1]` is less than `heap[3]`, it is violating the max-heap property. Thus, the key values of `heap[1]` and `heap[3]` will be interchanged, as shown in *Figure 9.34(b)*:

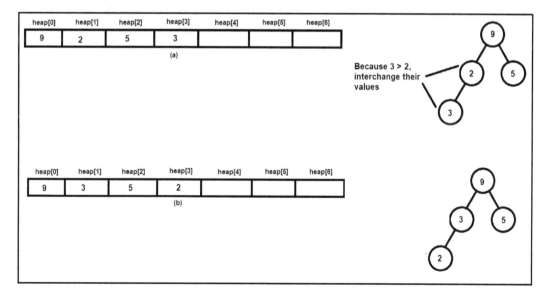

Figure 9.34

Now, 1 is added as the right child of node 3. In the array, the new value is inserted at the index location of `heap[4]`. Because the property of max-heap is still maintained, no interchanging is required:

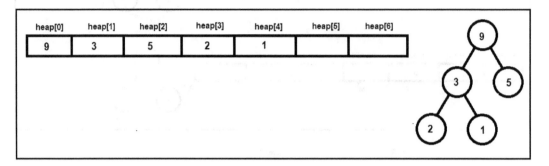

Figure 9.35

The next value is 4, which is added as the left child of node 5. In the array, the new value is inserted at the index location of `heap[5]`. Again, the property of max-heap is maintained, so no interchanging is required:

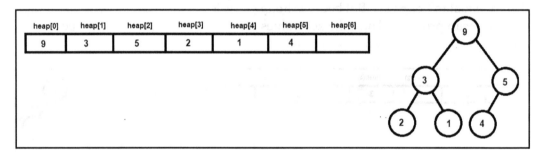

Figure 9.36

Next, 6 is added as the right child of node 5 (see *Figure 9.37 (a)*). In the array, it is inserted at the index location of `heap[6]`. Again, its parent element location is computed using the formula `(x-1)/2`. The parent element location is computed as 2. In keeping with the property of max-heap, `heap[2]` must be larger than or equal to `heap[6]`. But because `heap[2]` is less than `heap[6]`, it is violating the max-heap property; so the key values of `heap[2]` and `heap[6]` will be interchanged, as shown in *Figure 9.37(b)*:

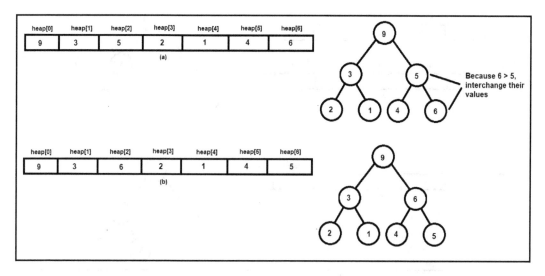

Figure 9.37

Once the max-heap is made, we perform heap sort by repeating the following three steps:

1. Removing its root element (and storing it in the sorted array)
2. Replacing the root element of the tree (array) by the last node value and removing the last node (decrementing the size of the array)
3. Reshuffling the key values to maintain the heap property

In the following *Figure 9.38(a)*, you can see that the root element, that is, 9, is deleted and is stored in another array called `arr`. The `arr` array will contain the sorted elements. The root element is replaced by the last element of the tree. The last element of the tree is 5, so it is removed from the `heap[6]` index location and is assigned to the root, that is, at `heap[0]`. Now, the property of heap is no longer true. So, the values of node elements 5 and 6 are interchanged (see *Figure 9.38(b)*):

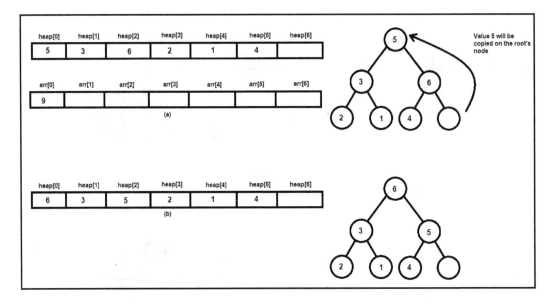

Figure 9.38

Now the process is repeated again, removing the key element of the root node and replacing its value with the last node and reshuffling the heap. That is, the root node element 6 is removed and is assigned to the sorted array, `arr`. And the root node is replaced by the last element of the tree that is by 4 (see *Figure 9.39(a)*). By putting the value 4 at the root, the property of heap is no longer true. So to maintain the property of heap, the value 4 is brought down that is the values of node elements 4 and 5 are interchanged, as shown in *Figure 9.39(b)*):

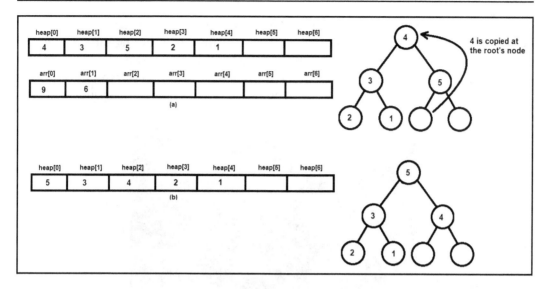

Figure 9.39

The steps are repeated to get the array sorted in descending order, as follows:

arr[0]	arr[1]	arr[2]	arr[3]	arr[4]	arr[5]	arr[6]
9	6	5	4	3	2	1

Figure 9.40

The program is compiled using GCC using the following statement:

```
gcc heapsort.c -o heapsort
```

Because no error appears on compilation, this means the heapsort.c program has successfully been compiled into the heapsort.exe file. On executing the file, it will ask us to specify how many numbers there are to be sorted. Following this, the program will prompt us to enter the numbers to be sorted. After entering the numbers, they will appear sorted in descending order, as shown in the following screenshot:

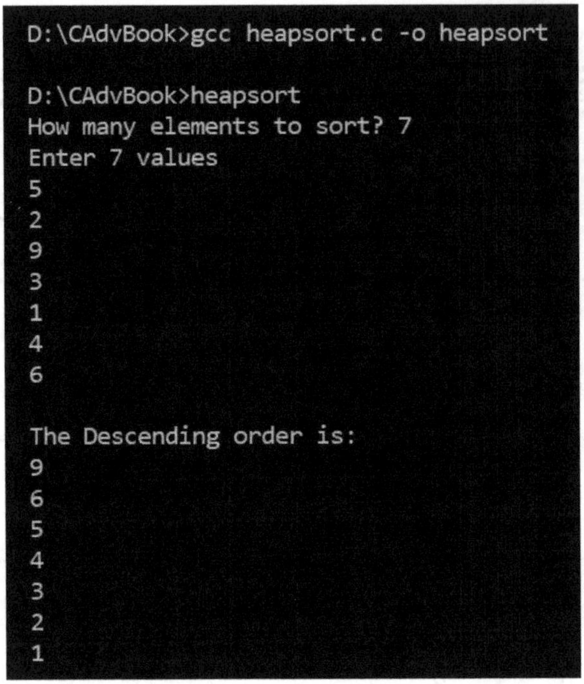

```
D:\CAdvBook>gcc heapsort.c -o heapsort

D:\CAdvBook>heapsort
How many elements to sort? 7
Enter 7 values
5
2
9
3
1
4
6

The Descending order is:
9
6
5
4
3
2
1
```

Figure 9.41

Voilà! We have successfully arranged numbers in descending order using heap sort.

See also

To learn more sorting methods like selection, merge, shell and radix sort visit *Appendix A* found on this link: https://github.com/PacktPublishing/Practical-C-Programming/blob/master/Appendix%20A.pdf.

10
Working with Graphs

Graphs show information in pictorial format. In graphs, certain information is plotted and then those plotted points are connected through lines or bars. Each plotted point is called a **vertex** (the plural of this is vertices), and the lines connecting them are called **edges**. Graphs have the ability to display large volumes of data in an easy-to-understand manner. Therefore, when comparing huge or enormous data, graphs are generally preferred.

Graphs can be used in several applications that include displaying a certain route of transmission or flow of data packets. Graphs can also be used to represent a kind of connection between two cities or stations, where stations can be represented by vertices and the route can be represented by edges. On social media, even friends can be connected in the form of graphs where each person can be represented by vertices and the edges between them ensure that they are friends. Similarly, graphs can be used for representing different networks.

In this chapter, we will learn how to represent graphs using different data structures. We will also learn to traverse the graphs and create a minimum spanning tree from graphs. To be able to do so, we are going to look at the following recipes:

- Creating an adjacency matrix representation of a directed graph
- Creating an adjacency matrix representation of an undirected graph
- Creating an adjacency list representation of a directed graph
- Carrying out the breadth-first traversal of a graph
- Carrying out the depth-first traversal of a graph
- Creating minimum spanning trees using Prim's algorithm
- Creating minimum spanning trees using Kruskal's algorithm

Before we begin with the recipes, let's have a quick introduction to the two main types of graphs.

Types of graphs

Based on directions, graphs can be of two types: directed and undirected. Let's review both of them briefly.

Directed graphs

In a directed graph, the edges clearly show the direction from one vertex to another. An edge in a directed graph is usually represented as (v1, v2), which means that the edge is pointing from vertex v1 toward vertex v2. In other words, a (v1, v2) pair indicates that v1 is the starting vertex and v2 is the ending vertex. A directed graph is very useful in real-world applications and is used in the **World Wide Web** (**WWW**), Google's PageRank algorithm, and more. Consider the following directed graph:

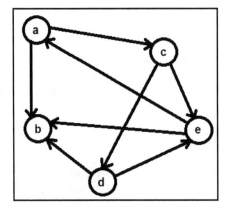

Figure 10.1

Here, you can see an edge between vertices **a** and **b**. Because the edge is pointing from vertex **a** toward **b**, vertex **a** is considered to be the starting vertex and vertex **b** is considered the ending vertex. This edge can be represented as (**a**,**b**). Similarly, there is an edge from vertices **a** to **c**, which, in turn, can be represented as (**a**,**c**). Therefore, we can say that the preceding graph has the following set of vertices:

```
(V) - { a,b,c,d,e}
```

Additionally, the graph has the following set of edges:

```
(E) - {(a,b), (a,c), (c,d), (c,e), (d,b), (d,e), (e,a), (e,b) }
```

Undirected graphs

An undirected graph is one in which the edges are present between vertices, but there is no specific direction identified – that is, there are no arrows at the end of the edges. Therefore, we cannot know which is the starting vertex and which one is the ending vertex. Undirected graphs are widely used in real-world applications such as Facebook and neural networks.

An edge between two vertices, **a** and **b**, in an undirected graph will mean that either of them can be a starting or ending vertex. Such an edge can be written as (**a,b**), that is, from **a** to **b**, as well as (**b,a**), that is, from **b** to **a**. The following diagram shows an undirected graph:

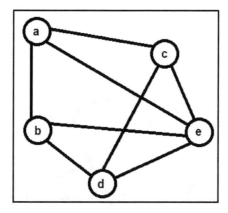

Figure 10.2

So, for this undirected graph, the following is the set of vertices:

```
(V) - { a,b,c,d,e}
```

Additionally, the graph will have the following set of edges:

```
(E) - {(a,b),  (b,a),  (a,c),  (c,a),  (a,e),  (e,a),  (b,e),  (e,b),  (b,d),
(d,b),  (c,d),  (d,c),  (c,e),  (e,c) }
```

Now, let's begin with the recipes.

Creating an adjacency matrix representation of a directed graph

An adjacency matrix is a square matrix that is used to represent a graph. The rows and columns of the matrix are labeled as per the graph vertices. So, if the graph vertices are **1,2,...5**, then the rows and columns of the adjacency matrix will be labeled as **1,2,...5**. Initially, the matrix is filled with all zeros (0). Then, the 0 at the `mat[i][j]` location (where `i` and `j` refer to the vertices) is replaced by 1 if there is an edge between the vertices of `i` and `j`. For example, if there is an edge from vertex **2** to vertex **3**, then at the `mat[2][3]` index location, the value of 0 will be replaced by **1**. In short, the elements of the adjacency matrix indicate whether pairs of vertices are adjacent or not in the graph.

Consider the following directed graph:

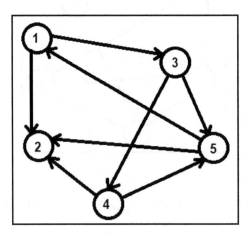

Figure 10.3

Its adjacency matrix representation is as follows:

5,5 5	1	2	3	4
1 0	0	1	1	0
2 0	0	0	0	0
3 1	0	0	0	1

4	0	1	0	0
1				
5	1	1	0	0
0				

The first row and the first column represent the vertices. If there is an edge between two vertices, then there will be a 1 value at the intersection of their respective row and column. The absence of an edge between them will be represented by 0. The number of nonzero elements of an adjacency matrix indicates the number of edges in a directed graph.

Here are two drawbacks of adjacency matrix representation:

- This representation requires n^2 elements to represent a graph having n vertices. If a directed graph has e edges, then (n^2-e) elements in the matrix would be zeros. Therefore, for graphs with a very low number of edges, the matrix becomes very sparse.
- Parallel edges cannot be represented by an adjacency matrix.

In this recipe, we will learn how to make an adjacency matrix representation of a directed graph.

How to do it...

Perform the following steps to create an adjacency matrix representation of a graph:

1. Ask the user for the number of vertices in the graph.
2. Define a square matrix that is equal to the number of vertices.
3. Initialize all the elements of the matrix to 0.
4. Ask the user to enter the edges. For each edge (i,j) entered by the user, replace 0 at the mat[i][j] index location.
5. Once all the edges are entered, display all of the elements of the adjacency matrix.

The code for creating an adjacency matrix representation of a graph is as follows:

```
//adjmatdirect.c

#include <stdio.h>

#define max 10
int main() {
  static int edg[max][max], i, j, v1, v2, numb;
  printf("How many vertices are there? ");
  scanf("%d", & numb);
  printf("We assume that the vertices are numbered from : ");
  for (i = 1; i <= numb; i++) printf("%d ", i);
  printf("\nEnter the edges of the graph. Like 1 4 if there is an
\n");
  printf("edge between vertex 1 and 4. Enter 0 0 when over\n");
  for (i = 1; i <= numb * (numb - 1); i++) {
    /* The for loop will run for at most numb*(numb-1) times because,
       the number of edges are at most numb*(numb-1) where numb is
       the number of vertices */
    scanf("%d %d", & v1, & v2);
    if (v1 == 0 && v2 == 0) break;
    edg[v1][v2] = 1;
  }
  printf("\nThe adjacency matrix for the graph is \n");
  for (i = 1; i <= numb; i++) printf("\t%d", i);
  printf("\n-----------------------------------------------------\n");
  for (i = 1; i <= numb; i++) {
    printf("%d |\t", i);
    for (j = 1; j <= numb; j++) {
      printf("%d\t", edg[i][j]);
    }
    printf("\n");
  }
  return 0;
}
```

Now, let's go behind the scenes to understand the code better.

How it works...

Assuming that the directed graphs the user will specify in this program will not be of more than 10 vertices, define a macro called `max` of value `10` and a two-dimensional matrix called `edg`, consisting of max rows and max columns. However, you can always increase the size of the macro if you think the user can specify a graph of more than 10 vertices.

In order to initialize all of the elements of the `edg` matrix to 0, define it as a static matrix. Thereafter, the user will be prompted to specify how many vertices there are in the graph. Suppose the user enters 5 to indicate that there are 5 vertices in the graph, then that value will be assigned to the `numb` variable.

To make the recipe easy to understand, we assume that the vertices are sequentially numbered from 1 to 5. The user is prompted to specify the edges between the vertices. This means that if there is an edge between vertices 1 and 3, then the user is supposed to enter the edge as 1,3. The vertices entered representing these edges are then assigned to the vertices of v1 and v2. Because the user is asked to specify the edges of the graph and to enter `0 0` when over, when the edge is assigned to the vertices of v1 and v2, we first ensure that the vertices are not 0 and 0. If they are, the program will stop asking for more edges and will branch to the statement from where the display of the adjacency matrix begins. If the vertices in the edge are not zero, then a value, 1, is assigned in the two-dimensional `edg` matrix at the index location of `[v1][v2]`. So, if there is an edge between vertices 1 and 2, then value 1 will be assigned at the `edg[1][2]` index location, replacing the value 0 that was initially there.

When all the edges of the graph are entered, the user will enter the vertices as `0 0` to indicate that all the edges have been entered. In that case, a nested `for` loop is executed and all the elements of the `edg` matrix are displayed on screen.

The program is compiled using GCC, as shown in the following screenshot. Because no error appears during the compilation, this means the `adjmatdirect.c` program has successfully compiled into the `adjmatdirect.exe` file. On executing the file, the user will be prompted to specify the number of vertices and its edges. Once the vertices and edges are entered, the program will display the adjacency matrix representation of the graph (take a look at the following screenshot):

```
D:\CAdvBook>gcc adjmatdirect.c -o adjmatdirect

D:\CAdvBook>adjmatdirect
How many vertices are there? 5
We assume that the vertices are numbered from : 1   2   3   4   5

Enter the edges of the graph. Like  1 4 if there is an
edge between vertex 1 and 4. Enter 0 0 when over
1 2
1 3
3 4
3 5
4 2
4 5
5 1
5 2
0 0

The adjacency matrix for the graph is
              1       2       3       4       5
    -----------------------------------------------------
1 |     0       1       1       0       0
2 |     0       0       0       0       0
3 |     0       0       0       1       1
4 |     0       1       0       0       1
5 |     1       1       0       0       0
```

Figure 10.4

Now, let's explore how to do the same thing for an undirected graph.

Creating an adjacency matrix representation of an undirected graph

By adding one more statement in this recipe's code, the same program can be used for creating the adjacency matrix representation of an undirected graph as well.

How to do it...

We refer to the same graph that was in the previous recipe; however, this time, there are no edges:

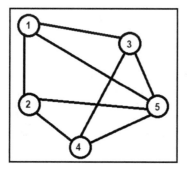

Figure 10.5

Its adjacency matrix representation is as follows:

5,5	1	2	3	4
5				
1	0	1	1	0
1				
2	1	0	0	1
1				
3	1	0	0	1
1				
4	0	1	1	0
1				
5	1	1	1	1
0				

The only difference between the programs of the directed and undirected graphs is that, in the latter, the edge is simply repeated. That is, if there is an edge between a and b, then it is considered to be two edges: one from a to b and the other from b to a.

The program for creating an adjacency matrix representation of an undirected graph is as follows:

```
//adjmatundirect.c

#include <stdio.h>
```

```
#define max 10

int main() {
  static int edg[max][max], i, j, v1, v2, numb;
  printf("How many vertices are there? ");
  scanf("%d", & numb);
  printf("We assume that the vertices are numbered from : ");
  for (i = 1; i <= numb; i++) printf("%d ", i);
  printf("\nEnter the edges of the graph. Like 1 4 if there is an
\n");
  printf("edge between vertex 1 and 4. Enter 0 0 when over\n");
  for (i = 1; i <= numb * (numb - 1); i++) {
    /* The for loop will run for at most numb*(numb-1) times because,
the
       number of edges are at most numb*(numb-1) where numb is the
number
       of vertices */
    scanf("%d %d", & v1, & v2);
    if (v1 == 0 && v2 == 0) break;
    edg[v1][v2] = 1;
    edg[v2][v1] = 1;
  }
  printf("\nThe adjacency matrix for the graph is \n");
  for (i = 1; i <= numb; i++) printf("\t%d", i);
  printf("\n-------------------------------------------------------
\n");
  for (i = 1; i <= numb; i++) {
    printf("%d |\t", i);
    for (j = 1; j <= numb; j++) {
      printf("%d\t", edg[i][j]);
    }
    printf("\n");
  }
  return 0;
}
```

How it works...

When you compare the preceding program with that of the directed graph, you will notice that only one extra statement has been added (marked in bold):

```
edg[v2][v1]=1;
```

That is, in the case of an edge from v1 to v2, an edge in reverse is also assumed, that is, from v2 to v1.

The program is compiled using GCC, as shown in the following screenshot. Because no error appears during the compilation, this means the adjmatundirect.c program has successfully compiled into the adjmatundirect.exe file. As expected, on running the file, the user will be prompted to specify the number of vertices and their edges. Once the number of vertices and edges are entered, the program will display the adjacency matrix representation of the undirected graph, as shown in the following screenshot:

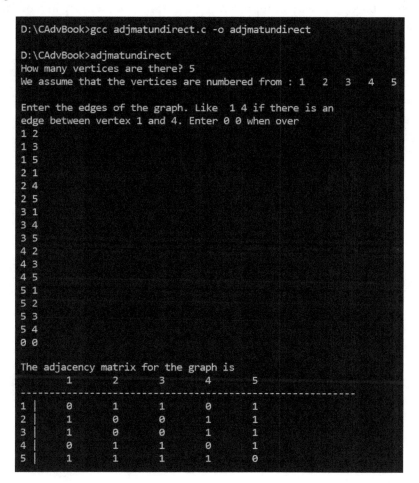

```
D:\CAdvBook>gcc adjmatundirect.c -o adjmatundirect

D:\CAdvBook>adjmatundirect
How many vertices are there? 5
We assume that the vertices are numbered from : 1    2    3    4    5

Enter the edges of the graph. Like  1 4 if there is an
edge between vertex 1 and 4. Enter 0 0 when over
1 2
1 3
1 5
2 1
2 4
2 5
3 1
3 4
3 5
4 2
4 3
4 5
5 1
5 2
5 3
5 4
0 0

The adjacency matrix for the graph is
            1       2       3       4       5
       ----------------------------------------------------
1 |        0       1       1       0       1
2 |        1       0       0       1       1
3 |        1       0       0       1       1
4 |        0       1       1       0       1
5 |        1       1       1       1       0
```

Figure 10.6

Now, let's move on to the next recipe!

Creating an adjacency list representation of a directed graph

In an adjacency list representation, linked lists are used to represent the adjacent vertices of a vertex. That is, a separate linked list is made for the adjacent vertices of each vertex, and, in the end, all the vertices of the graph are connected. Because linked lists are used, this way of representing a graph uses memory in a more optimized manner.

Consider the following directed graph:

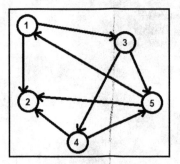

Figure 10.7

Its adjacency list representation is as follows:

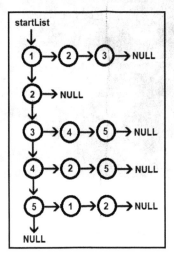

Figure 10.8

You can see in the preceding diagram that the adjacent vertices of vertex **1** are connected in the form of a linked list. Because there are no adjacent vertices for vertex **2**, its pointer is pointing to **NULL**. Similarly, the adjacent vertices of vertex **3**, that is, vertices **4** and **5**, are connected to vertex **3** in the form of a linked list. Once a linked list of all the vertices of the entire graph is created, all the vertices become connected through a link.

In this recipe, we will learn how to create the adjacency list representation of a directed graph.

How to do it...

Follow these steps to create an adjacency list representation of a graph:

1. Define a structure called `node` that contains three members. One member, `nme`, is for storing the vertex of the graph; another member, `vrt`, is for connecting vertices of the graph; and, finally, `edg` is for connecting the adjacent vertices of the vertex.
2. The user is asked to specify the count of the vertices in the graph.
3. A linked list is created where the `nme` member of each node contains the vertex of the graph.
4. All the nodes representing vertices of the graph are connected to each other using the `vrt` pointer.
5. Once all the vertices are entered, the user is prompted to enter the edges of the graph. The user can enter any number of edges and to indicate that all the edges are entered, the user can enter 0 0 for the edge.
6. When an edge is entered, for example, b, a `temp1` pointer is used and is set to point to vertex a.
7. A new node is created called `newNode`, and the vertex name b is assigned to the `nme` member of `newNode`.
8. One more pointer is used, called `temp2`, and is set to point to the last node that is connected to vertex a. Once `temp2` reaches the end of vertex a, the `edg` member of the `temp2` node is set to point to `newNode`, and hence establishing an edge between a and b.

The program for creating the adjacency list representation of a directed graph is as follows:

```c
//adjlistdirect.c

#include <stdlib.h>
#include <stdio.h>

struct node {
  char nme;
  struct node * vrt;
  struct node * edg;
};

int main() {
   int numb, i, j, noe;
   char v1, v2;
   struct node * startList, * newNode, * temp1, * temp2;
   printf("How many vertices are there ? ");
   scanf("%d", & numb);
   startList = NULL;
   printf("Enter all vertices names\n");
   for (i = 1; i <= numb; i++) {
     if (startList == NULL) {
        newNode = malloc(sizeof(struct node));
        scanf(" %c", & newNode - > nme); /* There is a space before %c
*/
        startList = newNode;
        temp1 = newNode;
        newNode - > vrt = NULL;
        newNode - > edg = NULL;
      } else {
        newNode = malloc(sizeof(struct node));
        scanf(" %c", & newNode - > nme);
        /* There is a space before %c */
        newNode - > vrt = NULL;
        newNode - > edg = NULL;
        temp1 - > vrt = newNode;
        temp1 = newNode;
     }
   }
   printf("Enter the edges between vertices. Enter v1 v2, if there is
an edge\n");
   printf("between v1 and v2. Enter 0 0 if over\n");
   noe = numb * (numb - 1);
   for (j = 1; j <= noe; j++) {
     scanf(" %c %c", & v1, & v2);
     /* There is a space before %c */
```

```
      if (v1 == '0' && v2 == '0') break;
    temp1 = startList;
    while (temp1 != NULL && temp1 - > nme != v1)
      temp1 = temp1 - > vrt;
    if (temp1 == NULL) {
      printf("Sorry no vertex exist by this name\n");
      break;
    }
    temp2 = temp1;
    while (temp2 - > edg != NULL) temp2 = temp2 - > edg;
    newNode = malloc(sizeof(struct node));
    newNode - > nme = v2;
    temp2 - > edg = newNode;
    newNode - > edg = NULL;
    newNode - > vrt = NULL;
  }
  printf("\nAdjacency List representation of Graph is\n");
  temp1 = startList;
  while (temp1 != NULL) {
    printf("%c\t", temp1 - > nme);
    temp2 = temp1 - > edg;
    while (temp2 != NULL) {
      printf("%c\t", temp2 - > nme);
      temp2 = temp2 - > edg;
    }
    printf("\n");
    temp1 = temp1 - > vrt;
  }
}
```

Now, let's go behind the scenes to understand the code better.

How it works...

Let's assume we are working with the following directed graph:

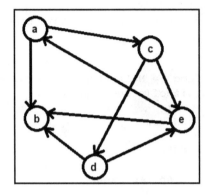

Figure 10.9

The adjacency list representation of this graph is as follows:

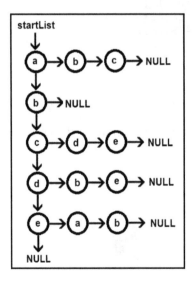

Figure 10.10

We define a structure called "node" comprising the following three members:

- nme: This is for storing the vertex.
- vrt: A pointer to connect all the vertices of the graph.

- edg: A pointer that connects all the vertices that are connected to the current vertex:

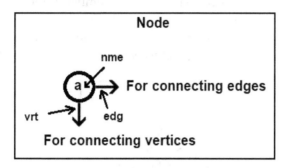

Figure 10.11

The user is prompted to specify the number of vertices. Assuming the user enters the value of 5, the value of 5 will be assigned to the numb variable. A startList pointer is defined as NULL. The whole adjacency list will be accessed through this startList pointer and it will be set to point to the first vertex of the graph. The user is first asked to enter the names of the vertices.

Initially, the startList pointer is NULL, so a new node called newNode is created and the vertex name, say a, entered by the user is assigned to the nme member of newNode. The startList pointer is set to point to newNode. To connect more vertices with newNode, the temp1 pointer is set to point to newNode. Initially, both the pointers, vrt and edg, are also set to NULL. Later, the vrt pointer will be set to point to other vertices and the edg pointer will be set to point to the vertices in which this current vertex is connected to. After the first iteration of the for loop, the node of the graph will look as follows:

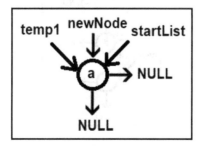

Figure 10.12

In the second iteration of the `for` loop, because the `startList` pointer is no longer NULL, the `else` block will execute and, again, a new node is created, called `newNode`. Next, the vertex name is assigned to the named member of the `newNode`. Again, the `vrt` and `edg` pointers of `newNode` are set to NULL. To connect `newNode` to the earlier vertex, we will take the help of the `temp1` pointer. The `vrt` pointer of the node, which is pointed to by the `temp1` pointer, is set to point to `newNode`, as follows:

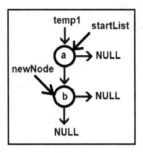

Figure 10.13

Then, the `temp1` pointer is set to point to `newNode`, and the process is repeated for the rest of the vertices. Essentially, the `temp1` pointer is used for connecting more vertices. At the end of the `for` loop, the nodes will appear connected as follows:

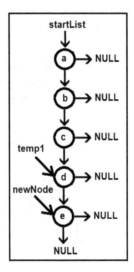

Figure 10.14

Once all the vertices of the graphs are entered, the user is asked to specify the edges between the vertices. Additionally, the user is asked to enter 0 0 when all the edges of the graph are entered. Suppose that the user enters a b to indicate there is an edge from vertex a to vertex b. The vertices are assigned to the v1 and v2 variables, respectively. We first ensure that the data in v1 and v2 is not 0. If yes, that means all the edges of the graph are entered and the program will jump to the statement from where the display of the adjacency list begins.

Then, to connect the a and b vertices, first, the temp1 pointer is set to point to startList. The temp1 pointer is set to find the node whose nme member is equal to the vertex entered in variable v1, that is, a. The temp1 pointer is already pointing to vertex a. Thereafter, you need to find the last node that is connected to temp1. The temp2 pointer is used for finding the last node connected to the node pointed to by temp1. Because this is the first edge being entered of vertex a, the edg member of the node pointed to by temp2 is already NULL. So, a new node is created called newNode, and the vertex name in variable v2, that is, b is assigned to the nme variable of newNode. The edg and vrt members of newNode are set to NULL, as follows:

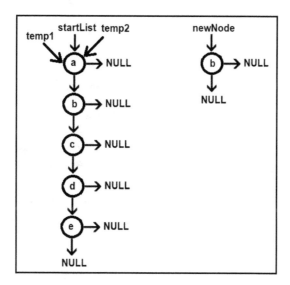

Figure 10.15

The edg member of temp2 is set to point to newNode as follows:

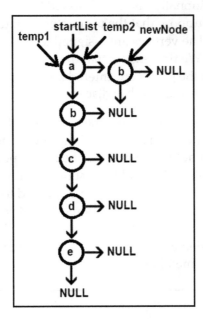

Figure 10.16

The procedure is repeated for the rest of the edges entered by the user.

The program is compiled using GCC, as shown in the following screenshot. Because no error appears during the compilation, this means the adjlistdirect.c program has successfully compiled into the adjlistdirect.exe file. On executing the executable file, the user will be prompted to specify the number of vertices and their edges. Once the vertices and edges are entered, the program will display the adjacency list representation of the directed graph, as shown in the following screenshot:

```
D:\CAdvBook>gcc adjlistdirect.c -o adjlistdirect

D:\CAdvBook>adjlistdirect
How many vertices are there ? 5
Enter all vertices names
a
b
c
d
e
Enter the edges between vertices. Enter v1 v2, if there is an edge
between v1 and v2. Enter 0 0 if over
a b
a c
c d
c e
d b
d e
e a
e b
0 0

Adjacency List representation of Graph is
a          b          c
b
c          d          e
d          b          e
e          a          b
```

Figure 10.17

Now, let's move on to the next recipe!

Carrying out the breadth-first traversal of a graph

The traversal of a graph refers to when you visit each of the vertices of a graph exactly once in a well-defined order. To ensure that each vertex of the graph is visited only once and to know which vertices have already been visited, the best way is to mark them. We will also look at how vertices are marked in this recipe.

Breadth-first traversal tends to create very short and wide trees. It operates by vertices in layers, that is, the vertices closest to the start are evaluated first, and the most distant vertices are evaluated last. Hence, it is referred to as the level-by-level traversal of the tree. The breadth-first traversal of a graph is very popularly used for finding the shortest path between two locations (vertices), that is, the path with the least number of edges. It is also used to find the linked pages of a web page, broadcasting information, and more.

In this recipe, we will learn how to carry out the breadth-first traversal of a graph.

How to do it...

Follow these steps to carry out the breadth-first traversal of a graph:

1. Add the first vertex of the graph into the queue. Any vertex can be chosen as a starting vertex.
2. Then, repeat the following *steps 3 to 8* until the queue is empty.
3. Take out the vertex from the queue and store it in a variable, say v.
4. Mark it as visited (the marking is done so that this vertex should not be traversed again).
5. Display the marked vertex.
6. Find out the adjacency vertices of the vertex v, and then perform *steps 7 to 8* on each of them.
7. If any of the adjacency vertices of v are not marked, mark it as visited.
8. Add the adjacency vertex to the queue.
9. Exit.

The program for the breadth-first traversal of a graph is as follows:

```c
//breadthfirsttrav.c

#include <stdlib.h>
#include <stdio.h>

#define max 20

enum Setmarked {
    Y,
    N
};
struct node {
    char nme;
```

```
    struct node * vrt;
    struct node * edg;
    enum Setmarked marked;
};

struct node * que[max];
int rear = -1, front = -1;
void queue(struct node * paramNode);
struct node * dequeue();

int main() {
    int numb, i, j, noe;
    char v1, v2;
    struct node * startList, * newNode, * temp1, * temp2, * temp3;
    printf("How many vertices are there ?");
    scanf("%d", & numb);
    startList = NULL;
    printf("Enter all vertices names\n");
    for (i = 1; i <= numb; i++) {
        if (startList == NULL) {
            newNode = malloc(sizeof(struct node));
            scanf(" %c", & newNode - > nme);
            /* There is a space before %c */
            startList = newNode;
            temp1 = newNode;
            newNode - > vrt = NULL;
            newNode - > edg = NULL;
            newNode - > marked = N;
        } else {
            newNode = malloc(sizeof(struct node));
            scanf(" %c", & newNode - > nme);
            /* There is a space before %c */
            newNode - > vrt = NULL;
            newNode - > edg = NULL;
            newNode - > marked = N;
            temp1 - > vrt = newNode;
            temp1 = newNode;
        }
    }
    printf("Enter the edges between vertices. Enter v1 v2, if there is
an edge\n");
    printf("between v1 and v2. Enter 0 0 if over\n");
    noe = numb * (numb - 1);
    for (j = 1; j <= noe; j++) {
        scanf(" %c %c", & v1, & v2);
        /* There is a space before %c */
        if (v1 == '0' && v2 == '0') break;
        temp1 = startList;
```

```
        while (temp1 != NULL && temp1 - > nme != v1)
          temp1 = temp1 - > vrt;
        if (temp1 == NULL) {
          printf("Sorry no vertex exist by this name\n");
          break;
        }
        temp2 = temp1;
        while (temp2 - > edg != NULL) temp2 = temp2 - > edg;
        newNode = malloc(sizeof(struct node));
        newNode - > nme = v2;
        temp2 - > edg = newNode;
        newNode - > edg = NULL;
        newNode - > vrt = NULL;
      }
    printf("\nAdjacency List representation of Graph is\n");
    temp1 = startList;
    while (temp1 != NULL) {
      printf("%c\t", temp1 - > nme);
      temp2 = temp1 - > edg;
      while (temp2 != NULL) {
        printf("%c\t", temp2 - > nme);
        temp2 = temp2 - > edg;
      }
      printf("\n");
      temp1 = temp1 - > vrt;
    }
    printf("\nBreadth First traversal of the graph is \n");
    temp1 = startList;
    if (temp1 == NULL)
      printf("Sorry no vertices in the graph\n");
    else
      queue(temp1);
    while (rear != -1) {
      temp3 = dequeue();
      temp1 = startList;
      while (temp1 - > nme != temp3 - > nme) temp1 = temp1 - > vrt;
      temp3 = temp1;
      if (temp3 - > marked == N) {
        printf("%c\t", temp3 - > nme);
        temp3 - > marked = Y;
        temp2 = temp3 - > edg;
        while (temp2 != NULL) {
          queue(temp2);
          temp2 = temp2 - > edg;
        }
      }
    }
  }
  return 0;
```

```
}

void queue(struct node * paramNode) {
    rear++;
    que[rear] = paramNode;
    if (front == -1) front = 0;
}

struct node * dequeue() {
    struct node * tempNode;
    if (front == rear) {
        tempNode = que[front];
        front = -1;
        rear = -1;
    } else {
        tempNode = que[front];
        front++;
    }
    return (tempNode);
}
```

Now, let's go behind the scenes to understand the code better.

How it works...

We are using the adjacency list representation of the directed graph from the previous recipe, *Creating an adjacency list representation of a directed graph*:

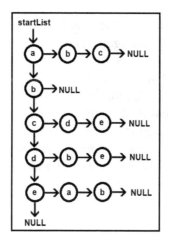

Figure 10.18

The `temp1` pointer is set to point to `startList`. That is, `temp1` is pointing to the node with vertex `a`. If `temp1` is not `NULL`, the node pointed to by the `temp1` pointer is added to the queue. The rear variable, which is -1 at the moment, is incremented to 0 and the `a` node is added to the array of `que` nodes at index location 0. Because the value of the front index location is -1 currently, the front is also set to 0, as follows:

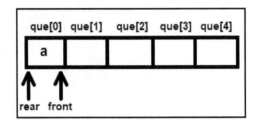

Figure 10.19

Thereafter, the dequeue function is invoked to remove a node from the queue. Unsurprisingly, the node at the `que[0]` index location, that is, `a`, is returned and, because the values of **front** and **rear** are the same, the values of the **front** and **rear** indices are set to -1, to indicate that the queue is empty again.

The node containing vertex `a` is returned from the queue and is assigned to the `temp3` pointer. The `temp1` pointer is set to point to the `startList` pointer. The marked member of the `temp3` node, that is, vertex `a`, is set to `N` initially. The vertex name stored in the `nme` member of the node is displayed, that is, vertex `a` is displayed on screen.

After displaying vertex `a`, its marked member is set to `Y` to indicate that the node is visited and should not be traversed again. The next step is to find the adjacent vertices of vertex `a`. To do so, the `temp2` pointer is set to point to where the `edg` pointer of `temp3` is pointing. The `edg` pointer of `temp3` is pointing at vertex `b`, so `temp2` is set to point at vertex `b`. Again, the procedure is repeated. If `temp2` is not `NULL`, the `b` node is queued, that is, it is added to the `que[0]` index location. Because all of the nodes that are connected to vertex `a` have to be queued, the `temp2` pointer is set to point to the location where its `edg` pointer is pointing. The `edg` pointer of node `b` (in the adjacency list) is pointing to node `c`, so node `c` is also inserted into the queue at the `que[1]` index location as follows:

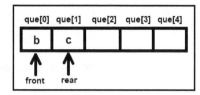

Figure 10.20

In the queue, nodes b and c are present. Now, again, the dequeue function is invoked; node b is removed from the queue and the temp3 pointer is set to point to it. The temp1 pointer is initially set to point to startList and, thereafter, by making use of its vrt pointer, the temp1 pointer is set to point to vertex b. Because the marked member of node b is N, its vertex name, b, is displayed on screen followed by setting its marked member to Y. A temp2 pointer is set to point to where the edg member of node b is pointing. The edg member of node b is pointing to NULL, so the next node in the queue is accessed, that is, node c is removed from the queue and the temp3 pointer is set to point to it. Because the queue is again empty, the values of the front and rear variables are set to -1.

Again, the temp1 pointer is set to point at vertex c, and the c node is displayed on screen, that is, it is traversed and its marked member is set to Y. So, up until now, nodes a, b, and c are displayed on screen. And the node that is attached to the edg member of c is added to the queue, that is, node d is added to the queue at the que[0] index location. Additionally, the node pointed to by the edg pointer of node d is accessed, that is, node e is also queued or, in other words, added at the que[1] index location as follows:

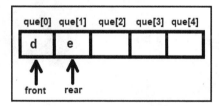

Figure 10.21

Node d is removed from the queue and displayed (traversed). The nodes pointed to by their edg member are accessed and, if any of them is marked, then N is added to the queue. The whole procedure is repeated until the queue becomes empty. The sequence in which the vertices are displayed on screen forms the breadth-first traversal of the graph.

The program is compiled using GCC, as shown in the following screenshot. Because no error appears during the compilation, this means the `breadthfirsttrav.c` program has successfully compiled into the `breadthfirsttrav.exe` file. On executing the file, the user will be prompted to specify the count of vertices in the graph, followed by entering the vertices' names. Thereafter, the user is asked to enter the edges of the graph and to enter `0 0` when completed. After the edges of the graph have been entered, the adjacency list representation of the graph will be displayed, followed by the breadth-first traversal of the graph, as shown in the following screenshot:

```
D:\CAdvBook>gcc breadthfirsttrav.c -o breadthfirsttrav

D:\CAdvBook>breadthfirsttrav
How many vertices are there ?5
Enter all vertices names
a
b
c
d
e
Enter the edges between vertices. Enter v1 v2, if there is an edge
between v1 and v2. Enter 0 0 if over
a b
a c
c d
c e
d b
d e
e a
e b
0 0

Adjacency List representation of Graph is
a        b        c
b
c        d        e
d        b        e
e        a        b

Breadth First traversal of the graph is
a        b        c        d        e
```

Figure 10.22

Now, let's move on to the next recipe!

Carrying out the depth-first traversal of a graph

In depth-first traversal (also called depth-first search), all nodes of a graph are visited by taking a path and going as deep as possible down that path. On reaching the end, you go back, pick up another path, and then repeat the process.

In this recipe, we will learn how to carry out the depth-first traversal of the graph.

How to do it...

Follow these steps for the depth-first traversal of a graph:

1. Push the first vertex of the graph into the stack. You can choose any vertex of the graph as the starting vertex.
2. Then, repeat the following *steps 3 to 7* until the stack is empty.
3. Pop the vertex from the stack and call it by any name, say, v.
4. Mark the popped vertex as visited. This marking is done so that this vertex should not be traversed again.
5. Display the marked vertex.
6. Find out the adjacency vertices of the v vertex, and then perform *step 7* on each of them.
7. If any of the adjacency vertices of v are not marked, mark them as visited and push them on to the stack.
8. Exit.

The program for the depth-first traversal of a graph is as follows:

//**depthfirsttrav.c**

```
#include <stdlib.h>
#include <stdio.h>
#define max 20

enum Setmarked {Y,N};
struct node {
    char nme;
    struct node * vrt;
    struct node * edg;
    enum Setmarked marked;
```

```
};

struct node * stack[max];
int top = -1;
void push(struct node * h);
struct node * pop();

int main() {
  int numb, i, j, noe;
  char v1, v2;
  struct node * startList, * newNode, * temp1, * temp2, * temp3;
  printf("How many vertices are there ?");
  scanf("%d", & numb);
  startList = NULL;
  printf("Enter all vertices names\n");
  for (i = 1; i <= numb; i++) {
    if (startList == NULL) {
      newNode = malloc(sizeof(struct node));
      scanf(" %c", & newNode - > nme);
      /* There is a white space before %c */
      startList = newNode;
      temp1 = newNode;
      newNode - > vrt = NULL;
      newNode - > edg = NULL;
      newNode - > marked = N;
    } else {
      newNode = malloc(sizeof(struct node));
      scanf(" %c", & newNode - > nme);
      /* There is a white space before %c */
      newNode - > vrt = NULL;
      newNode - > edg = NULL;
      newNode - > marked = N;
      temp1 - > vrt = newNode;
      temp1 = newNode;
    }
  }
  printf("Enter the edges between vertices. Enter v1 v2, if there is
an edge\n");
  printf("between v1 and v2. Enter 0 0 if over\n");
  noe = numb * (numb - 1);
  for (j = 1; j <= noe; j++) {
    scanf(" %c %c", & v1, & v2);
    /* There is a white space before %c */
    if (v1 == '0' && v2 == '0') break;
    temp1 = startList;
    while (temp1 != NULL && temp1 - > nme != v1)
      temp1 = temp1 - > vrt;
    if (temp1 == NULL) {
```

```
         printf("Sorry no vertex exist by this name\n");
         break;
      }
      temp2 = temp1;
      while (temp2 - > edg != NULL) temp2 = temp2 - > edg;
      newNode = malloc(sizeof(struct node));
      newNode - > nme = v2;
      temp2 - > edg = newNode;
      newNode - > edg = NULL;
      newNode - > vrt = NULL;
   }
   printf("\nAdjacency List representation of Graph is\n");
   temp1 = startList;
   while (temp1 != NULL) {
      printf("%c\t", temp1 - > nme);
      temp2 = temp1 - > edg;
      while (temp2 != NULL) {
         printf("%c\t", temp2 - > nme);
         temp2 = temp2 - > edg;
      }
      printf("\n");
      temp1 = temp1 - > vrt;
   }
   printf("\nDepth First traversal of the graph is \n");
   temp1 = startList;
   if (temp1 == NULL)
      printf("Sorry no vertices in the graph\n");
   else
      push(temp1);
   while (top >= 0) {
      temp3 = pop();
      temp1 = startList;
      while (temp1 - > nme != temp3 - > nme) temp1 = temp1 - > vrt;
      temp3 = temp1;
      if (temp3 - > marked == N) {
         printf("%c\t", temp3 - > nme);
         temp3 - > marked = Y;
         temp2 = temp3 - > edg;
         while (temp2 != NULL) {
            push(temp2);
            temp2 = temp2 - > edg;
         }
      }
   }
   return 0;
}

void push(struct node * h) {
```

```
    top++;
    stack[top] = h;
}

struct node * pop() {
    return (stack[top--]);
}
```

Now, let's go behind the scenes to understand the code better.

How it works...

We are using the adjacency list representation of the directed graph from the previous recipe, *Creating an adjacency list representation of a directed graph*:

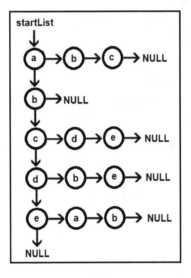

Figure 10.23

The `temp1` pointer is set to point to `startList`, that is, at node a, which we have assumed as the starting vertex of the graph. We then ensure that if `temp1` is not `NULL`, then the node pointed to by the `temp1` pointer is pushed to the stack. The value of `top`, which is initially -1, is incremented to 0 and node a is added to the array of the nodes stack at index location **0**, as follows:

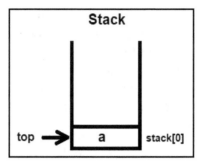

Figure 10.24

Thereafter, the `pop` function is invoked to remove the node from the stack. The node at the `stack[0]` index location is returned and the value of `top` is again decremented to -1.

The node containing vertex `a` is returned to the `temp3` pointer. The `temp1` pointer is set to point to the `startList` pointer. The marked member of the `temp3` node, that is, vertex `a`, is set to `N` initially. The vertex name stored in the `nme` member of the node is displayed, that is, vertex `a`, is displayed on screen. After displaying vertex `a`, its marked member is set to `Y` to indicate that the node is visited and should not be traversed again. The `temp2` pointer is set to point to where the `edg` pointer of `temp3` is pointing. The `edg` pointer of `temp3` is pointing to vertex `b`, so `temp2` is set to point to vertex `b`. Again, the procedure is repeated, that is, we check whether `temp2` is not `NULL`, and then node `b` is pushed to the stack at the `stack[0]` index location. Because all of the nodes that are connected to vertex `a` have to be pushed to the stack, the `temp2` pointer is set to point to the location that its `edg` pointer is pointing to. The `edg` pointer of node `b` (in the adjacency list) is pointing to node `c`, so node `c` is also pushed to the stack at the `stack[1]` index location, as follows:

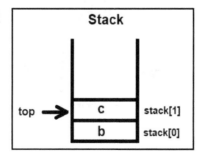

Figure 10.25

In the stack, nodes b and c are present. Now, again, the pop function is invoked, and the node, c, is popped from the stack and the temp3 pointer is set to point to it. The temp1 pointer is initially set to point to startList and, thereafter, by making use of its vrt pointer, the temp1 pointer is set to point to vertex c. Because the marked member of node c is N, its vertex name, c, is displayed on screen and its marked member is set to Y. So, up until now, nodes a and c are displayed on screen.

A temp2 pointer is set to point to where the edg member of node c is pointing. The edg member of node c is pointing to node d, so the d node is pushed to the stack and the next adjacent node of c is accessed. The next adjacent node of node c is node e, which is also pushed to the stack as follows:

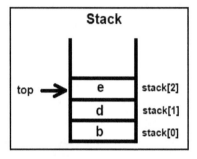

Figure 10.26

Again, the topmost node from the stack, node e, is popped, and the temp3 pointer is set to point to it. Again, the temp1 pointer is set to point to vertex e, and node e is displayed on screen, that is, it is traversed. Then, its marked member is set to Y, and the node that is attached to the edg member of e is pushed to the stack, that is, node a is pushed to the stack, followed by node b, as shown here:

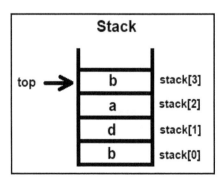

Figure 10.27

Node b is popped and the `temp3` pointer is set to point to it. The `temp1` pointer is set to point to node b. Because the marked member of node b is N, stating that it is not yet traversed, vertex b is displayed on screen and its marked member is set to Y. Since there is no adjacent member of vertex b, the next node, a, in the stack is popped. Because vertex a has already been visited, the next node from the stack is popped: node d. The procedure is repeated, and the sequence of vertices displayed is considered as the depth-traversal of the graph.

The program is compiled using GCC, as shown in the following screenshot. Because no error appears during the compilation, this means the `depthfirsttrav.c` program has successfully compiled into the `depthfirsttrav.exe` file. On executing the file, the user will be prompted to specify the count of vertices in the graph, followed by entering the vertices' names. Thereafter, the user is asked to enter the edges of the graph and enter `0  0` when completed. After the edges of the graph are entered, the adjacency list representation of the graph will be displayed, followed by the depth-first traversal of the graph, as shown in the following screenshot:

```
D:\CAdvBook>gcc depthfirsttrav.c -o depthfirsttrav

D:\CAdvBook>depthfirsttrav
How many vertices are there ?5
Enter all vertices names
a
b
c
d
e
Enter the edges between vertices. Enter v1 v2, if there is an edge
between v1 and v2. Enter 0 0 if over
a b
a c
c d
c e
d b
d e
e a
e b
0 0

Adjacency List representation of Graph is
a        b        c
b
c        d        e
d        b        e
e        a        b

Depth First traversal of the graph is
a        c        e        b        d
```

Figure 10.28

Now, let's move on to the next recipe!

Creating minimum spanning trees using Prim's algorithm

In this recipe, we will learn how to create a minimum spanning tree. A minimum spanning tree of a graph with n number of nodes will have n nodes. In a connected weighted graph, each edge of the graph is assigned a non-negative number called the "weight of the edge." Then, any spanning tree of the graph is assigned a total weight obtained by adding the weights of the edges in the tree. A minimum spanning tree of a graph is a spanning tree whose total weight is as small as possible.

There are a number of techniques that you can use to create a minimum spanning tree for a weighted graph. One of these methods is called Prim's algorithm.

Prim's algorithm is part of the category of greedy algorithms, where vertices are connected with edges that have the lowest weights. An arbitrary node is chosen initially as the tree root. In an undirected graph, any node can be considered as the tree root and the nodes adjacent to it as its children. The nodes of the graph are then appended to the tree, one at a time, until all of the nodes of the graph are included. The node of the graph added to the tree at each point is adjacent to a node of the tree by an arc of minimum weight. The arc of minimum weight becomes a tree arc connecting this new node to the tree. When all the nodes of the graph have been added to the tree, a minimum spanning tree is said to be made for the graph.

How to do it...

Follow these steps to implement Prim's algorithm:

1. Choose any vertex from the graph as the root of the minimum spanning tree. It can be any random vertex.
2. Find all of the edges from the vertex (or vertices in the tree) to other vertices in the graph. From those vertices, choose the vertex that has the edge with the minimum weight and add that vertex to the tree.
3. Repeat *step 2* until all the vertices of the graph are added to the minimum spanning tree.

Consider the following weighted graph:

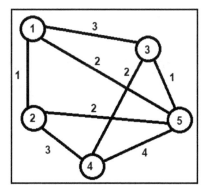

Figure 10.29

Now, to get the minimum spanning tree of this graph, we connect the vertices starting from vertex a (you can consider any vertex as the starting vertex of the graph). From the starting vertex, choose the nearest vertex having the lowest weight, and then repeat the procedure until all of the vertices are connected. In that way, we get the minimum spanning tree as follows:

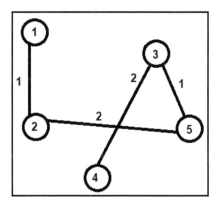

Figure 10.30

The preceding graph is called a tree because it is acyclic; it is called spanning because it covers every vertex.

The number of edges in a minimum spanning tree is *v-1*, where *v* is the number of vertices.

The program for creating a minimum spanning tree using Prim's algorithm is as follows:

```
//prims.c

#include <stdlib.h>
#include <stdio.h>
#define max 20
struct node
{
 int nme;
 int wt;
 struct node *vrt;
 struct node *edg;
 };

struct node *startList;

struct lst
{
 int u,v;
 int wt;
 struct lst *next;
}lst;

struct lst *pq=NULL;
struct lst *tr=NULL;
void addpqu(int a, int b, int w);
void maketree();
void disptree();
struct lst *delet();
int visited[max];
int n,nov=0;

int main()
{
 int i,j,noe,w;
 int a,b;
 struct node *newNode,*temp1,*temp2;
 printf ("How many vertices are there ?");
 scanf("%d",&n);
 printf("The vertices are named\n");
```

```
for(i=1;i<=n;i++)printf("%d\t",i);
printf("for convenience \n");
startList=NULL;
for(i=1;i<=n;i++)
{
    if (startList==NULL)
    {
        newNode =malloc(sizeof (struct node));
        newNode->nme=i;
        startList=newNode;
        temp1=newNode;
        newNode->vrt=NULL;
        newNode->edg=NULL;
    }
    else
    {
        newNode=malloc(sizeof (struct node));
        newNode->nme=i;
        newNode->vrt=NULL;
        newNode->edg=NULL;
        temp1->vrt=newNode;
        temp1=newNode;
    }
}
printf("Enter the edges between vertices. Enter 1 3, if there is an
edge\n");
printf("between 1 and 3. Enter 0 0 if over\n");
noe=n*(n-1);
for(j=1;j<=noe;j++)
{
    printf("Enter edge ");
    scanf("%d %d",&a,&b);
    if(a==0 && b==0)break;
    printf("Enter weight ");
    scanf("%d",&w);
    temp1=startList;
    while(temp1!=NULL && temp1->nme!=a)
    {
        temp1=temp1->vrt;
    }
    if(temp1==NULL)
    {
        printf("Sorry no vertex exist by this name\n");
        break;
    }
    temp2=temp1;
    while(temp2->edg!=NULL)temp2=temp2->edg;
    newNode=malloc(sizeof (struct node));
```

```
            newNode->nme=b;
            newNode->wt=w;
            temp2->edg=newNode;
            newNode->edg=NULL;
            newNode->vrt=NULL;
            temp1=startList;
            while(temp1!=NULL && temp1->nme!=b)
                temp1=temp1->vrt;
            if(temp1==NULL)
            {
                printf("Sorry no vertex exist by this name\n");
                break;
            }
            temp2=temp1;
            while(temp2->edg!=NULL)temp2=temp2->edg;
            newNode=malloc(sizeof (struct node));
            newNode->nme=a;
            newNode->wt=w;
            temp2->edg=newNode;
            newNode->edg=NULL;
            newNode->vrt=NULL;
    }
    printf ("Adjacency List representation of Graph is\n");
    temp1=startList;
    while (temp1!=NULL)
    {
        printf ("%d\t",temp1->nme);
        temp2=temp1->edg;
        while(temp2!=NULL)
        {
            printf("%d\t",temp2->nme);
            temp2=temp2->edg;
        }
        printf("\n");
        temp1=temp1->vrt;
    }
    temp1=startList;
    temp2=temp1->edg;
    while(temp2!=NULL)
    {
        addpqu(temp1->nme,temp2->nme, temp2->wt);
        temp2=temp2->edg;
    }
    maketree();
    disptree();
    return 0;
    }
```

```
void addpqu(int a, int b, int w)
{
 struct lst *lstNode,*findloc1,*findloc2;
 lstNode=malloc(sizeof(struct lst));
 lstNode->u=a;
 lstNode->v=b;
 lstNode->wt=w;
 lstNode->next=NULL;
 if(pq==NULL)
 {
     pq = lstNode;
 }
 else
 {
     if(lstNode->wt < pq->wt)
     {
         lstNode->next=pq;
         pq=lstNode;
     }
     else
     {
         findloc1=pq;
         while((findloc1!=NULL) && (findloc1->wt <= lstNode->wt))
         {
             findloc2=findloc1;
             findloc1=findloc1->next;
         }
         findloc2->next=lstNode;
         lstNode->next=findloc1;
     }
 }
}

struct lst *delet()
{
 struct lst *tempNode;
 if (pq !=NULL)
 {
     tempNode=pq;
     pq=pq->next;
     return tempNode;
 }
 else
     return NULL;
}

void maketree()
{
```

```
struct lst *lstNode,*tempNode1,*tempNode2;
struct node *x,*y;
int i,j;
while(nov <n)
{
    nxt: lstNode=delet();
    for(i=1;i<=nov;i++)
    {
        if(visited[i]==lstNode->u)
        {
            for(j=1;j<=nov;j++)
                if(visited[j]==lstNode->v) goto nxt;
        }
    }
    for(i=1;i<=nov;i++)
        if(visited[i]==lstNode->u) goto rpt;
    nov++;
    visited[nov]=lstNode->u;
    rpt: for(i=1;i<=nov;i++)
    {
        if(visited[i]==lstNode->v) goto rptt;
    }
    nov++;
    visited[nov]=lstNode->v;
    rptt: lstNode->next=NULL;
    if (tr==NULL)
    {
        tr=lstNode;
        tempNode1=tr;
    }
    else
    {
        tempNode1->next=lstNode;
        tempNode1=lstNode;
    }
    x=startList;
    while(x->nme!=lstNode->v)x=x->vrt;
    y=x->edg;
    pq=NULL;
    while(y!=NULL)
    {
        addpqu(x->nme,y->nme, y->wt);
        y=y->edg;
    }
}
}

void disptree()
```

```
{
  struct lst *t;
  t=tr;
  printf("Minimal Spanning tree with Prims Algorithm is \n");
  while(t!=NULL)
  {
      printf("%d %d\n",t->u,t->v);
      t=t->next;
  }
}
```

Now, let's go behind the scenes to understand the code better.

How it works...

The user is prompted to specify the number of vertices. Assuming the user enters 5, the value of 5 will be assigned to variable n. The vertices will be automatically named 1, 2, 3, 4, and 5 for convenience. A startList pointer of the node type is defined and is set to NULL initially. The startList pointer will be pointing to the first node of the adjacency linked list that will be created from the graph.

Two structures are defined: one is called node and the other is called lst. The node structure is for making the adjacency list representation of the graph and the lst structure is for creating a minimum spanning tree. Two pointers, pq and tr, are defined of the lst type and are defined as NULL.

To make the adjacency linked list representation, the first step is to create a linked list of the nodes, where each node represents a vertex of the graph. Because there are five vertices in the graph, a for loop is set to execute five times. Within the for loop, a node is created, called newNode, and the vertex number, 1, is assigned to its nme member. The startList pointer is set to point to newNode. The vrt and edg members of newNode are set to NULL. The temp1 pointer is also set to point to newNode. The startList pointer will keep pointing to the first node of the linked list, whereas the temp1 pointer will be used for connecting other nodes, that is, other vertices.

In the next iteration of the `for` loop, again, a new node is created, called `newNode`, and the vertex number, 2, will be assigned to it. The `vrt` and `edg` members of `newNode` are set to `NULL`. To connect with the existing vertices, 1, the `vrt` member of `temp1` is set to point to `newNode`. Thereafter, `temp1` is set to point to `NewNode`. The `for` loop will execute for the time equal to the number of vertices, that is, five, hence creating five nodes that contain their respective vertex numbers. By the time the `for` loop terminates, the vertices will be created and will appear as follows:

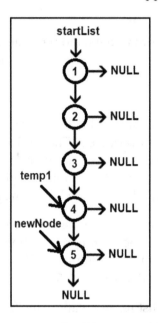

Figure 10.31

Once the vertices are created, the next step is to ask the user for the edges between the vertices. A graph having *n* vertices can, at most, have *n* * *(n-1)* edges. Because the number of vertices is five, so the node, that is, the number of edges variable, is initialized to 5*4=20. A `for` loop, `j`, is set to execute from 1 to 20, asking the user to enter the edges and their respective weights. Suppose that the user enters an edge as `1 2`, which will be assigned to the `a` and `b` variables, respectively; the weight entered is `1`, which is assigned to the `w` variable.

To create this edge, the `temp1` pointer is set to point to `startList`. To create a *(1,2)* edge, the `temp1` pointer is set to point to the node whose `nme` member is equal to 1. Currently, `temp1` is already pointing to vertex 1. The next step is to add vertex 2 at the end of vertex 1. To find the end of a vertex, we will take the help of another pointer, called `temp2`. The `temp2` pointer is first set to point to the node that the `temp1` pointer is pointing to. Thereafter, using its `edg` pointer, `temp2` is set to point to the last node of vertex 1. Then, a new node is created, called `newNode`, and the value of 2 is assigned to the `nme` member of `newNode`. The weight, 1, in the `w` variable is assigned to the `wt` member of `newNode`. The `edge` and `vrt` pointers of `newNode` are set to `NULL`. And, finally, the `edg` member of `temp2` is set to point to `newNode`. Therefore, vertices 1 and 2 are now connected.

This is an undirected graph, and edge *(1,2)* can also mean an edge from 2 to 1. So, we need an edge from vertex 2 to 1. The `temp1` pointer is set to point to `startList`. Using its `vrt` pointer, the `temp1` pointer is set to move further until it reaches vertex 2.

Once `temp1` reaches vertex 2, the next step is to set the `temp2` pointer to point to the last node of vertex 2. After doing so, a new node, called `newNode`, is created and the value of 1 is assigned to its `nme` member. Additionally, the weight in the `w` variable is assigned to the `wt` member of `newNode`. To connect these nodes that contain vertices 2 and 1, the edge pointer of `temp2` is set to point to `newNode`. The `edg` and `vrt` pointers of `newNode` are set to `NULL`. Therefore, vertices 2 and 1 are connected now too.

Displaying the adjacency linked list

After entering all of the edges along with their weights, the adjacency list has to be displayed. To do this, a `temp1` pointer is set to point to `startList`. A `while` loop will execute until the `temp1` pointer reaches `NULL`. So, the `temp1` pointer will point to vertex 1 initially. Thereafter, by taking the help of the second pointer, `temp2`, all the edges of the `temp1` pointer (that is, vertex 1) are accessed and displayed on screen. After displaying all the edges of vertex 1, by making use of the `vrt` member, the `temp1` pointer is set to point to the next vertex, that is, to vertex 2. Again, the `temp2` pointer is set to point at vertex 2, and, using its `edg` member, all the edges of vertex 2 are displayed. The procedure is repeated for all the vertices of the graph.

The adjacency list will appear as follows:

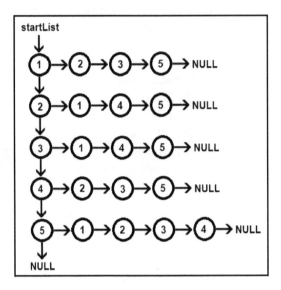

Figure 10.32

Creating the minimum spanning tree

To make the minimum spanning tree, we need to adjust the edges of the vertices in ascending order. The temp1 pointer is set to point at startList, that is, vertex 1. The temp2 pointer is set to point to where the edg pointer of temp1 is pointing to, that is, vertex 2.

Now, until temp2 becomes NULL, the addpqu function is invoked and vertices 1 and 2, and their weight, 1, are passed to it. In the addpqu function, a structure is created called lstNode of the lst type. The 1 and 2 vertices and their weight, 1, are assigned to the u, v, and wt members, respectively. The next pointer of lstNode is set to NULL. Additionally, a pointer, pq, is set to point to lstNode.

Following this, the `temp2` pointer is set to point to where its `edg` pointer is pointing, that is, vertex 3. Again, the `addpqu` function is called and vertices 1 and 3 and weight 3 are passed to it. In the `addpqu` function, again, a new node is creating, called `1stNode`, and vertices 1 and 3 and weight 3 are assigned to its `u`, `v`, and `wt` members, respectively. The next pointer of `1stNode` is set to `NULL`.

Because the nodes have to be arranged in ascending order of their weights, the `wt` member of `1stNode` and the previous node, `pq`, are compared. The `wt` member of `1stNode` is 3, which is greater than the `wt` member of the `pq` node, which is 1. So, the help of two pointers, `findloc1` and `findloc2`, is taken. One pointer is set to point to the weights of `1stNode`, and the `pq` nodes are compared.

Let's choose a vertex, 1, and add it to the minimum spanning tree:

Figure 10.33

Now, from vertex 1, there are edges to the vertices of 3, 2, and 5, but the edge with the minimum weight is to vertex 2. So, vertex 2 is also added to the minimum spanning tree:

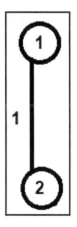

Figure 10.34

Again, from vertices 1 and 2 in the minimum spanning tree, we search for all the edges that lead to other vertices. We find that edges **(1,5)** and **(2,5)** have the same weight, so we can choose either of the vertices. Let's add edge **(2,5)** to the minimum spanning tree:

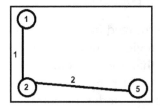

Figure 10.35

From the vertices of 1, 2, and 5 in the minimum spanning tree, we search for the edges with the lowest weights. Edge **(5,3)** has the minimum weight of 1, so edge **(5,3)** is added to the minimum spanning tree:

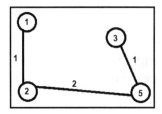

Figure 10.36

Now, we need to find the edge that leads to vertex 4 from the existing vertices in the minimum spanning tree. Edge **(3,4)** has the lowest weight and is, therefore, added to the minimum spanning tree:

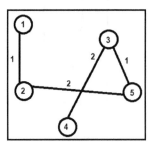

Figure 10.37

On compiling and running the program, you should get an output that is similar to the following screenshot:

```
D:\CAdvBook>gcc prims.c -o prims

D:\CAdvBook>prims
How many vertices are there ?5
The vertices are named
1       2       3       4       5          for convenience
Enter the edges between vertices. Enter 1 3, if there is an edge
between 1 and 3. Enter 0 0 if over
Enter edge 1 3
Enter weight 3
Enter edge 1 5
Enter weight 2
Enter edge 1 2
Enter weight 1
Enter edge 2 5
Enter weight 2
Enter edge 2 4
Enter weight 3
Enter edge 3 4
Enter weight 2
Enter edge 3 5
Enter weight 1
Enter edge 4 5
Enter weight 4
Enter edge 0 0
Adjacency List representation of Graph is
1       3       5       2
2       1       5       4
3       1       4       5
4       2       3       5
5       1       2       3       4
Minimal Spanning tree with Prims Algorithm is
1 2
2 5
5 3
3 4
```

Figure 10.38

Now, let's move on to the next recipe!

Creating minimum spanning trees using Kruskal's algorithm

In this recipe, we will learn how to make a minimum spanning tree using Kruskal's algorithm.

A minimum/minimal spanning tree of an undirected graph is a tree that is formed from graph edges that connect all of the vertices of the graph at the lowest total cost. A minimum spanning tree can exist if, and only if, the graph is connected. A graph is said to be connected if there exists a path between any two vertices.

Here, the nodes of the graph are initially considered as n distinct partial trees with one node each. At each step of the algorithm, two distinct partial trees are connected into a single partial tree by an edge of the graph. When only one partial tree exists (for instance, after $n-1$ such steps), it is a minimum spanning tree.

The connecting arc of minimum cost is used to connect two distinct trees. To do this, the arcs can be placed in a priority queue based on weight. The arc of lowest weight is then examined to see whether it connects two distinct trees. To determine whether an arc (x, y) connects two distinct trees, we can implement the trees with a father field in each node. Then, we can traverse all the ancestors of x and y to obtain the root of the tree connecting them. If the root of the two trees is the same node, and x and y are already in the same tree, then arc (x, y) is discarded, and the arc of the next lowest weight is examined.

How to do it...

Follow these steps to create a minimum spanning tree using Kruskal's algorithm:

1. Sort the edge list in ascending order of their weights.
2. Pick up the edge at the top of the edge list (with the smallest weight).
3. Remove this edge from the edge list.
4. Connect the two vertices with the given edge. If, by connecting the vertices, a cycle is made in the graph, then discard the edge.
5. Repeat the preceding *steps 2 to 4* until $n-1$ edges are added or the list of edges is complete.

The program for creating a minimum spanning tree using Kruskal's algorithm is as follows:

//kruskal.c

```
#include <stdlib.h>
#include <stdio.h>
#define max 20

struct node
{
 int nme;
 int wt;
 struct node *v;
 struct node *e;
};

typedef struct lst
{
 int u,v;
 int wt;
 struct lst *nxt;
}lst;

lst *pq=NULL;
lst *tr=NULL;
void addpqu(int a, int b, int w);
void maketree();
void disptree();
lst *delet();
int parent[max];

int main()
{
 int n,i,j,noe,w;
 int a,b;
 struct node *adj,*newNode,*p,*q;
 printf ("How many vertices are there ? ");
 scanf("%d",&n);
 for(i=1;i<=n;i++)parent[i]=0;
 printf("The vertices are named\n");
 for(i=1;i<=n;i++)printf("%d\t",i);
 printf("for convenience \n");
 for(i=1;i<=n;i++)
 {
     if (i==1)
     {
         newNode =malloc(sizeof (struct node));
```

```
            newNode->nme=i;
            adj=newNode;
            p=newNode;
            newNode->v=NULL;
            newNode->e=NULL;
        }
        else
        {
            newNode=malloc(sizeof (struct node));
            newNode->nme=i;
            newNode->v=NULL;
            newNode->e=NULL;
            p->v=newNode;
            p=newNode;
        }
    }
    printf("Enter the edges between vertices. Enter 1 3, if there is an
edge\n");
    printf("between 1 and 3. Enter 0 0 if over\n");
    noe=n*(n-1);
    for(j=1;j<=noe;j++)
    {
        printf("Enter edge: ");
        scanf("%d %d",&a,&b);
        if(a==0 && b==0)break;
        printf("Enter weight: ");
        scanf("%d",&w);
        p=adj;
        while(p!=NULL && p->nme!=a)
            p=p->v;
        if(p==NULL)
        {
            printf("Sorry no vertex exist by this name\n");
            break;
        }
        q=p;
        while(q->e!=NULL)q=q->e;
        newNode=malloc(sizeof (struct node));
        newNode->nme=b;
        newNode->wt=w;
        q->e=newNode;
        newNode->e=NULL;
        newNode->v=NULL;
        addpqu(a,b,w);
    }
    printf ("Adjacency List representation of Graph is\n");
    p=adj;
    while (p!=NULL)
```

```
    {
        printf ("%d\t",p->nme);
        q=p->e;
        while(q!=NULL)
        {
            printf("%d\t",q->nme);
            q=q->e;
        }
        printf("\n");
        p=p->v;
    }
    maketree();
    disptree();
    return 0;
}

void addpqu(int a, int b, int w)
{
lst *newNode,*k,*h;
newNode=(lst *)malloc(sizeof(lst));
newNode->u=a;
newNode->v=b;
newNode->wt=w;
newNode->nxt=NULL;
if(pq==NULL)
    pq = newNode;
else
{
    if(newNode->wt < pq->wt)
    {
        newNode->nxt=pq;
        pq=newNode;
    }
    else
    {
        k=pq;
        while((k!=NULL) && (k->wt <= newNode->wt))
        {
            h=k;
            k=k->nxt;
        }
        h->nxt=newNode;
        newNode->nxt=k;
    }
  }
}

lst *delet()
```

```
{
 lst *q;
 if (pq !=NULL)
 {
     q=pq;
     pq=pq->nxt;
     return q;
 }
 else
     return NULL;
 }

void maketree()
{
 lst *newNode,*p;
 int x,y,r1,r2;
 newNode=delet();
 while(newNode !=NULL)
 {
     newNode->nxt=NULL;
     x=newNode->u;
     y=newNode->v;
     while(x>0)
     {
         r1=x;
         x=parent[x];
     }
     while(y>0)
     {
         r2=y;
         y=parent[y];
     }
     if(r1 !=r2)
     {
         parent[r2]=r1;
         if (tr==NULL)
         {
             tr=newNode;
             p=tr;
         }
         else
         {
             p->nxt=newNode;
             p=newNode;
         }
     }
     newNode=delet();
 }
```

```
    }

void disptree()
{
  lst *t;
  t=tr;
  printf("Minimal Spanning tree with Kruskal Algorithm is \n");
  while(t!=NULL)
  {
      printf("%d %d\n",t->u,t->v);
      t=t->nxt;
  }
}
```

Now, let's go behind the scenes to understand the code better.

How it works...

Consider the following undirected graph:

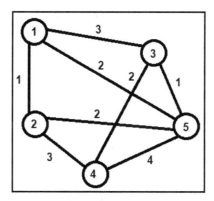

Figure 10.39

Because the graph has five vertices, the minimum spanning tree will have four edges. The first step in Kruskal's algorithm is that the edges of the graph are first sorted in ascending order of their weights:

```
Weight    Src    Dest
1         1      2
1         3      5
2         1      5
2         2      5
2         3      4
```

3	1	3
3	2	4
4	4	5

Now, we will pick up one edge at a time from the preceding table, and, if it does not make a cycle, we will include it in the minimum spanning tree. We begin with edge **(1,2)**. There is no cycle in this edge; therefore, it is included in the minimum spanning tree as follows:

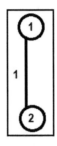

Figure 10.40

The next edge in the table is **(3,5)**. This edge also does not make a cycle, so it included in the minimum spanning tree:

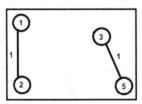

Figure 10.41

Next, pick edge **(1,5)**. Again, no cycle is made with this edge, so it is included in the minimum spanning tree:

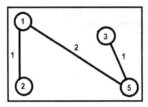

Figure 10.42

The next edge in the table is **(2,5)** but it does make a cycle, so it is discarded. The next edge in the table is **(3,4)**. Edge **(3,4)** does not make a cycle; therefore, it is added to the minimum spanning tree:

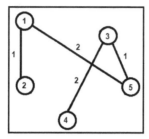

Figure 10.43

The number of vertices is 5, so the number of edges will be *v-1*, that is, 4, and we have 4 edges, so our minimum spanning tree is complete.

On compiling and running the `kruskal.c` program, we get an output that is similar to the following screenshot:

```
Adjacency List representation of Graph is
1        3        5        2
2        5        4
3        4        5
4        5
5
Minimal Spanning tree with Kruskal Algorithm is
1 2
3 5
1 5
3 4
```

Figure 3.44

As you can see, we get the adjacency list representation and the minimal spanning tree using Kruskal's algorithm in the output.

11
Advanced Data Structures and Algorithms

In this chapter, we will learn about advanced data structures and algorithms. We will learn how to use structures such as stacks, circular linked lists, doubly linked lists, and binary trees and their traversal.

In this chapter, we will cover the following recipes:

- Implementing a stack using a singly linked list
- Implementing a doubly or two-way linked list
- Implementing a circular linked list
- Making a binary search tree and doing inorder traversal recursively
- Performing postorder traversal of a binary tree non-recursively

Before we get into the recipes, it will be helpful for us to understand some of the structures and related terminologies we will be using in this chapter as well as in the other recipes in this book.

Stack

A stack is a data structure where all insertions and deletions are performed at one end. The end at which insertions and deletions are performed is called the **top of the stack (tos)**. The stack is also known as a **pushdown list** or **Last In First Out (LIFO)**; that is, the last item that is added to the stack is added at the top of all earlier items and will be the first item to be taken out of the stack.

The operations that can be performed on the stack are as follows:

- **Push**: This pushes the value onto the stack. Before pushing the value onto the stack, the value at the top is incremented to point at the new position where the new value can be pushed.
- **Pop**: This pops or fetches the value from the stack. The value at the top or the value pointed at by the top is taken out of the stack.
- **Peep**: This shows the value that is at the top of the stack, that is, the value that is pointed at by the stack, without taking that value out of the stack.

Doubly linked lists (two-way linked lists)

In doubly or two-way linked lists, two pointers are used in the structure, where one pointer points in the forward direction and the other points in the backward direction. These two pointers allow us to traverse a linked list in both ways, that is, in **First in First Out (FIFO)** order as well as LIFO order. In a singly linked list, traversal is only possible in one direction. The node of a doubly linked list looks like this:

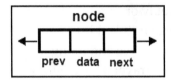

As we can see in the preceding diagram, there are two pointers, next and prev (you can give any name you like to these pointers). The next pointer is pointing at the next node, while the prev pointer is pointing at its previous node. To traverse the doubly linked list in both directions, we will make use of two other pointers called startList and endList. The startList pointer is set to point at the first node, while the endList pointer is set to point at the last node to allow for the traversal of the doubly linked list in both directions.

To traverse in FIFO order, we begin traversing from the node being pointed at by startList, moving further with the help of the next pointer. To traverse in LIFO order, we begin traversing the linked list from the node that's being pointed at by the endList pointer, then move backward with help of the prev pointer.

A doubly linked list that consists of certain nodes may look as follows:

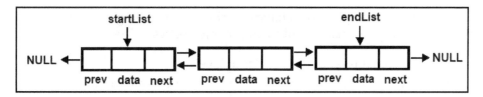

Note that the `prev` pointer of the first node and the `next` pointer of the last node is set to `NULL`. These `NULL` values help to terminate the traversing procedure.

Circular linked lists

In a linear linked list, the nodes are connected one after the other, and each node except the first has a unique predecessor and successor. The last node is set to point at `NULL` to indicate the termination of the linked list. But in the case of a circular linked list, the next pointer of the last node points back to the first node instead of pointing at `NULL`. In other words, a circular linked list has no `NULL` pointer, as can be seen in the following diagram:

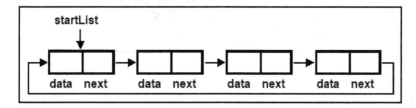

The advantage of a circular linked list over a linear linked list is that a circular linked list allows the pointer to move in reverse direction too. In real-world applications, the circular linked list is used in several places. For example, it can be used in an operating system while scheduling a CPU in a round-robin fashion, it can be used in a playlist of songs, and it can be used to track users in games.

Binary tree

A tree in which all of the nodes can have two children or siblings (at most) is called a binary tree. A binary tree has the following characteristics:

- A tree contains, at most, 2^l nodes at level l.
- If a binary tree contains m nodes at level l, it contains at most $2m$ nodes at level $l+1$.
- A tree contains $2d$ leaves and therefore $2d-1$ non-leaf nodes, where d is its depth.
- A binary tree with n internal nodes has $(n+1)$ external nodes.
- A binary tree with n nodes has exactly $n+1$ NULL links (see the following screenshot):

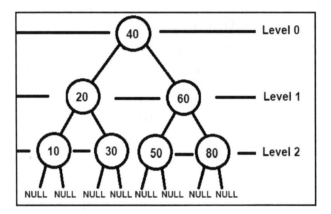

Binary search trees

A binary search tree is a tree in which the time to search an element is O(log2n) (which is faster than searching an element in a binary tree, where O(n)). But to support O(log2n) searching, we need to add a special property to the binary tree: we put all the nodes with values smaller than the value in the root into its left subtree and all of the nodes with values larger than the value in the root into its right subtree.

Traversing trees

Traversing means visiting the nodes of a tree. There are three ways of traversing a binary tree: preorder, inorder, and postorder. Since traversing a binary tree requires visiting the root and then its left and right child, these three ways of traversal only differ in the order in which visiting is performed. The tree traversal methods that are defined with the recursion method are as follows:

For preorder traversal, these are the steps:

1. Visit the root
2. Traverse the left subtree in preorder
3. Traverse the right subtree in preorder

 In preorder traversal, the root node of the binary tree is visited first.

For inorder traversal, these are the steps:

1. Traverse the left subtree in inorder
2. Visit the root
3. Traverse the right subtree in inorder

For postorder traversal, these are the steps:

1. Traverse the left subtree in postorder
2. Traverse the right subtree in postorder

Now that we've had a thorough introduction to the structures we will be looking at in this chapter, we can begin our journey.

Implementing a stack using a singly linked list

In this recipe, we will learn how to implement a stack that has a LIFO structure. LIFO means that whatever element was added to the stack last will be the first to be removed. The stack is a very important component of any compiler and operating system. The stack is used in branching operations, recursion, and many other system-level tasks. The stack can be implemented using arrays as well as through linked lists. In this recipe, we will learn how to implement a stack using a single linked list.

How to do it...

Follow these steps to implement a stack using a linked list:

1. A structure is defined called node. In this structure, besides a data member for storing content for the stack, a pointer is also defined that points to the next node.
2. The top pointer is initialized to NULL to indicate that the stack is currently empty.
3. A menu is displayed and the user is asked whether they want to push or pop from the stack. The user can enter 1 to indicate that they want to push a value to the stack or enter 2 to indicate that they want to pop a value from the stack. If the user enters 1, go to *step 4*. If they enter 2, go to *step 9*. If they enter 3, it means they want to quit the program, so go to *step 13*.
4. Allocate memory for the new node.
5. Ask the user for the value to be pushed and assign that value to the data member of the node.
6. Invoke the push function where the next pointer of the new node is set to point at top.
7. The top pointer is set to point at the new node.
8. Go to *step 3* to display the menu.
9. Check whether the top pointer is NULL. If yes, then display the message Stack is empty and go to *step 3* to display the menu. If top is not NULL, go to the next step.
10. A temporary pointer, temp, is set to point at the node where top is pointing.
11. The top pointer is set to point to where its next pointer is pointing.

12. Return the node that's being pointed at by `temp` as the popped node and display the data member of the popped node.

13. Exit the program.

The program for implementing a stack using a linked list is as follows:

```c
//stacklinkedlist.c

#include<stdio.h>

#include <stdlib.h>

struct node {
  int data;
  struct node * next;
};

void push(struct node * NewNode, struct node ** Top);
struct node * pop(struct node ** Top);

int main() {
  struct node * newNode, * top, * recNode;
  int n = 0;
  top = NULL;
  while (n != 3) {
    printf("\n1. Pushing an element into the stack\n");
    printf("2. Popping out an element from the stack\n");
    printf("3. Quit\n");
    printf("Enter your choice 1/2/3:");
    scanf("%d", & n);
    switch (n) {
    case 1:
      newNode = (struct node * ) malloc(sizeof(struct node));
      printf("Enter the value to push: ");
      scanf("%d", & newNode - > data);
      push(newNode, & top);
      printf("Value %d is pushed to stack\n", newNode - > data);
      break;
    case 2:
      recNode = pop( & top);
      if (recNode == NULL) printf("Stack is empty\n");
      else
        printf("The value popped is %d\n", recNode - > data);
      break;
    }
  }
  return 0;
```

```
    }
    void push(struct node * NewNode, struct node ** Top) {
      NewNode - > next = * Top;
      * Top = NewNode;
    }

    struct node * pop(struct node ** Top) {
      struct node * temp;
      if ( * Top == NULL) return (NULL);
      else {
        temp = * Top;
        ( * Top) = ( * Top) - > next;
        return (temp);
      }
    }
```

Now, let's go behind the scenes so that we can understand the code.

How it works...

First, a structure is defined, called a node, that consists of two members: one is the data and the other is a pointer called next. Because we want our stack to only store integer values, the data member of the structure is defined as an integer for storing integers and the next pointer is used to connect other nodes. Initially, the top pointer is set to NULL.

A while loop is set to execute, within which a menu is displayed. The menu is set to display three options: 1, to push into the stack; 2, to pop from the stack; and 3, to quit. Until the user enters 3 in the menu, the while loop will continue executing and keep displaying the menu, prompting the user to enter the desired option. If the user enters 1 to push a value to the stack, a new node is created by newNode. The user is prompted to enter the value to be pushed to the stack. Suppose the data that's being entered by the user is 10. Here, that value will be assigned to the data member of newNode, as follows:

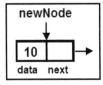

Thereafter, the `push` function is invoked and `newNode` and the `top` pointer are passed to it. In the `push` function, the next pointer of `newNode` is set to point at the `top` pointer, which is `NULL`, and then the top pointer is set to point at X, as follows:

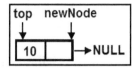

The `top` pointer must always point to the last inserted node. Due to this, it is set to point at `newNode`. After completing the `push` function, control goes back to the `main` function, where the menu will be displayed once more.

Let's assume that the user enters 1 to push another value to the stack. Again, a new node is created by `newNode`. The user is asked to enter the value to push. Assuming that the user enters 20, the value 20 will be assigned to the data member of `newNode`. The `push` function is invoked and `newNode` and the `top` pointer are passed to it. Here, the `top` pointer is pointing at the node that was pushed earlier, as follows:

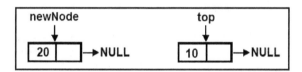

In the `push` function, the next pointer of `newNode` is set to point at the node where the `top` pointer is pointing to, as follows:

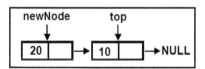

Then, the `top` pointer is set to point at `newNode`, as follows:

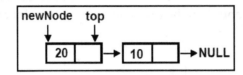

After executing the `push` function, the menu will be displayed again. Let's assume that the user wants to *pop* a value from the stack. To do this, they will enter 2 in the menu. The `pop` function will be invoked and the top pointer will be passed to it. In the `pop` function, it's ensured that the `top` pointer is not NULL because if it is, this means the stack is already empty; a value can't be popped out from an empty stack. To get the value from the stack, we will use a temporary pointer called `temp`. The `temp` pointer is set to point at the node that's being pointed to by the `top` pointer:

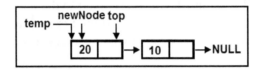

Thereafter, the `top` pointer is set to move to the next node, that is, the node where its next pointer is pointing to. The node that's being pointed at by the `temp` pointer is returned to the `main` function:

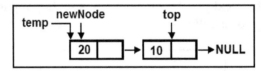

In the `main` function, the node that's returned by the `pop` function is assigned to `recNode`. First, it's confirmed that `recNode` is not NULL. Then, the value in its data member is displayed on the screen. So, 20 will be displayed on the screen.

After executing the pop function, the menu will be displayed once more, asking the user to enter the desired option. Let's assume that the user presses 2 to pop another value from the stack. Again, the pop function will be invoked. In the pop function, we check that the top pointer is not NULL and that it's pointing to a node. Because the top pointer is pointing at a node and is not NULL, a temporary pointer, temp, is set to point at the node that's being pointed to by the top pointer:

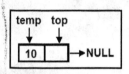

Thereafter, the top pointer is set to point to where its next pointer is pointing. The next pointer of top is pointing at NULL, so the top pointer will be set to NULL and the node that is being pointed to by the temp pointer is returned to the main function.

In the main function, the returned node from the pop function is assigned to the recNode pointer. After confirming that recNode is not pointing at NULL, the value in the data member of recNode is displayed on the screen. So, the value 10 will appear on the screen. After executing the pop function, the menu will be displayed again on the screen.

Let's assume that the user wants to pop the stack once more. But at this point, we know that the stack is empty. When the user presses 2 on the menu, the pop function will be invoked. However, since the value of the top pointer is NULL, the pop function will return a NULL value to the main function. In the main function, the NULL value that was returned by the pop function is assigned to the recNode pointer. Because the recNode pointer is assigned NULL, a message stating stack is empty will be displayed on the screen. Again, the menu will be displayed, prompting the user to enter a choice. Upon entering 3, the program will terminate.

The program is compiled using GCC. Because no error appears on compilation, this means the `stacklinkedlist.c` program has successfully compiled into the `stacklinkedlist.exe` file. On executing the file, we get a menu, prompting us to push or pop from the stack, as shown in the following screenshot:

```
D:\CAdvBook>gcc stacklinkedlist.c -o stacklinkedlist

D:\CAdvBook>stacklinkedlist

1. Pushing an element into the stack
2. Popping out an element from the stack
3. Quit
Enter your choice 1/2/3:1
Enter the value to push: 10
Value 10 is pushed to stack

1. Pushing an element into the stack
2. Popping out an element from the stack
3. Quit
Enter your choice 1/2/3:1
Enter the value to push: 20
Value 20 is pushed to stack

1. Pushing an element into the stack
2. Popping out an element from the stack
3. Quit
Enter your choice 1/2/3:2
The value popped is 20

1. Pushing an element into the stack
2. Popping out an element from the stack
3. Quit
Enter your choice 1/2/3:2
The value popped is 10

1. Pushing an element into the stack
2. Popping out an element from the stack
3. Quit
Enter your choice 1/2/3:2
Stack is empty

1. Pushing an element into the stack
2. Popping out an element from the stack
3. Quit
Enter your choice 1/2/3:3

D:\CAdvBook>
```

While popping from the stack, you must have noticed that the stack is a LIFO structure where the value that was pushed last was the first to be popped out.

Now, let's move on to the next recipe!

Implementing a doubly or two-way linked list

In this recipe, we will learn how to create a doubly linked list and how to traverse its elements in FIFO and LIFO order. As we explained in the introduction to this chapter, the node of a doubly linked list consists of two pointers: one points forward, while the other points backward. The pointer pointing forward is usually called `next` and is used to point at the next node. The other, which is pointing backward, is usually called `prev` and is used to point at the previous node.

Traversal in FIFO order means the elements of the doubly linked list are displayed in the order in which they were added to the list. Traversal is done by making use of the `next` pointer of the node.

Traversal in LIFO order means the elements are displayed in reverse or backward direction, and this traversal is done with the help of the `prev` pointer.

How to do it...

In this doubly linked list, I will be making use of two pointers, `startList` and `endList`, where `startList` will point at the first node and `endList` will point at the last node. The `startList` pointer will help to traverse the list in FIFO order, while the `endList` pointer will help to traverse it in LIFO order. Follow these steps to create a doubly linked list and traverse it in either direction:

1. Define a structure called `node`. To store content for the doubly linked list, define a data member in the node structure. Define two pointers called `next` and `prev`.

2. A menu is displayed that shows four options: 1, to create a doubly linked list; 2, to display the elements of the list in LIFO order; 3, for displaying the elements in FIFO order; and 4, to quit. If the user enters 1, go to *step 3*. If the user enters 2, go to *step 10*. If the user enters 3, go to *step 15*. Finally, if the user enters 4, then it means they want to quit the program, so go to *step 19*.

3. Initialize the `startList` pointer to `NULL`.

4. Allocate memory for the new node.

5. Ask the user for the value to be added to the doubly linked list. The value that's entered by the user is assigned to the data member of the node.

6. Set the `next` and `prev` pointers of the node to `NULL`.

7. If this node is the first node of the doubly linked list, set the `startList` pointer to point at the new node. If this node is not the first node, don't disturb the `startList` pointer and let it point at the node that it is currently pointing to.

8. If this is the first node of the doubly linked list, set the `endList` pointer to at new node. If this is not the first node, perform the following steps:

    1. Set the `next` pointer of the new node to `NULL`.

    2. Set the `prev` pointer of the new node so that it points at the node pointed at by `endList`.

    3. Set the `next` pointer of `endList` so that it points at the new node.

    4. Set `endList` so that it points at the new node.

9. Ask the user whether more elements have to be added to the doubly linked list. If the user wants to enter more, go to *step 4*; otherwise, display the menu by going to *step 2*.

10. To display the linked list in LIFO order, let the `temp` pointer point at the node being pointed at by `endList`.

11. Let *step 12* and *step 13* run until the `temp` pointer reaches `NULL`.

12. Display the data member of the node being pointed at by `temp`.

13. Set the `temp` pointer so that it points to where its `prev` pointer is pointing.

14. The doubly linked list's content is displayed in LIFO order. Now, go to *step 2* to display the menu again.

15. Make the `temp` pointer point at the node being pointed at by the `startList` pointer.

16. If the `temp` pointer is not `NULL`, display the data member of the node being pointed at by `temp`.

17. Let the `temp` point at the node that its next pointer is pointing to.

18. If `temp` has reached NULL, this means all of the nodes of the doubly linked list have been traversed. Now, you can display the menu by jumping to *step 2*. If `temp` has not reached NULL, then go to *step 16* to display the rest of the elements of the doubly linked list.

19. Exit the program.

The program for implementing a doubly or two-way linked list is as follows:

//**doublylinkedlist.c**

```c
#include <stdio.h>

#include <stdlib.h>

#include <string.h>

struct node {
  int data;
  struct node * next, * prev;
};

struct node * startList, * endList;
void createdoubly();
void list_lifo();
void list_fifo();

int main() {
  int n = 0;
  while (n != 4) {
    printf("\n1. Creating a doubly linked list\n");
    printf("2. Displaying elements in L.I.F.O. order\n");
    printf("3. Displaying elements in F.I.F.O. order\n");
    printf("4. Quit\n");
    printf("Enter your choice 1/2/3/4: ");
    scanf("%d", & n);
    switch (n) {
    case 1:
      createdoubly();
      break;
    case 2:
      list_lifo();
      break;
    case 3:
      list_fifo();
      break;
    }
  }
```

```
      return 0;
}

void createdoubly() {
  char k[10];
  struct node * newNode;
  startList = NULL;
  strcpy(k, "yes");
  while (strcmp(k, "yes") == 0 || strcmp(k, "Yes") == 0) {
    if (startList == NULL) {
      newNode = (struct node * ) malloc(sizeof(struct node));
      printf("Enter the value to add: ");
      scanf("%d", & newNode - > data);
      newNode - > next = NULL;
      newNode - > prev = NULL;
      startList = newNode;
      endList = startList;
    } else {
      newNode = (struct node * ) malloc(sizeof(struct node));
      printf("Enter the value to add: ");
      scanf("%d", & newNode - > data);
      newNode - > next = NULL;
      newNode - > prev = endList;
      endList - > next = newNode;
      endList = newNode;
    }
    printf("Want to add more yes/no? ");
    scanf("%s", k);
  }
  printf("Doubly linked list is created\n");
}
void list_lifo() {
  struct node * temp;
  temp = endList;
  if (temp != NULL) {
    printf("The elements of the doubly linked list in L.I.F.O. order
:\n");
    while (temp != NULL) {
      printf("%d\n", temp - > data);
      temp = temp - > prev;
    }
  } else
    printf("The doubly linked list is empty\n");
}

void list_fifo() {
  struct node * temp;
  temp = startList;
```

```
     printf("The elements of the doubly linked list in F.I.F.O. order:
\n");
     while (temp != NULL) {
       printf("%d\n", temp - > data);
       temp = temp - > next;
     }
   }
```

Now, let's go behind the scenes so that we can understand the code.

How it works...

When implementing a doubly linked list, a structure is defined, called a node, that consists of an integer called data and two pointers, next and prev. Because a doubly linked list can be traversed from either end—that is, forward or backward—the two pointers are required. The next pointer will point at the node after it, whereas the prev pointer will point at the node just before it.

A menu is displayed on the screen showing four options: 1, for creating the doubly linked list; 2, for displaying the elements of the doubly linked list in LIFO order; 3, for displaying elements in FIFO order; and 4, to quit the program.

Let's assume that the user enters 1. The createdoubly function will be invoked. In this function, the startList pointer is set to NULL and a string variable, k, is assigned the yes string. A while loop is set to execute while k has yes assigned to it. Here, the user can keep adding more elements to the doubly linked list by entering yes whenever they are prompted to continue. The startList pointer will be set to point at the first node of the doubly linked list, while the endList pointer will be set to point at the last node.

The procedure for adding the first node is different from adding the rest of the nodes. Due to this, if else blocks are made in the code. When startList is NULL while creating the first node, an if block will be executed; otherwise, an else block will be executed. In the if block, a new node is created called newNode. The user is asked to enter a value for the doubly linked list. Suppose the user enters the value 10; this will be assigned to the data member of newNode, and the next and prev pointers of newNode will be set to NULL:

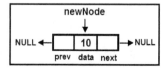

The `startList` pointer is set to point at `newNode`, and the `endList` pointer is also set to point at `newNode`:

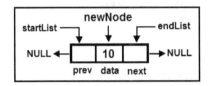

`endList` will not stay on this first node; instead, it will keep moving forward and will point at the last node of this doubly linked list. After executing the `if` block, the user is asked whether more nodes have to be added. If the user enters yes, the `while` loop will execute again. Now, `startList` isn't `NULL` and is pointing at `newNode`; so, instead of the `if` block, the `else` block will execute. In the `else` block, a new node is created called `newNode`. The user is prompted to enter a value to be added to the doubly linked list. Assuming the user enters a value of 20, the value will be assigned to the data member of `newNode`:

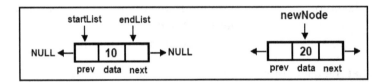

The `prev` pointer of `newNode` is set to point at `endList`, while the `next` pointer of `newNode` is set to `NULL`. The `next` pointer of `endList` is set to point at `newNode`, as follows:

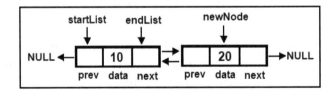

Thereafter, the `endList` pointer is set to point at `newNode`, but the `startList` pointer will be kept pointing at the first node, as follows:

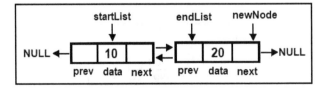

Once again, the user is asked whether they want to add more elements to the doubly linked list. Suppose the user doesn't want to add more elements to the list, so the text they enter is no. The text no will be assigned to k and, consequently, the while loop will terminate. The createdoubly function ends and control will be returned to the main function. In the main function, the menu will be displayed with the aforementioned four options.

Let's assume that the user enters 2 to display the elements of the doubly linked list in LIFO order. Here, the list_lifo function will be invoked. In the list_lifo function, a temporary pointer called temp is used and is set to point at the last node that was pointed at by the endList pointer:

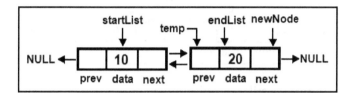

A while loop is set to execute until the temp pointer reaches NULL. The value in the data member of the node being pointed at by the temp pointer is displayed on the screen. Here, a value of 20 will appear on the screen. After that, the temp pointer is set to point to the node being pointed to by its prev pointer:

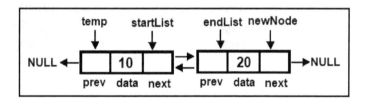

Again, the value of the temp pointer is checked. Because the temp pointer isn't NULL, the while loop will execute again. Within the while loop, the value in the data member of the node being pointed at by the temp pointer is displayed on the screen. Here, a value of 10 will appear on the screen. Thereafter, the temp pointer is set to point at the node that its prev pointer is pointing to. The prev pointer of temp is pointing at NULL, so the temp pointer is set to point at NULL. Now, because temp is pointing at NULL, the while loop will terminate, the list_lifo function ends, and control goes back to the main function.

In the `main` function, the menu will be displayed again asking the user to enter the desired option. Now, let's assume that the user enters 3 to display the elements of the doubly linked list in FIFO order. On entering 3, the `list_fifo` function will be invoked. In the `list_fifo` function, the `temp` pointer is set to point at the node being pointed at by the `startList` pointer, as shown previously. The `while` loop is set to execute until the `temp` pointer points at `NULL`. Because `temp` is not `NULL`, the value in the data member of the node being pointed at by the `temp` pointer is displayed on the screen. Here, a value of 10 will appear on the screen. Thereafter, the `temp` pointer is set to point at the node that is being pointed to by its `next` pointer, as follows:

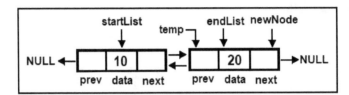

Because the `temp` pointer is still not pointing at `NULL`, the `while` loop will execute once more. Within the `while` loop, the value in the data member of the node being pointed at by the `temp` pointer is displayed on the screen; a value of 20 will appear. Again, the `temp` pointer is set to point at the node that its next pointer is pointing to. The next pointer of `temp` is pointing at the `NULL` pointer, so `temp` will point at `NULL`. Because the `temp` pointer is pointing at `NULL`, the `while` loop will terminate; hence, the `list_fifo` function ends and control goes back to the `main` function. Here, the menu is displayed once more, asking the user to enter the desired option. Let's assume the user enters 4 to quit the program. Upon entering 4, the program will terminate.

The program is compiled using GCC. Because no error appears upon compilation, this means the `doublylinkedlist.c` program has successfully compiled into the `doublylinkedlist.exe` file. On executing the file, we get a menu asking for options for creating a doubly linked list and for traversing the doubling linked list in LIFO as well as in FIFO order. By doing this, we get the following output:

```
D:\CAdvBook>gcc doublylinkedlist.c -o doublylinkedlist

D:\CAdvBook>doublylinkedlist

1. Creating a doubly linked list
2. Displaying elements in L.I.F.O. order
3. Displaying elements in F.I.F.O. order
4. Quit
Enter your choice 1/2/3/4: 1
Enter the value to add: 10
Want to add more yes/no? yes
Enter the value to add: 20
Want to add more yes/no? no
Doubly linked list is created

1. Creating a doubly linked list
2. Displaying elements in L.I.F.O. order
3. Displaying elements in F.I.F.O. order
4. Quit
Enter your choice 1/2/3/4: 2
The elements of the doubly linked list in L.I.F.O. order :
20
10

1. Creating a doubly linked list
2. Displaying elements in L.I.F.O. order
3. Displaying elements in F.I.F.O. order
4. Quit
Enter your choice 1/2/3/4: 3
The elements of the doubly linked list in F.I.F.O. order:
10
20

1. Creating a doubly linked list
2. Displaying elements in L.I.F.O. order
3. Displaying elements in F.I.F.O. order
4. Quit
Enter your choice 1/2/3/4: 4

D:\CAdvBook>
```

The preceding screenshot shows the benefit of using a doubly linked list that is traversing its elements in FIFO, as well as in LIFO, order.

Implementing a circular linked list

In this recipe, we will learn how to implement a circular linked list. The difference between a linear linked list and a circular linked list is that where the last node of the linear linked list points at NULL, the pointer of the last node in a circular linked list points back to the first node, hence allowing the pointer to traverse in a backward direction too.

How to do it...

Follow these steps to implement a circular linked list:

1. Define a structure called node. To store data in a circular linked list, define a data member in the node structure. Besides a data member, define a pointer that will point at the next node.

2. A pointer called startList is initialized to NULL. The startList pointer will designate the start of the circular linked list.

3. A menu is displayed and the user is asked to press 1 to add elements to the circular linked list, 2 to display elements of the circular linked list, and 3 to quit the program. If the user enters 1, go to *step 4*. If they enter 2, go to *step 16*. If they enter 3, it means they want to quit the program, so go to *step 23*.

4. The user is prompted to specify how many numbers they want to add to the circular linked list. A loop is set to execute for the specified number of times; that is, *steps 5 to 14* are repeated for the specified number of times.

5. Allocate memory for the new node.

6. Ask the user for the value to be added to the circular linked list. The value that's entered by the user is assigned to the data member of the node.

7. If startList is NULL—that is, if it is the first node of the circular linked list—then make the startList pointer point at a new node.

8. To make a linked list appear as circular, make the next pointer of startList point at startList.

9. If startList is not NULL—that is, if it is not the first node of the circular linked list—follow *steps 10 to 14*.

10. Make the temp pointer point at startList.

11. Until the next pointer of temp is equal to startList, make the temp pointer point to where its next pointer is pointing; that is, set the temp pointer so that it points at the last node of the circular linked list.

12. Once the `temp` pointer reaches the last node of the circular linked list, the next pointer of `temp` is set to point at the new node.
13. Then, the `temp` pointer is set to point at the new node.
14. The next pointer of `temp` is set to point at `startLIst`.
15. Go to *step 3* to display the menu.
16. The previous step ensures `startList` is not NULL. If `startList` is NULL, it means the circular linked list is empty. In that case, a message is displayed, informing the user that the circular linked list is empty. Then, control jumps to *step 3* to display the menu.
17. If `startList` is not NULL, the data member of the node being pointed at by the `startList` pointer is displayed on the screen.
18. A temporary pointer, `temp`, is set to point to where the next pointer of `startList` is pointing to.
19. Repeat *steps 20* and *21* until the `temp` pointer reaches the node being pointed at by the `startList` pointer.
20. Display the contents of the node being pointed at by the data member of `temp`.
21. The `temp` pointer is set to point to where its next pointer is pointing.
22. Jump to *step 3* to display the menu.
23. Terminate the program.

The program for implementing a circular linked list is as follows:

```
//circularlinkedlist.c

#include <stdio.h>

#include <stdlib.h>

struct node {
  int data;
  struct node * next;
};

struct node * startList = NULL;

void addlist(struct node ** h);
void disp();

int main() {
  struct node * newNode;
  int n = 0, i, k;
```

```
    while (n != 3) {
      printf("\n1. Adding elements to the circular linked list\n");
      printf("2. Displaying elements of the circular linked list\n");
      printf("3. Quit\n");
      printf("Enter your choice 1/2/3: ");
      scanf("%d", & n);
      switch (n) {
      case 1:
        printf("How many values are there ");
        scanf("%d", & k);
        printf("Enter %d values\n", k);
        for (i = 1; i <= k; i++) {
          newNode = (struct node * ) malloc(sizeof(struct node));
          scanf("%d", & newNode - > data);
          addlist( & newNode);
        }
        printf("Values added in Circular Linked List \n");
        break;
      case 2:
        disp();
        break;
      }
    }
    return 0;
}

void addlist(struct node ** NewNode) {
  struct node * temp;
  if (startList == NULL) {
    startList = * NewNode;
    startList - > next = startList;
  } else {
    temp = startList;
    while (temp - > next != startList)
      temp = temp - > next;
    temp - > next = * NewNode;
    temp = * NewNode;
    temp - > next = startList;
  }
}

void disp() {
  struct node * temp;
  if (startList == NULL)
    printf("The circular linked list is empty\n");
  else {
    printf("Following are the elements in circular linked list:\n");
    printf("%d\n", startList - > data);
```

```
    temp = startList - > next;
    while (temp != startList) {
      printf("%d\n", temp - > data);
      temp = temp - > next;
    }
  }
}
```

Now, let's go behind the scenes so that we can understand the code.

How it works...

A structure is defined, called a node, that consists of two members: an integer and a pointer called next. I am creating a circular linked list comprised of integer numbers, which is why I have taken an integer member. However, you can use any number of members you want, as well as any data type.

We define a pointer called startList and initialize it to NULL. The startList pointer will be used to point at the first node of the circular linked list.

A menu is displayed on the screen that shows three options: 1, to add elements to the circular linked list; 2, to display elements of the circular linked list; and 3, to quit. Obviously, the first step is to add elements to the circular linked list. Let's assume that the user enters 1. On entering 1, the user will be asked to specify how many values they want to enter in the list. The limit that's entered by the user will be assigned to a variable called k. Assuming that the user wants to enter five elements in the list, a for loop is set to run five times. Within the for loop, a new node is created called newNode. The value that's entered by the user is assigned to the data member of newNode. Assuming the value that's entered by the user is 10, it will be assigned to the data member of newNode, as follows:

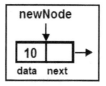

The `addlist` function will be invoked and `newNode` will be passed to it as an argument. In the `addlist` function, it is confirmed whether it is the first node of the circular linked list or not; that is, if `startList` is NULL, it is set to point at `newNode`:

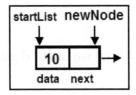

To make it a circular linked list, the next pointer of `startList` is set to point at `startList` itself:

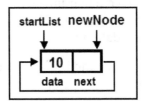

The `addlist` function ends. Control goes back to the main function and resumes the `for` loop's execution. Within the `for` loop, a `newNode` node is created. The value that's entered by the user is assigned to the data member of `newNode`. Assuming that the user has entered a value of 20, it will be assigned to the data member of `newNode`:

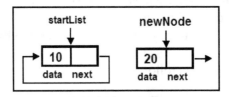

Again, the `addlist` function is invoked and `newNode` is passed to it. In the `addlist` function, because the `startList` pointer is no longer NULL, the `else` block will be executed. In the `else` block, a temporary pointer called `temp` is set to point at `startList`. A `while` loop is set to execute until the next pointer of `temp` points at `startList`; that is, until the `temp` pointer reaches the last node of the circular linked list, the `temp` pointer will keep moving further so that it points at its next node. Because there is only a single node in the circular linked list, the `temp` pointer is already pointing at the last node of the list:

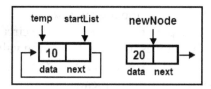

Once the `temp` pointer reaches the last node of the circular linked list, the next pointer of `temp` is set to point at `newNode`:

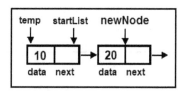

Thereafter, the `temp` pointer is set to point at `newNode`:

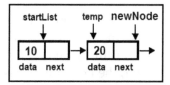

Finally, to make the linked list appear circular, the next pointer of `temp` is set to point at `startList`:

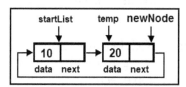

This procedure is repeated for the other three elements of the circular linked list. Assuming the other the three elements that are entered are 30, 40, and 50, the circular linked list will appear as follows:

After creating the circular linked list, the user will see the display menu again. Assuming the user wants to display the elements of the circular linked list, they will enter a value as per the menu choices. Upon entering the value, the disp function will be invoked. In the disp function, it's ensured that the startList pointer is NULL. If the startList pointer is NULL, it means the circular linked list is empty. In that case, the disp function will terminate after displaying the message that the circular linked list is empty. If the startList pointer is not empty, the value in the data member of the node being pointed at by the startList pointer is displayed on the screen; that is, a value of 10 will appear on the screen. A temporary pointer, temp, is set to point at the node being pointed at by the next pointer of startList:

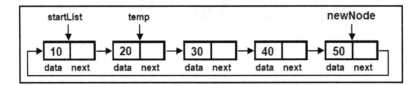

A while loop is set to execute until the temp pointer reaches the node being pointed at by the startList pointer. Within the while loop, the data member of the node being pointed at by the temp pointer is displayed on the screen; that is, a value of 20 will appear on the screen. Thereafter, the temp pointer is set to point at the node that its next pointer is pointing to. This way, the while loop will execute and display all of the elements of the circular linked list. When the while loop ends, the disp function also ends. Control goes back to the main function, where the menu will be displayed once more. To exit the program, the user has to enter 3. On entering 3, the program will terminate.

The program is compiled using GCC. Because no error appears on compilation, this means the circularlinkedlist.c program has successfully compiled into the circularlinkedlist.exe file. On executing the file, we get a menu that will not only add elements to the circular linked list but will display them too. By doing this, we get the output shown in the following screenshot:

```
D:\CAdvBook>gcc circularlinkedlist.c -o circularlinkedlist

D:\CAdvBook>circularlinkedlist

1. Adding elements to the circular linked list
2. Displaying elements of the circular linked list
3. Quit
Enter your choice 1/2/3: 1
How many values are there 5
Enter 5 values
10
20
30
40
50
Values added in Circular Linked List

1. Adding elements to the circular linked list
2. Displaying elements of the circular linked list
3. Quit
Enter your choice 1/2/3: 2
Following are the elements in circular linked list:
10
20
30
40
50

1. Adding elements to the circular linked list
2. Displaying elements of the circular linked list
3. Quit
Enter your choice 1/2/3: 3

D:\CAdvBook>
```

Voilà! We have successfully implemented a circular linked list. Now, let's move on to the next recipe!

Creating a binary search tree and performing an inorder traversal on it recursively

In this recipe, we will ask the user to enter a few numbers and build a binary tree from those numbers. Once the binary tree has been created, its inorder traversal is performed. These steps will be divided into two parts: creating the binary tree and traversing the binary tree in inorder.

How to do it... – binary tree

Follow these steps to create the binary tree:

1. Create a node with the following structure: data for storing tree elements, a right pointer to point at the right child of the tree, and a left pointer to point at the left child of the tree.

2. Create the root node of the tree. To do this, allocate memory space for a new node and set the root pointer to point at it.

3. Prompt the user to enter the tree elements. The value that's entered by the user is assigned to the data member of the root node.

4. The left and right pointers of the root node are set to NULL.

5. The root node is created. Next, prompt the user to specify the number of elements in the tree.

6. Repeat *steps 7 to 22* for the number of elements specified by the user.

7. Allocate memory space for a new node and set the new pointer so that it points at it.

8. Prompt the user to enter the tree element. The tree element that's entered by the user is assigned to the data member of the new node.

9. The left and right pointers of the new node are set to NULL.

10. To connect the root node to the new node, we need to find a location where it can be connected. To do so, set the temp pointer so that it points at the root node. Compare the values in the data members of the new node and temp node.

11. If new ->data > temp->data, go to *step 12*; otherwise, go to *step 16*.

12. If the right link of `temp` is NULL—that is, if there is no child on the right of the `temp` node—then, the new node is added to the right link of the `temp` node.

13. The new node is added as the right child of the `temp` node. Jump to *step 7* to add more tree elements.

14. If the right link of the root is not NULL, the `temp` pointer is set to point where the `right` pointer of `temp` is pointing to.

15. Go to *step 11* for more comparisons.

16. If `new->data < root->data`, go to *step 17*; otherwise, go to *step 21*.

17. If the left link of the node is NULL—that is, there is no child on the left of the temp node—then the new node is added to the left link.

18. The new node is added as the left child of the `temp` node. Jump to *step 7* to add more tree elements.

19. If the left link of the root is not NULL, the `temp` pointer is set to point to where its `left` pointer is pointing.

20. Go to *step 11* for more comparisons.

21. If `new->data = temp->data`, this means the value in the new node is a duplicate and cannot be added to the tree.

22. Go to *step 7* to add more tree elements.

23. For inorder traversal, we will follow the algorithm that's provided in the next section. The `inorder` function is called recursively and the root node of the binary tree is passed to this function.

How to do it... – inorder traversal of the tree

Because it's a recursive form, the function will be called recursively. The function is as follows:

```
inorder(node)
```

Here, `inorder` is the function that will be recursively called and `node` is the node of the binary tree that's being passed to it. Initially, the node will be the root of the binary tree, whose inorder traversal is required. Follow these steps:

1. If node is NULL, go to *step 2*; otherwise, return to the caller function.

2. Call the same function (the `inorder` function) with the node's left child set as an argument:

```
call inorder(node->leftchild)
```

3. Display the content in the node:

```
display node->info
```

4. Call the same function itself (the `inorder` function) with the node's right child set as an argument:

```
call inorder(node->rightchild)
```

The program for creating a binary search tree and traversing it in inorder is as follows:

//**binarysearchtree.c**

```c
#include <stdio.h>

#include <stdlib.h>

#define max 20
struct tree {
   int data;
   struct tree * right;
   struct tree * left;
};
void build(int Arr[], int Len);
struct tree * makeroot(int val);
void rightchild(struct tree * rootNode, int val);
void leftchild(struct tree * rootNode, int val);
void travino(struct tree * node);
int main() {
   int arr[max], i, len;
   printf("How many elements are there for making the binary search
tree? ");
   scanf("%d", & len);
   printf("Enter %d elements in array \n", len);
   for (i = 0; i < len; i++)
     scanf("%d", & arr[i]);
   build(arr, len);
   return 0;
}

void build(int Arr[], int Len) {
   struct tree * temp, * rootNode;
```

```
    int j;
    rootNode = makeroot(Arr[0]);
    for (j = 1; j < Len; j++) {
      temp = rootNode;
      while (1) {
        if (Arr[j] < temp - > data) {
          if (temp - > left != NULL) {
            temp = temp - > left;
            continue;
          }
          leftchild(temp, Arr[j]);
        }
        if (Arr[j] > temp - > data) {
          if (temp - > right != NULL) {
            temp = temp - > right;
            continue;
          }
          rightchild(temp, Arr[j]);
        }
        break;
      }
    }
    printf("Binary Search Tree is created\n");
    printf("The inorder traversal of the tree is as follows:\n");
    travino(rootNode);
}

struct tree * makeroot(int val) {
    struct tree * rootNode;
    rootNode = (struct tree * ) malloc(sizeof(struct tree));
    rootNode - > data = val;
    rootNode - > right = NULL;
    rootNode - > left = NULL;
    return rootNode;
}

void leftchild(struct tree * rootNode, int val) {
    struct tree * newNode;
    newNode = (struct tree * ) malloc(sizeof(struct tree));
    newNode - > data = val;
    newNode - > left = NULL;
    newNode - > right = NULL;
    rootNode - > left = newNode;
}

void rightchild(struct tree * rootNode, int val) {
    struct tree * newNode;
    newNode = (struct tree * ) malloc(sizeof(struct tree));
```

```
    newNode - > data = val;
    newNode - > left = NULL;
    newNode - > right = NULL;
    rootNode - > right = newNode;
}

void travino(struct tree * node) {
  if (node != NULL) {
    travino(node - > left);
    printf("%d\t", node - > data);
    travino(node - > right);
  }
}
```

Now, let's go behind the scenes so that we can understand the code.

How it works... – binary tree

We created a structure called `tree` consisting of the following members:

- `data`: An integer member for storing integer data. Here, we're assuming that our tree only consists of integer elements.
- `right` and `left` pointers: These are used to point at the left and right child, respectively.

Internally, the tree will be maintained through an array; an integer array is defined of the size 20. For our purposes, let's assume that the user doesn't enter more than 20 elements for the tree. However, you can always increase the size of the macro to any larger number you desired.

The user is prompted to specify the number of elements they want to enter for the tree. Let's say the user wants to enter seven elements for the tree; here, the value 7 will be assigned to the `len` variable. The user is prompted to enter the seven integers and the values entered by them will be assigned to the `arr` array, as shown in the following screenshot:

arr[0]	arr[1]	arr[2]	arr[3]	arr[4]	arr[5]	arr[6]
40	20	60	80	30	50	10

The `build` function is invoked and the array, `arr`, containing the tree elements and the length of the array, `len`, are passed to it. In the `build` function, we need to create a root node of the tree. To create a root node of the tree, the `makeroot` function is invoked and the first element of the array, `arr`, is passed to it as an argument. In the `makeroot` function, a node called `rootNode` is created and the value of the first array element is assigned to its data member. Because the root node of the tree is not pointing at any other node at the moment, the right and left child of the root node are set to `NULL`:

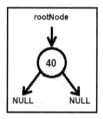

The `makeroot` function ends and `rootNode` is returned to the `build` function. In the `build` function, a `temp` pointer is set to point at `rootNode`. All of the array elements from index 1 and above are compared with the data members of the `temp` node, that is, the root node. If the array element is smaller than the data member of the `temp` node, the array element will be added as the left child of the root node. Also, if the array element is larger than the data member of the `temp` node, it will be added as the right child of the root node, for example, if the second array element is 20 and the root node is 40. Because 20 is smaller than 40, it is checked whether the `left` pointer of the `temp` node is `NULL`. Because the `left` pointer of `temp` is `NULL`, the `leftchild` function is invoked and 20 is passed to it. In the `leftchild` function, a new node is created called `newNode`. Here, the second array element (20) is assigned to the data member of `newNode`. The `left` and `right` pointers of `newNode` are set to `NULL`. The `left` pointer of `temp` is set to point at `newNode`, as follows:

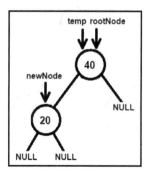

Control goes back to the `build` function, where the `for` loop will pick up the next array element for building the tree. Let's say the next array element is 60. Again, a `temp` pointer is set to point at the root node. The value 60 is compared with the root node, which is 40. Because the value of the array element, 60, is greater than the root node, 40, the right child of the root node is checked. Because the right child of the root node is NULL, the `rightchild` function is invoked and the `temp` pointer and the array element, 60, are passed to it. In the `rightchild` function, a new node is created called `newNode` and the value 60 is passed to it, which is assigned to its data member. The `left` and `right` pointers of `newNode` are set to NULL. The `right` pointer of `rootNode` is set to point at `newNode`, as follows:

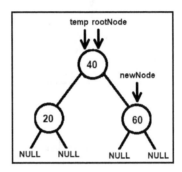

After completing the `rightchild` function, control goes back to the `build` function, where the `for` loop picks up the next array element for building the tree. The next array element is 80. A temporary pointer, `temp`, is set to point at the root node. The root node, 40 is compared with the new element to be added, 80. Because 80 > 40, the right child of the `temp` node is checked. The `right` pointer of the `temp` node is not NULL, so the `temp` pointer is set to point at its right node, as follows:

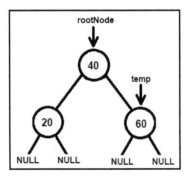

Now, the `right` pointer of `temp` is checked again. This procedure is repeated until the `right` pointer of `temp` is found to be NULL. The `right` pointer of 60 is NULL, so the `rightchild` function is invoked and `temp`, 60, and the new element, 80, are passed to it. In the `rightchild` function, a new node is created called `newNode` and the value 80 is assigned to it. The right and left pointers of `newNode` are set to NULL. The `right` pointer of `temp` is set to point at `newNode`, as follows:

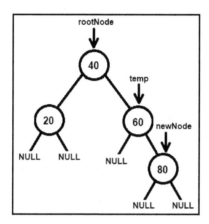

After completing the `rightchild` function, control jumps back to the `build` function, where the `for` loop picks up the next array element for building the tree. After all of the array elements have been used, the binary search tree will look as follows:

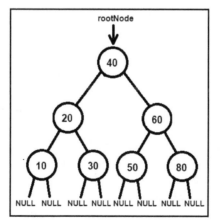

Once the binary search tree has been created, the `travino` function is invoked for inorder traversal of the binary tree and the root node is passed to it.

How it works... – inorder traversal of the tree

The `travino` function is a recursive function. First, it ensures the supplied node is not NULL. If the node is not NULL, a recursive call to the `travino` function is made with the node's left child. The node is checked to ensure it's not NULL. If it isn't, again, a recursive call to the `travino` function is made with its left child. If the node is NULL, the value in the data member of the node is displayed on the screen and a recursive call to the `travino` function is made with the node's right child. This procedure is repeated until all of the nodes that are displayed on the screen have been visited.

The inorder traversal is described as *L,V,R*, as follows:

- L means visiting the left child
- V means visiting the node that is displaying its content
- R means visiting the right child

On each node of the binary tree, LVR operations are applied, beginning from the root node. Our binary tree has already been created and looks as follows. At node 40, three operations—L,V, and R—are applied. L means visiting its left child, so we move to the left child of node 40, but two of its operations, V and R, still need to be completed on the node left. So, node 40 is pushed onto the stack with V and R attached to it:

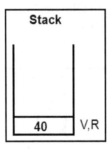

The left child of node 40 is node 20. Again, at node 20, three operations—L,V, and R—are applied. First, L (the left child) is visited. Only two operations, V and R, are left. So, again, node 20 is pushed onto the stack with V and R attached to it. The left child of node 20 is node 10. Again, at this node L, V, and R are applied. Since its left child is NULL, the second operation, V, is applied; that is, the node is displayed or we can say it is traversed. After that, we go to its right child. The right child of node 10 is NULL and since all three operations (L,V, and R) have been applied on this node, it is not pushed to the stack:

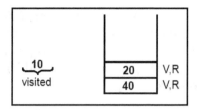

Now, node 20 is popped from the stack. Its two operations, V and R, are pending. First, it is visited (displayed) and then we go to its right child:

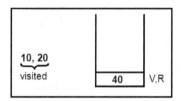

The right child of node 20 is 30. Again, at node 30, three operations—L,V, and R—are applied. First L (the left child) is visited. Since it has no left child, the second operation, V, is applied; that is, node 30 is visited (displayed), and then we go to its right child. It has no right child either and since all three operations (L,V, and R) have been applied on this node, 30 is not pushed to the stack:

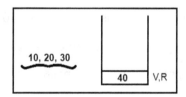

Now, node 40 is popped from the stack. Its two operations, V and R, are pending. First, it is visited (displayed) and then we go to its right child. The right child of node 40 is node 60. At node 60, the three operations—L,V, and R—are applied. First, L (the left child) is visited. V and R are left. Here, node 60 is pushed to the stack with V and R attached to it:

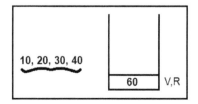

The left child of node 60 is node 50. Again at this node, L, V, and R are applied. Since its left child is NULL, the second operation, V, is applied; that is, node 50 is displayed or we can say it is traversed. After that, we go to its right child. The right child of node 50 is NULL and since all three operations (L,V, and R) have been applied to this node, it is not pushed to the stack:

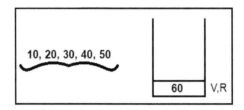

Now, node 60 is popped from the stack. Its two operations, V and R, are pending. First, it is visited (displayed) and then we go to its right child. So, the visited nodes will be 10, 20, 30, 40, 50, and 60.

The right child of node 60 is 80. Again, at node 80, three operations—L,V, and R—are applied. First, L (its left child) is visited. Since it has no left child, the second operation, V, is applied; that is, node 80 is visited (displayed), and then we go to its right child. It has no right child either and since all three operations (L,V, and R) have been applied to this node, 80 is not pushed to the stack.

So, the final inorder traversal of the tree is 10, 20, 30, 40, 50, 60, and 80.

The program is compiled using the GCC compiler using the following statement:

```
D:\CAdvBook>GCC binarysearchtree.c - binarysearchtree
```

As shown in the following screenshot, no error appears when we compile. This means the binarysearchtree.c program has successfully compiled into a .exe file called binarysearchtree.exe. Let's run the executable file and enter some elements to create a binary tree and see its inorder traversal. By doing this, we get the following output:

```
D:\CAdvBook>binarysearchtree
How many elements are there for making the binary search tree? 7
Enter 7 elements in array
40
20
60
80
30
70
10
Binary Search Tree is created
The inorder traversal of the tree is as follows:
10      20      30      40      60      70      80
```

Performing postorder traversal of a binary tree non-recursively

In this recipe, we will perform postorder traversal of a binary tree without recursion. This will be done through non-recursive calls to the function.

Getting started

To create a binary tree, refer to the *Creating a binary search tree and performing an inorder traversal on it recursively* recipe. We will be performing postorder traversal on the same binary tree we created in this recipe.

How to do it...

For postorder traversal of a binary tree, we need to apply three tasks—L, R, and V—on each of the tree nodes. These tasks are as follows:

- L means visit the left link
- R means visit the right link
- V means visit the node

To find out which tasks between L, R, and V are pending and which have already been performed, we will use two stacks: one for storing the node and another for storing an integer value of 0 or 1. Let's go over what 0 and 1 indicate:

- The value 0 indicates that the L task is done, while the R and V tasks are pending on the node.
- The value 1 means that the L and R tasks have been performed on the node and that only V is pending.

Follow these steps to perform postorder tree traversal:

1. A temporary node called `temp` is set to point at the root node of the tree.
2. Push the node that's being pointed at by `temp` to `nodeArray` and the value 0 to `valueArray`. The integer 0 in `valueArray` indicates that the R and V tasks are pending on the node.
3. Make the `temp` node point at the node where its `left` pointer is pointing.
4. If the `temp` is not pointing at `NULL`, go to *step 2*.
5. If `temp` reaches `NULL`, go to *step 6*.
6. Pop the node from `nodeArray`.
7. Pop the integer from `valueArray`.
8. If the popped integer value is 1, visit the node that is displaying the data member of the node. Then, go to *step 6*.
9. If the popped integer value is 0, go to *step 10*.
10. Push the node to `nodeArray`.
11. Push the integer 1 to `valueArray` to indicate that the L and R operations have been performed and that only V is pending.
12. Make the `temp` pointer point to where its `right` pointer is pointing.
13. If the `temp` pointer does not reach `NULL`, go to *step 2*.
14. If the `temp` pointer reaches `NULL`, go to *step 6*.

The program for creating a binary search tree and traversing it in postorder non-recursively is as follows:

```c
//postordernonrec.c

#include <stdio.h>

#include <stdlib.h>

struct tree {
  int data;
  struct tree * right;
  struct tree * left;
};

struct stackstruc {
  int valueArray[15];
  struct tree * nodeArray[15];
};

struct stackstruc stack;
int top = -1;

struct tree * makeroot(int val);
void rightchild(struct tree * rootNode, int val);
void leftchild(struct tree * rootNode, int val);
void nontravpost(struct tree * node);
void pushNode(struct tree * node, int val);
struct tree * popNode();
int popVal();

int main() {
  struct tree * temp, * rootNode;
  int val;
  printf("Enter elements of tree and 0 to quit\n");
  scanf("%d", & val);
  rootNode = makeroot(val);
  scanf("%d", & val);
  while (val != 0) {
    temp = rootNode;
    while (1) {
      if (val < temp - > data) {
        if (temp - > left != NULL) {
          temp = temp - > left;
          continue;
        }
        leftchild(temp, val);
      }
```

```
        if (val > temp - > data) {
          if (temp - > right != NULL) {
            temp = temp - > right;
            continue;
          }
          rightchild(temp, val);
        }
        break;
      }
      scanf("%d", & val);
    }
    printf("\nTraversal of tree in Postorder without using recursion:
\n");
    nontravpost(rootNode);
}

struct tree * makeroot(int val) {
    struct tree * rootNode;
    rootNode = (struct tree * ) malloc(sizeof(struct tree));
    rootNode - > data = val;
    rootNode - > right = NULL;
    rootNode - > left = NULL;
    return rootNode;
}

void leftchild(struct tree * rootNode, int val) {
    struct tree * newNode;
    newNode = (struct tree * ) malloc(sizeof(struct tree));
    newNode - > data = val;
    newNode - > left = NULL;
    newNode - > right = NULL;
    rootNode - > left = newNode;
}

void rightchild(struct tree * rootNode, int val) {
    struct tree * newNode;
    newNode = (struct tree * ) malloc(sizeof(struct tree));
    newNode - > data = val;
    newNode - > left = NULL;
    newNode - > right = NULL;
    rootNode - > right = newNode;
}

void nontravpost(struct tree * node) {
    struct tree * temp;
    int val;
    temp = node;
    while (1) {
```

```
      while (temp != NULL) {
        pushNode(temp, 0);
        temp = temp - > left;
      }
      while (top >= 0) {
        temp = popNode();
        val = popVal();
        if (val == 0) {
          if (temp - > right != NULL) {
            pushNode(temp, 1);
            temp = temp - > right;
            break;
          }
        }
        printf("%d\n", temp - > data);
        continue;
      }
      if ((temp == NULL) || (top < 0)) break;
      else continue;
    }
}

void pushNode(struct tree * node, int val) {
  top++;
  stack.nodeArray[top] = node;
  stack.valueArray[top] = val;
}

struct tree * popNode() {
  return (stack.nodeArray[top]);
}

int popVal() {
  return (stack.valueArray[top--]);
}
```

Now, let's go behind the scenes so that we can understand the code.

How it works...

Postorder traversal requires the L, R, and V tasks to be applied to each node of the binary tree. Here, L means visiting the left child, R means visiting the right child, and V means visiting the node that is displaying its content.

The question is, how will we know which tasks have already been performed on a node and which tasks are left to be performed? To do so, we will use two arrays, `nodeArray` and `valueArray`. `nodeArray` contains the node that the tasks are to be performed one, while `valueArray` is used to indicate what task has been left on the corresponding node. `valueArray` can have one of the following two values:

- **Value 0**: This indicates that the left link of the node has been traversed and that two tasks are pending: traversing the node being pointed to by its `right` pointer and visiting the node.
- **Value 1**: This indicates that the node being pointed to by its `right` pointer has been traversed. Only the task of visiting the node is pending.

Once the binary search tree has been created, the `nontravpost` function is invoked for postorder traversal of the binary tree and the root node is passed to the function as an argument. The `nontravpost` function is a non-recursive function.

A temporary pointer, `temp`, is set to point at the root node. A `while` loop is set to execute until `temp` is not `NULL`. Within the `while` loop, the `pushNode` function is called and the node being pointed to by `temp` is passed to it, along with a value of 0.

In the `pushNode` function, the value of top that was initialized to -1 is incremented to 0 and the node, 40, and the value 0 are pushed into the `nodeArray` and `valueArray` arrays at index location being pointed to by `top` (the index location, 0):

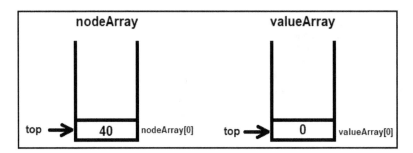

The `pushNode` function ends and control jumps back to the `nontravpost` function, where the `temp` pointer is set to point at its left node. The `left` pointer of temp is pointing at node 20, so `temp` will now point at node 20. The `while` loop will keep executing until the `temp` pointer reaches the `NULL` pointer. Again, within the `while` loop, the `pushNode` function is called and node 20 and value 0 are passed to it. In the `pushNode` function, the value of the `top` pointer is incremented to 1 and node 20 and the value 0 are pushed to the `nodeArray[1]` and `valueArray[1]` array index locations, as follows:

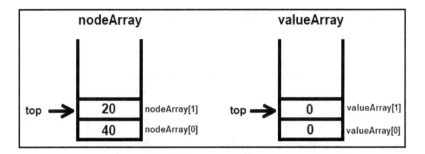

This process is repeated for the next node that's on the left of the `temp` node. On the left of node 20 is node 10. Upon pushing node 10, the `nodeArray` and `valueArray` arrays will look as follows:

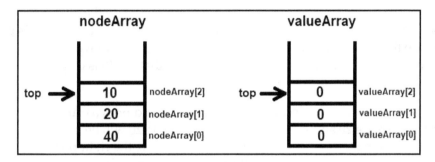

Because temp has reached the NULL pointer, the first `while` loop will terminate and the next `while` loop will execute while the value of `top` is greater than or equal to 0. The `popNode` function is invoked, which returns the node in the `nodeArray` array that's being pointed at by the `top` index. The value of the `top` index is currently 2, so the node at the index location of `nodeArray[2]`, that is, 10, is accessed and returned to the `nontravpost` function. In the `nontravpost` function, node 10 will be assigned to the `temp` pointer. Next, the `popVal` function is invoked, which returns the value in the `valueArray` array that's being pointed to by the `top` index. This happens at the `valueArray[2]` index location. That is, the value 0 at the `valueArray[2]` index location is returned by the `popVal` function and is assigned to the `val` variable. The value of `top` is now decremented to 1. Because the value in the `val` variable is 0, an `if` block is executed in the `nontravpost` function. The `if` block checks whether the right child of the node being pointed at by the `temp` pointer isn't NULL; if so, the `pushNode` function is called and the node being pointed to by `temp`, that is, 10 and integer value 1, is passed to it as an argument.

In the `pushNode` function, the value of `top` is incremented to 2 and node 10 and the value 1 are pushed to the `nodeArray[2]` and `valueArray[2]` index locations, respectively:

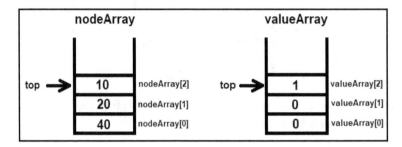

After executing the `pushNode` function, control jumps back to the `nontravpost` function, where the `temp` pointer is set to point to where its `right` pointer is pointing. But because the `right` pointer of `temp` is `NULL`, the `while` loop will break and the data member of the node being pointed to by `temp` (that is, 10) is displayed on the screen.

Again, the `while` loop will execute and the `popNode` and `popVal` functions will execute to pop node 20 and value 0, respectively. Node 20 will be pointed to by the `temp` pointer. Because the value that's being popped is 0, the right pointer of the node being pointed to by `temp` is searched. If the `right` pointer of node 20 is pointing at node 30, the `pushNode` function is invoked and node 20 is pushed, along with the value 1:

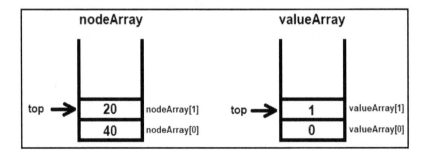

Next, the `temp` pointer is set to point to where its `right` pointer is pointing, that is, node 30. The `pushNode` function is invoked and node 30 and an integer value of 0 are pushed to the `nodeArray` and `valueArray` arrays, respectively:

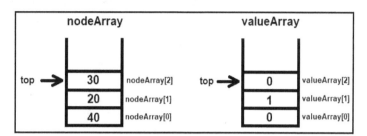

This procedure is repeated until the stacks are empty.

The program is compiled with GCC using the following statement:

```
D:\CAdvBook>GCC postordernonrec.c - postordernonrec
```

If no error appears upon compilation, then the `postordernonrec.c` program has successfully compiled into the `postordernonrec.exe` file. Let's run this file and enter some new elements that will build a binary tree and get its postorder traversal using a non-recursive approach. By doing this, we will get the following output:

```
D:\CAdvBook>gcc postordernonrec.c -o postordernonrec

D:\CAdvBook>postordernonrec
Enter elements of tree and 0 to quit
40
20
60
80
30
50
10
0

Traversal of tree in Postorder without using recursion:
10
30
20
50
80
60
40
```

See also

To learn how to implement queues and circular queues using arrays and dequeues using circular queues, visit *Appendix B* found on this link: `https://github.com/PacktPublishing/Practical-C-Programming/blob/master/Appendix%20B.pdf`.

12
Creativity with Graphics

OpenGL (short for **Open Graphics Library**) is a cross-platform **application program interface** (**API**) used for rendering two- and three-dimensional graphics; it works independently of operating systems. It provides several built-in routines for displaying graphics and for applying special effects, anti-aliasing, and different transformations.

OpenGL had a library called the **OpenGL Utility Toolkit** (**GLUT**), but it has not been supported for several years. FreeGLUT, a free, open source piece of software, is used as an alternative in its place. GLUT was very popularly used in graphics applications as it is highly portable and is very simple to use. It has a large library of functions for creating windows, different graphical shapes, event handling, and more. If FreeGLUT is not installed on your computer and you have Windows OS on your computer, you can download `freeglut 3.0.0` for MinGW and extract it. On Ubuntu, you need to give the following command to install FreeGLUT:

```
sudo apt-get install freeglut3-dev
```

In this chapter, we will learn to do the following recipes:

- Drawing four graphical shapes
- Drawing a circle
- Drawing a line between two mouse clicks
- Making a bar graph of the supplied values
- Making an animated bouncing ball

List of OpenGL functions

Before we delve into the recipes, let's have a quick overview of some OpenGL functions that we will be using in this chapter. The following are some of the most frequently used OpenGL functions:

Function	Description
glutInit	Used to initialize GLUT.
glutCreateWindow	Used for creating a top-level window. You can supply the window name as a label while creating the window.
glutInitWindowSize	Used to define the window size. The width and height of the window are specified in pixels while defining the window size.
void glutInitWindowPosition	Used to set the initial window position. The window's x and y locations are specified in terms of pixels.
glutDisplayFunc	Used to specify the callback function to be executed to display graphics in the current window. For redisplaying the content in the window too, the specified callback function is executed.
glutMainLoop	This is an entry point for the GLUT event processing loop.
glClearColor	Used to specify clear values for the color buffers. You need to specify the red, green, blue, and alpha values used when the color buffers are cleared. The initial values are all 0.
glClear	Used to clear the buffers to preset values. Certain masks can be used to specify the buffers to be cleared. The following are three masks that can be used.
GL_COLOR_BUFFER_BIT	This mask represents the buffers that are currently being used for applying colors.
GL_DEPTH_BUFFER_BIT	This mask represents the depth buffer.
GL_STENCIL_BUFFER_BIT	This mask represents the stencil buffer.
glBegin	Used for grouping statements that lead to a specific shape. You can create different shapes such as points, lines, triangles, rectangles, and more, by grouping the required vertices within this grouping statement. The shape that you want to create can be specified by specifying any of the modes: GL_POINTS, GL_LINES, GL_LINE_STRIP, GL_LINE_LOOP, GL_TRIANGLES, GL_TRIANGLE_STRIP, GL_TRIANGLE_FAN, GL_QUADS, GL_QUAD_STRIP, and GL_POLYGON.
glEnd	Used to end the group of statements.

glColor3f	Used to set the current color for drawing graphics. The values for the red, green, and blue colors (in this strict sequence) can be specified to set the color. The values of these colors can be between 0 and 1, where 0 is the lowest intensity and 1 is the highest intensity of the color.
glVertex	Used to specify coordinates for the point, line, and polygon vertices. This function has to be enclosed between a glBegin/glEnd pair. There might be a suffix of 2, 3, or 4 after glVertex, depending on the number of coordinates required for defining the vertex. For example, if two coordinates, x and y, are required to specify the vertex, then a value of 2 will be added as a suffix to glVertex making it glVertex2. Similarly, 3 and 4 can be suffixed if the coordinates required for specifying the vertex are 3 and 4, respectively. Also, one more suffix can be added, such as s, i, f, or d if the vertex coordinates are of the short, int, float or double data types respectively. For example, glVertex2f() can be used to specify the vertex with x and y coordinates, and the coordinate values will be of the float data type.
glLineWidth	Used to specify the width of the line to be drawn. The width of the line can be specified in terms of pixels. The default width is 1.
glPointSize	Used to specify the diameter of rasterized points. The default diameter is 1.
glFlush	The commands sometimes get buffered depending on the resource utilization and networking situation. The glFlush function empties all the buffers and ensures that the commands are executed as early as possible.
glutSwapBuffers	This function is used for swapping the front buffer with the back buffer. The front buffer displays the image or frame on the screen and the back buffer is where the image (or frame) hasn't yet been rendered. Once the image or frame is rendered in the back buffer, then this function swaps the front and back buffers, displaying the image that is now ready in the back buffer.
glutReshapeFunc	Used for specifying the reshape callback function for the current window. The function is invoked automatically during these situations: when a window is reshaped, before a window's first display callback, and after a window is created.

`glViewport`	Used to set the viewport, that is, the vicinity of the window in which we want the rendered image to appear. Four arguments are passed to the function. The first two arguments represent the lower-left corner of the viewport rectangle in terms of pixels. The third and fourth arguments represent the width and height of the viewport. The width and height of the viewport are usually set to be equal to the dimensions of the window or less in size.
`glMatrixMode`	Used to specify which matrix is the current matrix. The vertices are rendered on the basis of the current state of the matrix, so a matrix must be chosen so that it serves our needs. The following are the two main options.
`GL_MODELVIEW`	This is the default matrix option. This option is used when the user wants to perform translation, rotation, or similar operations.
`GL_PROJECTION`	This option is used when the user wants to perform parallel projection, perspective projection, and so on.
`glLoadIdentity`	Used to replace the current matrix with the identity matrix.
`gluOrtho2D`	Used to set up a two-dimensional orthographic viewing region. Four arguments are passed to this function. The first two coordinates represent the left and right vertical clipping planes. The last two specify the coordinates for the bottom and top horizontal clipping planes.
`glutMouseFunc`	Used to set the mouse callback function for the current window. That is, whenever the mouse button is pressed or released, each action invokes the mouse callback function. In the callback function, the following three arguments are automatically passed.
`button`	It represents any of the three buttons, `GLUT_LEFT_BUTTON`, `GLUT_MIDDLE_BUTTON`, or `GLUT_RIGHT_BUTTON`, depending on which of the mouse buttons is pressed.
`state`	The state can be either `GLUT_UP` or `GLUT_DOWN` depending on whether the callback was invoked because of the mouse release or mouse press, respectively.
`x and y`	Represents the window's relative coordinates when the mouse button state changes.
`glutIdleFunc`	Used to set the global idle callback, mainly used for performing background processing tasks. The idle callback is continuously called even if no event is occurring. The `NULL` parameter is sent to this function to disable the generation of the idle callback.

You need to initialize the **X Window System (X11)** for working with graphics. X11 provides a GUI environment, that is, it enables the displaying of windows and graphics, and provides an environment for interacting with a mouse and keyboard. The command used for starting the X11 is the `xinit` command.

Drawing four graphical shapes

In this recipe, we will learn to draw four different shapes: a square, a triangle, points, and a line.

How to do it...

The following are the steps to make different graphical shapes:

1. Initialize GLUT, define the window size, create the window, and set the position of the window.
2. Define the callback function that will be automatically invoked after displaying the window.
3. To draw a square, first, define its color.
4. Draw a square by defining its four vertices and enclosing them within `glBegin` and `glEnd` statements along with the `GL_QUADS` keyword.
5. To draw a line, set the width and color of the line.
6. Group a pair of vertices within `glBegin` and `glEnd` with the `GL_LINES` keyword to draw a line.
7. To draw the points, set the point size to 3 px and also set their color.
8. The vertices are where the points have to be displayed. Group them into a pair of `glBegin` and `glEnd` with the `GL_POINTS` keyword.
9. To draw a triangle, group three vertices into `glBegin` and `glEnd` statements along with the `GL_TRIANGLES` keyword.
10. The `glFlush` function is invoked to empty all the buffered statements and get the shapes drawn quickly.

The program for drawing the preceding four shapes is as follows:

```
//opengldrawshapes.c

#include <GL/glut.h>

void drawshapes() {
  glClearColor(0.0 f, 0.0 f, 0.0 f, 1.0 f);
  /* Making background color black as first
   All the 3 arguments R, G, B are 0.0 */
  glClear(GL_COLOR_BUFFER_BIT);
  glBegin(GL_QUADS);
  glColor3f(0.0 f, 0.0 f, 1.0 f);
  /* Making picture color blue (in RGB mode), as third argument is 1.
*/
  glVertex2f(0.0 f, 0.0 f);
  glVertex2f(0.0 f, .75 f);
  glVertex2f(-.75 f, .75 f);
  glVertex2f(-.75 f, 0.0 f);
  glEnd();
  glLineWidth(2.0);
  glColor3f(1.0, 0.0, 0.0);
  glBegin(GL_LINES);
  glVertex2f(-0.5, -0.5);
  glVertex2f(0.5, -0.5);
  glEnd();
  glColor3f(1.0, 0.0, 0.0);
  glPointSize(3.0);
  /* Width of point size is set to 3 pixel */
  glBegin(GL_POINTS);
  glVertex2f(-.25 f, -0.25 f);
  glVertex2f(0.25 f, -0.25 f);
  glEnd();
  glBegin(GL_TRIANGLES);
  glColor3f(0, 1, 0);
  glVertex2f(0, 0);
  glVertex2f(.5, .5);
  glVertex2f(1, 0);
  glEnd();
  glFlush();
}

int main(int argc, char ** argv) {
  glutInit( & argc, argv);
  glutCreateWindow("Drawing some shapes");
  /* Giving title to the window */
  glutInitWindowSize(1500, 1500);
  /* Defining the window size that is width and height of window */
```

```
    glutInitWindowPosition(0, 0);
    glutDisplayFunc(drawshapes);
    glutMainLoop();
    return 0;
}
```

Now, let's go behind the scenes to understand the code better.

How it works...

The first step, as expected, is that GLUT is initialized, followed by creating a top-level window, and the label supplied for the window is Drawing some shapes. However, you can give it any label. The window is defined with a width of 1,500 px and height of 1,500 px. The initial position of the window is set at 0,0, that is, at the coordinates of *x=0* and *y=0*. The drawshapes callback function is invoked for displaying different shapes in the window.

In the drawshapes function, the values of the color buffers are cleared, followed by clearing the buffers to preset values.

The first shape that we are drawing is a square, so a group of statements for drawing a square are enclosed within glBegin and glEnd statements. The GL_QUADS keyword is supplied with the glBegin statement because a quad refers to any shape that comprises 4 vertices. The glColor3f function is invoked to create a square filled with the color blue. The four sets of vertices are supplied to make a square. A vertex comprises *x* and *y* coordinates.

Next, we will draw lines. The glLineWidth function is invoked to specify the width of the lines to be drawn as 2 px wide. The glColor3f function is invoked to make the lines appear in the color red. Two vertices are grouped within glBegin and glEnd with the GL_LINES keyword to draw a line.

Next, we will draw two points. To make the points clearly visible, the point size is set to 3 px, and the color in which the points will be drawn is set to red (or any color except black). The two vertices where we want the points to be displayed are supplied after being grouped into a pair of glBegin and glEnd statements. The GL_POINTS keyword is supplied with the glBegin statement to draw the points.

Finally, we draw a triangle by grouping three triangle vertices into glBegin and glEnd statements. The GL_TRIANGLES keyword is supplied with glBegin to indicate that the vertices that are specified in the group are meant for drawing a triangle. glColor3f is invoked to make sure the triangle will be filled with the color green.

Finally, the `glFlush` function is invoked to empty all the buffered statements and get them executed quickly to display the desired shapes.

To compile the program, we need to open the Command Prompt and change the directory to the folder where the program is saved. Then, we execute the `xinit` command at the command prompt to start the X server (X11).

Once X server starts, give the following command to compile the program. Remember that the program has to be linked with `-lGL -lGLU -lglut` while compiling the program.

The syntax is as follows:

```
gcc filename.c -lGL -lGLU -lglut
```

Here, `filename.c` is the name of the file.

We will use the following command to compile our program:

```
gcc opengldrawshapes.c -lGL -lGLU -lglut -lm -o opengldrawshapes
```

If no error appears, this means the `opengldrawshapes.c` program has successfully been compiled into an executable file: `opengldrawshapes.exe`. This file is executed using the following command:

```
$./opengldrawshapes
```

We will get the output as shown in the following screenshot:

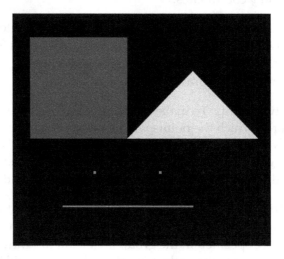

Figure 12.1

Voilà! We have successfully drawn four different graphical shapes: a square, triangle, points, and a line. Now let's move on to the next recipe!

Drawing a circle

The procedure for drawing a circle is completely different from the other graphical shapes, hence it gets its own dedicated recipe. It needs a `for` loop to draw small points or lines at 0 to 360 degrees. So, let's learn to draw a circle.

How to do it...

The following are the steps for drawing a circle:

1. Initialize GLUT, define the size of a top-level window, and create it. Also, set the initial position of the window for displaying our circle.
2. Define a callback function that is auto-invoked after creating the window.
3. In the callback function, color buffers are cleared and the color for displaying the circle is set.
4. The statements for drawing a circle are grouped within a pair of `glBegin` and `glEnd` functions along with the `GL_LINE_LOOP` keyword.
5. Use a `for` loop to draw small lines from 0 to 360 to give the shape of a circle.

The program for drawing a circle is as follows:

```
//opengldrawshapes2.c
```

```
#include <GL/glut.h>
#include<math.h>
#define pi 3.142857

void drawshapes() {
    glClearColor(0.0f, 0.0f, 0.0f, 1.0f);
    glClear(GL_COLOR_BUFFER_BIT);
    glColor3f(0.0f, 1.0f, 0.0f);
    glBegin(GL_LINE_LOOP);
        for (int i=0; i <360; i++)
        {
            float angle = i*pi/180;
            glVertex2f(cos(angle)*0.5,sin(angle)*0.5);
    }
```

```
        glEnd();
        glFlush();
    }

    int main(int argc, char** argv) {
        glutInit(&argc, argv);
        glutCreateWindow("Drawing some shapes");
        glutInitWindowSize(1500, 1500);
        glutInitWindowPosition(0, 0);
        glutDisplayFunc(drawshapes);
        glutMainLoop();
        return 0;
    }
```

Now, let's go behind the scenes to understand the code better.

How it works...

GLUT is initialized and a top-level window is created with the label, `Drawing some shapes`. The size of the window is defined as 1,500 px wide and 1,500 px in height. The initial position of the window is set at 0, 0, that is, at the *x=0* and *y=0* coordinate location. The `drawshapes` callback function is invoked for drawing a circle in the window.

In the `drawshapes` function, the values of the color buffers are cleared, followed by clearing the buffers to preset values. The `glColor3f` function is invoked to set the color in which we want to draw the circle. I have set the color to green to draw the circle but you can choose any color. A group of statements meant for drawing a circle is collected within a pair of `glBegin` and `glEnd` functions. The `glBegin` function is supplied to the `GL_LINE_LOOP` keyword to indicate that the circle that we are going to draw will be made up of several small lines.

Within the `glBegin` and `glEnd` functions, a `for` loop is used that executes from value 0 to 360; that is, a very small line will be drawn at every degree from 0 until 360 to give it the shape of a circle. The degree is first converted into radians and the line is drawn at the vertex location, *cos(angle) * radius, sin(angle)* radius*. When such small lines are drawn at every degree, it will give it the appearance of a circle on the screen.

To compile the program, start the X server and give the following command to compile the program:

```
gcc opengldrawshapes2.c –lGL –lGLU –lglut –lm –o opengldrawshapes2
```

If no error appears, that means the `opengldrawshapes2.c` program has successfully compiled into an executable file: `opengldrawshapes2.exe`. This file is executed using the following command:

```
$./opengldrawshapes2
```

We will get the output as shown in the following screenshot:

Figure 12.2

Voilà! We have successfully learned how to draw a circle. Now let's move on to the next recipe!

Drawing a line between two mouse clicks

In this recipe, we will learn to draw a line between two mouse clicks. A mouse click is considered a procedure of pressing the mouse button and releasing it. You can draw as many lines as you want between a pair of mouse press and release events.

How to do it...

The following are the steps to draw a line between two mouse clicks:

1. Initialize GLUT, define the size of the top-level window, and display the window.

2. Define a `drawLine` callback function that draws a line if any mouse click event occurs.

3. In the `drawLine` function, the clear values for the clear buffers are specified.

4. The `glutSwapBuffers()` function is invoked to swap the front and back buffers to display any frame that is rendered in the back buffer and is ready to be displayed.

5. The `glutReshapeFunc` function is invoked to specify the reshape callback function that will be auto-invoked whenever the window is reshaped to redraw the lines.

6. Because the vertices of the line are rendered on the basis of the current state of the matrix, a matrix is set as the current matrix for the viewing and modeling transformations.

7. A two-dimensional orthographic viewing region is also set up.

8. A mouse callback function is set up with the name `mouseEvents`. The callback is invoked whenever the mouse button is pressed or released.

9. As per the coordinates where the mouse button is pressed and released, the `drawLine` function will be invoked to draw the lines between the two coordinates.

The program for drawing a line between two mouse clicks is as follows:

`//openglmouseclick.c`

```
#include <GL/glut.h>

int noOfClicks = 0;
int coord[2][2];
int leftPressed = 0;

void drawLine(void)
{
    glClearColor(0.0, 0.0, 0.0, 1.0);
    glClear(GL_COLOR_BUFFER_BIT);
    glBegin(GL_LINES);
        for(int i=0; i<noOfClicks; i++) {
            glVertex2f(coord[i][0],coord[i][1]);
        }
    glEnd();
    glutSwapBuffers();
}

void projection(int width, int height)
```

```
{
    glViewport(0, 0, width, height);
    glMatrixMode(GL_PROJECTION);
    glLoadIdentity();
    gluOrtho2D(0, width, height, 0);
    glMatrixMode(GL_MODELVIEW);
}

void mouseEvents(int button, int state, int x, int y)
{
    switch (button) {
        case GLUT_LEFT_BUTTON:
            if (state == GLUT_DOWN) {
                leftPressed = 1;
            }
            if (state == GLUT_UP) {
                if(leftPressed) {
coord[noOfClicks][0]=x;
coord[noOfClicks][1]=y;
noOfClicks++;
leftPressed = 0;
}
glutIdleFunc(NULL);
            }
            break;
        default:
            break;
    }
    drawLine();
}

int main(int argc, char **argv)
{
    glutInit(&argc, argv);
    glutInitWindowSize(1000, 1000);
    glutCreateWindow("Displaying lines between two mouse clicks");
    glutDisplayFunc(drawLine);
    glutReshapeFunc(projection);
    glutMouseFunc(mouseEvents);
    glutMainLoop();
    return 0;
}
```

Now, let's go behind the scenes to understand the code better.

How it works...

GLUT is initialized and a top-level window is created with the label, `Displaying lines between two mouse clicks`. The window size is specified as 1,000 px wide and 1,000 px in height. The `drawLine` callback function is invoked for drawing lines if any mouse click event has occurred.

In the `drawLine` function, the clear values for the clear buffers are specified. Also, the buffers are cleared to preset values so that colors can be applied to them. Because no mouse click has occurred yet, the value of `noOfClicks` global variable is 0, and hence no line will be drawn at the moment.

The `glutSwapBuffers()` function is invoked to swap the front and back buffers to display any frame that is rendered in the back buffer and is ready to be displayed. Because no mouse click has been made yet, nothing will happen with this function.

Then, the `glutReshapeFunc` function is invoked to specify the reshape callback function for the current window. The callback function projection will be invoked automatically whenever the window is reshaped, before the window's first display callback and after the window is created. In the projection callback, a viewport is set to define the vicinity in which we want the lines to be drawn. Thereafter, a matrix is set as the current matrix for the viewing and modeling transformations. Also, the vertices are rendered on the basis of the current state of the matrix, so the matrix is chosen accordingly.

Besides this, a two-dimensional orthographic viewing region is also set up. The mouse callback function is set up with the name `mouseEvents`, so whenever a mouse button is pressed or released, the `mouseEvents` callback function will be automatically invoked. In the callback function, the information about which mouse button is pressed and whether the mouse button is pressed or released is passed. Also, the x and y coordinates where the mouse action takes place are also passed to the `mouseEvents` callback function.

In the `mouseEvents` function, first, it checks whether the left mouse button is pressed. If yes, then the location where the mouse button is released, that location's x and y coordinates are picked up and assigned to the `coord` array. Basically, the mouse button has to be pressed and then released to store the coordinate values. When two mouse clicks and releases are observed, the `drawLine` function is invoked to draw the lines between the two coordinates.

To compile the program, start the X server and give the following command to compile the program:

```
gcc openglmouseclick.c -1GL -1GLU -1glut -1m -o openglmouseclick
```

If no error appears, that means the `openglmouseclick.c` program has successfully compiled into an executable file: `openglmouseclick.exe`. This file is executed using the following command:

```
$./openglmouseclick
```

We will get the output as shown in the following screenshot:

Figure 12.3

Once you implement this functionality, you can draw as many lines as you want.

Now let's move on to the next recipe!

Making a bar graph of the supplied values

In this recipe, we will learn to draw bar charts. Let's assume we have data about the percentage of profit growth of a company for the last three years. We will assign that percentage of profit growth to an array, and on the basis of the values in the array, we will draw a bar chart with three bars on the screen.

How to do it...

The following are the steps for drawing a bar chart with the values defined in an array:

1. Initialize GLUT, define the size of the top-level window, set its initial position for display, and display the window on the screen.
2. Define the callback function that is auto-invoked after creating a window for drawing the bar chart.
3. An array is defined in the callback that defines the height of the bar chart. The width of the bar chart is fixed at 2 px.
4. A two-dimensional orthographic viewing region is set up, that is, coordinates are set up for horizontal and vertical clipping planes.
5. To display the horizontal and vertical x and y axes, the vertices for the two lines are grouped in a glBegin and glEnd pair with the GL_LINES keyword.
6. In order to display three bars, a for loop is set to execute three times. To display bars one beside the other, the x axis of the next bar is computed. The height of each bar is computed on the basis of the array defined in *step 3*.
7. The bar chart is displayed using the four vertices that are grouped in the glBegin and glEnd pair with the GL_POLYGON keyword.

The program for drawing a bar chart on the basis of values in an array is as follows:

```
//opengldrawbar.c

#include <GL/glut.h>

void display(){
    float x,y,width, result[] = {10.0, 15.0, 5.0};
    int i, barCount = 3;
    x=1.0;
    y = 0.0;
```

```
        width = 2.0;
        glColor3f(1.0, 0.0, 0.0);
        glClearColor(1.0, 1.0, 1.0, 1.0);
        gluOrtho2D(-5, 20, -5, 20);
        glBegin(GL_LINES);
            glVertex2f(-30, 0.0);
            glVertex2f(30, 0.0);
            glVertex2f(0.0, -30);
            glVertex2f(0.0, 30);
        glEnd();
        for(i=0; i<barCount; i++){
            x = (i * width) + i + 1;
            glBegin(GL_POLYGON);
                glVertex2f(x, y);
                glVertex2f(x, y+result[i]);
                glVertex2f(x+width, y+result[i]);
                glVertex2f(x+width, y);
            glEnd();
        }
        glFlush();
    }

int main(int argc, char *argv[]){
    glutInit(&argc, argv);
    glutInitWindowPosition(0, 0);
    glutInitWindowSize(500, 500);
    glutCreateWindow("Drawing Bar Chart");
    glutDisplayFunc(display);
    glutMainLoop();
    return 0;
}
```

Now, let's go behind the scenes to understand the code better.

How it works...

GLUT is initialized and a top-level window is created with the label, Displaying Bar Chart. The initial position of the window is set at 0,0, that is, at the $x=0$ and $y=0$ coordinate location. The window size is specified as 500 px in width and 500 px in height. The display callback function is invoked for drawing the bar chart.

In the display callback, a result array is initialized to three values. Basically, the values in the resulting array represent the growth in profit percentage of the company in the last three years. Let's assume the growth in the profit percentage of the company in 2019, 2018, and 2017 was 10%, 15%, and 5%, respectively. We want the three bars corresponding to this data to rest on the x axis, so the y coordinate is set to 0. To make the first bar appear after some space, the x coordinate value is set to 1. The width of each bar is set to 2. The color for the bar chart is set to red.

A two-dimensional orthographic viewing region is set up, that is, coordinates are set up for the horizontal and vertical clipping planes. Before drawing the bar chart, the horizontal and vertical x and y axes have to be drawn, so vertices for two lines are grouped in the glBegin and glEnd pair with the GL_LINES keyword.

After drawing the x and y axes, a for loop is set to execute three times because we need to draw three bars. Within the for loop, the bars are given a fixed width of 2 px, and, after every bar chart, the x axis of the next bar is computed. Also, the height of the bar – that is, the y coordinate – is computed on the basis of the profit percentage mentioned in each result array. The bar chart is displayed using the four vertices that are grouped in the glBegin and glEnd pair with the GL_POLYGON keyword.

To compile the program, start the X server and give the following command to compile the program:

```
gcc opengldrawbar.c –lGL –lGLU –lglut –lm –o opengldrawbar
```

If no error appears, that means the opengldrawbar.c program has successfully compiled into an executable file: opengldrawbar.exe. This file is executed using the following command:

```
$./opengldrawbar
```

We will get the output as shown in the following screenshot:

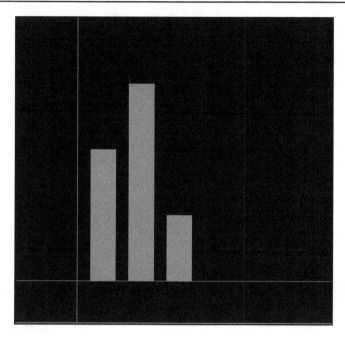

Figure 12.4

Voilà! We have successfully created a bar chart using data entered in an array. Now let's move on to the next recipe!

Making an animated bouncing ball

In this recipe, we will learn to create an animation of a bouncing ball. The ball will be made to appear as if it is falling on the floor and then bouncing back up. To make the ball appear as falling to the floor, the ball is displayed at certain *x, y* coordinates; after drawing the ball, it is cleared from its current place and redrawn just below its original location. This process of drawing of the ball, erasing it, and redrawing at a lower *y* coordinate location in quick succession will make the ball appear as if it is falling to the ground. The reverse procedure can be used to show the ball bouncing back up.

How to do it...

The following are the steps to make a small animation of a bouncing ball:

1. GLUT is initialized, the top-level window is defined as being of a specific size, its position is set, and, finally, the top-level window is created.
2. The callback function is invoked to display a bouncing ball.
3. In the callback function, the color buffers are cleared and the color of the bouncing ball is set to green.
4. The `glPointSize` is set to 1 px because the circle will be drawn with the help of small points or dots.
5. The `GL_PROJECTION` is set as the current matrix in order to enable parallel and perspective projections. Also, a two-dimensional orthographic viewing region is set up.
6. To make the falling section of the animation, a ball is drawn at some *x, y* coordinate. After drawing that ball, the screen is cleared, and the ball is redrawn at a lower location (at a lower *y* coordinate).
7. The preceding step is repeated in quick succession to give the appearance of a falling ball.
8. To make the ball bounce back up, the ball is drawn, then the screen is cleared, and the ball is redrawn at a higher *y* coordinate that is just above the *ground* location.

The program for making an animated bouncing ball is as follows:

```
//ballanim.c

#include<stdio.h>
#include<GL/glut.h>
#include<math.h>
#define pi 3.142857

void animball (void)
{
    int x,y;
    glClearColor(0.0, 0.0, 0.0, 1.0);
    glColor3f(0.0, 1.0, 0.0);
    glPointSize(1.0);
    glMatrixMode(GL_PROJECTION);
    glLoadIdentity();
    gluOrtho2D(-350, 350, -350, 350);
    for (float j = 0; j < 1000; j += 0.01)
    {
```

```
        glClear(GL_COLOR_BUFFER_BIT);
        glBegin(GL_POINTS);
            for (int i=0; i <360; i++)
            {
                x = 100 * cos(i);
                y = 100 * sin(i);
                /* If 100 is radius of circle, then circle is defined
as
                x=100*cos(i) and y=100*sin(i)  */
                glVertex2i(x / 2 - 1 * cos(j), y / 2 - 150* sin(j));
            }
        glEnd();
        glFlush();
    }
}

int main (int argc, char** argv)
{
    glutInit(&argc, argv);
    glutCreateWindow("Animating a ball");
    glutInitWindowSize(1000, 1000);
    glutInitWindowPosition(0, 0);
    glutDisplayFunc(animball);
    glutMainLoop();
}
```

Now, let's go behind the scenes to understand the code better.

How it works...

GLUT is initialized and a top-level window is created with the label, `Animating a ball`. The initial position of the window is set at *0,0*, that is, at *x=0* and *y=0* coordinate location. The window size is specified with 1,000 px of width and 1,000 px of height. The callback function, `animball`, is invoked to display a bouncing ball.

In the `animball` callback function, the values of the color buffers are cleared. The color for drawing the bouncing ball is set to green. Because the ball will be drawn using small points or dots, the `glPointSize` is set to 1 px.

The `GL_PROJECTION` is set as the current matrix in order to enable parallel and perspective projections. Also, a two-dimensional orthographic viewing region is set up, defining the left and right vertical clipping planes and the bottom and top horizontal clipping planes.

To display a bouncing ball, we first make the ball drop down on the floor and then bounce back up. To make the falling ball, we draw a ball at some *x, y* coordinate. After drawing that ball, we clear the screen and redraw the ball just below the original coordinate, that is, after lowering the *y* coordinate. Clearing and redrawing the ball with successively falling *y* coordinates repetitively and swiftly will make the ball appear as if it's falling. We will do the reverse to make the ball bounce up. That is, the ball is drawn, the screen is cleared, and the ball is redrawn at successively higher *y* coordinates. The radius of the ball is assumed to be 100 px (but it can be any radius).

To compile the program, start the X server and give the following command to compile the program:

```
gcc ballanim.c -lGL -lGLU -lglut -lm -o ballanim
```

If no error appears, that means the `ballanim.c` program has successfully compiled into an executable file: `ballanim.exe`. This file is executed using the following command:

```
$./ballanim
```

We will get the output as shown in the following screenshot:

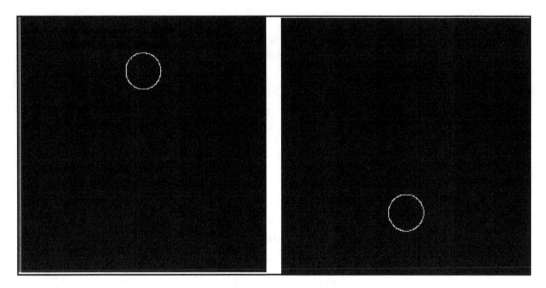

Figure 12.5

Voilà! We have successfully created an animated bouncing ball.

13
Using MySQL Database

MySQL is one of the most popular database management systems in recent times. Databases, as we all know, are used for storing data that's going to be used in the future when required. The data in a database can be secured through encryption and can be indexed for faster access. Where the volume of data is too high, a database management system is preferred over a traditional sequential and random file handling system. Storing data in a database is a very important task in any application.

This chapter is focused on understanding how table rows are managed in the database tables. In this chapter, you will learn about the following recipes:

- Displaying all the built-in tables in a default MySQL database
- Storing information into MySQL database
- Searching desired information in the database
- Updating information in the database
- Deleting data from the database using C

We will review the most commonly used functions in MySQL before we move on to the recipes. Also, ensure that you read *Appendix B* and *Appendix C* to install Cygwin and MySQL Server before implementing the recipes in this chapter.

Functions in MySQL

While accessing and working with MySQL database in C programming, we will have to use several functions. Let's go through them.

mysql_init()

This initializes a MYSQL object that can be used in the `mysql_real_connect()` method. Here is its syntax:

```
MYSQL *mysql_init(MYSQL *object)
```

If the object parameter that's passed is NULL, then the function initializes and returns a new object; otherwise, the supplied object is initialized and the address of the object is returned.

mysql_real_connect()

This establishes a connection to a MySQL database engine running on the specified host. Here is its syntax:

```
MYSQL *mysql_real_connect(MYSQL *mysqlObject, const char *hostName,
const char *userid, const char *password, const char *dbase, unsigned
int port, const char *socket, unsigned long flag)
```

Here:

- `mysqlObject` represents the address of an existing MYSQL object.
- `hostName` is where the hostname or IP address of the host is provided. To connect to a local host, either NULL or the string *localhost* is provided.
- `userid` represents a valid MySQL login ID.
- `password` represents the password of the user.
- `dbase` represents the database name to which the connection has to be established.
- `port` is where either value 0 is specified or the port number for the TCP/IP connection is supplied.
- `socket` is where either NULL is specified or the socket or named pipe is supplied.
- `flag` can be used to enable certain features, such as handling expired passwords and applying compression in the client/server protocol, but its value is usually kept at 0.

The function returns a MYSQL connection handler if the connection is established; otherwise, it returns NULL.

mysql_query()

This function executes the supplied SQL query. Here is its syntax:

```
int mysql_query(MYSQL *mysqlObject, const char *sqlstmt)
```

Here:

- `mysqlObject` represents the `MYSQL` object
- `sqlstmt` represents the null-terminated string that contains the SQL statement to be executed

The function returns `0` if the SQL statement executes successfully; otherwise, it returns a non-zero value.

mysql_use_result()

After successful execution of an SQL statement, this method is used to save the result set. This means that the result set is retrieved and returned. Here is its syntax:

```
MYSQL_RES *mysql_use_result(MYSQL *mysqlObject)
```

Here, `mysqlObject` represents the connection handler.

If no error occurs, the function returns a `MYSQL_RES` result structure. In case of any error, the function returns `NULL`.

mysql_fetch_row()

This function fetches the next row from a result set. The function returns `NULL` if there are no more rows in the result set to retrieve or if an error occurs. Here is its syntax:

```
MYSQL_ROW mysql_fetch_row(MYSQL_RES *resultset)
```

Here, the `resultset` parameter is the set from which the next row has to be fetched. You can access values in the column of the row by using the subscript `row[0]`, `row[1]`, and so on, where `row[0]` represents the data in the first column, `row[1]` represents the data in the second column, and so on.

mysql_num_fields()

This returns the number of values; that is, columns in the supplied row. Here is its syntax:

```
unsigned int mysql_num_fields(MYSQL_ROW row)
```

Here, the parameter row represents the individual row that is accessed from the resultset.

mysql_free_result()

This frees the memory allocated to a result set. Here is its syntax:

```
void mysql_free_result(MYSQL_RES *resultset)
```

Here, resultset represents the set whose memory we want to free up.

mysql_close()

This function closes the previously opened MySQL connection. Here is its syntax:

```
void mysql_close(MYSQL *mysqlObject)
```

It de-allocates the connection handler that's represented by the mysqlObject parameter. The function returns no value.

This covers the functions that we need to know for using the MySQL database for our recipes. From the second recipe onward, we will be working on a database table. So, let's get started and create a database and a table inside it.

Creating a MySQL database and tables

Open the Cygwin Terminal and open the MySQL command line by giving the following command. Through this command, we want to open MySQL through the user ID root and try to connect with the MySQL server running at the localhost (127.0.0.1):

```
$ mysql -u root -p -h 127.0.0.1
Enter password:
Welcome to the MariaDB monitor.  Commands end with ; or \g.
```

```
Your MySQL connection id is 12
Server version: 5.7.14-log MySQL Community Server (GPL)
Copyright (c) 2000, 2017, Oracle, MariaDB Corporation Ab and others.
Type 'help;' or '\h' for help. Type '\c' to clear the current input
statement.
MySQL [(none)]>
```

The preceding MySQL prompt that appears confirms that the `userid` and `password` have been entered correctly and that you are successfully connected to a running MySQL server. Now, we can go ahead and run SQL commands.

Create database

The `create database` statement creates the database with the specified name. Here is the syntax:

```
Create database database_name;
```

Here, `database_name` is the name of the new database to be created.

Let's create a database by the name `ecommerce` for our recipes:

```
MySQL [(none)]> create database ecommerce;
Query OK, 1 row affected (0.01 sec)
```

To confirm that our `ecommerce` database has been successfully created, we will use the `show databases` statement to see the list of existing databases on the MySQL server:

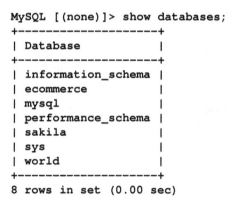

```
MySQL [(none)]> show databases;
+--------------------+
| Database           |
+--------------------+
| information_schema |
| ecommerce          |
| mysql              |
| performance_schema |
| sakila             |
| sys                |
| world              |
+--------------------+
8 rows in set (0.00 sec)
```

In the preceding database listing, we can see the name `ecommerce`, which confirms that our database has been successfully created. Now, we will apply the `use` statement to access the `ecommerce` database, as shown here:

```
MySQL [(none)]> use ecommerce;
Database changed
```

Now, the `ecommerce` database is in use, so whatever SQL commands we will give will be applied to the `ecommerce` database only. Next, we need to create a table in our `ecommerce` database. For creating a database table, the `Create table` command is used. Let's discuss it next.

Create table

This creates a database table with the specified name. Here is its syntax:

```
CREATE TABLE table_name (column_name column_type,column_name
column_type,.....);
```

Here:

- `table_name` represents the name of the table that we want to create.
- `column_ name` represents the column names that we want in the table.
- `column_type` represents the data type of the column. Depending on the type of data we want to store in the column, the `column_type` can be `int`, `varchar`, `date`, `text`, and so on.

The `create table` statement creates a `users` table with three columns: `email_address`, `password`, and `address_of_delivery`. Assuming that this table will contain information of the users who have placed orders online, we will be storing their email address, password, and the location where the order has to be delivered:

```
MySQL [ecommerce]> create table users(email_address varchar(30),
password varchar(30), address_of_delivery text);
Query OK, 0 rows affected (0.38 sec)
```

To confirm that the table has been successfully created, we will use the `show tables` command to display the list of existing tables in the currently opened database, as shown here:

```
MySQL [ecommerce]> show tables;
+---------------------+
| Tables_in_ecommerce |
+---------------------+
| users               |
+---------------------+
1 row in set (0.00 sec)
```

The output of the `show tables` command displays the `users` table, thus confirming that the table has indeed been created successfully. To see the table structure (that is, its column names, column types, and column width), we will use the `describe` statement. The following statement displays the structure of the `users` table:

```
MySQL [ecommerce]> describe users;
+--------------------+-------------+------+-----+---------+-------+
| Field              | Type        | Null | Key | Default | Extra |
+--------------------+-------------+------+-----+---------+-------+
| email_address      | varchar(30) | YES  |     | NULL    |       |
| password           | varchar(30) | YES  |     | NULL    |       |
| address_of_delivery | text       | YES  |     | NULL    |       |
+--------------------+-------------+------+-----+---------+-------+
3 rows in set (0.04 sec)
```

So, now that we have learned about some basic commands to work with our database, we can begin with the first recipe of this chapter.

Displaying all the built-in tables in a default mysql database

The MySQL server, when installed, comes with certain default databases. One of those databases is `mysql`. In this recipe, we will learn to display all the table names that are available in the `mysql` database.

How to do it...

1. Create a MySQL object:

   ```
   mysql_init(NULL);
   ```

2. Establish a connection to the MySQL server running at the specified host. Also, connect to the desired database:

   ```
   mysql_real_connect(conn, server, user, password, database, 0,
   NULL, 0)
   ```

3. Create an execute SQL statement, comprised of show tables:

   ```
   mysql_query(conn, "show tables")
   ```

4. Save the result of the executing SQL query (that is, the table information of the mysql database) into a resultset:

   ```
   res = mysql_use_result(conn);
   ```

5. Fetch one row at a time from the resultset in a while loop and display only the table name from that row:

   ```
   while ((row = mysql_fetch_row(res)) != NULL)
         printf("%s \n", row[0]);
   ```

6. Free up the memory that is allocated to the resultset:

   ```
   mysql_free_result(res);
   ```

7. Close the opened connection handler:

   ```
   mysql_close(conn);
   ```

The mysql1.c program for displaying all the tables in the built-in mysql database is as follows:

```
#include <mysql/mysql.h>
#include <stdio.h>
#include <stdlib.h>

void main() {
      MYSQL *conn;
      MYSQL_RES *res;
      MYSQL_ROW row;
      char *server = "127.0.0.1";
```

```
        char *user = "root";
        char *password = "Bintu2018$";
        char *database = "mysql";
        conn = mysql_init(NULL);
        if (!mysql_real_connect(conn, server,
            user, password, database, 0, NULL, 0)) {
            fprintf(stderr, "%s\n", mysql_error(conn));
            exit(1);
        }
        if (mysql_query(conn, "show tables")) {
            fprintf(stderr, "%s\n", mysql_error(conn));
            exit(1);
        }
        res = mysql_use_result(conn);
        printf("MySQL Tables in mysql database:\n");
        while ((row = mysql_fetch_row(res)) != NULL)
            printf("%s \n", row[0]);
        mysql_free_result(res);
        mysql_close(conn);
    }
```

Now, let's go behind the scenes to understand the code better.

How it works...

We will start by establishing a connection with the MySQL server and for that, we need to invoke the mysql_real_connect function. But we have to pass a MYSQL object to the mysql_real_connect function and we have to invoke the mysql_init function to create the MYSQL object. Hence, the mysql_init function is first invoked to initialize a MYSQL object by the name conn.

We will then supply the MYSQL object conn to the mysql_real_connect function, along with the valid user ID, password, and the host details. The mysql_real_connect function will establish a connection to the MySQL server running at the specified host. Besides this, the function will link to the supplied mysql database and will declare conn as the connection handler. This means that conn will be used in the rest of the program whenever we want to perform some action to the specified MySQL server and the mysql database.

If any error occurs in establishing the connection to the MySQL database engine, the program will terminate after displaying an error message. If the connection to the MySQL database engine is established successfully, the mysql_query function is invoked and the SQL statement show tables and the connection handler conn are supplied to it. The mysql_query function will execute the supplied SQL statement. To save the resulting table information of the mysql database, the mysql_use_result function is invoked. The table information that's received from the mysql_use_result function will be assigned to resultset res.

Next, we will invoke the mysql _fetch_row function in a while loop that will extract one row at a time from the resultset res; that is, one table detail will be fetched at a time from the resultset and assigned to the array row. The array row will contain complete information of one table at a time. The table name stored in the row[0] subscript is displayed on the screen. With every iteration of the while loop, the next piece of table information is extracted from resultset res and assigned to the array row. Consequently, all the table names in the mysql database will be displayed on the screen.

Then, we will invoke the mysql_free_result function to free up the memory that is allocated to resultset res and, finally, we will invoke the mysql_close function to close the opened connection handler conn.

Let's use GCC to compile the mysql1.c program, as shown here:

```
$ gcc mysql1.c -o mysql1 -I/usr/local/include/mysql -
L/usr/local/lib/mysql -lmysqlclient
```

If you get no errors or warnings, that means the mysql1.c program has compiled into an executable file, mysql1.exe. Let's run this executable file:

```
$ ./mysql1
MySQL Tables in mysql database:
columns_priv
db
engine_cost
event
func
general_log
gtid_executed
help_category
help_keyword
help_relation
help_topic
innodb_index_stats
```

```
innodb_table_stats
ndb_binlog_index
plugin
proc
procs_priv
proxies_priv
server_cost
servers
slave_master_info
slave_relay_log_info
slave_worker_info
slow_log
tables_priv
time_zone
time_zone_leap_second
time_zone_name
time_zone_transition
time_zone_transition_type
user
```

Voila! As you can see, the output shows the list of built-in tables in the `mysql` database. Now, let's move on to the next recipe!

Storing information in MySQL database

In this recipe, we will learn how to insert a new row into the `users` table. Recall that at the beginning of this chapter, we created a database called `ecommerce`, and in that database, we created a table called `users` with the following columns:

```
email_address varchar(30)
password varchar(30)
address_of_delivery text
```

We will be inserting rows into this `users` table now.

How to do it...

1. Initialize a MYSQL object:

```
conn = mysql_init(NULL);
```

2. Establish a connection to the MySQL server running at the localhost. Also, connect to the database that you want to work on:

```
mysql_real_connect(conn, server, user, password, database, 0,
NULL, 0)
```

3. Enter the information of the new row that you want to insert into the users table in the ecommerce database, which will be for the new user's email address, password, and address of delivery:

```
printf("Enter email address: ");
scanf("%s", emailaddress);
printf("Enter password: ");
scanf("%s", upassword);
printf("Enter address of delivery: ");
getchar();
gets(deliveryaddress);
```

4. Prepare an SQL INSERT statement comprising this information; that is, the email address, password, and address of delivery of the new user:

```
strcpy(sqlquery,"INSERT INTO users(email_address, password,
address_of_delivery)VALUES (\'");
strcat(sqlquery,emailaddress);
strcat(sqlquery,"\', \'");
strcat(sqlquery,upassword);
strcat(sqlquery,"\', \'");
strcat(sqlquery,deliveryaddress);
strcat(sqlquery,"\')");
```

5. Execute the SQL INSERT statement to insert a new row into the users table in the ecommerce database:

```
mysql_query(conn, sqlquery)
```

6. Close the connection handler:

```
mysql_close(conn);
```

The adduser.c program for inserting a row into a MySQL database table is shown in the following code:

```
#include <mysql/mysql.h>
#include <stdio.h>
#include <stdlib.h>
#include <string.h>
```

```
void main() {
    MYSQL *conn;
    char *server = "127.0.0.1";
    char *user = "root";
    char *password = "Bintu2018$";
    char *database = "ecommerce";
    char emailaddress[30],
    upassword[30],deliveryaddress[255],sqlquery[255];
    conn = mysql_init(NULL);
    if (!mysql_real_connect(conn, server, user, password,
database, 0,
    NULL, 0)) {
        fprintf(stderr, "%s\n", mysql_error(conn));
        exit(1);
    }
    printf("Enter email address: ");
    scanf("%s", emailaddress);
    printf("Enter password: ");
    scanf("%s", upassword);
    printf("Enter address of delivery: ");
    getchar();
    gets(deliveryaddress);
    strcpy(sqlquery,"INSERT INTO users(email_address, password,
    address_of_delivery)VALUES (\'");
    strcat(sqlquery,emailaddress);
    strcat(sqlquery,"\', \'");
    strcat(sqlquery,upassword);
    strcat(sqlquery,"\', \'");
    strcat(sqlquery,deliveryaddress);
    strcat(sqlquery,"\')");
    if (mysql_query(conn, sqlquery) != 0)
    {
        fprintf(stderr, "Row could not be inserted into users
    table\n");
        exit(1);
    }
    printf("Row is inserted successfully in users table\n");
    mysql_close(conn);
}
```

Now, let's go behind the scenes to understand the code better.

How it works...

We start by invoking the mysql_init function to initialize a MYSQL object by the name conn. The initialized MYSQL object conn is then supplied for invoking the mysql_real_connect function, along with the valid user ID and password, which in turn will establish a connection to the MySQL server running on the localhost. In addition, the function will link to our ecommerce database.

If any error occurs in establishing the connection to the MySQL database engine, an error message will be displayed and the program will terminate. If the connection to the MySQL database engine is established successfully, then conn will act as a connection handler for the rest of the program.

You will be prompted to enter information for the new row that you want to insert into the users table in the ecommerce database. You will be prompted to enter the information for the new row: the email address, password, and address of delivery. We will create an SQL INSERT statement comprising this information (email address, password, and address of delivery), which is supposed to be entered by users. Thereafter, we will invoke the mysql_query function and pass the MySQL object conn and the SQL INSERT statements to it to execute the SQL statement and insert a new row into the users table.

If any error occurs while executing the mysql_query function, an error message will be displayed on the screen and the program will terminate. If the new row is successfully inserted into the users table, the message Row is inserted successfully in users table will be displayed on the screen. Finally, we will invoke the mysql_close function and pass the connection handler conn to it to close the connection handler.

Let's open the Cygwin Terminal. We will require two Terminal windows; on one window, we will run SQL commands and on the other, we will compile and run C. Open another Terminal window by pressing *Alt+F2*. In the first Terminal window, invoke the MySQL command line by using the following command:

```
$ mysql -u root -p -h 127.0.0.1
Enter password:
Welcome to the MariaDB monitor.  Commands end with ; or \g.
Your MySQL connection id is 27
Server version: 5.7.14-log MySQL Community Server (GPL)
Copyright (c) 2000, 2017, Oracle, MariaDB Corporation Ab and others.
Type 'help;' or '\h' for help. Type '\c' to clear the current input
statement.
```

To work with our `ecommerce` database, we need to make it the current database. So, open the `ecommerce` database by using the following command:

```
MySQL [(none)]> use ecommerce;
Reading table information for completion of table and column names
You can turn off this feature to get a quicker startup with -A
Database changed
```

Now, `ecommerce` is our current database; that is, whatever SQL commands we will execute will be applied to the `ecommerce` database only. Let's use the following SQL `SELECT` command to see the existing rows in the `users` database table:

```
MySQL [ecommerce]> select * from users;
Empty set (0.00 sec)
```

The given output confirms that the `users` table is currently empty. To compile the C program, switch to the second Terminal window. Let's use GCC to compile the `adduser.c` program, as shown here:

```
$ gcc adduser.c -o adduser -I/usr/local/include/mysql -
L/usr/local/lib/mysql -lmysqlclient
```

If you get no errors or warnings, that means the `adduser.c` program has compiled into an executable file, `adduser.exe`. Let's run this executable file:

```
$ ./adduser
Enter email address: bmharwani@yahoo.com
Enter password: gold
Enter address of delivery: 11 Hill View Street, New York, USA
Row is inserted successfully in users table
```

The given C program output confirms that the new row has been successfully added to the `users` database table. To confirm this, switch to the Terminal window where the MySQL command line is open and use the following command:

```
MySQL [ecommerce]> select * from users;
+----------------------+----------+-------------------------------------
+
| email_address        | password | address_of_delivery
|
+----------------------+----------+-------------------------------------
+
| bmharwani@yahoo.com  | gold     | 11 Hill View Street, New York, USA
|
+----------------------+----------+-------------------------------------
+
1 row in set (0.00 sec)
```

Voila! The given output confirms that the new row that was entered through C has been successfully inserted into the `users` database table.

Now, let's move on to the next recipe!

Searching for the desired information in the database

In this recipe, we will learn how to search for information in a database table. Again, we assume that a `users` table comprising three columns, `email_address`, `password`, and `address_of_delivery`, already exists (please see the section, *Creating a MySQL database and tables*, of this chapter, where we created an `ecommerce` database and a `users` table in it). On entering an email address, the recipe will search the entire `users` database table for it, and if any row is found that matches the supplied email address, that user's password and address of delivery will be displayed on the screen.

How to do it...

1. Initialize a MYSQL object:

   ```
   mysql_init(NULL);
   ```

2. Establish a connection to the MySQL server running at the specified host. Also, establish a connection to the `ecommerce` database:

   ```
   mysql_real_connect(conn, server, user, password, database, 0,
   NULL, 0)
   ```

3. Enter the email address of the user whose details you want to search for:

   ```
   printf("Enter email address to search: ");
   scanf("%s", emailaddress);
   ```

4. Create an SQL `SELECT` statement that searches the row in the `users` table that matches the email address that was entered by the user:

   ```
   strcpy(sqlquery,"SELECT * FROM users where email_address like
   \'");
   strcat(sqlquery,emailaddress);
   strcat(sqlquery,"\'");
   ```

5. Execute the SQL SELECT statement. Terminate the program if the SQL query does not execute or some error occurs:

```
if (mysql_query(conn, sqlquery) != 0)
{
fprintf(stderr, "No row found in the users table with this
email      address\n");
    exit(1);
}
```

6. If the SQL query executes successfully then the row(s) that matches the specified email address are retrieved and assigned to a resultset:

```
resultset = mysql_use_result(conn);
```

7. Use a while loop to extract one row at a time from the resultset and assign it to the array row:

```
while ((row = mysql_fetch_row(resultset)) != NULL)
```

8. The information of the entire row is shown by displaying the subscripts row[0], row[1], and row[2], respectively:

```
printf("Email Address: %s \n", row[0]);
printf("Password: %s \n", row[1]);
printf("Address of delivery: %s \n", row[2]);
```

9. Memory that's allocated to the resultset is freed up:

```
mysql_free_result(resultset);
```

10. The opened connection handler is closed:

```
mysql_close(conn);
```

The searchuser.c program for searching in a specific row in a MySQL database table is shown in the following code:

```
#include <mysql/mysql.h>
#include <stdio.h>
#include <stdlib.h>
#include <string.h>

void main() {
    MYSQL *conn;
    MYSQL_RES *resultset;
    MYSQL_ROW row;
```

```
    char *server = "127.0.0.1";
    char *user = "root";
    char *password = "Bintu2018$";
    char *database = "ecommerce";
    char emailaddress[30], sqlquery[255];
    conn = mysql_init(NULL);
    if (!mysql_real_connect(conn, server, user, password, database, 0,
    NULL, 0)) {
        fprintf(stderr, "%s\n", mysql_error(conn));
        exit(1);
    }
    printf("Enter email address to search: ");
    scanf("%s", emailaddress);
    strcpy(sqlquery,"SELECT * FROM users where email_address like
\'");
    strcat(sqlquery,emailaddress);
    strcat(sqlquery,"\'");
    if (mysql_query(conn, sqlquery) != 0)
    {
        fprintf(stderr, "No row found in the users table with this
    email address\n");
        exit(1);
    }
    printf("The details of the user with this email address are as
    follows:\n");
    resultset = mysql_use_result(conn);
    while ((row = mysql_fetch_row(resultset)) != NULL)
    {
        printf("Email Address: %s \n", row[0]);
        printf("Password: %s \n", row[1]);
        printf("Address of delivery: %s \n", row[2]);
    }
    mysql_free_result(resultset);
    mysql_close(conn);
}
```

Now, let's go behind the scenes to understand the code better.

How it works...

We will start by invoking the `mysql_init` function to initialize a `MYSQL` object by the name `conn`. Thereafter, we will invoke the `mysql_real_connect` function and pass the `MYSQL` object `conn` to it along with the valid user ID, password, and the host details. The `mysql_real_connect` function will establish a connection to the MySQL server running at the specified host and will also connect to the supplied database, `ecommerce`. The `MYSQL` object `conn` will act as the connection handler for the rest of the program. Wherever a connection to the MySQL server and `ecommerce` database is required, referring to `conn` will suffice.

If any error occurs in establishing a connection to the MySQL database engine or the `ecommerce` database, an error message will be displayed and the program will terminate. If a connection to the MySQL database engine is established successfully, you will be prompted to enter the email address of the user whose details you want to search for.

We will create an SQL `SELECT` statement that will search the row in the `users` table that matches the email address entered by the user. Then, we will invoke the `mysql_query` function and pass the created SQL `SELECT` statement to it, along with the connection handler `conn`. If the SQL query does not execute or some error occurs, the program will terminate after displaying an error message. If the query is successful, then the resulting row(s) that satisfy the condition (that is, the row(s) that match the supplied email address) will be retrieved by invoking the `mysql_use_result` function and will be assigned to the result set, `resultset`.

We will then invoke the `mysql _fetch_row` function in a `while` loop that will extract one row at a time from the `resultset`; that is, the first row from the `resultset` will be accessed and assigned to the array row.

Recall that the `users` table contains the following columns:

- `email_address varchar(30)`
- `password varchar(30)`
- `address_of_delivery text`

Consequently, the array row will contain complete information of the accessed row, where the subscript `row[0]` will contain the data of the `email_ address` column, `row[1]` will contain the data of the column password, and `row[2]` will contain the data of the `address_of_delivery` column. The information of the entire row will be displayed by displaying the subscripts `row[0]`, `row[1]`, and `row[2]`, respectively.

At the end, we will invoke the `mysql_free_result` function to free up the memory that was allocated to the `resultset`. Then, we will invoke the `mysql_close` function to close the opened connection handler `conn`.

Let's open the Cygwin Terminal. We will require two Terminal windows; on one window, we will run SQL commands and on the other, we will compile and run C. Open another Terminal window by pressing *Alt+F2*. In the first Terminal window, invoke the MySQL command line by using the following command:

```
$ mysql -u root -p -h 127.0.0.1
Enter password:
Welcome to the MariaDB monitor.  Commands end with ; or \g.
Your MySQL connection id is 27
Server version: 5.7.14-log MySQL Community Server (GPL)
Copyright (c) 2000, 2017, Oracle, MariaDB Corporation Ab and others.
Type 'help;' or '\h' for help. Type '\c' to clear the current input
statement.
```

To work with our `ecommerce` database, we need to make it the current database. So, open the `ecommerce` database by using the following command:

```
MySQL [(none)]> use ecommerce;
Reading table information for completion of table and column names
You can turn off this feature to get a quicker startup with -A
Database changed
```

Now, `ecommerce` is our current database; that is, whatever SQL commands we will execute will be applied to the `ecommerce` database only. Let's use the following SQL `SELECT` command to see the existing rows in the `users` database table:

```
MySQL [ecommerce]> select * from users;
+---------------------+----------+-------------------------------------
+
| email_address       | password | address_of_delivery |
+---------------------+----------+-------------------------------------
+
| bmharwani@yahoo.com | gold     | 11 Hill View Street, New York, USA

| harwanibm@gmail.com | diamond  | House No. xyz, Pqr Apartments, Uvw
Lane, Mumbai, Maharashtra                |
| bintu@gmail.com     | platinum | abc Sea View, Ocean Lane, Opposite
Mt. Everest, London, UKg
+---------------------+----------+-------------------------------------
+
3 rows in set (0.00 sec)
```

The given output shows that there are three rows in the `users` table.

To compile the C program, switch to the second Terminal window. Let's use GCC to compile the `searchuser.c` program, as shown here:

```
$ gcc searchuser.c -o searchuser -I/usr/local/include/mysql -
L/usr/local/lib/mysql -lmysqlclient
```

If you get no errors or warnings, that means the `searchuser.c` program has compiled into an executable file, `searchuser.exe`. Let's run this executable file:

```
$ ./searchuser
Enter email address to search: bmharwani@yahoo.com
The details of the user with this email address are as follows:
Email Address:bmharwani@yahoo.com
Password: gold
Address of delivery: 11 Hill View Street, New York, USA
```

Voila! We can see that complete information of the user with their email address, `bmharwani@yahoo.com`, is displayed on the screen.

Now, let's move on to the next recipe!

Updating information in the database

In this recipe, we will learn how to update information in a database table. We assume that a `users` database table already exists, comprising of three columns—`email_address`, `password`, and `address_of_delivery` (please see the beginning of this chapter, where we learned to create a database and a table in it). On entering an email address, all the current information of the user (that is, their password and address of delivery) will be displayed. Thereafter, the user will be prompted to enter a new password and address of delivery. This new information will be updated against the current information in the table.

How to do it...

1. Initialize a `MYSQL` object:

```
mysql_init(NULL);
```

2. Establish a connection to the MySQL server running at the specified host. Also, generate a connection handler. The program will terminate if some error occurs in establishing the connection to the MySQL server engine or to the `ecommerce` database:

```
if (!mysql_real_connect(conn, server, user, password,
database, 0, NULL, 0))
    {
        fprintf(stderr, "%s\n", mysql_error(conn));
        exit(1);
    }
```

3. Enter the email address of the user whose information has to be updated:

```
printf("Enter email address of the user to update: ");
scanf("%s", emailaddress);
```

4. Create an SQL SELECT statement that will search the row in the `users` table that matches the email address that was entered by the user:

```
strcpy(sqlquery,"SELECT * FROM users where email_address like
\'");
strcat(sqlquery,emailaddress);
strcat(sqlquery,"\'");
```

5. Execute the SQL SELECT statement. The program will terminate if the SQL query does not execute successfully or some other error occurs:

```
if (mysql_query(conn, sqlquery) != 0)
    {
        fprintf(stderr, "No row found in the users table with
this            email address\n");
        exit(1);
    }
```

6. If the SQL query executes successfully, then the row(s) that match the supplied email address will be retrieved and assigned to the `resultset`:

```
resultset = mysql_store_result(conn);
```

7. Check if there is at least one row in the `resultset`:

```
if(mysql_num_rows(resultset) >0)
```

8. If there is no row in the `resultset`, then display the message that no row was found in the `users` table with the specified email address and exit from the program:

```
printf("No user found with this email address\n");
```

9. If there is any row in the `resultset`, then access it and assign it to the array row:

```
row = mysql_fetch_row(resultset)
```

10. Information about the user (that is, the email address, password, and address of delivery, which are assigned to the subscripts `row[0]`, `row[1]`, and `row[2]`, respectively) are displayed on the screen:

```
printf("Email Address: %s \n", row[0]);
printf("Password: %s \n", row[1]);
printf("Address of delivery: %s \n", row[2]);
```

11. The memory allocated to the `resultset` is freed:

```
mysql_free_result(resultset);
```

12. Enter the new updated information of the user; that is, the new password and the new address of delivery:

```
printf("Enter new password: ");
scanf("%s", upassword);
printf("Enter new address of delivery: ");
getchar();
gets(deliveryaddress);
```

13. An SQL UPDATE statement is prepared that contains the information of the newly entered password and address of delivery:

```
strcpy(sqlquery,"UPDATE users set password=\'");
strcat(sqlquery,upassword);
strcat(sqlquery,"\', address_of_delivery=\'");
strcat(sqlquery,deliveryaddress);
strcat(sqlquery,"\' where email_address like \'");
strcat(sqlquery,emailaddress);
strcat(sqlquery,"\'");
```

14. Execute the SQL UPDATE statement. If any error occurs in executing the SQL UPDATE query, the program will terminate:

```
if (mysql_query(conn, sqlquery) != 0)
{
fprintf(stderr, "The desired row in users table could not be
    updated\n");
    exit(1);
}
```

15. If the SQL UPDATE statement executes successfully, display a message on the screen informing that the user's information has been updated successfully:

```
printf("The information of user is updated successfully in
users table\n");
```

16. Close the opened connection handler:

```
mysql_close(conn);
```

The updateuser.c program for updating a specific row of a MySQL database table with new content is shown in the following code:

```
#include <mysql/mysql.h>
#include <stdio.h>
#include <stdlib.h>
#include <string.h>

void main() {
    MYSQL *conn;
    MYSQL_RES *resultset;
    MYSQL_ROW row;
    char *server = "127.0.0.1";
    char *user = "root";
    char *password = "Bintu2018$";
    char *database = "ecommerce";
    char emailaddress[30], sqlquery[255],
    upassword[30],deliveryaddress[255];
    conn = mysql_init(NULL);
    if (!mysql_real_connect(conn, server, user, password, database, 0,
NULL, 0)) {
        fprintf(stderr, "%s\n", mysql_error(conn));
        exit(1);
    }
    printf("Enter email address of the user to update: ");
    scanf("%s", emailaddress);
```

```
    strcpy(sqlquery,"SELECT * FROM users where email_address like
\'");
    strcat(sqlquery,emailaddress);
    strcat(sqlquery,"\'");
    if (mysql_query(conn, sqlquery) != 0)
    {
        fprintf(stderr, "No row found in the users table with this
        email address\n");
        exit(1);
    }
    resultset = mysql_store_result(conn);
    if(mysql_num_rows(resultset) >0)
    {
        printf("The details of the user with this email address are as
        follows:\n");
        while ((row = mysql_fetch_row(resultset)) != NULL)
        {
            printf("Email Address: %s \n", row[0]);
            printf("Password: %s \n", row[1]);
            printf("Address of delivery: %s \n", row[2]);
        }
        mysql_free_result(resultset);
        printf("Enter new password: ");
        scanf("%s", upassword);
        printf("Enter new address of delivery: ");
        getchar();
        gets(deliveryaddress);
        strcpy(sqlquery,"UPDATE users set password=\'");
        strcat(sqlquery,upassword);
        strcat(sqlquery,"\', address_of_delivery=\'");
        strcat(sqlquery,deliveryaddress);
        strcat(sqlquery,"\' where email_address like \'");
        strcat(sqlquery,emailaddress);
        strcat(sqlquery,"\'");
        if (mysql_query(conn, sqlquery) != 0)
        {
            fprintf(stderr, "The desired row in users table could not
            be updated\n");
            exit(1);
        }
        printf("The information of user is updated successfully in
        users table\n");
    }
    else
        printf("No user found with this email address\n");
    mysql_close(conn);
}
```

Now, let's go behind the scenes to understand the code better.

How it works...

In this program, we first ask the user to enter the email address they want to update. Then, we search the users table to see if there is any row with the matching email address. If we find it, we display the current information of the user; that is, the current email address, password, and address of delivery. Thereafter, we ask the user to enter a new password and new address of delivery. The new password and address of deliver will replace the old password and address of delivery, thereby updating the users table.

We will start by invoking the mysql_init function to initialize a MYSQL object by the name conn. Then, we will pass the MYSQL object conn to the mysql_real_connect function that we invoked to establish a connection to the MySQL server running at the specified host. Several other parameters will also be passed to the mysql_real_connection function, including a valid user ID, password, host details, and the database with which we want to work. The mysql_real_connect function will establish the connection to the MySQL server running at the specified host and will declare the MYSQL object conn as the connection handler. This means that conn can connect to the MySQL server and the ecommerce database wherever it is used.

The program will terminate after displaying an error message if some error occurs while establishing the connection to the MySQL server engine or to the ecommerce database. If the connection to the MySQL database engine is established successfully, you will be prompted to enter the email address of the user whose record you want to update.

As we mentioned earlier, we will first display the current information of the user. So, we will create an SQL SELECT statement and we will search the row in the users table that matches the email address that's entered by the user. Then, we will invoke the mysql_query function and pass the created SQL SELECT statement to it, along with the connection handler conn.

Again, the program will terminate after displaying an error message if the SQL query does not execute successfully or some other error occurs. If the query executes successfully, then the resulting row(s) (that is, the row(s) that match the supplied email address), will be retrieved by invoking the mysql_use_result function and will be assigned to the resultset.

We will then invoke the `mysql_num_rows` function to ensure that there is at least one row in the `resultset`. If there is no row in the `resultset`, this means that no row was found in the `users` table that matches the given email address. In this case, the program will terminate after informing that no row was found in the `users` table with the given email address. If there is even a single row in the `resultset`, we will invoke the `mysql _fetch_row` function on the `resultset`, which will extract one row from the `resultset` and assign it to the array row.

The `users` table contains the following three columns:

- `email_address varchar(30)`
- `password varchar(30)`
- `address_of_delivery text`

The array row will contain the information of the accessed row, where the subscripts `row[0]`, `row[1]`, and `row[2]` will contain the data of the columns `email_ address`, `password`, and `address_of_delivery`, respectively. The current information of the user is displayed by displaying the information assigned to the aforementioned subscripts. Then, we will invoke the `mysql_free_result` function to free up the memory that is allocated to the `resultset`.

At this stage, the user will be asked to enter the new password and the new address of delivery. We will prepare an SQL UPDATE statement that contains the information of the newly entered password and address of delivery. The `mysql_query` function will be invoked and the SQL UPDATE statement will be passed to it, along with the connection handler `conn`.

If any error occurs in executing the SQL UPDATE query, again, an error message will be displayed and the program will terminate. If the SQL UPDATE statement executes successfully, a message informing that the user's information has been updated successfully will be displayed. Finally, we will invoke the `mysql_close` function to close the opened connection handler `conn`.

Let's open the Cygwin Terminal. We will require two Terminal windows; on one window, we will run SQL commands and on the other, we will compile and run C. Open another Terminal window by pressing *Alt+F2*. In the first Terminal window, invoke the MySQL command line by using the following command:

```
$ mysql -u root -p -h 127.0.0.1
Enter password:
Welcome to the MariaDB monitor.   Commands end with ; or \g.
Your MySQL connection id is 27
```

```
Server version: 5.7.14-log MySQL Community Server (GPL)
Copyright (c) 2000, 2017, Oracle, MariaDB Corporation Ab and others.
Type 'help;' or '\h' for help. Type '\c' to clear the current input
statement.
```

To work with our `ecommerce` database, we need to make it the current database. So, open the `ecommerce` database by using the following command:

```
MySQL [(none)]> use ecommerce;
Reading table information for completion of table and column names
You can turn off this feature to get a quicker startup with -A
Database changed
```

Now, `ecommerce` is our current database; that is, whatever SQL commands we will execute will be applied to the `ecommerce` database only. Let's use the following SQL `SELECT` command to see the existing rows in the `users` database table:

```
MySQL [ecommerce]> select * from users;
+---------------------+----------+-----------------------------------
+
| email_address       | password | address_of_delivery|
+---------------------+----------+-----------------------------------
+
| bmharwani@yahoo.com | gold     | 11 Hill View Street, New York, USA|
| harwanibm@gmail.com | diamond  | House No. xyz, Pqr Apartments, Uvw
Lane, Mumbai, Maharashtra|
| bintu@gmail.com     | platinum | abc Sea View, Ocean Lane, Opposite
Mt. Everest, London, UKg
+---------------------+----------+-----------------------------------
+
3 rows in set (0.00 sec)
```

We can see from the preceding output that there are three rows in the `users` table. To compile the C program, switch to the second Terminal window. Let's use GCC to compile the `updateuser.c` program, as shown here:

```
$ gcc updateuser.c -o updateuser -I/usr/local/include/mysql -
L/usr/local/lib/mysql -lmysqlclient
```

If you get no errors or warnings, that means the `updateuser.c` program has compiled into an executable file, `updateuser.exe`. Let's run this executable file:

```
$ ./updateuser
Enter email address of the user to update: harwanibintu@gmail.com
No user found with this email address
```

Let's run the program again and enter an email address that already exists:

```
$ ./updateuser
Enter email address of the user to update: bmharwani@yahoo.com
The details of the user with this email address are as follows:
Email Address: bmharwani@yahoo.com
Password: gold
Address of delivery: 11 Hill View Street, New York, USA
Enter new password: coffee
Enter new address of delivery: 444, Sky Valley, Toronto, Canada
The information of user is updated successfully in users table
```

So, we have updated the row of the user with the email address, bmharwani@yahoo.com. To confirm that the row has been updated in the users database table too, switch to the Terminal window where the MySQL command line is running and issue the following SQL SELECT command:

```
MySQL [ecommerce]> MySQL [ecommerce]> select * from users;
+---------------------+----------+------------------------------------
+
| email_address       | password | address_of_delivery|
+---------------------+----------+------------------------------------
+
| bmharwani@yahoo.com | coffee   | 444, Sky Valley, Toronto, Canada
|
| harwanibm@gmail.com | diamond  | House No. xyz, Pqr Apartments, Uvw
Lane, Mumbai, Maharashtra
|
| bintu@gmail.com     | platinum | abc Sea View, Ocean Lane, Opposite
Mt. Everest, London, UKg
+---------------------+----------+------------------------------------
+
```

Voila! We can see that the row of the users table with the email address bmharwani@yahoo.com has been updated and is showing the new information.

Now, let's move on to the next recipe!

Deleting data from the database using C

In this recipe, we will learn how to delete information from a database table. We assume that a `users` table comprising three columns, `email_address`, `password`, and `address_of_delivery`, already exists (please see the beginning of this chapter, where we created an `ecommerce` database and a `users` table in it). You will be prompted to enter the email address of the user whose row has to be deleted. On entering an email address, all the information of the user will be displayed. Thereafter, you will again be asked to confirm if the displayed row should be deleted or not. After your confirmation, the row will be permanently deleted from the table.

How to do it...

1. Initialize a `MYSQL` object:

   ```
   mysql_init(NULL);
   ```

2. Establish a connection to the MySQL server running at the specified host. Also, generate a connection handler. If any error occurs in establishing a connection to the MySQL server engine, the program will terminate:

   ```
   if (!mysql_real_connect(conn, server, user, password,
   database, 0,
       NULL, 0)) {
          fprintf(stderr, "%s\n", mysql_error(conn));
          exit(1);
       }
   ```

3. If the connection to the MySQL database engine is established successfully, you will be prompted to enter the email address of the user whose record you want to delete:

   ```
   printf("Enter email address of the user to delete: ");
   scanf("%s", emailaddress);
   ```

4. Create an SQL `SELECT` statement that will search the row from the `users` table that matches the email address that's entered by the user:

   ```
   strcpy(sqlquery,"SELECT * FROM users where email_address like
   \'");
   strcat(sqlquery,emailaddress);
   strcat(sqlquery,"\'");
   ```

5. Execute the SQL SELECT statement. The program will terminate after displaying an error message if the SQL query does not execute successfully:

```
if (mysql_query(conn, sqlquery) != 0)
{
    fprintf(stderr, "No row found in the users table with this email
    address\n");
    exit(1);
}
```

6. If the query executes successfully, then the resulting row(s) that match the supplied email address will be retrieved and assigned to the resultset:

```
resultset = mysql_store_result(conn);
```

7. Invoke the mysql_num_rows function to ensure that there is at least one row in the resultset:

```
if(mysql_num_rows(resultset) >0)
```

8. If there is no row in the resultset, that means no row was found in the users table that matches the given email address; hence, the program will terminate:

```
printf("No user found with this email address\n");
```

9. If there is any row in the result set, that row is extracted from the resultset and will be assigned to the array row:

```
row = mysql_fetch_row(resultset)
```

10. The information of the user is displayed by displaying the corresponding subscripts in the array row:

```
printf("Email Address: %s \n", row[0]);
printf("Password: %s \n", row[1]);
printf("Address of delivery: %s \n", row[2]);
```

11. The memory that's allocated to the resultset is freed up:

```
mysql_free_result(resultset);The user is asked whether he/she
really want to delete the shown record.
printf("Are you sure you want to delete this record yes/no:
");
scanf("%s", k);
```

12. If the user enters `yes`, an SQL `DELETE` statement will be created that will delete the row from the `users` table that matches the specified email address:

```
if(strcmp(k,"yes")==0)
{
    strcpy(sqlquery, "Delete from users where email_address
like
    \'");
    strcat(sqlquery,emailaddress);
    strcat(sqlquery,"\'");
```

13. The SQL `DELETE` statement is executed. If there are any error occurs in executing the SQL `DELETE` query, the program will terminate:

```
if (mysql_query(conn, sqlquery) != 0)
{
    fprintf(stderr, "The user account could not be
deleted\n");
    exit(1);
}
```

14. If the SQL `DELETE` statement is executed successfully, a message informing that the user account with the specified email address is deleted successfully is displayed:

```
printf("The user with the given email address is successfully
deleted from the users table\n");
```

15. The opened connection handler is closed:

```
mysql_close(conn);
```

The `deleteuser.c` program for deleting a specific row from a MySQL database table is shown in the following code:

```
#include <mysql/mysql.h>
#include <stdio.h>
#include <stdlib.h>
#include <string.h>

void main() {
MYSQL *conn;
MYSQL_RES *resultset;
MYSQL_ROW row;
char *server = "127.0.0.1";
char *user = "root";
```

```
char *password = "Bintu2018$";
char *database = "ecommerce";
char emailaddress[30], sqlquery[255],k[10];
conn = mysql_init(NULL);
if (!mysql_real_connect(conn, server, user, password, database, 0,
NULL, 0)) {
    fprintf(stderr, "%s\n", mysql_error(conn));
    exit(1);
}
printf("Enter email address of the user to delete: ");
scanf("%s", emailaddress);
strcpy(sqlquery,"SELECT * FROM users where email_address like \'");
strcat(sqlquery,emailaddress);
strcat(sqlquery,"\'");
if (mysql_query(conn, sqlquery) != 0)
{
    fprintf(stderr, "No row found in the users table with this email
    address\n");
    exit(1);
}
resultset = mysql_store_result(conn);
if(mysql_num_rows(resultset) >0)
{
    printf("The details of the user with this email address are as
    follows:\n");
    while ((row = mysql_fetch_row(resultset)) != NULL)
    {
        printf("Email Address: %s \n", row[0]);
        printf("Password: %s \n", row[1]);
        printf("Address of delivery: %s \n", row[2]);
    }
    mysql_free_result(resultset);
    printf("Are you sure you want to delete this record yes/no: ");
    scanf("%s", k);
    if(strcmp(k,"yes")==0)
    {
        strcpy(sqlquery, "Delete from users where email_address like
        \'");
        strcat(sqlquery,emailaddress);
        strcat(sqlquery,"\'");
        if (mysql_query(conn, sqlquery) != 0)
        {
            fprintf(stderr, "The user account could not be
deleted\n");
            exit(1);
        }
        printf("The user with the given email address is successfully
        deleted from the users table\n");
```

```
        }
    }
    else
        printf("No user found with this email address\n");
        mysql_close(conn);
    }
```

Now, let's go behind the scenes to understand the code better.

How it works...

We will start by invoking the mysql_init function to initialize a MYSQL object by the name conn. We will then pass the MYSQL object conn to the mysql_real_connect function that we invoked to establish a connection to the MySQL server running at the specified host. Several other parameters will also be passed to the mysql_real_connection function, including a valid user ID, password, host details, and the database with which we want to work. The mysql_real_connect function will establish a connection to the MySQL server running at the specified host and will declare a MYSQL object conn as the connection handler. This means thar conn can connect to the MySQL server and the commerce database wherever it is used.

The program will terminate after displaying an error message if some error occurs while establishing a connection to the MySQL server engine or to the ecommerce database. If the connection to the MySQL database engine is established successfully, you will be prompted to enter the email address of the user whose record you want to delete.

We will first display the information of the user and thereafter will seek permission from the user as to whether they really want to delete that row or not. So, we will create an SQL SELECT statement that will search the row from the users table that matches the email address that was entered by the user. Then, we will invoke the mysql_query function and pass the created SQL SELECT statement to it, along with the connection handler conn.

Again, the program will terminate after displaying an error message if the SQL query does not execute successfully or some other error occurs. If the query executes successfully, then the resulting row(s) (that is, the row(s) that match the supplied email address) will be retrieved by invoking the mysql_use_result function and will be assigned to the resultset.

We will invoke the `mysql_num_rows` function to ensure that there is at least one row in the `resultset`. If there is no row in the `resultset`, that means no row was found in the `users` table that matches the given email address. In that case, the program will terminate after informing that no row was found in the `users` table with the given email address. If there is even a single row in the `resultset`, we will invoke the `mysql _fetch_row` function on the `resultset`, which will extract one row from the `resultset` and assign it to the array row.

The `users` table contains the following three columns:

- `email_address varchar(30)`
- `password varchar(30)`
- `address_of_delivery text`

The array row will contain information of the accessed row, where the subscripts `row[0]`, `row[1]`, and `row[2]` will contain the data of the columns `email_ address`, `password`, and `address_of_delivery`, respectively. The current information of the user will be displayed by displaying the current email address, password, and address of delivery that's assigned to the subscripts `row[0]`, `row[1]`, and `row[2]`. Then, we will invoke the `mysql_free_result` function to free up the memory that is allocated to the `resultset`.

At this stage, the user will be asked to confirm whether they really want to delete the shown record. The user is supposed to enter `yes`, all in lowercase, to delete the record. If the user enters `yes`, an SQL DELETE statement will be created that will delete the row from the `users` table that matches the specified email address. The `mysql_query` function will be invoked and the SQL DELETE statement will be passed to it, along with the connection handler `conn`.

If any error occurs in executing the SQL DELETE query, again an error message will be displayed and the program will terminate. If the SQL DELETE statement executes successfully, a message informing that the user account with the specified mail address has been deleted successfully is displayed. Finally, we will invoke the `mysql_close` function to close the opened connection handler `conn`.

Let's open the Cygwin Terminal. We will require two Terminal windows; on one window, we will run MySQL commands and on the other, we will compile and run C. Open another Terminal window by pressing *Alt+F2*. In the first Terminal window, invoke the MySQL command line by giving the following command:

```
$ mysql -u root -p -h 127.0.0.1
Enter password:
```

```
Welcome to the MariaDB monitor.  Commands end with ; or \g.
Your MySQL connection id is 27
Server version: 5.7.14-log MySQL Community Server (GPL)
Copyright (c) 2000, 2017, Oracle, MariaDB Corporation Ab and others.
Type 'help;' or '\h' for help. Type '\c' to clear the current input
statement.
```

To work with our `ecommerce` database, we need to make it the current database. So, open the `ecommerce` database by using the following command:

```
MySQL [(none)]> use ecommerce;
Reading table information for completion of table and column names
You can turn off this feature to get a quicker startup with -A
Database changed
```

Now, `ecommerce` is our current database; that is, whatever SQL commands we will execute will be applied to the `ecommerce` database only. Let's use the following SQL `SELECT` command to see the existing rows in the `users` database table:

```
MySQL [ecommerce]> select * from users;
+---------------------+-----------+-------------------------------------
+
| email_address | password | address_of_delivery |
+---------------------+-----------+-------------------------------------
+
| bmharwani@yahoo.com | coffee | 444, Sky Valley, Toronto, Canada
|
| harwanibm@gmail.com | diamond | House No. xyz, Pqr Apartments, Uvw
Lane, Mumbai, Maharashtra |
| bintu@gmail.com | platinum | abc Sea View, Ocean Lane, Opposite Mt.
Everest, London, UKg
+---------------------+-----------+-------------------------------------
+
3 rows in set (0.00 sec)
```

From the preceding output, we can see that there are three rows in the `users` table. To compile the C program, switch to the second Terminal window. Let's use GCC to compile the `deleteuser.c` program, as shown here:

```
$ gcc deleteuser.c -o deleteuser -I/usr/local/include/mysql -
L/usr/local/lib/mysql -lmysqlclient
```

If you get no errors or warnings, that means the `deleteuser.c` program has compiled into an executable file, `deleteuser.exe`. Let's run this executable file:

```
$ ./deleteuser
Enter email address of the user to delete: harwanibintu@gmail.com
No user found with this email address
```

Now, let's run the program again with a valid email address:

```
$ ./deleteuser
Enter email address of the user to delete: bmharwani@yahoo.com
The details of the user with this email address are as follows:
Email Address: bmharwani@yahoo.com
Password: coffee
Address of delivery: 444, Sky Valley, Toronto, Canada
Are you sure you want to delete this record yes/no: yes
The user with the given email address is successfully deleted from the
users table
```

So, the row of the user with the email address bmharwani@yahoo.com will be deleted from the `users` table. To confirm that the row has been deleted from the `users` database table too, switch to the Terminal window where the MySQL command line is running and issue the following SQL SELECT command:

```
MySQL [ecommerce]> select * from users;
+----------------------+-----------+------------------------------------
+
| email_address        | password  | address_of_delivery
|
+----------------------+-----------+------------------------------------
+
| harwanibm@gmail.com  | diamond   | House No. xyz, Pqr Apartments, Uvw
Lane, Mumbai, Maharashtra
|
| bintu@gmail.com      | platinum  | abc Sea View, Ocean Lane, Opposite
Mt. Everest, London, UKg
+----------------------+-----------+------------------------------------
+
```

Voila! We can see that now there are only two rows left in the `users` table, confirming that one row has been deleted from the `users` table.

14
General-Purpose Utilities

In this chapter, we are going to learn about the different functions that are used when performing different tasks. We will learn how to register functions that execute automatically when a program terminates. We will learn about functions that measure the clock ticks and CPU seconds required for the execution of certain tasks. We will also learn how to allocate memory at runtime, and then free it up when its task is over. Finally, we will learn how to handle different signals.

In this chapter, we will dive into the following recipes:

- Registering a function that is called when a program exits
- Measuring the clock ticks and CPU seconds required in the execution of a function
- Performing dynamic memory allocation
- Handling signals

However, before we proceed, a small introduction to dynamic memory allocation and some related functions is in order.

Dynamic memory allocation

As the name suggests, **dynamic memory allocation** is the concept of allocating memory at runtime. Unlike static memory allocation, where the memory is prebooked, dynamic memory allocation can be booked as and when required. The size of memory that is statically allocated cannot be increased or decreased, whereas the size of dynamically allocated memory blocks can be increased and decreased as per your requirements. Additionally, when processing is over, the dynamically allocated memory can be freed so that it can be used by other applications. The following subsections describe several functions that are required in dynamic memory allocation.

malloc()

This function allocates memory dynamically, that is, during runtime. A block of memory of a given size in bytes is allocated and a pointer pointing to that block is returned. Here is its syntax:

```
pointer = (data_type*) malloc(size_in_bytes)
```

This function doesn't initialize the allocated memory, as that memory block initially contains some garbage values.

calloc()

This function allocates multiple blocks of memory and returns a pointer pointing to that memory block. Here is its syntax:

```
pointer=(data_type*) calloc( size_t num_of_blocks, size_t
size_of_block )
```

This function initializes the allocated memory blocks to zero.

realloc()

As the name suggests, this function is used to reallocate or resize the allocated memory. The reallocation of memory will not result in the loss of the existing data. Here is its syntax:

```
pointer= realloc(void *pointer, size_t new_blocksize);
```

Here, `pointer` is a pointer to the existing allocated memory block. `new_blocksize` represents the new size of the block in bytes and can be smaller or larger than the existing allocated block size.

free()

When the job or task assigned to the allocated block of memory is over, that memory block needs to be freed up so that it can be used by another application. To free up the dynamically allocated memory, the `free` function is used. Here is its syntax:

```
free(pointer);
```

Here, `pointer` represents the pointer to the allocated memory.

Let's now begin with our first recipe!

Registering a function that is called when a program exits

Our first recipe will be to register a function that executes automatically when a program terminates normally. For this recipe, we will be using the `atexit()` function.

The `atexit` function is set to point to a function; this function is automatically called without arguments when the program terminates. If more than one `atexit` function is defined in a program, then these functions will be called in the **Last In, First Out (LIFO)** order, that is, the function pointed to last by the `atexit` function will be executed first, followed by the second to last one, and so on.

The `atexit` function accepts a single mandatory parameter: the pointer to the function to be called on program termination. Additionally, the function returns 0 if the function is registered successfully, that is, the function to be invoked is successfully pointed. The function returns a nonzero value if it is not registered.

In this recipe, we will dynamically allocate some memory for accepting a string from the user. The string entered is displayed on the screen, and, when the program terminates, the registered function is automatically executed, which frees up the dynamically allocated memory.

How to do it...

Follow these steps to create a recipe that registers a function that executes automatically when a program terminates normally:

1. Register a function using the `atexit` function.
2. Allocate some memory dynamically and allow that memory to be pointed to by a pointer.
3. Ask the user to enter a string and assign the string to the dynamically allocated memory block.
4. Display the entered string on the screen.

5. When the program terminates, the function registered via the `atexit` function is invoked automatically.

6. The registered function simply frees up the dynamically allocated memory so that it can be used by other applications.

The program for registering a function that automatically executes when a program terminates is as follows (`atexistprog1.c`):

```c
#include <stdio.h>
#include <stdlib.h>

char *str;
void freeup()
{
    free(str);
    printf( "Allocated memory is freed  \n");
}

int main()
{
    int retvalue;
    retvalue = atexit(freeup);
    if (retvalue != 0) {
        printf("Registration of function for atexit () function
            failed\n");
        exit(1);
    }
    str = malloc( 20 * sizeof(char) );
    if( str== NULL )
    {
        printf("Some error occurred in allocating memory\n");
        exit(1);
    }
    printf("Enter a string ");
    scanf("%s", str);
    printf("The string entered is %s\n", str);
}
```

Now, let's go behind the scenes to understand the code better.

How it works...

Using the `atexit` function, register a function called `freeup`, ensuring that the `freeup` function will be invoked if the program terminates normally. The value returned by the `atexit` function is checked to see that it is zero only. If the value returned by the `atexit` function is a nonzero value, then that means the function is not registered successfully and the program will terminate after displaying an error message.

If the function is registered successfully, 20 bytes are dynamically allocated and the allocated memory block is assigned to a character pointer, `str`. If the `str` pointer is `NULL`, then this means an error has occurred in the allocation of the memory block. If it is confirmed that the `str` pointer is not `NULL` and is pointing to a memory block, the user will be asked to enter a string. The string entered by the user is assigned to the memory block pointed to by the `str` pointer. The string entered by the user is then displayed on the screen, and, finally, the program terminates. However, before the program terminates, the function that is registered using the `atexit` function, `freeup`, is invoked. The `freeup` function frees the memory allocated to the `str` pointer and displays a message: `Allocated memory is freed`.

The program is compiled using GCC, as shown in the following screenshot. Because no error appears during compilation, the `atexistprog1.c` program has successfully compiled into a `.exe` file: `atexistprog1.exe`. Upon executing this file, the user is prompted to enter a string that is assigned to the dynamically allocated memory. On program termination, the function registered with `atexit` is executed, which frees up the dynamically allocated memory, as is confirmed by the text message in the following screenshot:

```
D:\CAdvBook>gcc atexistprog1.c -o atexistprog1

D:\CAdvBook>atexistprog1
Enter a string Pizza
The string entered is Pizza
Allocated memory is freed
```

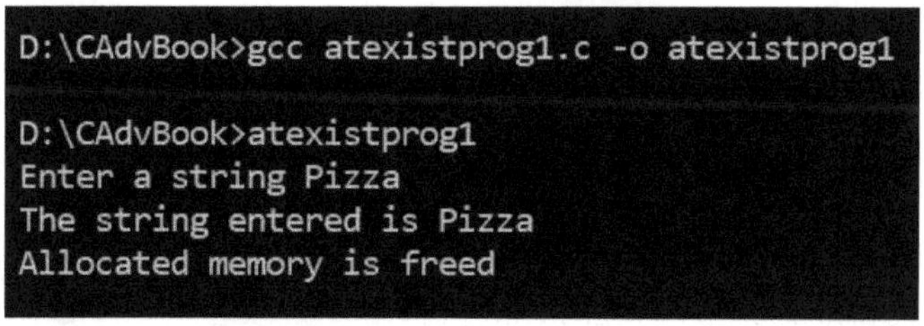

Figure 14.1

Voilà! We have successfully registered a function that is called when the program exits.

There's more...

If there is more than one function that is registered via the atexit function, then these functions will be executed in LIFO order. To understand this, let's modify the preceding atexistprog1.c program to register two functions via the atexit function. We will save the modified program as atexistprog2.c as follows (atexistprog2.c):

```c
#include <stdio.h>
#include <stdlib.h>

char *str;
void freeup1()
{
    free(str);
    printf( "Allocated memory is freed  \n");
}

void freeup2()
{
    printf( "The size of dynamic memory can be increased and decreased
\n");
}

int main()
{
    int retvalue;
    retvalue = atexit(freeup1);
    if (retvalue != 0) {
        printf("Registration of function freeup1() for atexit ()
          function failed\n");
        exit(1);
    }
    retvalue = atexit(freeup2);
    if (retvalue != 0) {
        printf("Registration of function freeup2() for atexit ()
          function failed\n");
        exit(1);
    }
    str = malloc( 20 * sizeof(char));
    if( str== NULL )
    {
        printf("Some error occurred in allocating memory\n");
        exit(1);
    }
    printf("Enter a string ");
    scanf("%s", str);
```

```
    printf("The string entered is %s\n", str);
}
```

On compiling and executing the program, we get the following output:

```
D:\CAdvBook>gcc atexistprog2.c -o atexistprog2

D:\CAdvBook>atexistprog2
Enter a string Pizza
The string entered is Pizza
The size of dynamic memory can be increased and decreased
Allocated memory is freed
```

Figure 14.2

This output confirms that the last registered function, freeup2, is executed first, followed by the first registered function, freeup1.

Now, let's move on to the next recipe!

Measuring the clock ticks and CPU seconds required in the execution of a function

In this recipe, we will learn how to find out the clock ticks and CPU seconds that are required in the execution of a function. We will create a program that contains a function. This function will simply run a nested loop and we will find out the time required to run it. To do so, we will make use of the clock() function.

The clock() function returns the processor time that is consumed by the program. Essentially, this time is dependent on the technique that the operating system uses in allocating the resources to the process. More precisely, the function returns the number of clock ticks elapsed from the time the program is invoked. The function does not require any parameters and returns either the processor time that is required in running certain statements or returns –1 if there is any failure.

The time returned by the function is measured in
CLOCKS_PER_SECs of a second, where CLOCKS_PER_SEC varies as
per the operating system and its value is around 1,000,000. So, in
order to find the number of seconds used by the CPU, the number of
clock ticks returned by the function is divided by CLOCKS_PER_SEC.

The value returned by the clock() function is of the clock_t data
type. The clock_t data type is used to represent the processor time.

How to do it...

Follow these steps to find out the number of clock ticks and CPU seconds required to
run a function:

1. Define two variables of the clock_t data type for saving processor time.
2. Invoke the clock() function to discern the number of clock ticks elapsed
   from the time the program is invoked. The clock ticks are saved in one of
   the variables.
3. Invoke a function whose processing time has to be established.
4. Again, invoke the clock() function and then save the returned number of
   clock ticks to another variable.
5. Subtract the number of clock ticks in the two variables to discern the
   number of clock ticks required to execute the function.
6. Divide the number of clock ticks returned in the preceding steps
   by CLOCKS_PER_SEC to identify the number of seconds used by the
   function.
   1. Both the number of clock ticks and the CPU seconds required to
      execute the function are displayed on the screen.

The program for knowing the number of clock ticks and CPU seconds required in
executing a function is as follows (timecalc.c):

```
#include <time.h>
#include <stdio.h>

void somefunction()
{
    for (int i=0; i<32000; i++)
    {
        for (int j=0; j<32000; j++) ;
    }
}
```

```
}

int main()
{
    clock_t clocktickstart, clocktickend;
    double timeconsumed;
    clocktickstart = clock();
    somefunction();
    clocktickend = clock();
    timeconsumed = (double)(clocktickend - clocktickstart) /
       CLOCKS_PER_SEC;
    printf("Number of clocks ticks required in running the function is
       : %.3f\n",  (double)(clocktickend - clocktickstart));
    printf("Time taken by program is : %.2f sec\n", timeconsumed);
    return 0;
}
```

Now, let's go behind the scenes to understand the code better.

How it works...

Define two variables, clocktickstart and clocktickend, of the clock_t data type, as they will be used to represent the processor time. The main idea of this program is to ascertain the time consumed during the execution of a function.

The clock function is invoked to know the number of clock ticks elapsed from the time the program is invoked. Assign the number of clock ticks returned to a clocktickstart variable. Then, invoke a somefunction() function, which includes a nested for loop. The idea of using nested loops is just to make the CPU invest some time in executing these loops. After the somefunction function is over, invoke the clock() function, and assign the number of clock ticks elapsed from the time the program is invoked to the clocktickend variable. The difference between the clocktickend and clocktickstart variables will give us the number of clock ticks used in executing the somefunction function. The number of clock ticks is then divided by CLOCKS_PER_SEC to distinguish the number of CPU seconds used to execute the function. Finally, the number of clock ticks used in executing the somefunction function and the CPU seconds used by it are displayed on the screen.

The program is compiled using GCC, as shown in the following screenshot. Because no error appears during compilation, the `timecalc.c` program is successfully compiled into a `.exe` file: `timecalc.exe`. Upon executing this file, the number of clock ticks and the number of CPU seconds required in the execution of the specific function in the program are displayed on the screen as follows:

```
D:\CAdvBook>gcc timecalc.c -o timecalc

D:\CAdvBook>timecalc
Number of clocks ticks required in running the function is : 2500.000
Time taken by program is : 2.50 sec
```

Figure 14.3

Now, let's move on to the next recipe!

Performing dynamic memory allocation

In this recipe, we will learn how to dynamically allocate some memory. We will also learn how to increase the number of memory blocks, how to decrease the number of allocated memory blocks, and how to free up memory.

How to do it...

We will ask the user how many memory blocks need to be allocated, and we will dynamically allocate that number of memory blocks. The user will then be asked to assign integer values to those memory blocks. After that, the user will be asked how many more additional blocks need to be allocated. Similarly, the user will be asked how many memory blocks need to be reduced too. The following are the steps to be performed in order to dynamically allocate memory, by increasing and decreasing memory blocks:

1. The user is asked to enter an integer value, and that number of memory blocks will be dynamically allocated by invoking the `calloc` function. Each allocated memory block will be capable of storing a numerical of the integer data type.
2. The user is then asked to enter values in the dynamically allocated memory blocks.

3. Display the integer values on the screen that are assigned to the memory blocks.

4. Ask the user how many more memory blocks need to be added.

5. Invoke the `realloc` function to increase the number of allocated memory blocks.

6. Ask the user to enter the integer values in the newly added memory blocks.

7. Display all the integer values assigned to the memory blocks.

8. Ask the user how many of the available memory blocks are required.

9. Again, invoke the `realloc` function to reduce the number of allocated memory blocks.

10. Display the integer values available in the existing memory blocks.

11. Free up all of the memory blocks so that they can be used by other applications.

The program for showing the benefits of dynamic memory allocation, that is, how the memory can be allocated at runtime, and how its size can be increased or decreased and is freed, is as follows (`dynamicmem.c`):

```c
#include <stdio.h>
#include <stdlib.h>

int main()
{
    int* ptr;
    int m,n, i;

    printf("How many elements are there? ");
    scanf("%d", &n);
    ptr = (int*)calloc(n, sizeof(int));
    if (ptr == NULL) {
        printf("Memory could not be allocated.\n");
        exit(0);
    }
    printf("Enter %d elements \n", n);
    for (i = 0; i < n; ++i)
        scanf("%d",&ptr[i]);
    printf("\nThe elements entered are: \n");
    for (i = 0; i < n; ++i)
        printf("%d\n", ptr[i]);
    printf("\nHow many elements you want to add more? ");
    scanf("%d",&m);
    ptr = realloc(ptr, (m+n) * sizeof(int));
    printf("Enter values for %d elements\n",m);
    for (i = n; i < (m+n); ++i)
```

```
        scanf("%d",&ptr[i]);
    printf("\nThe complete set of elements now are: \n");
    for (i = 0; i < (m+n); ++i)
        printf("%d\n", ptr[i]);
    printf("\nHow many elements you want to keep ? ");
    scanf("%d", &m);
    ptr = realloc(ptr, (m) * sizeof(int));
    printf("\nThe new set of elements now are: \n");
    for (i = 0; i < m; ++i)
        printf("%d\n", ptr[i]);
    free(ptr);
    return 0;
}
```

Now, let's go behind the scenes to understand the code better.

How it works...

The user will be asked to specify the number of elements. The value entered by the user will be assigned to the variable n. Let's assume the value entered by the user is 4, which is then assigned to the variable n. Using the `calloc` function, 4 memory blocks are dynamically allocated, where the size of each memory block is equal to the size consumed by an `int` data type. In other words, a memory block that can store four integer values is dynamically allocated and a pointer, `ptr`, is set to point to it. If the `ptr` pointer is NULL, then this means that the memory could not be allocated and the program will terminate after displaying an error message.

If the memory is successfully allocated, the user will be asked to enter four integer values. The values entered will be assigned to individual memory blocks pointed to by the pointer, `ptr`. The integer values entered by the user are then displayed on the screen. The user will then be asked if they want to add more elements. Assuming that the user wants to add two more memory blocks to the existing allocated ones, the value of 2 entered by the user will be assigned to the variable m.

Using the `realloc` function, the quantity of the memory blocks increases from four to six, where each memory block is able to store an integer number. The user will be asked to enter the integer values for two newly added memory blocks. To indicate that the size of memory blocks has increased from four to six, all of the six integers assigned to the memory blocks are displayed on the screen. Thereafter, the user will be asked how many blocks they want to keep out of the six memory blocks. Let's assume the value entered by the user is 3; that is, the user wants to keep the integers in the first three memory blocks and discard the rest.

The value of 3 entered by the user will be assigned to the variable m. Again, the realloc function is invoked to reduce the number of memory blocks from six to three. Finally, the integers in the three memory blocks are displayed on the screen.

The program is compiled using GCC, as shown in the following screenshot. Because no error appears during compilation, the dynamicmem.c program has successfully compiled into a .exe file: dynamicmem.exe. Upon executing this file, the user is prompted to define how many memory blocks they want to dynamically allocate. After that, the user is asked how many additional memory blocks they want. The user is also asked whether they want to keep some memory blocks active from the total, thereby reducing the number of allocated memory blocks, and, finally, all the memory blocks are freed. All of the actions appear as follows:

```
D:\CAdvBook>gcc dynamicmem.c -o dynamicmem

D:\CAdvBook>dynamicmem
How many elements are there? 4
Enter 4 elements
25
10
35
9

The elements entered are:
25
10
35
9

How many elements you want to add more? 2
Enter values for 2 elements
28
20

The complete set of elements now are:
25
10
35
9
28
20

How many elements you want to keep ? 3

The new set of elements now are:
25
10
35
```

Figure 14.4

Now, let's move on to the next recipe!

Handling signals

In this recipe, we will learn signal handling. We will learn how to automatically raise a signal, how signals are raised by user actions, and how signals are directed to specific signal-handling functions. Signal handling is required to take necessary action when the signal occurs. The actions may include ignoring the signal, terminating the process, blocking or suspending a process, resuming a process, and many more.

Let's start with a quick overview of signals before we dive into the recipe.

Signals

A signal is an indicator that is generated through software and is used to stop the usual execution of the program, and through a branch of CPU to perform some specific tasks. The signal can be generated either by a process or when the user presses *Ctrl + C*. When something goes wrong or some error occurs while executing an operation, the signal acts as a medium of communication between the process and the operating system. The signal is raised by the operating system and is forwarded to the process to take necessary actions. Essentially, a corresponding signal handler is executed as a corrective measure.

The following are some of the important signals that you should be aware of:

- **SIGABRT (Signal Abort)**: This signal reports the abnormal termination of the program. The signal is raised in the case of critical errors; for example, if an assertion fails or memory could not be allocated, or any similar memory heap errors.
- **SIGFPE (Signal Floating-Point Exception)**: This signal reports an arithmetic error. Any arithmetic error, including overflow or divide by zero, is covered by this signal.
- **SIGILL (Signal Illegal Instruction)**: This signal reports illegal instructions. Such a signal is raised when the program tries to execute data or an executable file is corrupted. In other words, the signal is raised when the program is trying to execute a nonexecutable instruction.
- **SIGINT (Signal Interrupt)**: This is a program interrupt signal that is generated by the user by pressing *Ctrl + C*.

- **SIGSEGV (Signal Segmentation Violation)**: This signal is raised when the program tries to write into read-only memory or into a block that does not have write permissions. The signal is also raised when a program tries to read or write into memory that is outside the range that is allocated to it.
- **SIGTERM (Signal Terminate)**: This is a termination signal that is sent to a process in order to terminate it.

To handle signals in a program, the `signal()` function is used. Let's look at a quick introduction to the signal function.

signal()

The signal function directs the occurrence of the signal to any of the following signal handlers:

- `SIG_IGN`: This will result in the signal being ignored.
- `SIG_DFL`: This will result in invoking the default action that is associated with the raised signal.
- `user_defined_function`: This will result in the invoking of the user-defined function when the signal is raised.

Now, let's begin with the recipe.

How to do it...

The following are the steps for associating signals to signal-handling functions, automatically raise the signals, and get the desired actions performed when signals are raised by user actions:

1. Associate a signal interrupt, `(SIGINT)`, to a function. This function will act as a signal handler.
2. Write some code in the signal handler function.
3. In the `main` function, make a `while` loop that executes 5 times. You can make the `while` loop run for as many times as you want. The `while` loop is set to display a text message after a delay of 1 second.
4. The idea is to automatically raise the signal after 5 seconds. So, after its 5 iterations, the `while` loop ends and the interrupt signal is automatically raised.

5. The associated signal handler function is executed.
6. After executing the code in the signal handler, in the `main` function, again, associate a signal interrupt, (`SIGINT`), with another signal handler function.
7. Set an infinite `while` loop to execute, which displays a text message after each delay of 1 second.
8. If the user presses *Ctrl + C* , the signal interrupt is raised and the associated signal handler is raised.
9. In the signal handler, we associate the signal interrupt with its default action.
10. Consequently, if the user presses *Ctrl + C* again, that is, if the signal interrupt is raised again, the default action will take place: the program will terminate.

The program for showing how the signals are automatically raised, how signals are raised by the user, and how they are handled, is as follows (`signalhandling.c`):

```
#include <stdio.h>
#include <unistd.h>
#include <stdlib.h>
#include <signal.h>

void sighandler1(int signum) {
    printf("Ctrl + C is auto pressed \n");
}

void sighandler2(int signum) {
    printf("You have pressed Ctrl+c\n");
    printf("Press Ctrl+c again to exit\n");
    (void) signal(SIGINT, SIG_DFL);
}

int main () {
    int x=1;
    signal(SIGINT, sighandler1);
    while(x<=5) {
        printf("Signal will be raised automatically after 5
          seconds\n");
        x++;
        sleep(1);
    }
    raise(SIGINT);
    signal(SIGINT, sighandler2);
    while(1) {
        printf("Infinite loop, press Ctrl+C to raise signal\n");
```

```
        sleep(1);
    }
    return(0);
}
```

Now, let's go behind the scenes to understand the code better.

How it works...

Using the `signal` function, a signal interrupt, `(SIGINT)`, is associated with a function called `signalhandler1`. That is, if the interrupt is autogenerated or is generated by the user, the `sighandler1` function will be invoked. A counter, x, is initialized to 1 and a while loop is set to execute until the value of counter x becomes larger than 5. Within the `while` loop, the following text is displayed: `Signal will be raised automatically after 5 seconds`. In addition to this, the value of counter x is incremented by 1 within the `while` loop. A delay of 1 second is inserted in the `while` loop. In short, the `while` loop will display a text message after a gap of 1 second each. After displaying the text message 5 times, the `raise` function is invoked to raise the `SIGINT` signal.

On raising the `SIGINT` signal, the `signalhandler1` function will be invoked. The `signalhandler1` function does nothing other than display a text message: `Ctrl+C is auto pressed`. After executing the `signalhandler1` function, the control resumes executing the statements in the `main` function. Again, the `signal` function is invoked and the `SIGINT` signal is associated with the `sighandler2` function. Once more, a `while` loop is set to execute; however, this time, the loop will run indefinitely. Within the `while` loop, a text message, `Infinite loop, press Ctrl+C to raise signal`, is displayed. After displaying the text message, a delay of 1 second is inserted; that is, the text message will keep on displaying indefinitely after a gap of 1 second. If the user presses *Ctrl + C*, the signal interrupt will be raised and the `sighandler2` function will be invoked.

In the `sighandler2` function, a text message, `You have pressed Ctrl+C`, is displayed on one line and, on the next line, `Press Ctrl+C again to exit` is displayed. Thereafter, the `signal` function is invoked to set the `SIGINT` signal to take the default action. The default action of the `SIGINT` interrupt is to terminate and exit from the program. This means that if the user again presses *Ctrl + C*, the program will terminate.

The program is compiled using GCC, as shown in the following screenshot. Because no error appears during compilation, the signalhandling.c program has successfully compiled into a .exe file: signalhandling.exe. Upon executing this file, five text messages are displayed on the screen through the first while loop. After that, the signal is automatically raised and the text message from the first signal handler appears on the screen. Thereafter, a text message from the infinite while loop appears. Finally, the output from the second signal handler appears, which is executed when the signal interrupt is generated by the user. All of the actions appear as follows:

```
D:\CAdvBook>gcc signalhandling.c -o signalhandling

D:\CAdvBook>signalhandling
Signal will be raised automatically after 5 seconds
Signal will be raised automatically after 5 seconds
Signal will be raised automatically after 5 seconds
Signal will be raised automatically after 5 seconds
Signal will be raised automatically after 5 seconds
Ctrl + C is auto pressed
Infinite loop, press Ctrl+C to raise signal
Infinite loop, press Ctrl+C to raise signal
Infinite loop, press Ctrl+C to raise signal
Infinite loop, press Ctrl+C to raise signal
You have pressed Ctrl+c
Press Ctrl+c again to exit
Infinite loop, press Ctrl+C to raise signal
Infinite loop, press Ctrl+C to raise signal
Infinite loop, press Ctrl+C to raise signal
```

Figure 14.5

Voilà! We have successfully handled signals.

15
Improving the Performance of Your Code

In this chapter, we will learn how to speed up the execution of any C program. We will learn to keep the frequently used content in CPU registers, and we will learn how to take input faster from the user. We will also learn to apply loop unrolling in C programs.

The following are the recipes we will work through in this chapter:

- Using the `register` keyword in C code for better efficiency
- Taking input faster in C
- Applying loop unrolling for faster results

Let's begin with the first recipe.

Using the register keyword in C code for better efficiency

The access time when using registers is quite a bit lower than that of accessing content from any memory variable. So, to take advantage of this, content that is frequently used in any program is kept in registers. The `register` keyword is used to indicate the content that needs to be kept in these registers.

In this recipe, we will find out the cost of renting a car for a specified distance. The car rent not only depends on the distance but also on the type of car, that is, whether the car has **air conditioning** (**AC**) or not. The rent of the AC car per kilometer, the rent of the non-AC car per kilometer, and the service tax percentage values are all stored in register variables.

How to do it...

The steps for finding total car rent for a specified distance with a specified car type using register variables are as follows:

1. The user is asked to enter the distance of the planned journey.
2. The user is asked to specify the type of the car, that is, whether the car should have AC or not.
3. Two register variables are defined to indicate the rent per kilometer for the AC and non-AC car, respectively.
4. One more register variable is defined that is set to represent the service tax percentage.
5. On the basis of the type of the car chosen by the user, the distance value is multiplied by the respective register variable to find out the total amount.
6. The service tax is computed and added to the total amount. The service tax percentage is accessed from the respective register variable.
7. The total rent of the car is displayed on the screen.

The program for computing the total rent of the car for the specified car type and journey length using the register variables is as follows:

```
//tourvehicle.c

#include <stdio.h>
#include <string.h>

int main() {
    int distance;
    char car_type[20];
    register int Acperkm,Nonacperkm,servicetax;
    float carRent, totalrent;

    printf("How many kilometers? ");
    scanf("%d", &distance);
    printf("AC car or non AC ac/non? ");
```

```
    scanf("%s", car_type);
    Acperkm=3;
    Nonacperkm=2;
    servicetax=1;
    if(strcmp(car_type, "ac")==0)
        carRent=distance*Acperkm;
    else
        carRent=distance*Nonacperkm;
    totalrent=carRent + (carRent*servicetax/100);
    printf("The total rent for the car will be $ %.2f\n",totalrent);
    return 0;
}
```

Now, let's go behind the scenes to understand the code better.

How it works...

The user is asked to specify how many kilometers the vehicle is required to be rented for. The value entered by the user is assigned to the distance variable. Thereafter, the user is asked to specify what kind of car they want to rent: an AC car or a non-AC car. The option entered by the user is assigned to the car_type variable. Three register variables are defined by the names Acperkm, Nonacperkm, and servicetax.

Because the register variables stay closer to the CPU and their access time is very low when compared to accessing content from memory variables, the register variables are used for those values that are frequently required in computation. The three register variables, Acperkm, Nonacperkm, and servicetax, are initialized to 3, 2, and 1, respectively, to indicate that the rate for an AC car is $3 per kilometer and that of a non-AC car is $2 per kilometer. The service tax is assumed to be 1% of the total amount.

String comparison is done to know the type of car that is specified by the user. If the type of car selected is an AC car, the values in the distance variable and the Acperkm register variable are multiplied.

Similarly, if the type of car selected is a non-AC car, the values in the distance and Nonacperkm variables are multiplied together. The result of the multiplication is the total amount to be assigned to the carRent variable. To this total amount, a 1% service tax rate is added to find out the total rent. The total rent of the car for the specified distance and type of car is then displayed on the screen.

The program is compiled using GCC, as shown in the following screenshot. Because no errors appear on compilation, that means the `tourvehicle.c` program has successfully been compiled into an EXE file, `tourvehicle.exe`. On executing the file, the user is prompted to enter the number of kilometers for which the car is required on rent. The user will also be asked to specify the type of car that is required on rent. The program then displays the total rent of the car, as shown in the screenshot:

```
D:\CAdvBook>gcc tourvehicle.c -o tourvehicle

D:\CAdvBook>tourvehicle
How many kilometers? 927
AC car or non AC ac/non? ac
The total rent for the car will be $ 2808.81
```

Figure 15.1

Voilà! We have successfully used register variables to speed up processing in C. Now let's move on to the next recipe!

Taking input faster in C

In this recipe, we will learn to take input faster from the user. We will ask the user to enter a number and the entered number will be displayed on the screen. We will make use of the `getchar_unlocked()` function for this purpose.

The `getchar_unlocked()` function works similarly to `getchar()` function, with the difference that it is not thread-safe. As a result, it overlooks certain input constraints and so is quite a bit faster than `getchar()`. It is used for taking long input data in a situation where a single thread is being used for handling input and other streams.

How to do it...

The steps for taking a number from the user using a faster input approach are as follows:

1. The user is asked to enter a number.

2. The number that will be entered by the user is accepted by the `getchar_unlocked()` function. Only one digit at a time is accepted by this function.

3. The value entered by the user is first checked to ensure that it is a digit only. If it is not, the user is asked to re-enter the value.

4. If the value entered by the user is a digit, its ASCII value is saved in the variable. This is because `getchar_unlocked()` assigns the ASCII value of the entered value to the variable.

5. From the ASCII of the entered value, 48 is subtracted to convert it into the actual digit that the user has entered.

6. If the digit is the first digit entered by the user, then it is simply assigned to another variable. But if it is not the first digit, then the existing digit in the variable is multiplied by 10 and the new digit is then added to the variable.

7. *Steps* 2 through 7 are repeated for every digit entered by the user until the user presses the *Enter* key.

8. The number in the variable is the actual number entered by the user and, hence, is displayed on the screen.

The program for entering a number using a fast input technique is as follows:

```
//fastinp.c

#include <stdio.h>

int getdata() {
    char cdigit = getchar_unlocked();
    int cnumb = 0;
    while(cdigit<'0' || cdigit>'9') cdigit = getchar_unlocked();
    while(cdigit >='0' && cdigit <='9') {
        cnumb = 10 * cnumb + cdigit - 48;
        cdigit = getchar_unlocked();
    }
    return cnumb;
}

int main()
{
```

```
        int numb;
        printf("Enter a number ");
        numb=getdata();
        printf("The number entered is %d\n",numb);
        return 0;
    }
```

Now, let's go behind the scenes to understand the code better.

How it works...

The user is asked to enter a number. A user-defined getdata() function is invoked and the value returned by the function is assigned to the numb variable, which in return is then displayed on the screen. The getdata function will keep asking for the digits of the number and will return the number when the *Enter* key is pressed.

Let's assume that the user wants to enter 20. Within the getdata function, the getchar_unlocked() function is invoked. So, on entering the first digit, 2 (of the number 20), it will be assigned to the cdigit variable, which is of the character data type. The ASCII value of 2 is 50, so the value 50 is actually assigned to the cdigit variable.

Before proceeding further, we ensure that the value entered by the user is a digit, and not a character or some other symbol. If the user enters something other than a digit, the getchar_unlocked() function is again invoked, asking the user to enter a valid digit. If the value entered is a digit, then 48 is subtracted from its ASCII value to convert it to its actual value. This is because the ASCII value of 2 is 50; on subtracting 48 from 50, the result will be 2, which is the actual digit that was entered by the user. The value of 2 is assigned to the cnumb variable.

Since the next digit of the number 20 is 0, the getchar_unlocked () function is invoked and the value 0 is assigned to the cdigit variable. Again, it is checked that the value entered by the user is a digit and nothing else. The ASCII value of 0 is 48. From the ASCII value of 0, the value 48 is subtracted to make its value 0. The current value in cnumb is 2, which is then multiplied by 10 and the value of cdigit is added to the result. The result of this computation will be 20 and it is assigned to the cnumb variable. The value in the cnumb variable is returned to the main function to be displayed.

In short, whatever digit is entered by the user, its ASCII value is assigned to the variable and the numerical value 48 is subtracted from the ASCII value of the digit to convert it into the actual digit that was entered by the user.

The program is compiled using GCC, as shown in the following screenshot. Because no error appears on compilation, that means the `fastinp.c` program has successfully been compiled into an EXE file, `fastinp.exe`. On executing the file, the user is prompted to enter a number. The number is accepted using a fast input technique. After entering all the digits of the number, when the user presses the *Enter* key, the entered number is displayed on the screen as shown in the following screenshot:

```
D:\CAdvBook>gcc fastinp.c -o fastinp

D:\CAdvBook>fastinp
Enter a number 2049
The number entered is 2049
```

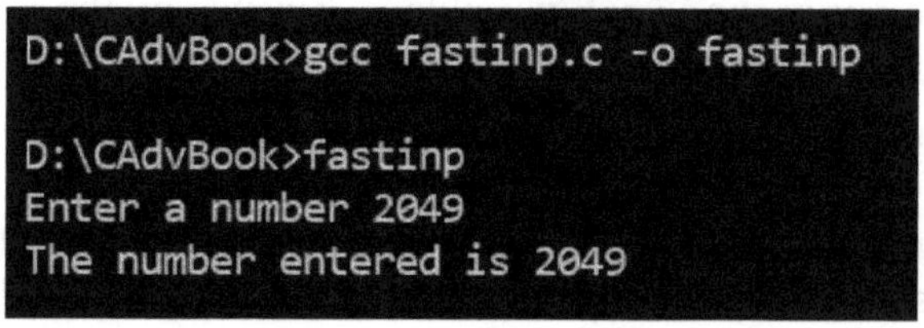

Figure 15.2

Voilà! We have successfully configured faster input of numbers in C. Now let's move on to the next recipe!

Applying loop unrolling for faster results

In this recipe, we will learn to print the sum of a sequence of numbers from 1 to a limit entered by the user using the loop unrolling technique. Loop unrolling means reducing or removing the loops from the program to reduce overheads applied while running the loops. Basically, for running a loop, the operating system has to manage two overheads – the first overhead is to maintain the count of the loop and the second overhead is to do conditional branching. Loop unrolling helps in avoiding these two overheads. Let's see how.

How to do it...

The steps for finding the sum of the first *n* sequence of numbers using the loop unrolling technique are as follows:

1. The `sum` variable in which the addition of sequence numbers will be stored is initialized to 0.

2. The user is asked to enter the limit up to which the sum of the sequence of numbers is desired. The value entered by the user is assigned to the `limit` variable.

3. We need to find the number between 9 to 1 that perfectly divides the value in the `limit` variable. To find this, we set a `for` loop to execute from 9 to 1.

4. Within the `for` loop, the value in the `limit` variable is divided by the `for` loop variable.

5. If the number in the `limit` variable is divisible by the `for` loop variable, the `for` loop will break.

6. If the number in the `limit` variable is not divisible by the `for` loop variable, the next iteration of the loop is executed with a reduced value, that is, with the value of 8. The steps are repeated until the value in the `limit` variable is perfectly divisible by the `for` loop variable.

7. Once we get the integer by which the limit is divisible, we reduce the number of `for` loops by that integer, that is, the increment of the `for` loop is set to that integer value.

8. Within the `for` loop, a `while` loop is used that adds the sequence of numbers into the `sum` variable.

9. Finally, the addition of the sequence of numbers in the `sum` variable is displayed on the screen.

The program for printing the sum of a sequence of numbers using the loop unrolling technique is as follows:

```
//loopunrolling.c

#include <stdio.h>

int main() {
    int sum,i,limit,rem,quot,incr,x, count;
    sum = 0;
    printf("Enter limit ");
    scanf("%d", &limit);
    for(i=9;i>=1;i--)
    {
        rem=limit % i;
        if (rem==0) break;
    }
    incr=i;
    count=0;
    for(i=1;i<=limit; i+=incr)
    {
        x=0;
```

```
        while(x<incr)
        {
            sum += i+x;
            x++;
        }
        count++;
    }
    printf("The sum of first %d sequence numbers is %d\n",limit, sum);
    printf("The loop executed for %d number of times\n",count);
    return 0;
}
```

Now, let's go behind the scenes to understand the code better.

How it works...

This program finds the sum of sequence numbers from 1 up to the limit entered by the user. The user is asked to enter the limit, and the value entered by the user is assigned to the limit variable. For adding the sequence numbers, we will make use of a for loop. To do loop unrolling or to reduce the number of iterations of the loop, we find the integer by which the limit can be divided. That is, we divide the value in the limit variable by integers from 9 to 1. Once we get the integer by which the limit is divisible, we reduce the number of for loops by that integer.

Let's assume that the user enters a limit of 40, which is assigned to the limit variable. A for loop is set to run from the values 9 to 1, and every value from 9 to 1 will be used to try to divide the value in the limit variable. On any division, if the remainder appears as 0, the for loop will break; else, the next iteration will execute with the decreased value. Currently, the value in the limit variable is 40 and the value of i in the first iteration is 9. The remainder of dividing 40 by 9 is a non zero value, so the next iteration of the for loop will begin with the next decreased value, 8.

Because, on dividing 40 by 8, you get a remainder of 0, the for loop will break and the control will jump to the statement immediately after the for loop. The value of i at that time is 8, so the value of 8 is assigned to the incr variable. That is, the for loop will increment by a value of 8. It also means that we are applying loop unrolling by reducing the iterations of the for loop by 8 times. In other words, the for loop will be set to run from 1 until the limit, which is 40, with an increment of 8 after every iteration.

In the first iteration, the value of i is 1. The sum variable, in which the addition of the sequence of numbers will be computed, is initialized to 0. The value of i is added to the sum variable. As said earlier, the next iteration of the for loop will increment the value of i by 8. So, within the for loop, a while loop is used. Within the while loop, a variable, x, is used that executes from 0 to the value of the incr variable (that is, until the value of 8). In other words, the while loop will add the sequence of numbers from 1 to 8 into the sum variable.

Once the sum of the first eight values of the sequence of numbers is computed and assigned to the sum variable, the next iteration of the for loop will begin with the value of i incremented to 9. Again within the for loop, the while loop will execute to compute the sum of the sequence of numbers from 9 to 16. Again, the next iteration of the for loop will increase the value of i to 17. The process continues until the for loop completes. In short, the for loop is unrolled to the value assigned to the incr variable. Finally, the sum of the sequence of numbers is displayed on the screen.

The program is compiled using GCC, as shown in the following screenshot. Because no error appears on compilation, that means the loopunrolling.c program has successfully been compiled into an EXE file, loopunrolling.exe. On executing the file, the user is prompted to enter the limit up to which the sum of the sequence of numbers is desired. The program will not only print the sum of the sequence of numbers but will also print how many loop iterations it took for the sum to be computed, as shown in the following screenshot:

```
D:\CAdvBook>gcc loopunrolling.c -o loopunrolling

D:\CAdvBook>loopunrolling
Enter limit 40
The sum of first 40 sequence numbers is 820
The loop executed for 5 number of times
```

Figure 15.3

Voilà! We have successfully executed loop unrolling to generate a faster result.

16
Low-Level Programming

Sometimes, for precise results and in order to overcome the limitations of a programming language, you need to control the content of CPU registers at the bit level. In such situations, you can make use of two things: bitwise operators and assembly language programming.

In this chapter, we will learn how to perform the following recipes in order to carry out low-level programming in C:

- Converting a binary number into a decimal using a bitwise operator
- Converting a decimal into binary using a bitwise operator
- Converting a decimal number into binary using bit masking
- Multiplying two numbers using the inline assembly language in C
- Dividing two numbers using assembly code in C

Introduction to bitwise operators

Every number that we enter into any variable is internally stored in the form of binary digits. To perform bit-level operations, C provides the following bitwise operators.

& (binary AND)

This results in a binary 1 if both the operands are 1. If either of the bits is 0, then the result of the & operation is 0.

Assuming that operand A has a value of 1010 and operand B has a value of 0111, then A&B will be as follows:

A	1010
B	0111
A&B	0010

| (binary OR)

This results in a binary 1 if either of the operands is 1. If both of the bits are 0, then the result of the | operation is 0.

Assuming that operand A has a value of 1010 and operand B has a value of 0111, then A|B will be as follows:

A	1010
B	0111
A|B	1111

^ (binary XOR)

This results in a binary 1 if either of the operands is 1 but not both. If both of the bits are 0, or if both are 1, then the result of the ^ operation is 0.

Assuming that operand A has a value of 1010 and operand B has a value of 0111, then A^B will be as follows:

A	1010
B	0111
A^B	1111

~ (binary complement)

This negates or inverses the binary digits of the operand. That is, the binary digit 1 will be converted to 0 and vice versa. Assuming that operand A has a value of 1010, then ~A will be as follows:

A	1010
~A	0101

<< (binary shift left)

This left-shifts the binary digits of the operand by the specified number of bits, and the empty space created after the least significant bits is filled with 0s.

Assuming that operand A has a value of 00001010, then left-shifting A by 2 bits (A<<2) will give us the following:

A	00001010
A<<2	00101000

On every left-shift, the value of the operand is multiplied by powers of 2. That is, if the operand is left-shifted by 2 bits, that means it is multiplied by 2 x 2, that is, 4.

>> (binary shift right)

This right-shifts the binary digits of the operand by the specified number of bits, and the empty space created after the most significant bits is filled with 0s.

Assuming that operand A has a value of 00001010, then right-shifting A by 2 bits (A>>2) will give us the following:

A	00001010
A>>2	00000010

You can see that on right-shifting, the least significant bits are dropped off. On every right-shift, the value of the operand is divided by powers of 2. That is, if the operand is right-shifted by 2 bits, that means it is divided by 2 x 2, that is, 4.

Let's go on to gain some practical knowledge by making some working recipes. The first recipe is next.

Converting a binary number into a decimal using a bitwise operator

In this recipe, you will learn how to convert a binary number into a decimal.

How to do it...

To convert a binary number into a decimal, perform the following steps:

1. Enter a binary number.
2. Apply a mod 10 (`% 10`) operator to the binary digits of the binary number to isolate the last bit of the binary number.
3. Left-shift the binary digit isolated in *step 2* to multiply it by the power of 2.
4. Add the product of the previous multiplication to the variable that will store the result, that is, the decimal number. Let's call the variable `dec`.
5. The last digit of the binary number is truncated.
6. Repeat *step 2* to *step 4* until all the bits of the binary digits are over.
7. Display the decimal in the `dec` variable.

The program for converting a binary number into a decimal is as follows:

```
binintodec.c
#include <stdio.h>
void main()
{
    int num,bin,temp,dec=0,topower=0;
    printf("Enter the binary number: ");
    scanf("%d",&bin);
    temp=bin;
    while(bin >0)
    {
        num=bin %10;
        num=num<<topower;
        dec=dec+num;
        topower++;
        bin=bin/10;
    }
    printf("The decimal of %d is %d\n",temp,dec);
}
```

Now, let's go behind the scenes to understand the code better.

How it works...

You will be prompted to enter a binary number. The number you enter will be assigned to the `bin` variable. The binary number is temporarily assigned to a `temp` variable. A `while` loop is executed until the binary number in the `bin` variable becomes 0.

Let's assume that the binary number entered in the `bin` variable is `1101`. Then, we will apply the `mod` (`%`) operator to the binary digits in the `bin` variable in order to isolate its last bit. In fact, the `%` operator divides by the specified number and returns the remainder. That is, when `%  10` is applied to `1  1  0  1`, it will return `1`, which is then assigned to the `num` variable.

A `topower` variable is initialized to `0`. The purpose of the `topower` variable is to left-shift the digits, that is, to multiply the binary digits by the power of 2. The binary digit `1` in the `num` variable is added to another variable called `dec`. The value of the `topower` variable is incremented to `1`. The binary number `1  1  0  1` in the `bin` variable is truncated to `1  1  0` by dividing it by `10` and removing the fraction.

Again, the whole procedure is repeated. The last digit in the `bin` variable is isolated by the application of the `%10` operator; that is, `0` will be isolated from `1  1  0` and assigned to the `num` variable. The binary digit `0` is left-shifted by `1` bit, making it `0  0`. So, a value of `0` is then added to the value in the `dec` variable; that is, the value in the `dec` variable remains `1`. The value of `topower` is incremented to `2`. The last digit of the binary digit `1  1  0` in the `bin` variable is removed by dividing it by `10`; therefore, the binary digit in the `bin` variable will become `1  1`.

Once again, apply `%10` to `1  1`; the remainder will be `1`, which will be assigned to the `num` variable. The binary digit `1` is left-shifted by `2` bits, making it `1  0  0`. The binary value `1  0  0` represents `4`, which is then added to the value in the `dec` variable. The value in the `dec` variable was `1`, and after adding `4` to it, the total in the `dec` variable will become `5`. Again, the value in the `topower` variable will be incremented, making its value `3`. The last digit of the binary digits (`1  1`) in the `bin` variable will be truncated by dividing it by `10`. Hence, the digit in the `bin` variable will become `1`.

Again, `%10` is applied to binary digit `1` in the `bin` variable. As a result of this, `1` will be assigned to the `num` variable. The binary digit `1` in the `num` variable is left-shifted by `3` bits, making it `1  0  0  0`. The binary value `1  0  0  0` represents `8`, which is then added to the value in the `dec` variable. The current value in the `dec` variable is `5`. On adding `8` to it, the value in the `dec` variable will become `13`. The value of the `topower` variable is incremented to `4`. The binary value `1` in the `bin` variable is divided by `10`, making it `0`. The `while` loop will terminate and the decimal value `13` in the `dec` variable is displayed on the screen.

The whole procedure can be illustrated as follows:

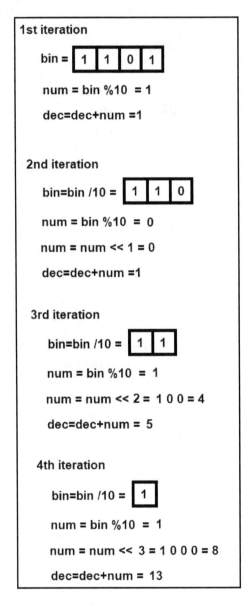

Figure 16.1

Let's use GCC to compile the `binintodec.c` program as follows:

```
D:\CBook>gcc binintodec.c -o binintodec
```

If you get no errors or warnings, this means the `binintodec.c` program has compiled into an executable file, `binintodec.exe`. Let's run this executable file as follows:

```
D:\CBook>binintodec
Enter the binary number: 1101
The decimal of 1101 is 13
```

Voilà! We've successfully converted a binary number to a decimal using a bitwise operator. Now, let's move on to the next recipe!

Converting a decimal into binary using a bitwise operator

In this recipe, we will learn to convert a decimal number into a binary number by making use of a bitwise operator. Bitwise operators operate on the binary digits of a number and enable us to do precise manipulation as desired.

How to do it...

To convert a decimal number into a binary number by making use of a bitwise operator, perform the following steps:

1. Enter a decimal number. This number is internally stored in the form of binary digits.
2. Isolate the least significant bit of the decimal number by applying a logical AND operation between the entered decimal number and value 1.
3. The least significant bit that results from *step 2* is stored in an array.
4. Right-shift the binary digits of the decimal number by 1 bit. On shifting to the right, the second least significant bit will become the least significant bit.
5. Repeat *steps 2* to *4* until all the binary digits of the decimal number are placed into the array.
6. The binary digits assigned to the array are the binary version of the entered decimal number. Display the binary digits in an array to get the result.

The program for converting a decimal into a binary number using a bitwise operator is as follows:

```
convertintobin.c
#include <stdio.h>
void main()
{
    int num,i,x,temp;
    int p[10];
    printf("Enter Decimal Number : ");
    scanf("%d",&num);
    temp=num;
    x=0;
    while(num > 0)
    {
        if((num & 1) == 0 )
        {
            p[x]=0;
x++;
        }
        else
        {
            p[x]=1;
            x++;
        }
        num = num >> 1;
    }
    printf("Binary of %d is ",temp);
    for(i=x-1;i>=0;i--)printf("%d",p[i]);
}
```

Now, let's go behind the scenes.

How it works...

You will be prompted to enter a decimal number. The number you enter is assigned to the num variable. The value entered in the num variable is temporarily assigned to another variable, temp. A while loop is set to execute until the value of num becomes 0. Apply the logical AND operation to isolate each binary digit of the number. For example, if the value entered in variable num is 13, then, internally, it will be stored in a binary format as follows:

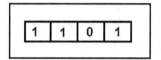

Figure 16.2

Now, the least significant bit is isolated by applying the AND operation. That is, the binary digits of 13 are ANDed with 1 as follows. The ANDed means the AND operation is applied on binary digits of 13 and 1 :

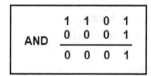

Figure 16.3

The application of AND on binary digits 1 and 1 results in 1. If either of the binary digits is 0, then the result of AND will be 0. So, the output of num AND 1 will be **1**, which will be stored into array p at index location 0 as shown in the following screenshot:

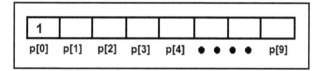

Figure 16.4

After that, right-shift the digits in the num variable by 1 bit. On shifting to the right, the least significant bit, 1, will be dropped off and a 0 will be added to the most significant bit. Again, the new set of binary digits in the num variables is ANDed with 1, that is, the AND operation is applied between the new set of binary digits in num variable and 1. The output of num AND 1 will be 0, which is then assigned to array p at index location 1; that is, 0 will be assigned to the p[1] location as shown in the figure:

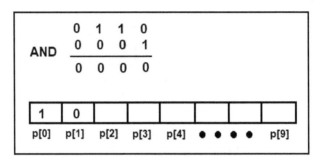

Figure 16.5

Again, right-shift the digits in the num variable by 1 bit. Again, the least significant bit, 0, will be dropped off and a 0 will be added to the most significant bit. Once more, the new set of binary digits in the num variables is ANDed with 1, as shown in *Figure 16.6(a)*. The output of the num variable AND 1 will be 1, which is then assigned to array p at index location 2. Thereafter, right-shift the digits in the num variable again by 1 bit. The most significant bit in the num variable, 1, will be dropped off and a 0 bit will be added to the most significant bit location. The binary digits in num are once more ANDed with 1 . ANDed here means, the AND operation is applied between the binary digits in num and 1. The output of the AND operation will be 1, which will be assigned to array p at index location p[3] (*Figure 16.6(b)*):

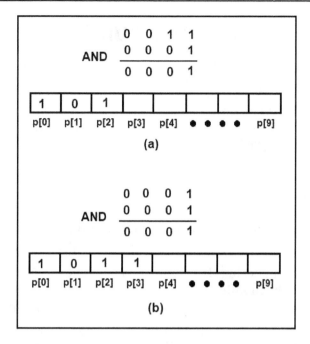

Figure 16.6 (a) and (b)

Now, the binary digits assigned to array p are the binary conversion of the number assigned to variable num. Simply display the binary digits in array p in reverse order to get the result. Hence, 1 1 0 1 is the binary conversion of 13.

Let's use GCC to compile the convertintobin.c program as follows:

```
D:\CBook>gcc convertintobin.c -o convertintobin
```

If you get no errors or warnings, that means the convertintobin.c program has compiled into an executable file, convertintobin.exe. Let's run this executable file as follows:

```
D:\CBook>convertintobin
Enter Decimal Number : 13
Binary of 13 is 1101
```

Voilà! We've successfully converted a decimal number into a binary number using a bitwise operator. Now, let's move on to the next recipe!

Converting a decimal number into binary using bit masking

In this recipe, we will learn how to convert a decimal number into a binary number by masking certain bits of a register. Masking means isolating or separating out the desired binary digits. Masking hides the undesired binary digits and makes only the desired binary digits visible.

How to do it...

To convert a decimal number into a binary number using bit masking, perform the following steps:

1. Enter a decimal value. The decimal number entered is internally stored in the form of binary digits.
2. Assign a number 1 followed by 31 zeros to a variable called mask.
3. Mask each of the binary digits of the decimal number one by one, beginning from the most significant bit. Apply an AND operation between the binary digits of the entered decimal number and the binary digits in the mask variable.
4. Right-shift the binary digits in the mask variable by 1 bit making it 0 1 followed by 30 zeros.
5. Repeat this procedure. Apply the AND operation between the entered decimal number and the mask variable and the resultant binary digit is displayed on the screen. The procedure is repeated until the value in the mask variable becomes 0.

The program for converting a decimal number into binary using bit masking is as follows:

```
decintobin.c
#include <stdio.h>
void main()
{
    int i, totbits;
    unsigned mask,num;
    printf("Enter decimal value: ");
    scanf("%d", &num);
    totbits=32;
    mask = 1 << (totbits - 1);
```

```
for(i = 0; i < totbits; i++)
{
    if((num & mask) == 0 )
        printf("0");
    else
        printf("1");
    mask >>= 1;
}
}
```

Now, let's go behind the scenes.

How it works...

You will be prompted to enter a decimal value. The decimal value you entered will be assigned to the num variable. Let's assume that you have entered a value of 13. This value will be internally stored in the form of binary digits in the num variable as follows:

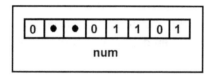

Figure 16.7

We will set a totbits variable to 32 bits because an int data type in C consists of 32 bits, and we have to mask each bit of the number in the num variable to display its binary version. We will define a mask variable and assign a value of 1 to it. To make the value 1 in the mask variable appear as 10000...00, that is, 1 followed by 31 zeros, we will left-shift value 1 by 31 bits as follows:

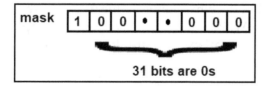

Figure 16.8

Now, we will execute a `for` loop 32 times to mask or isolate each bit in the `num` variable and display it. Within the `for` loop, we will apply an AND operation on the `num` and `mask` variables. Consequently, each of the binary digits of the two variables will be ANDed. We know that, in the AND operation, the output is 1 only when both of the bits are 1. If either of the bits is 0, the AND operation will return 0.

Figure 16.9 shows the application of the AND operation on the `num` and `mask` variables:

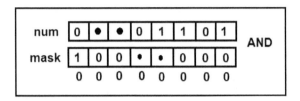

Figure 16.9

Hence, the value 0 is returned. Thereafter, we will right-shift the binary digits in the `mask` variable by 1 bit, making it 0 1 followed by 30 zeros. Again, when the AND operation is applied between the `num` and `mask` variables, the result will be 0 (refer to the following figure), which is then displayed on the screen. So, up until now, we have 0 0 displayed on the screen:

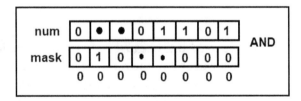

Figure 16.10

Again, we will right-shift the binary digits in the `mask` variable by 1 bit, making 0 0 1 followed by 29 zeros. Again, when the AND operation is applied between the `num` and `mask` variables, the result will be 0, which is then displayed on the screen.

The procedure and output will be the same for the next 25 bits; that is, we will get 28 zeros on the screen. After that, when we apply another right-shift operation on the binary digits of the mask variable, it will become 1 0 0 0. On the application of the AND operation on the num and mask variables, we will get an output of 1, which is then displayed on the screen. So, for now, we have 28 zeros followed by 1 bit on the screen:

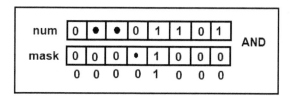

Figure 16.11

As we keep repeating the procedure, we will get the outputs shown in *Figure 16.12*. We will have 28 zeros followed by 1 1 bits on the screen (*Figure 16.12 (a)*). After another repetition, we will have 28 zeros followed by 1 1 0 bits on the screen (*Figure 16.12 (b)*). In the final execution of the for loop, the final binary version of the number assigned to the num variable will be 28 zeros followed by 1 1 0 1 (*Figure 16.12 (c)*):

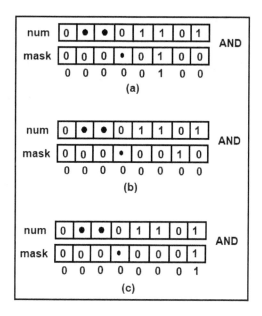

Figure 16.12 (a), (b), and (c)

Let's use GCC to compile the `decintobin.c` program as follows:

```
D:\CBook>gcc decintobin.c -o decintobin
```

If you get no errors or warnings, that means the `decintobin.c` program has compiled into an executable file, `decintobin.exe`. Let's run this executable file as follows:

```
D:\CBook>decintobin
Enter decimal value: 13
00000000000000000000000000001101
```

Voilà! We've successfully converted a decimal number into binary using bit masking.

Introduction to assembly coding

The x86 processors have eight 32-bit general-purpose registers. The names of some of these general-purpose registers are EAX, EBX, ECX, and EDX. These registers can be used in subsections. For example, the least significant 2 bytes of EAX can be used as a 16-bit register called AX. Again, the least significant byte of AX can be used as an 8-bit register called AL and the most significant byte of AX can be used as an 8-bit register called AH. Similarly, the BX register can be used in the form of the BH and BL registers, and so on.

We will be writing inline assembly code in this chapter because this code is easily integrated with C code during code generation. Consequently, the C and assembly code is optimized by the compiler to produce efficient object code.

The syntax for using inline assembly code is as follows:

```
asm [volatile] (
asm statements
: output statements
: input statements
);
```

The `asm` statements are enclosed within quotes, and the outputs and inputs are in the form of `"constraint"` (name) pairs separated by commas. The constraints can be any of the following:

Constraint	Usage
g	Compiler will decide the register to be used for the variable
r	Load into any available register
a	Load into the `eax` register
b	Load into the `ebx` register
c	Load into the `ecx` register
d	Load into the `edx` register
f	Load into the floating-point register
D	Load into the `edi` register
S	Load into the `esi` register

The outputs and inputs are referenced by numbers.

Multiplying two numbers using the inline assembly language in C

In this recipe, we will learn how to multiply two numbers using the inline assembly language in C. By making use of inline assembly code, we can have better control over CPU registers, manipulate their values up to the bit level, and take advantage of C as well.

How to do it...

To multiply two numbers using the inline assembly language in C, perform the following steps:

1. Load the two values to be multiplied into `eax` and `ebx` registers
2. Multiply the contents of the `eax` and `ebx` registers and store the result in the `eax` register
3. Display the content of the `eax` register on the screen

The program for multiplying two digits using inline assembly code is as follows:

```c
#include <stdio.h>
#include <stdint.h>
int main(int argc, char **argv)
{
    int32_t var1=10, var2=20, multi = 0;
    asm volatile ("imull %%ebx,%%eax;"
        : "=a" (multi)
        : "a" (var1), "b" (var2)
    );
    printf("Multiplication = %d\n", multi);
    return 0;
}
```

Now, let's go behind the scenes.

How it works...

Let's assign the two numbers that we want to multiply to two integer variables, var1 and var2. Thereafter, we will load the contents of the var1 variable into the eax register and the contents of the var2 variable into the ebx register. We will multiply the contents of the eax and ebx registers and store the result in the eax register.

The content of the eax register is assigned to the multi variable. The content in this variable, which contains the multiplication of two variables, is displayed on the screen.

Let's use GCC to compile the multiasm.c program as follows:

```
D:\CBook>gcc multiasm.c -o multiasm
```

If you get no errors or warnings, that means the multiasm.c program has compiled into an executable file, multiasm.exe. Let's run this executable file as follows:

```
D:\CBook>multiasm
Multiplication = 200
```

Voilà! We've successfully multiplied two numbers using the inline assembly language in C. Now, let's move on to the next recipe!

Dividing two numbers using assembly code in C

In this recipe, we will learn to divide two numbers using the inline assembly language in C. The assembly language provides us with better control over CPU registers, so we have to manually place the divisor and dividend in their respective registers. Additionally, after the division, the quotient and remainder will be automatically saved in their respective registers.

How to do it...

To divide two numbers using assembly code in C, perform the following steps:

1. Load the dividend into the `eax` register.
2. Load the divisor into the `ebx` register.
3. Initialize the `edx` register to zero.
4. Execute the `divl` assembly statement to divide the content of the `eax` register by the content of the `ebx` register. By doing this division, the quotient will be assigned to any available register and the remainder will be assigned to the `ebx` register.
5. The quotient is retrieved from the available register and the remainder is retrieved from the `ebx` register, and both are displayed on the screen.

The program for dividing two digits using inline assembly code is as follows:

asmdivide.c
```c
#include <stdio.h>
void main() {
    int var1=19,var2=4, var3=0, remainder, quotient;
    asm("divl %%ebx;"
        "movl %%edx, %0"
        : "=b" (remainder) , "=r" (quotient)
        : "a" (var1), "b" (var2), "d" (var3)
    );
    printf ("On dividing %d by %d, you get %d quotient and %d
remainder\n", var1, var2, quotient, remainder);
}
```

Now, let's go behind the scenes.

How it works...

Let's assign the two numbers to be divided to the two variables var1 and var2. Assign the dividend to var1 and the divisor to var2. Thereafter, we will load the dividend from the var1 variable into the eax register and the divisor from the var2 variable into the ebx register.

The edx register has to be initialized to zero. To do this, we will initialize a var3 variable to zero. From var3, the zero value is loaded into the edx register. Then, we will execute the divl assembly statement to divide the content of the eax register by the content of the ebx register. By doing this division, the quotient will be assigned to any available register and the remainder will be assigned to the ebx register.

The quotient from the available register is loaded into a variable called quotient, and the remainder from the ebx register is loaded into another variable called remainder. Finally, the quotient and remainder values are displayed on the screen.

Let's use GCC to compile the asmdivide.c program as follows:

```
D:\CBook>gcc asmdivide.c -o asmdivide
```

If you get no errors or warnings, that means the asmdivide.c program has compiled into an executable file, asmdivide.exe. Let's run this executable file as follows:

```
D:\CBook>asmdivide
On dividing 19 by 4, you get 4 quotient and 3 remainder
```

Voilà! We've successfully divided two numbers using assembly code in C.

Embedded Software and IoT

17

When it comes to doing specific tasks more efficiently and precisely, embedded systems are preferred. They work as independent components, and they can be collectively combined into larger pieces of equipment. The internet is a vast and endless source of information; consequently, the **Internet of Things (IoT)** plays a major role in making embedded devices smarter so that they can be managed and controlled remotely.

In this chapter, we'll deep dive into the following recipes related to embedded software and IoT:

- Toggling the port of a microcontroller in Embedded C (blinking LED)
- Incrementing the value of a port in Embedded C
- Toggling the voltage in an output pin using Arduino (blinking LED)
- Taking input from the serial port using Arduino
- Sensing the temperature using Arduino with the LM35 sensor

Technical requirements

For embedded programming in C, we will use Keil MDK, which provides a software development environment for a wide range of ARM Cortex-M-based microcontroller devices. MDK provides the very easy-to-use µVision IDE, an Arm C/C++ compiler, and other libraries. You can download Keil MDK from the following URL: `https://www.keil.com/download/`. Let's take a look at the following steps:

1. Download the following three executable files. You may not find the files with exactly the same names, but they will be somewhat similar:
    - `mdk526.exe`: This provides a development environment for ARM devices.
    - `c251v560.exe`: This provides development tools for all 80251 devices.

- `c51v959.exe`: This provides development tools for all 8051 devices.

2. Double-click on these executable files one by one and follow the setup dialog boxes to install these three Keil products.

Following the successful installation of these products, you will find an icon called Keil uVision5 on the desktop. The icon represents the **Integrated Development Environment** (**IDE**) that enables us to write, edit, debug, and compile programs. The compiler converts the source code into a HEX file, which, in return, can be fused onto the target chip.

In order to work with Arduino, you have to buy the Arduino board and download the Arduino IDE from `https://www.arduino.cc/en/main/software`.

At the time of writing this chapter, the latest version of the Arduino IDE that is available is 1.8.8. The downloaded executable file will be `arduino-1.8.8-windows.exe`. Connect the Arduino board to your PC and simply double-click on the executable file to install the Arduino IDE. When it has successfully installed, you will find the Arduino IDE icon on the desktop.

Introduction to embedded systems

An embedded system is a combination of computer hardware and software designed to do specific functions within larger equipment. The heavy equipment used in industries, automobiles, medical procedures, household appliances, and mobile devices use embedded systems. Most embedded systems use a RISC family microcontroller, such as PIC 16F84, Atmel 8051, or Motorola 68HC11. Several input and output devices can be connected to the embedded system's microcontrollers, such as an LCD display, keypad, printer, and sensor. These devices can control several other devices such as fans, motors, bulbs, washing machines, ovens, AC controllers, cars, printers, and so much more.

To program a microcontroller to do a specific task, the microcontroller is interfaced with a PC by connecting it to a slot. An assembly program, or Embedded C, can be used to write and burn the program onto the microcontroller. The programs can be stored in the microcontroller's **EPROM** (short for **Erasable Programmable Read-Only Memory**). It's an internal, read-only memory that can be programmed and erased when exposed to an ultraviolet light source. We will be developing applications for embedded systems using Embedded C with software such as Keil.

Introduction to IoT

IoT is an architecture that comprises hardware and software systems or devices that are connected to the internet using various means such as WiFi, Ethernet, and more. The web API and other protocols, when combined, provide an environment that allows smart embedded devices to be connected to the internet. Consequently, it enables us to access data from remote areas and control or trigger certain actions on various devices via the internet. In other words, IoT is a system of interrelated embedded computing devices that have the ability to transfer data over a network and take necessary actions. Arduino is considered to be the best starting point for embedded IoT. For Arduino to be able to work as an IoT device, Android with an Ethernet shield is required.

Let's quickly learn a little more about Arduino.

Introduction to Arduino

Arduino is an architecture that includes the Atmel microcontroller family along with standard hardware. The pin diagram of Arduino is as follows:

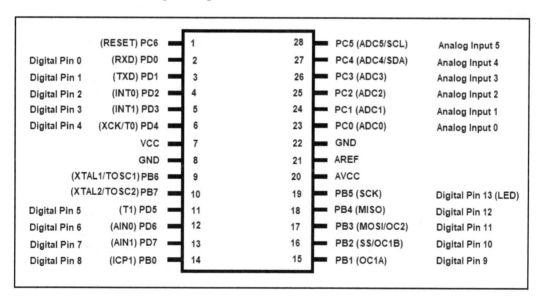

Arduino includes 14 digital pins that can operate with 5V:

- Pins **0** (**RXD**) and **1** (**TXD**) are the serial pins used to transfer TTL serial data.
- Pins **2** and **3** are the external interrupt pins used to activate an interrupt.
- Pins **3**, **5**, **6**, **9**, **10**, and **11** are used to provide the PWM output.
- Pins **10**, **11**, **12**, and **13** are **SPI** pins (short for the **Serial Peripheral Interface**). Named **SS**, **MOSI**, **MISO**, and **SCK**, these pins are used for SPI communication.
- Pin **13** is an LED pin. A HIGH digital value, when supplied to this pin, will make the LED glow.
- Analog pins **4** and **5**—called **SDA** and **SCL**, respectively—are used in the communication of **TWI** (short for the **Two-Wire Interface**).
- The **AREF** (short for **Analog Reference**) pin is used to connect to some reference voltage from an external power supply.
- The **RESET** (**RST**) pin is used to reset the microcontroller.

As far as software is concerned, Arduino comes with an IDE that we can use to write and edit applications and can even upload them to do specific tasks. This IDE includes support for the C and C++ programming languages for programming microcontrollers. It contains several libraries that make the job of a software developer quite easy. Besides this, the IDE provides communication windows in order to enter data into the board as well as to get output.

The Arduino board provides ports to connect LCDs, relays, and much more to its output pin and provides input pins to input information from sensors, relays, and much more. The Arduino board can be powered either by a USB or by connecting a 9V battery.

While working with Arduino programming, we will be using the following functions:

- `Serial.begin()` is used to set the data rate while establishing communication between the Arduino board and the PC. In order to communicate with the computer through serial data transmission, we need to first set the data rate in bits per second (baud). We can use any of the baud rates, such as 300, 600, 1200, 2400, 4800, 9600, 14400, 19200, 28800, 38400, 57600, or 115200.
- `Serial.println()` is used to display a message to the serial port in a human-readable format. It displays the message in ASCII text followed by a newline character on the serial monitor. You will need to press *Ctrl* + *Shift* + *M* to open the serial monitor.

- `Serial.available()` checks whether the data, in terms of bytes from the serial port, is available for reading. Essentially, the data to be read from the serial port is stored in the serial receive buffer and this method checks whether the data has arrived in this buffer. This method returns the number of bytes available to read:

- `Serial.read()` reads incoming serial data and returns the first byte of incoming serial data available. The method returns -1 if no data is available to read.

- `analogRead()` reads the value from the specified analog pin. The Arduino board contains a multichannel, 10-bit analog-to-digital converter. As a result of this, it will map input voltages between 0 and the operating voltage (5V or 3.3V) into integer values between 0 and 1023.

For example, if you're using a 5V Arduino and a sensor is connected to its analog pin, then the following formula is used to convert the 10-bit analog reading into a temperature:

```
Voltage at pin in milli volts = Reading from ADC * 5000/1024
```

This formula converts the number 0-1023 from the ADC into 0-5000 mV.

If you're using a 3.3V Arduino, then the following formula is used to convert the analog reading into a temperature:

```
Voltage at pin in milli volts = Reading from ADC * 3300/1024
```

This formula converts the number 0-1023 from the ADC into 0-3300 mV.

To convert the number of millivolts retrieved from the preceding formula into a temperature, the following formula is used:

```
Centigrade temperature = Analog voltage in mV / 10
```

That wraps up our introduction to embedded systems and IoT. We'll now review the required technical software and hardware we need to complete the recipes in this chapter. After that, we will begin with the first recipe.

Toggling the port of a microcontroller in Embedded C (blinking LED)

In this recipe, we will learn how to send HIGH and LOW signals to a specific port that is connected to an LED, and make the LED blink. The idea behind this exercise is to learn how to control a device that is connected to a specific port of the microcontroller.

How to do it...

To toggle the port of a microcontroller in Embedded C, perform the following steps:

1. We will carry out this recipe using Keil; double-click on the Keil uVision5 icon to activate the IDE.
2. Create a new project by clicking on the **Project** | **New uVision Project** option.
3. When prompted, specify the project name and the folder where you want to create the new project.
4. Give the new project the name `LedBlinkProject` and then click on the **Save** button.
5. The device selection window will open and you will be prompted to select a device.
6. From the **Device** combo box, select the **Legacy Device Database [no RTE]** option. You will get the list of devices in the lower-left pane (refer to the following screenshot).
7. Click on the **Microchip** node to expand it and display the list of devices in it.
8. Because we want to program the Atmel microcontroller, from the **Microchip** node, select the **AT89C51** device. The description of the selected device will appear in the description pane on the right. Click on **OK** to move further:

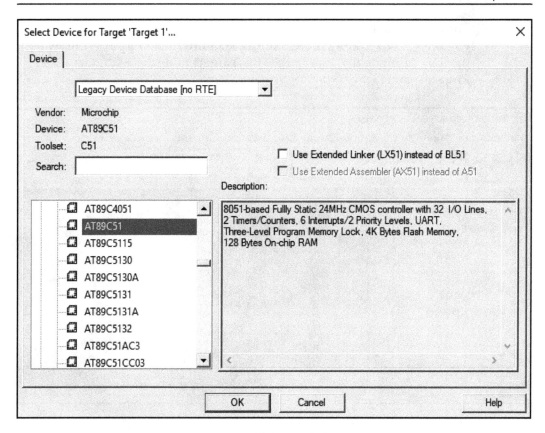

3. You will be asked whether you want to copy the STARTUP.A51 file to the project folder (refer to the following screenshot). The startup file will be required for running the project, so click on the **Yes** button to add the file and move further:

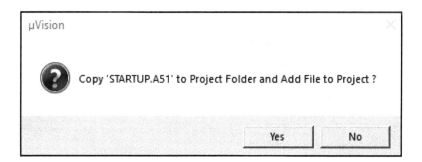

4. The IDE will appear as follows. You can see three
   windows: **Project Workspace**, **Editing Window**, and **Output Window** in
   the IDE. Additionally, you can see the **Target1** node created under the
   Project space:

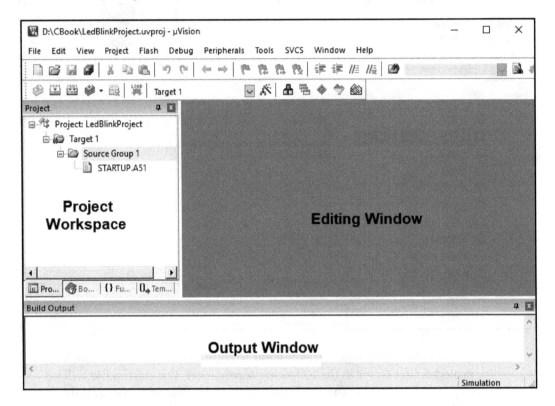

5. Add a C file. Right-click on **Source Group1** under the **Target1** node and
   click on the **Add New item to Group 'Source Group 1'** option. From the list
   box, select the **C File (.c)** option. Specify the filename as blinkingLed (or
   any other name), and then click on the **Add** button (refer to the following
   screenshot):

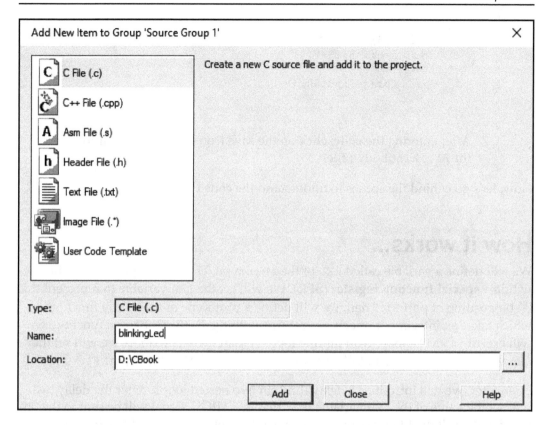

6. The `blinkingLed.c` file is added to **Source Group 1**. Enter the following code in the editor window:

```
#include<reg52.h>

sbit LED = P1^0;
void Delay(int);
void main (void)
{
    while(1)
    {
        LED = 0;
        Delay(500);
        LED = 1;
        Delay(500);
    }
}

void Delay(int n)
```

```
        {
            int i,j;
            for(i=0;i<n;i++)
            {
                for(j=0;j<100;j++);
            }
        }
```

7. After entering the code, click on the save icon from the toolbar to save the `blinkingLed.c` file.

Now, let's go behind the scenes to understand the code better.

How it works...

We will define a variable called `LED` of the `sbit` type. The `sbit` type defines a bit within a **special function register** (**SFR**). We will set the `LED` variable to represent the 0th-bit position of port `P1`. Then, we will define a prototype of the `Delay` function, which takes an integer parameter but returns nothing. Within the `main` function, we will execute a `while` loop in an infinite loop. Within the `while` loop, we will set the `LED` variable to `0`, that is, a LOW signal will be sent to the 0th bit of port `P1`.

Thereafter, we will introduce a delay through two nested loops. After the delay, we will set the value of the `LED` variable to `1`, that is, a HIGH signal will be sent to the 0th bit of port `P1`. If the LED is connected to the 0th bit of port `1`, the LED will glow and, after some delay, it will go off. Again, after some delay, the LED will glow again; therefore, we get a blinking LED.

Press *F7* or click on the **Build** button to start compiling the code. If there is no error, you can move on to the next step. You can either generate a HEX file to infuse into the desired hardware, or you can use the simulation technique to see whether the program is giving the desired output. In order to generate a HEX file, right-click on the **Target1** node and select **Options for Target 'Target 1'**. We will get a dialog box showing different options. Click on the **Output** tab, and check the **Create HEX File** box (refer to the following screenshot). Additionally, click on the **Device** tab to confirm that the device selected is **AT89C51**. Then, click on the **OK** button:

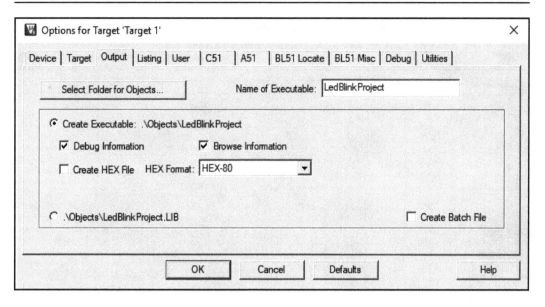

Figure 5.5

Keil's built-in **Debug** option can be used for code simulation. To do this, click on **Debug | Start/Stop Debug Session**; alternatively, you can press *Ctrl + F5* as the shortcut key, or click on the **Start/Stop Debug Session** icon (it appears in the form of d) in the toolbar. The free version of the Keil tool has a condition that the running code size should not be more than 2 KB. You will get the following dialog box indicating that the running code has an upper limit of 2 KB:

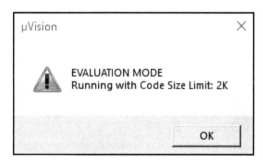

Figure 5.6

Click on the **OK** button to move further. Now the **Project** workspace window shows most of the SFRs as well as the GPRs, **r0** to **r7**, as follows:

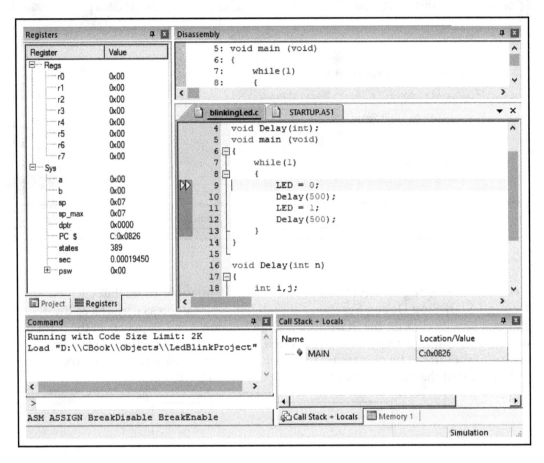

Figure 5.7

Click on the **Run** icon from the toolbar or press *F5*. To see the output on ports go to **Peripherals** | **Select I/O ports** | **Port 1**. You will get the blinking LED on Port1, as shown in the following screenshot. You can see that there is a LOW signal in bit0 of the Port1 and a HIGH signal on the same bit:

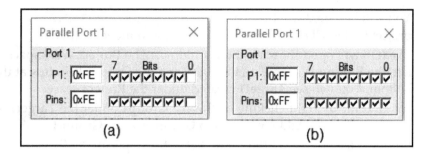

Figure 5.8

Voilà! We've successfully created a blinking LED using a microcontroller port. Now, let's move on to the next recipe!

Incrementing the value of a port in Embedded C

In this recipe, we will learn how to display values from 0 to 255 on a specific port of a microcontroller and make the value increment like a counter.

How to do it...

To increment the value of a port in Embedded C, perform the following steps:

1. Launch the Keil uVision5 IDE.
2. Create a new project by clicking on the **New Project | New uVision Project** option.
3. Specify the project name and folder location when prompted. Let's give the new project the name `CounterApp`; click on **Save**.
4. The device selection window will open and you will be prompted to select a device. From the **Device** combo box, select **Legacy Device Database [no RTE]**.
5. You will get the list of devices in the lower-left pane. Click on the **Microchip** node to expand it and display the list of devices in it.
6. From the **Microchip** node, select the **AT89C51** device. The description of the selected device will appear in the description pane on the right. Click on **OK** to move further.

6. You will be asked whether you want to copy the STARTUP.A51 file to the project folder. Click on **Yes** to add the file and move further.

7. The IDE will open showing three windows: The **Project Workspace** on the left, the **Editing Window** on the right, and the **Output Window** at the bottom. You will see **Target1** created under the **Project** space.

8. Add a C file by right-clicking on **Source Group1** under the **Target1** node and then click on **Add New item to Group 'Source Group 1'**.

9. From the list box, select the **C File (.c)** option. Specify the filename as showcounter and then click on **Add**.

10. The showcounter.c file will be added to **Source Group 1**. Enter the following code in the editor window:

```c
#include<stdio.h>
#include<reg52.h>
void delay(void);
void main()
{
    unsigned char i;
    i=0x00;
    while(++i)
    {
        P3=i;
        delay();
    }
}

void delay(void)
{
    int j;
    int i;
    for(i=0;i<1000;i++)
    {
        for(j=0;j<10000;j++)
        {
        }
    }
}
```

8. After entering the code, click on the **SAVE** icon in the toolbar to save the showcounter.c file.

Now, let's go behind the scenes to understand the steps better.

How it works...

We will define a variable, i, of the unsigned char type; a variable of the unsigned char type can store 256 bits, whereas that of a signed char can store only 128 bits. The i variable is assigned the HEX value of 0. We will set a while loop to execute infinitely. With every iteration of the while loop, the value of the i variable will increment by 1. Within the while loop, we will assign the value of the i variable, that is, 0, to port P3.

We will introduce a delay by using two nested for loops. Thereafter, we will execute a while loop again, incrementing the value of the i variable, making it 1. Again, we will assign the value of the i variable to port P3 for display. And, we will reintroduce some delay, followed by executing the while loop again. This process continues infinitely; consequently, port P3 will display the counter from 0 until 255 repeatedly.

Press *F7* or click on the **Build** button to compile the code. If there is no error, you can move ahead to the next step; otherwise, first, debug the code. In order to see the output of the code through simulation, we will use Keil's built-in **Debug** option for simulation of the code. To do this, click on **Debug | Start/Stop Debug Session**. Alternatively, you can press *Ctrl + F5* as the shortcut key, or click on the **Start/Stop Debug Session** icon (it appears in the form of a D) in the toolbar.

On the free version of Keil, there is a condition that the running code size should not be more than 2 KB, so you will get a dialog box indicating that the running code has an upper limit of 2 KB. Click on **OK** to move further. The project workspace window shows most of the SFRs as well as the GPRs, from **r0** to **r7**. Click on the **Run** icon from the toolbar or press the *F5* key. You can see the output of the ports under **Peripherals | Select I/O ports | Port 3**. You will see the bits of the ports showing the counter from 0 to 255.

In the following screenshot, **(a)** shows the bits set to a value of 5. The binary value of 5 is 101, so, accordingly, the first and third bits are set to a HIGH signal and the remaining bits are set to a LOW signal. Similarly, **(b)** shows the bits displaying the counter value of 10. The bits of the port will be set showing the values from 0 to 255:

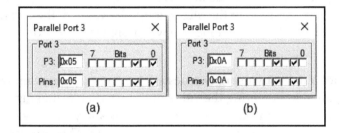

(a)   (b)

Figure 5.9

Voilà! We've successfully created a counter using Embedded C. Now, let's move on to the next recipe!

Toggle voltage in output pin using Arduino (blinking LED)

In this recipe, we will learn how to make an LED that is connected to the output pins of the Arduino board blink.

How to do it...

To make an LED that is connected to the output pins of the Arduino board blink, perform the following steps:

1. Open the Arduino IDE. Arduino opens up with a file showing the default content, as follows:

```
void setup() {
// put your setup code here, to run once:
}

void loop() {
// put your main code here, to run repeatedly:

}
```

2. Connect the Arduino board to the PC.

3. From the **Tools** menu, select **Port** and confirm whether it shows COM3 (Arduino/Genuino Uno) or whatever Arduino board you have attached to your PC. Additionally, confirm whether the **Board** option from the **Tools** menu indicates the Arduino board that is attached to your PC. In my case, the **Board** option will show **Arduino/Genuino Uno**.

4. Remember, the LEDs have polarity; hence, they will only glow when they are connected properly. The long leg is positive and should connect to a digital pin on the Arduino board. I am using the 13th pin of the Arduino board for the output, so connect the long leg of the LED to the 13th pin of the Arduino board (refer to *Figure 5.10*). Then, connect the short leg of the LED, which is negative, to the GND on the Arduino board.

5. Type the following program in the editor window:

```
int Led = 13;

void setup() {
pinMode(Led, OUTPUT);
}

void loop() {
digitalWrite(Led, HIGH);
        delay(1000);
        digitalWrite(Led, LOW);
        delay(1000);

}
```

6. Save the application by clicking on **File** | **Save As**. Specify the application name when prompted. Select the desired folder location and specify the application name. Let's name the application `ArduinoLedBlink`. A folder will be created with the specified application name (`ArduinoLedBlink`), and, within the `ArduinoLedBlink` folder, the application will be created with the filename `ArduinoLedBlink.ino`.

7. Upload the application to Arduino by clicking on the **Upload** icon in the toolbar.

Now, let's go behind the scenes to understand the steps better.

How it works...

We will start by defining a `Led` variable and setting it to represent pin 13 of the Arduino. By invoking the `pinMode` function, the `Led` variable will be indicated as the output pin, that is, it will be connected to an output device for display or to do some task.

Within the `loop` function, we will invoke the `digitalWrite` method to send a HIGH signal to variable `Led`. By doing so, the LED that is connected to output pin 13 will be switched on. Thereafter, we will introduce a time delay of 1,000 milliseconds.

Once more, we will invoke the `digitalWrite` method and send a LOW signal, this time to variable `Led`. As a result, the LED connected to output pin 13 will be switched off. Again, we will introduce a delay of 1,000 milliseconds. The commands in the `loop` function will execute infinitely making the connected LED to keep blinking.

On uploading the program to Arduino, the LED connected to the 13th pin of the Arduino will start blinking, as follows:

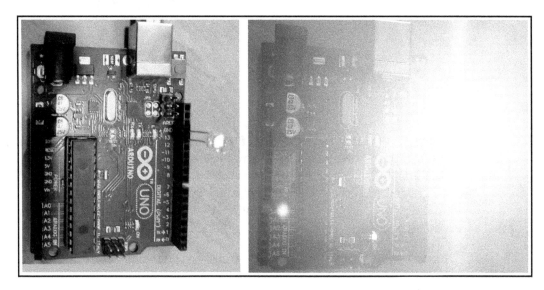

Figure 5.10

Voilà! We've successfully toggled the voltage in an output pin on the Arduino board to make a blinking LED.

Now, let's move on to the next recipe!

Taking input from the serial port using Arduino

In this recipe, we will be attaching an LED to the Arduino board and will prompt the user to press either 0 or 1. The user can input a value using the serial port. If the value entered by the user is 0, it will switch off the LED and if the value entered by the user is 1, it will make the LED glow.

How to do it...

To take input from the serial port using Arduino, perform the following steps:

1. Invoke the Arduino IDE. Arduino opens up with a file showing its default content, as follows:

```
void setup() {
// put your setup code here, to run once:

}

void loop() {
// put your main code here, to run repeatedly:

}
```

2. Connect the Arduino board to your PC.
3. From the **Tools** menu, select **Port** and confirm whether it shows COM3 (Arduino/Genuino Uno) or whatever Arduino board you have attached to your PC. Additionally, confirm whether the **Board** option from the **Tools** menu indicates the Arduino board that is attached to your PC. In my case, the **Board** option will show **Arduino/Genuino Uno**.
4. We will be attaching the LED to the output pin 13 of Arduino. Because the LEDs have polarity and need to be connected properly, we will connect the long leg of the LED (also known as the positive pin) to the 13th digital pin on the Arduino board. Additionally, we will connect the short leg of the LED (also known as the negative pin) to the GND on the Arduino board.

5. Type the following program in the editor window:

```
int Led = 13;
void setup() {
                pinMode(Led,OUTPUT);
                Serial.begin(9600);
                Serial.println("Enter 0 to switch Off LED and
1 to
                switch it On");
}

void loop() {
if(Serial.available())
                {
                                        int input=Serial.read();
                                        input=input-48;
                                        if(input==0)
                                        {
Serial.println("LED
                                                        is OFF");
digitalWrite(Led,LOW);
                                        }
                                        else if(input==1)
                                        {
Serial.println("LED
                                                        is ON");
digitalWrite(Led,HIGH);
                                        }
                                        else
                                        {
Serial.println("Enter 0 to switch Off
 LED and 1 to switch it On");
                                        }
                }
}
```

6. Save the application by clicking on the **File | Save As** option. Specify the application name when prompted. Let's name the application ArduinoTakinginput. A folder will be created with the specified application name, and, within the ArduinoLedBlink folder, the application will be created with the filename ArduinoTakinginput.ino.

7. Upload the application to Arduino by clicking on the **Upload** icon from the toolbar (refer to the following screenshot):

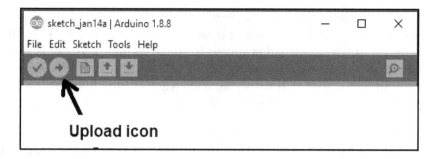

Upload icon

Now, let's go behind the scenes to understand the steps better.

How it works...

We will define a Led variable and set it to represent pin 13 of Arduino. By invoking the pinMode function, the Led variable is declared as the output pin and, hence, we will use it for connecting to an output device in order to perform a desired action. In this application, the output device will be an LED.

Because we want our PC to communicate with Arduino using serial communication, we need to set the data rate in terms of bits per second. So, we will call the Serial.begin function to set the serial data transmission speed at 9,600 bits per second (however, it can be any baud rate). Thereafter, we will display a message on the serial port in a human-readable format, informing the user that 0 can be pressed to switch off the connected LED and 1 can be pressed to switch on the LED.

Within the loop function of Arduino, we will invoke the Serial.available function to check whether any data is available in the serial port to read from. That is, the serial receive buffer will be checked to see whether some data or bytes are available there to be read. The data can be available in the serial receive buffer only when the user presses any key. It also means that no output will appear until the user presses any key. The moment the user presses any key, that byte will go into the serial receive buffer and the Serial.available function will return the Boolean value true. As a result of this, the if block will execute.

Within the `if` block, we will invoke the `Serial.read` function to read the serial data from the serial port. The data or byte that is read from the serial port will be assigned to the variable input. The byte read is always in ASCII format. The user is supposed to press either 0 or 1; their corresponding ASCII values are 48 and 49, respectively. So, if the user presses 0, its ASCII value, 48, will be assigned to the variable input. And if the user presses 1, its ASCII value, 49, will be assigned to the variable input.

To get the actual value of the number entered by the user, the value of 48 is subtracted from the variable input. If the user presses 0, a specified `if` block will execute. Within that `if` block, we will invoke the `Serial.println` function to display the message **LED is OFF** to inform the user. And we will invoke the `digitalWrite` method to send a LOW signal to output pin 13 where the LED is connected. Consequently, the LED, if it is glowing, will be switched off.

If the user presses 1, then another `if` block will execute; in this case, we will invoke the `Serial.println` function to display the message **LED is On**. And we will invoke the `digitalWrite` function to send a HIGH signal to output pin 13 to make the LED glow. If the user has not pressed either 0 or 1, we will display a message asking them to press either 0 or 1 only.

After uploading the program to Arduino, we can press *Ctrl* + *Shift* + *M* to open the serial monitor. In the serial monitor, we will get the following message: **Enter 0 to switch off LED and 1 to switch it On** (refer to the first dialog box in *Figure 5.11*). After pressing 0 in the serial monitor, we will get the message **LED is OFF** and, again, you will be prompted to enter either 0 or 1 (refer to the second dialog box in *Figure 5.11*). Besides the message in the serial monitor, the LED that is connected to the 13th pin of the Arduino board will also get switched off (if it was glowing). On pressing 1, the message **LED is ON** will be displayed in the serial monitor. Additionally, a message will appear prompting us to enter either 0 or 1 (refer to the third dialog box in *Figure 5.11*). Also, the LED connected to the Arduino board will glow:

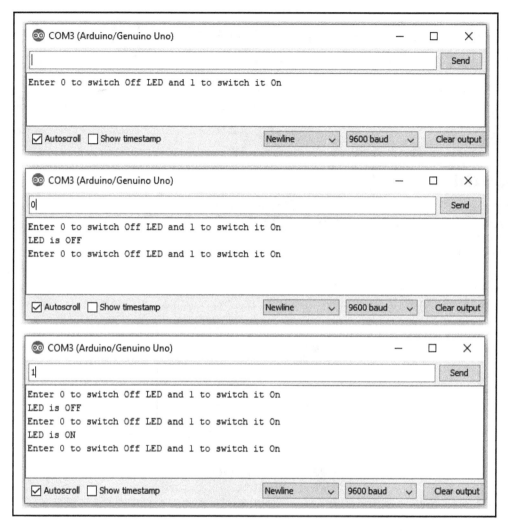

Figure 5.11

Voilà! We've successfully made an LED switch on and off on the basis of the input made to the serial port using Arduino.

Now, let's move on to the next recipe!

Sensing the temperature using Arduino with the LM35 sensor

In this recipe, we will learn how to sense temperature using the LM35 sensor connected to the Arduino board and will display the temperature in Celsius and Fahrenheit.

Getting ready...

For this recipe, we will require the following three components: a breadboard, Arduino Uno R3, and an LM35 sensor.

The LM35 is a temperature sensor that produces an output voltage that is linearly proportional to centigrade temperature. It does not require any external calibration or trimming to provide an accurate temperature. It has three terminals, **Vs**, **Vout**, and **Ground**, as shown in the following diagram:

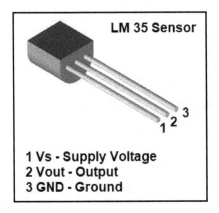

Figure 5.12

We will connect the LM35 sensor to the Arduino board as follows:

1. Connect the +Vs terminal to +5v on your Arduino board.
2. Connect the Vout terminal to Analog0 or A0 on the Arduino board.
3. Connect the GND terminal with the GND terminal on Arduino.

The following diagram makes this clearer:

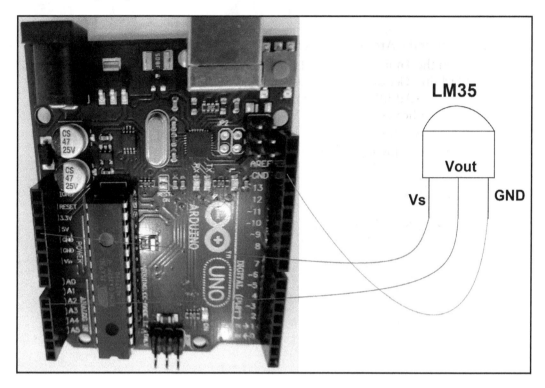

Figure 5.13

Now that the LM35 sensor is connected to the Arduino board, let's perform the steps listed next.

How to do it...

To sense temperature using the LM35 sensor connected to the Arduino board, perform the following steps:

1. Invoke the Arduino IDE. Arduino will open up with a file showing its default content, as follows:

```
void setup() {
// put your setup code here, to run once:
}

void loop() {
```

```
    // put your main code here, to run repeatedly:

}
```

2. Connect the Arduino board to the PC.

3. From the **Tools** menu, select **Port** and confirm whether it shows COM3 (Arduino/Genuino Uno) or whatever Arduino board you have attached to your PC. Additionally, confirm whether the **Board** option from the **Tools** menu indicates the Arduino board that is attached to your PC. In my case, the **Board** option will show **Arduino/Genuino Uno**.

4. Type the following program into the editor window:

```
float voltage;
int tempPin = 0;

void setup() {
    Serial.begin(9600);
}

void loop() {
    voltage = analogRead(tempPin);
    float tempInCelsius = voltage * 0.48828125;
    float tempinFahrenheit = (tempInCelsius*9)/5 + 32;
    Serial.print("Temperature in Celsius is: ");
    Serial.print(tempInCelsius);
    Serial.print("*C");
    Serial.println();
    Serial.print("Temperature in Fahrenheit is: ");
    Serial.print(tempinFahrenheit);
    Serial.print("*F");
    Serial.println();
    delay(1000);
}
```

5. Save the application by clicking on the **File** | **Save As** option. Specify the application name when prompted. Let's name the application SensorApp. A folder will be created with the name SensorApp and, within that folder, the application will be created with the filename SensorApp.ino.

6. Upload the application to Arduino by clicking on the **Upload** icon in the toolbar.

How it works...

We define a variable called `voltage`, of the float data type, and a variable called `tempPin`, of the integer type; we will set the latter to represent pin 0 of Arduino. In order to make our PC communicate with Arduino using serial communication, we need to set the data rate in terms of bits per second. So, we will call the `Serial.begin` function to set the serial data transmission speed to 9,600 bits per second (however, it can be any baud rate).

Within the `loop` function, we will invoke the `analogRead` function to read the value from the specified analog pin, 0. Recall that the Arduino boards contain a multichannel, 10-bit analog to digital converter that maps input voltages between 0 and the operating voltage (5V or 3.3V) into integer values between 0 and 1023. The value read from the analog pin, 0, is assigned to the `voltage` variable.

We are using a 5V Arduino and an LM35 sensor is already connected to its analog pin. We will use the following formula to convert the 10-bit analog reading into a temperature:

```
Voltage at pin in milliVolts = Reading from ADC * 5000/1024
```

This formula converts the numbers 0-1023 from the ADC into 0-5000 mV. To convert millivolts retrieved from this formula into temperature, we will use another formula:

```
Centigrade temperature = Analog voltage in mV / 10
```

The two previously mentioned formulas can be rewritten as follows:

```
Centigrade temperature = Reading from ADC * 0.48828125;
```

Using this formula, the value read into the voltage variable is converted into temperature in Celsius and is assigned to the `tempInCelsius` variable. To convert temperature in Celsius (°C) into Fahrenheit (°F), the following formula is used:

```
F=(C*9)/5+32
```

Using this formula, the temperature in Celsius found in the `tempInCelsius` variable is converted into Fahrenheit and assigned to the `tempinFahrenheit` variable.

Temperatures in °C and °F are displayed to the serial port by invoking. The temperature reading can be seen by opening the serial monitor. Press *Ctrl + Shift + M* to open the serial monitor and display the temperature. You can also press the LM35 sensors in your thumbs to see the rise and fall in temperature.

We will introduce a delay of 1,000 milliseconds between every temperature display by invoking the `delay` function. That is, the application will keep displaying the temperature in °C and °F infinitely with a delay of 1,000 milliseconds in between.

After uploading the program to Arduino, we can press *Ctrl + Shift + M* to open the serial monitor. In the serial monitor, we will get the temperature in Celsius as well as in Fahrenheit. You will keep getting a temperature reading continuously with a delay of 1,000 milliseconds in between:

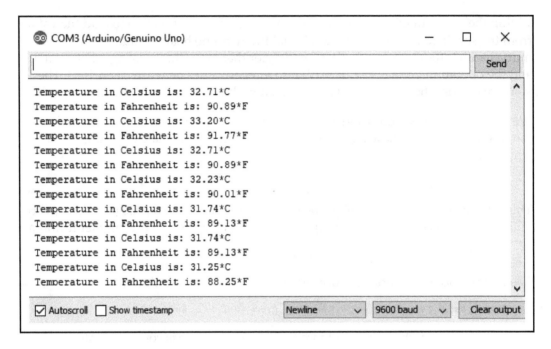

Figure 5.14

In the following photograph, you can see the LM35 sensor attached to the Arduino board. You can press the LM35 sensor in your thumbs to see the rise in the temperature readings:

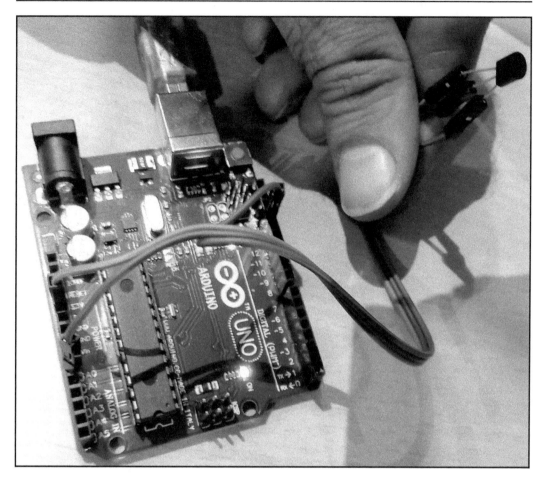

Figure 5.15

Voilà! We've successfully created a temperature sensor with an LM35 sensor using Arduino.

18
Applying Security in Coding

While coding, sometimes you may use functions that don't check or constrain the data entered by the user. The user either may enter incorrect data or content that might be larger than the capacity of the receiving variable. In such a situation, a buffer overflow or segmentation fault may occur. Consequently, the program will give an erroneous output.

In this chapter, we will use the following recipes to see how we can error-proof the entering of data in a program:

- Avoiding buffer overflow while reading strings from the keyboard
- Writing secure code while copying strings
- Avoiding errors while string formatting
- Avoid vulnerabilities while accessing files in C

Buffer overflow

The most common vulnerability in C programming is buffer overflows. The buffer, as the name suggests, represents a temporary area of memory storage in the RAM that a program uses to run itself. Usually, all the variables used in a program are assigned temporary buffer storage for keeping the values assigned to them. Some functions don't limit the data within the buffer boundaries while assigning larger values (larger than the assigned buffer) to the variables, leading to overflowing of the buffer. The overflowing data corrupts or overwrites data of other buffers.

These buffer overflows might be used by hackers or malicious users to damage files or data or to extract sensitive information. That is, an attacker might enter such an input that leads to buffer overflows.

While assigning values to an array, there are no bounds checks and the code might work, whether the memory being accessed belongs to your program or not. In most cases, it leads to a segmentation fault, overwriting data in another memory region.

We will be using some terms and functions repeatedly in this program. Let's do a quick overview of them.

gets()

The gets() function reads characters from the standard input device and assigns them to the specified string. Reading of characters stops when the newline character is reached. This function does not check for buffer length and always results in a vulnerability. Here is its syntax:

```
char *gets ( char *str);
```

Here, str represents the pointer to the string (array of characters) to which the read characters are assigned.

On successful execution, the function returns str and NULL if any error occurs.

fgets()

The fgets() function is used for reading a string from the specified source, where the source can be any file, keyboard, or another input device. Here is its syntax:

```
char *fgets(char *str, int numb, FILE *src);
```

The numb number of bytes are read from the specified source src and assigned to the string pointed to by str. The function either reads numb-1 bytes, or until a newline (\n) is reached, or an end of file is encountered, whichever happens first.

The function also appends the null character (\0) to the string that is read to terminate the string. If executed successfully, the function returns a pointer to str and returns NULL if an error occurs.

fpurge(stdin)

The fpurge(stdin) function is used to flush or clear out the input buffer of the stream. Sometimes, after feeding data for some variables, the data (which might be in the form of spaces or a newline character) is left behind in the buffer and is not cleared. In such cases, this function is used. If executed successfully, the function returns zero, else it returns EOF.

Here is its syntax:

```
fpurge(stdin)
```

sprintf()

The sprintf() function is used for assigning formatted text to a string. Here is its syntax:

```
int sprintf(char *str, const char *format, ...)
```

Here, str is a pointer to the string where the formatted string has to be assigned, and format is the same as in a printf statement, where different formatting tags such as %d and %s can be used to format the content.

snprintf()

The snprintf() function formats the given content and assigns it to the specified string. Only the specified number of bytes will be assigned to the destination string. Here is its syntax:

```
int snprintf(char *str, size_t numb, const char *format, ...);
```

Here's a breakdown of what the preceding code represents:

- *str: Represents the pointer that points to the string where formatted content will be assigned.
- numb: Represents the maximum number of bytes that can be assigned to the string.
- format: Like the printf statement, several formatting tags such as %d and %s can be used to format the content.

Note: `snprintf` automatically appends a null character to the formatted string.

strcpy()

The `strcpy()` function is used for copying the content from one string to another. Here is its syntax:

```
char* strcpy(char* dest, const char* src);
```

Here, `src` represents the pointer to the source string from where the content has to be copied and `dest` represents the pointer to the destination string to which the content has to be copied.

strncpy( )

The `strncpy()` function is used for copying the specified number of bytes from one string into another. Here is its syntax:

```
char * strncpy ( char * dest, const char *src, size_t numb);
```

Here's a breakdown of what the preceding code represents:

- `dest`: Represents the pointer to the destination string to where the bytes have to be copied
- `src`: Represents the pointer to the source string from where the bytes have to be copied
- `numb`: Represents the number of bytes to be copied from source to the destination string

If the value of the `numb` parameter is larger than the length of the source string, the destination string will be padded with null bytes. If the length of the destination string is smaller than the `numb` parameter, then the string will be truncated to be equal to the length of the destination string.

Let's now begin our journey for secure coding with the first recipe.

Understanding how a buffer overflow occurs

In this recipe, we will learn to get input from the user and will see the situations that lead to a buffer overflow and result in ambiguous output. We will also learn the procedure to avoid a buffer overflow.

Basically, we will make a structure comprising two members and in one of the members, we will deliberately enter text that is larger than its capacity, as a result of which a buffer overflow will occur. This will lead to the overwriting of the content of another member of the structure.

How to do it...

Here are the steps to make a program that will lead to a buffer overflow:

1. Define a structure consisting of two members, name and orderid.
2. Define two variables of the structure type defined in *step 1*. In one of the structure variables, we will deliberately generate a buffer overflow by entering a large amount of data.
3. Prompt the user to enter a value for the orderid member for the first structure.
4. Invoke the fpurge function to empty out the input stream buffer before invoking the gets function.
5. Invoke the gets function to enter data for the name member for the first structure. Enter text that is larger than the length of the name member.
6. Repeat *steps 3* to *5* to enter data for the orderid and name members for the second structure. This time, enter data within the capacity of the name member.
7. Display data assigned to the orderid and name members of the first structure. Buffer overflow will occur in the case of the first structure and you will get an ambiguous output while displaying the orderid value.
8. Display data assigned to the orderid and name member of the second structure. No buffer overflow takes place in this structure and you get exactly the same data that was entered for both the members.

The following program will take the name and order number values for two structures. In one member of the structure, we will enter data that is larger than its capacity to generate a buffer overflow:

```c
//getsproblem.c

#include <stdio.h>

struct users {
  char name[10];
  int orderid;
};
int main(void) {
  struct users user1, user2;
  printf("Enter order number ");
  scanf("%d", & user1.orderid);
  fpurge(stdin);
  printf("Enter first user name ");
  gets(user1.name);
  printf("Enter order number ");
  scanf("%d", & user2.orderid);
  fpurge(stdin);
  printf("Enter second user name ");
  gets(user2.name);
  printf("Information of first user - Name %s, Order number %d\n",
    user1.name, user1.orderid);
  printf("Information of second user - Name %s, Order number %d\n",
    user2.name, user2.orderid);
}
```

Now, let's go behind the scenes to understand the code better.

How it works...

The program will ask for two pairs of names and order numbers. In the first pair, we will deliberately generate a buffer overflow by entering text that is longer than the variable size, whereas for the second pair, we will enter the data within the specified range. Consequently, the information of the first user (pair) will be displayed incorrectly, that is, the data will not appear exactly the same as it was entered, whereas that of the second user will appear correctly.

So, we will define a structure called users with two fields or members called name and orderid, where name is defined as a string of size 10 bytes and orderid is defined as an int variable of 2 bytes. Then, we will define two variables user1 and user2 of the users structure type; that means both the user1 and user2 variables will get a name and orderid member each.

You will be prompted to enter the username and order number twice. The first pair of names and the order numbers entered will be assigned to user1 and the second to user2. The entered information of the two users is then displayed on the screen.

Let's use GCC to compile the getsproblem.c program. If you get no errors or warnings, it means the getsproblem.c program has compiled into an executable file: getsproblem.exe. Let's run this file:

```
$ gcc getsproblem.c -o getsproblem
$ ./getsproblem
Enter order number 101
Enter first user name bintu mohan harwani
Enter order number 102
Enter second user name chirag
Information of first user - Name bintu mohan harwani, Order number 2003984744
Information of second user - Name chirag, Order number 102
```

Figure 18.1

We can see in the preceding output that because of the buffer overflow made by the name member in the first structure, the value of the orderid member, which was 101, is overwritten. Consequently, we get a garbage value for the orderid of the first structure. The output of the second structure is correct because the value entered for its members is within their capacity.

To avoid overflow while entering data, we simply replace the gets function with the fgets function. With the fgets function, we can specify the maximum number of characters that can be allowed in the specified string. The extra text will be truncated and will not be assigned to the specified string.

Learning how to avoid a buffer overflow

In the previous recipe, we defined two structure variables because we wanted to show that if data entered is larger in size than the member field allows, it will result in ambiguous output; and if data is entered within the capacity of the receiving variables, it will generate the correct output.

In the following recipe, we don't need two structure variables as we will be using the fgets function to address our concern. This function never results in a buffer overflow.

How to do it...

Here are the steps for avoiding a buffer overflow using the fgets function:

1. Define a structure consisting of two members, name and orderid.
2. Define a variable of the structure type defined in *step 1*.
3. Prompt the user to enter a value for the orderid member of the structure.
4. Invoke the fpurge function to empty out the input stream buffer before invoking the fgets function.
5. Invoke the fgets function to enter data for the name member of the structure. In order to constrain the size of the text to be assigned to name member, its length is computed by invoking the sizeof function and that length of string is supplied to the fgets function.
6. Add a null character to the string, if one is not already there, to terminate the string.
7. Display data assigned to the orderid and name members of the structure to verify that there is no buffer overflow.

The following program defines a structure consisting of two members and explains how a buffer overflow can be avoided while entering data through the keyboard:

```
//getssolved.c

#include <stdio.h>
#include <string.h>
#include <stdlib.h>

struct users {
  char name[10];
  int orderid;
```

```
};

int main(void) {
    struct users user1;
    int n;
    printf("Enter order number ");
    scanf("%d", & user1.orderid);
    fpurge(stdin);
    printf("Enter user name ");
    fgets(user1.name, sizeof(user1.name), stdin);
    n = strlen(user1.name) - 1;
    if (user1.name[n] == '\n')
        user1.name[n] = '\0';
    printf("Information of the user is - Name %s, Order number %d\n",
        user1.name, user1.orderid);
}
```

Now, let's go behind the scenes to understand the code better.

How it works...

In the program, the fgets function takes input from the standard input device and the maximum number of characters that will be read from the input device will be equal to the number of bytes allowed in the name variable of the user1 structure. As a result, even if the user enters a larger string, only the specified number of bytes from the input will be picked up; that is, only the first 10 characters in the input will be picked up and assigned to the name member of the user1 structure.

The fgets function appends the null character (\0) to the string, provided the number of characters entered is one less than the maximum length specified in the function. But for the string that is larger than the specified length, we need to insert the null character at the end of the string. To do so, we need to check if the newline character is there as the last character of the string. If yes, then we replace the newline character in the string with the null character to terminate the string.

Let's use GCC to compile the `getssolved.c` program. If you get no errors or warnings, it means the `getssolved.c` program has compiled into an executable file: `getssolved.exe`. Let's run this file:

```
$ gcc getssolved.c -o getssolved
$ ./getssolved
Enter order number 101
Enter user name bintu mohan harwani
Information of the user is - Name bintu moh, Order number 101
```

Figure 18.2

We can see in the preceding output that the larger text assigned to the `name` member of the structure is truncated as per the member's size, hence no buffer overflow occurs.

Understanding how a vulnerability occurs while copying strings

In this recipe, we will see the vulnerability that might occur while copying a string. We will also see how to avoid that vulnerability. We will first define a structure consisting of two members. In one of the members, we will be copying a text that is larger than its capacity, which will result in overwriting the content of another member.

In the next recipe, we will learn how to avoid this problem.

How to do it...

Here are the steps to understand how a vulnerability occurs while copying a string:

1. Define a structure consisting of two members, `name` and `orderid`.
2. Define a variable of the structure type defined in *step 1*.
3. Assign any integer value to the `orderid` member of the structure.

4. Invoke the `strcpy` function to assign text to the `name` member of the structure. In order to generate a buffer overflow, assign a larger text to it.

5. Display data assigned to the `orderid` and `name` members of the structure to confirm if the ambiguous output is generated, which verifies that a buffer overflow has occurred.

The program that shows a vulnerability when copying a string is as follows:

```
//strcpyproblem.c

#include <stdio.h>
#include <string.h>

struct users {
  char name[10];
  int orderid;
};

int main(void) {
  struct users user1;
  char userid[] = "administrator";
  user1.orderid = 101;
  strcpy(user1.name, userid);
  printf("Information of the user - Name %s, Order number %d\n",
    user1.name, user1.orderid);
}
```

Now, let's go behind the scenes to understand the code better.

How it works...

To enter the name and order number of a customer, define a structure called users with two members, `name` and `orderid`. The `name` member is a character array or string of 10 bytes in length, and the `orderid` member is a variable of the `int` data type consisting of 2 bytes.

A variable, user1, is defined as the users structure type; hence, the user1 structure will get two members, name and orderid. An integer value 101 is assigned to the orderid member of user1 structure. Also, a string, administrator, is assigned to the name member of user1. Because the string administrator is larger than the size of the name member, a buffer overflow will occur, overwriting the memory of the next memory location, that is, of the orderid member. Consequently, while displaying the information of the user, though the data in the name member may appear correctly, the content of orderid member will appear incorrectly, as its content is overwritten.

Let's use GCC to compile the strcpyproblem.c program. If you get no errors or warnings, it means the strcpyproblem.c program has compiled into an executable file: strcpyproblem.exe. Let's run this file:

```
$ gcc strcpyproblem.c -o strcpyproblem
$ ./strcpyproblem
Information of the user - Name administrator, Order number 114
```

Figure 18.3

In the preceding output, you can see that because the name member is assigned a string that is larger than its size, this results in it overwriting the content of another member, orderid. The content of the name member appears the same as entered by the user, whereas that of orderid is displayed incorrectly.

Learning how to write secure code while copying strings

To avoid the buffer overflow that occurs when using the strcpy function, simply replace the strcpy function with the strncpy function. strncpy will copy only the specified number of bytes into the destination string, hence buffer overflows don't occur in this function. Let's see how it is done.

How to do it...

Here are the steps to make secure code while copying a string:

1. Define a structure consisting of two members, name and orderid.
2. Define a variable of the structure type defined in *step 1*.
3. Assign any integer value to the orderid member of the structure.
4. Determine the length of the name member of the structure to find the maximum number of characters that it can accommodate.
5. Invoke the strncpy function for copying a text to the name member of the structure. Pass the length of the name member, too, to the strncpy function to truncate the text if it is larger than the capacity of the name member.
6. Add a null character to the string, if it is not there already, to terminate it.
7. Display data assigned to the orderid and name members of the structure to verify that a buffer overflow does not occur and the same data is displayed as was entered.

The program that is secure enough for copying strings is as follows:

//strcpysolved.c

```
#include <stdio.h>
#include <string.h>

struct users {
  char name[10];
  int orderid;
};

int main(void) {
  int strsize;
  struct users user1;
  char userid[] = "administrator";
  user1.orderid = 101;
  strsize = sizeof(user1.name);
  strncpy(user1.name, userid, strsize);
  if (user1.name[strsize - 1] != '\0')
    user1.name[strsize - 1] = '\0';
  printf("Information of the user - Name %s, Order number %d\n",
    user1.name, user1.orderid);
}
```

Now, let's go behind the scenes to understand the code better.

How it works...

In this recipe, everything is the same as the previous recipe. The point of difference is that we invoke the strncpy function. When this function is invoked, only the strsize number of bytes from the administrator text is assigned to the name member of the user1 structure. Because strsize contains the maximum length of the name member, no buffer overflow will occur in this case.

Finally, we check if the null character, \0, exists as the last character in the name member. If not, then the null character is added at its end to terminate the string. On displaying the information of the user, we see that because the length of the name member is 10, only the first 9 characters from the text administrator are assigned to the name member, followed by a null character. As a result of this, the value of the orderid member will also appear correctly, exactly the same as was entered.

Let's use GCC to compile the strcpysolved.c program. If you get no errors or warnings, it means the strcpysolved.c program has compiled into an executable file: strcpysolved.exe. Let's run this file:

```
$ gcc strcpysolved.c -o strcpysolved

$ ./strcpysolved
Information of the user - Name administr, Order number 101
```

Figure 18.4

You can see in the preceding output that whatever value is entered for the two members, we get exactly the same output.

Understanding the errors that occur while formatting strings

In this recipe, we will understand what kind of error might occur while formatting strings. We will also see how to avoid that error. We will define a structure consisting of two members, and to one member, we will be assigning a formatted string. Let's see what error we come across.

In the next recipe, we will see how to avoid it.

How to do it...

Here are the steps to make a program in which an error occurs due to string formatting:

1. Define a structure consisting of two members, name and orderid.
2. Define a variable of the structure type defined in *step 1*.
3. Assign any integer value to the orderid member of the structure.
4. Invoke the sprintf function to assign formatted text to the name member of the structure. In order to generate a buffer overflow, assign a larger text to it.
5. Display data assigned to the orderid and name members of the structure to confirm if the ambiguous output is generated to verify whether buffer overflow has occurred.

The following is the program that generates an erroneous output because of applying string formatting:

```c
//sprintfproblem.c

#include <stdio.h>

struct users {
    char name[10];
    int orderid;
};

int main(void) {
    struct users user1;
    user1.orderid = 101;
    sprintf(user1.name, "%s", "bintuharwani");
    printf("Information of the user - Name %s, Order number
    %d\n", user1.name, user1.orderid);
}
```

Now, let's go behind the scenes to understand the code better.

How it works...

We want to enter information about the customer's name and the order placed by them. So, we define a structure called `users` with two members, `name` and `orderid`, where the `name` member is defined as a character array of length 10 bytes, and the `orderid` member is defined of the int data type consisting of 2 bytes. A variable, `user1`, is defined of the `users` structure type, hence the `user1` structure will get two members, `name` and `orderid`. An integer of value `101` is assigned to the `orderid` member of the `user1` structure.

Using the `sprintf` function, a string, `bintuharwani`, is assigned to the `name` member of the `user1` structure. The `bintuharwani` string is larger than the `name` member, hence a buffer overflow will occur, overwriting the memory of the next memory location, that is, the memory of the `orderid` member. So, while displaying the information of the user, the name will appear correctly but you will get a different or ambiguous value for the `orderid` member.

Let's use GCC to compile the `sprintfproblem.c` program. If you get no errors or warnings, it means the `sprintfproblem.c` program has compiled into an executable file: `sprintfproblem.exe`. Let's run this file:

```
$ gcc sprintfproblem.c -o sprintfproblem

$ ./sprintfproblem
Information of the user - Name bintuharwani, Order number 0
```

Figure 18.5

In the output, you can see that the order number is displayed incorrectly; that is, instead of the assigned value, `101`, it displays the value `0`. This is because on assigning the `bintuharwani` string to the `name` member, the fact that the string is larger in size than the capacity of the `name` member leads to a buffer overflow that overwrites the value of the `orderid` member.

Learning how to avoid errors while formatting strings

In this recipe, we will use the snprintf function. The snprintf function will assign the formatted text to the name member but will limit the size of the string assigned to it. The difference between the sprintf and snprintf functions is that sprintf simply assigns the complete formatted text to the destination string no matter what its capacity, whereas snprintf allows us to specify the maximum length of the text that can be assigned to the destination string. Therefore, a buffer overflow will not occur as only the specified size of the text is assigned to the destination string.

How to do it...

Here are the steps to make a program in which an error occurs due to string formatting:

1. Define a structure consisting of two members, name and orderid.
2. Define a variable of the structure type defined in *step 1*.
3. Assign any integer value to the orderid member of the structure.
4. Invoke the snprintf function to assign formatted text to the name member of the structure. Pass the length of the name member to the snprintf function, as well, to truncate the text if it is larger than the capacity of the name member.
5. Display data assigned to the orderid and name members of the structure to verify that a buffer overflow does not occur and the same data is displayed as was entered.

The following program shows how the error related to string formatting can be avoided:

```
//sprintfsolved.c

#include <stdio.h>

struct users {
  char name[10];
  int orderid;
};

int main(void) {
```

```
    struct users user1;
    user1.orderid = 101;
    snprintf(user1.name, sizeof(user1.name), "%s", "bintuharwani");
    printf("Information of the user - Name %s, Order number
      %d\n", user1.name, user1.orderid);
}
```

Now, let's go behind the scenes to understand the code better.

How it works...

To constrain the size of the content assigned to the name member of the user1 structure, we will make use of the snprintf function. You can see that through the snprintf function, only the first 10 characters from the text bintuharwani are assigned to the name member. Because the length of the name member is 10, it is capable of storing 10 characters and hence no buffer overflow occurs and the value assigned to the orderid member will remain intact and undisturbed. On displaying the values of the orderid and name members, both of their values will be displayed correctly.

Let's use GCC to compile the sprintfsolved.c program. If you get no errors or warnings, it means the sprintfsolved.c program has compiled into an executable file: sprintfsolved.exe. Let's run this file:

```
$ gcc sprintfsolved.c -o sprintfsolved
$ ./sprintfsolved
Information of the user - Name bintuharw, Order number 101
```

Figure 18.6

In the preceding output, we can see that the extra formatted text that is assigned to the name member is truncated, hence the correct output of the name and orderid members is displayed on the screen.

Understanding how vulnerabilities occur while accessing files in C

Let's assume that you wrote a program to create a text file named `file1.txt`. In such programs, a malicious user or hacker might add some soft links to some important or sensitive file in the file that you want to create. As a result, it will lead to overwriting of the important file.

How to do it...

We will start by assuming that some important file by the name of `file2.txt` already exists on your computer and contains some sensitive information. Here are the steps that a malicious user or hacker can use in your program to create a file to overwrite `file2.txt`:

1. A file pointer is defined.
2. The hacker might create a soft link and attach a sensitive file to the file that we want to create.
3. Open the file to which we want to write the content. But in reality, the sensitive file that is attached to our file will be opened in write-only mode.
4. Prompt the user to enter the lines of text to be written into the file.
5. Write the lines entered by the user into the file.
6. Repeat *steps 4* and *5* until the user enters `stop`.
7. Close the file pointed to by the file pointer, `fp`.

Following is the program that a malicious user can use to link some important file to the file that you want to create, and hence can overwrite and destroy that important file on your system:

```
//fileproblem.c

#include <stdio.h>
#include <string.h>
#include <stdlib.h>
#include <unistd.h>

#define BUFFSIZE 255

void main(int argc, char * argv[]) {
  FILE * fp;
```

```
    char str[BUFFSIZE];
    if (symlink("file2.txt", "file1.txt") != 0) {
      perror("symlink() error");
      unlink("file2.txt");
      exit(1);
    } else {
      fp = fopen("file1.txt", "w");
      if (fp == NULL) {
        perror("An error occurred in creating the file\n");
        exit(1);
      }
      printf("Enter content for the file\n");
      gets(str);
      while (strcmp(str, "stop") != 0) {
        fputs(str, fp);
        gets(str);
      }
    }
    fclose(fp);
  }
```

Now, let's go behind the scenes to understand the code better.

How it works...

A file pointer is defined by the name fp. At this stage, a hacker or malicious user might invoke the symlink function to create a soft link named file1.txt to the file named file2.txt. In this program, file2.txt can be replaced by the password file or some other sensitive file that the malicious user may want to overwrite or destroy.

Because the program is for creating a new file, the program invokes the fopen function to open file1.txt in write-only mode and the opened file will be pointed at by fp, the file pointer. But because file1.txt and file2.txt are linked, file2.txt will be actually opened instead of file1.txt, and in write-only mode, and will be pointed at by the file pointer, fp. The program will terminate if the file cannot be opened in write-only mode or some other error occurs.

The user is prompted to enter lines of text for the file. The lines entered by the user are assigned to the `str` string. The `fputs` function is invoked to write the content assigned to the `str` string into the file pointed at by the file pointer, `fp`. Consequently, the sensitive file will be overwritten. The user can enter as many lines of text as desired and can enter `stop` when they are done. So a `while` loop is set to execute that will keep taking lines of text from the user and will keep writing them into the file until `stop` is entered. Finally, the file pointed to by the file pointer, `fp`, is closed.

Let's use GCC to compile the `fileproblem.c` program as shown in the following screenshot. If you get no errors or warnings, it means the `fileproblem.c` program has compiled into an executable file: `fileproblem.exe`. Let's run this file:

```
$ gcc fileproblem.c -o fileproblem
$ ./fileproblem
Enter content for the file
global warming has become a problem today
stop
```

Figure 18.7

The preceding text will not go into the desired file, `file1.txt`, but will overwrite the sensitive file, `file2.txt`, deleting its earlier content, if any. If we look at the content of the `file2.txt` file, we will see the content that was supposed to be written into `file1.txt`:

```
$ cat file2.txt
global warming has become a problem today
```

Figure 18.8

Now, let's rewrite the program to remove the file vulnerabilities.

Learning how to avoid vulnerabilities while writing a file in C

The special care we will take in this recipe is that we will unlink all the links (if any) to the file that we are going to create. We will also ensure that our program does not overwrite any file if it already exists.

How to do it...

Here are the steps to write a program to avoid vulnerabilities while creating a file in C:

1. A file pointer is defined.
2. The hacker might create a soft link and attach a sensitive file to the file that we want to create.
3. Remove the links from the file that you want to write in.
4. Open the file using the flags that check whether the file already exists or not. If the file exists, it should be overwritten.
5. Associate the file descriptor with the file stream.
6. Prompt the user to enter the lines of text to be written into the file.
7. Write the lines entered by the user into the file.
8. Repeat *steps 5* and *6* until the user enters `stop`.
9. Close the file pointed to by the file pointer, `fp`.

The following is the program that removes vulnerabilities while creating a text file:

```
//filesolved.c

#include <stdio.h>
#include <string.h>
#include <fcntl.h>
#include <stdlib.h>
#include <unistd.h>

#define BUFFSIZE 255

void main(int argc, char * argv[]) {
    int ifp;
    FILE * fp;
    char str[BUFFSIZE];
    if (symlink("file2.txt", "file1.txt") != 0) {
```

```
        perror("symlink() error");
        unlink("file2.txt");
        exit(1);
    } else {
      unlink("file1.txt");
      ifp = open("file1.txt", O_WRONLY | O_CREAT | O_EXCL, 0600);
      if (ifp == -1) {
        perror("An error occurred in creating the file\n");
        exit(1);
      }
      fp = fdopen(ifp, "w");
      if (fp == NULL) {
        perror("Could not be linked to the stream\n");
        exit(1);
      }
      printf("Enter content for the file\n");
      gets(str);
      while (strcmp(str, "stop") != 0) {
        fputs(str, fp);
        gets(str);
      }
    }
    fclose(fp);
}
```

Now, let's go behind the scenes to understand the code better.

How it works...

You can see in the program that a file pointer is defined by the name fp. We are expecting that a hacker or malicious user might have created a soft link called file1.txt to the existing file, file2.txt. file2.txt is a sensitive file that we don't want to be overwritten or destroyed. To make the program free from any vulnerability, the unlink() function is invoked to remove any links to the file1.txt. This will avoid overwriting of any sensitive file that might be linked with file1.txt.

Also, the open function is invoked to open the file instead of the traditional fopen function. The open function opens the file1.txt file in write-only mode with the O_CREAT and O_EXCL flags, which will fail the open function if the file already exists. This will ensure that no existing sensitive file will be overwritten accidentally in case it is linked to file1.txt. The open function will return a file descriptor for the opened file that will be assigned to the ifp variable.

To work with the file, we need a file stream. So the `fdopen` function is invoked to associate a file stream with the `ifp` file descriptor that is generated through the `open` function. The `fdopen` function returns a pointer to the file stream that is assigned to the file pointer, `fp`. In addition, the `w` mode is used in the `fdopen` function because although it opens the file in write mode, it will never cause truncation of the file. This makes the program much safer and avoids the accidental deletion of any file.

Thereafter, the program is the same as the previous program. It asks the user to enter certain lines, which are then written in `file1.txt`. Finally, the file pointed to by the file pointer, `fp`, is closed.

Let's use GCC to compile the `filesolved.c` program, as shown in the following screenshot. If you get no errors or warnings, it means the `filesolved.c` program has compiled into an executable file: `filesolved.exe`. Let's run this file:

```
$ gcc filesolved.c -o filesolved

$ ./filesolved
Enter content for the file
World is getting warmer. Global warming is a very big problem
stop
```

Figure 18.9

We can verify whether the content entered while running the program has gone into `file1.txt` or not. To do so, we will open `file1.txt` to see its contents as follows:

```
$ cat file1.txt
World is getting warmer. Global warming is a very big problem
```

Figure 18.10

We can see that the content entered by the user has gone into `file1.txt`.

The contents of `file2.txt` are intact as follows:

```
$ cat file2.txt
A fighter aircraft is a military aircraft designed primarily for air-to-air
 combat against other aircraft, as opposed to bombers and attack aircraft,
whose main mission is to attack ground targets. The hallmarks of a fighter
are its speed, maneuverability, and small size relative to other combat air
craft.
```

Figure 18.11

Other Books You May Enjoy

If you enjoyed this book, you may be interested in these other books by Packt:

Hands-On Network Programming with C
Lewis Van Winkle

ISBN: 978-1-78934-986-3

- Uncover cross-platform socket programming APIs
- Implement techniques for supporting IPv4 and IPv6
- Understand how TCP and UDP connections work over IP
- Discover how hostname resolution and DNS work
- Interface with web APIs using HTTP and HTTPS
- Explore Simple Mail Transfer Protocol (SMTP) for electronic mail transmission
- Apply network programming to the Internet of Things (IoT)

Extreme C

Kamran Amini

ISBN: 978-1-78934-362-5

- Build advanced C knowledge on strong foundations, rooted in first principles
- Understand memory structures and compilation pipeline and how they work, and how to make most out of them
- Apply object-oriented design principles to your procedural C code
- Write low-level code that's close to the hardware and squeezes maximum performance out of a computer system
- Master concurrency, multithreading, multi-processing, and integration with other languages
- Unit Testing and debugging, build systems, and inter-process communication for C programming

Leave a review - let other readers know what you think

Please share your thoughts on this book with others by leaving a review on the site that you bought it from. If you purchased the book from Amazon, please leave us an honest review on this book's Amazon page. This is vital so that other potential readers can see and use your unbiased opinion to make purchasing decisions, we can understand what our customers think about our products, and our authors can see your feedback on the title that they have worked with Packt to create. It will only take a few minutes of your time, but is valuable to other potential customers, our authors, and Packt. Thank you!

Index

executing 255

D

data
  deleting, from database using C 474, 475,
    476, 478, 480
  reading, sent from server 244, 245, 246
  sending, to client 242, 243
database
  desired information, searching 460, 461,
    463, 464, 465
  table information, updating 465, 466, 468,
    470, 471, 472, 473
deadlock
  about 212
  avoiding 218, 219, 220, 222, 223
  creating 212, 213, 214, 216, 217
depth-first traversal
  performing, of graph 343, 346, 347, 348,
    349
desired information
  searching, in database 460, 461, 463, 464,
    465
directed graph
  about 316
  adjacency list representation, creating of 326,
    327, 330, 331, 333, 334
  adjacency matrix representation, creating of
    318, 319, 321, 322
directives
  used, for performing conditional compilation
    106, 107, 109, 110, 111
divide and conquer approach 272
doubly linked list 374, 375
dynamic memory allocation
  about 483
  functions 484
  performing 492, 494
  working 494, 495

E

element
  deleting, from array 14, 15
  entering, of matrices 22, 23
  inserting, in array 9, 10, 11, 12, 13

Embedded C
  port of microcontroller, toggling 536, 537,
    538, 539, 540, 541
  value of port, incrementing 543, 544, 545,
    546
embedded systems 532
Erasable Programmable Read-Only Memory
    (EPROM) 532
errors
  avoiding, while formatting strings 577, 578
  catching, with compile-time assertions 118,
    119, 120, 121
  defining, while formatting strings 574, 576
external sorting 271

F

fclose() function 169
fgets() function 169, 562
file handling
  functions 168
file
  encrypting 191, 192, 194, 195, 196
  number of vowels, counting in 181, 182, 184,
    185
First in First out (FIFO)
  about 226
  data, reading 235, 236
  data, writing 233, 234
  used, for communicating processes 233
fopen() function 168
fork() function 228
fpurge(stdin) function 563
fputs() function 169
free() function 484
fseek() function 170
ftell() function 171
ftok() function 256
function
  registering, called on program exit 487
functions in IPC, with shared memory and
    message queues
  about 256
  ftok() 256
  msgget() 258
  msgrcv() 259

item
   searching, binary search used 272, 274, 275, 276, 278

K

Kruskal's algorithm
   used, for creating minimum spanning trees 364, 365, 369, 370, 371

L

Last In First Out (LIFO) 73, 373, 378, 485
line
   drawing, between mouse clicks 433, 434, 436, 437
linear searching 271
listen() function 240
loop unrolling
   applying, for faster result 507, 508, 509, 510

M

macros
   advantages 105
   disadvantages 105
malloc() function 484
matrices
   element, entering of 22, 23
   multiplying 16, 17, 18, 20, 21
   sparse matrix, detecting 36, 37, 38, 39, 40
max-heap
   creating 304
   deleting 305, 307, 308, 310, 312, 314
memory leak 131
memset() function 239
message
   passing from one process to another, with message queue 255
   reading, from message queue 263, 265
   writing, into message queue 261
minimum spanning tree
   adjacency linked list, displaying 359
   creating 360, 362, 363
   creating, with Kruskal's algorithm 364, 365, 369, 370, 371
   creating, with Prim's algorithm 350, 351, 352, 357, 358, 359

mkfifo() function 227
msgget() function 258
msgrcv() function 259
multiple tasks
   performing, with multiple threads 203, 204, 205, 206
multithreading 198
mutex
   about 199
   used, to share data between threads 206, 207, 208, 209, 210, 211
mutual exclusion 198, 199
MySQL database
   creating 448, 449
   information, storing 455, 456, 458, 459
MySQL tables
   creating 448, 450, 451
MySQL
   database, creating 450
   functions 445
   mysql_fetch_row() 447
mysql_close() function 448
mysql_fetch_row() function 447
mysql_free_result() function 448
mysql_init() function 446
mysql_num_fields() function 448
mysql_query() function 447
mysql_real_connect() function 446
mysql_use_result() function 447

N

numbers
   arranging in ascending order, with bubble sort 278, 280, 282, 284
   arranging in ascending order, with insertion sort 285, 286, 287, 290
   arranging in ascending order, with quick sort 291

O

OpenGL
   functions 424, 426